D1219011

CIVIL WAR *Album*

COMPLETE PHOTOGRAPHIC HISTORY

OF THE CIVIL WAR

CIVIL WAR

Album

Complete Photographic History of the Civil War

Fort Sumter to Appomattox

Edited by
William C. Davis and Bell L. Wiley
Under the direction of
The National Historic Society

New York

Originally published in six separate volumes as:

The Image of War 1861-1865, volume One: Shadows of the Storm
The Image of War 1861-1865, volume Two: The Guns of '62
The Image of War 1861-1865, volume Three: the Embattled Confederacy
The Image of War 1861-1865, volume Four: Fighting for Time
The Image of War 1861-1865, volume Five: The South Besieged
The Image of War 1861-1865, volume Six: The End of an Era

Published by Tess Press
151 West 19th Street
New York, NY 10011

Manufactured in Hong Kong

ISBN 1-57912-142-X

Library of Congress Cataloging-in-Publication Data

Civil War album: complete photographic history of the Civil War: Fort Sumter to Appomottox/ edited by William C. Davis and Bell I. Wiley; under the direction of the National Historical Society; with a new introduction by William C. Davis.
cm.
Originally published 198101984 in 6 separate vols. As the series, The image of war, 1861–1865
Includes index.
ISBN 1-57912-157-8 (alk. Paper)
1. United States—History—Civil War, 1861–1865—Pictorial works. I. Davis, WilliamC., 1946–II. Wiley, Bell Irvin, 1906– III. National Historical Society.

E468.7.C573 2000
973.7—dc21 00-056767

The Editors

Editor
William C. Davis

Senior Consulting Editor
Bell I. Wiley

Photographic Consultants
William A. Frassanito
Manuel kean
Lloyd Ostendorf
Frederick ray

Editorial Assistants
Deborah A. Berrier
Karen K. Kennedy
Denise Mummert
James Rietmulder

Contents

Introduction

WILLIAM C. DAVIS

The origins of the *Civil War Times Illustrated History of the Civil War* are just about as obscure and unlikely as they could be. At their remotest distance, they date from 1960 in a cramped two-bedroom bungalow in Sebatopol, California, in the heart of redwood and wine country. Not exactly a place one associates with the Civil War.

But there I was, aged almost fourteen, having read perhaps two books on the "late unpleasantness," and vaguely aware that I found the general subject interesting. Then I saw and advertisement in the now long-defunct "True Magazine". It was for a book titled *Campfire and Battlefield of the Civil War*, and emphasized that the volume included almost 1,000 photographs from the conflict. In fact, though the ad did not bother to say so, it was a reprint of one of the very first Civil War photographic books, put together by Rossiter Johnson and first published at the turn of the century when the development of the halftone process made it practical to reproduce photographs in books and magazines.

To a typical fourteen-year-old—meaning one with no job and no money—the terms were alluring. The book cost $15.00 plus postage and handling, could be ordered on approval with no money down, and paid for in four installments of $3.95 each. Remember, this is 1960, and begging even $3.95 a month from financially hard-pressed parents was no easy feat. As I recall, I ordered the book unilaterally, trusting that I would find the money somewhere later on.

When the book arrived I experienced something like unto an epiphany. Day after day I poured over the book. I never read the text then or later. To this day I have not read it, nor would I advise anyone else to do so, for intervening years of experience have taught me how unreliable was most of the material being written at the time.

But the photographs transfixed me. The reproduction was awful. Even the originals were not too clear, for halftone printing was still fairly primitive when Campfire and Battlefield first appeared. The reprint I bought was merely photographed from an original copy, and with little given to quality. Nevertheless, it was what was in the photos, and not their quality, that seized me. Here were the actual faces and figures of the men and women of the Civil War, their weapons, their homes, their forts and railroads. These were not just stilted paintings or crude woodcuts at the time, but the faces of the Civil War exactly as they appeared to each other.

I treasured that book, and have it still. It was the very first Civil War book I ever bought (eventually someone made those $3.95 payments, though I cannot remember who). More to the point, it inaugurated a fascination with the photographic record of the conflict that has lasted to this day, and that along the way has produced some of the most exhilarating moments of my life, and with them this new volume of the *Civil War Times' The Civil War Album*.

No one is interested in the life stories of historians, and wisely, I might add, so I will skip the next eighteen years and pick up the story in 1978. Through a series of accidents, fortuitous circumstances, and only occasional design, by then I was editor of "Civil War Times Illustrated", the nation's largest and leading magazine devoted to the conflict, and living in central Pennsylvania where it is published. One of the happiest aspects of editing that magazine was that almost every week, thanks to its wide circulation and reputation, the magazine's editorial offices received letters out of the blue regarding new discoveries in Civil War photography. Collectors sent in copies of the treasures they uncovered in flea markets and antique stores. Dusty attics disgorged long hidden images of the great and small. And in the course of researching illustrations for articles, our editors and art director constantly found overlooked rarities in public archives.

With no particular object in mind, I filed all of this in the back of my mind along with all the rest of the clutter that a historian carries around. Then in 1978 the thunderbolt struck. At nearby Carlisle sat the United States Military History Institute, the Army's chief repository of books and documents. In that year the Institute received an incredible bequest. A defunct Civil War veterans organization, the Massachusetts commandery of the Military Order of the Loyal Legion of the United States, seeking a secure home for its fabulous collections of documents and artifacts before they were vandalized into oblivion, turned most of the material over to the Army. Among the donation were some photographs.

About 40,000 to be exact! The Massachusetts MOLLUS commandery—the acronym by which the group was known—had accumulated in the last two decades of the nineteenth century the greatest collection of Civil War photographs in existence, yet for years it had been virtually unknown outside the MOLLUS membership. Even the people at "Civil War Times Illustrated", which by then had been publishing for almost two decades, had never heard of the collection. I'll never forget the day the100 and more leather-bound volumes arrived at the institute. Colonel George Pappas, then director of the Institute, piled them on a metal trolley and wheeled load after load into the archives room, where I and a couple of other expectant Institute staff attacked them greedily. Almost every page yielded something new, something never-before-published. Here were portraits of generals we had never known to exist, regiment after regiment standing at attention for the camera, nurses at work in the hospitals, even photos of the photographers themselves at work. The magnitude of the collection was staggering, dwarfing by several multiples of the largest known holdings of the time.

As near as I can recall, that same evening, stunned by what I had seen, I lay awake most of the night turning over in my mind just what could be done with that collection. It was out of that sleepless night, whose own roots went all the way back to a fire lit in 1960, that the *Civil War Times Illustrated Photographic History of the Civil War* eventually emerged.

Shadows of the Storm

The Coming of the War

T. HARRY WILLIAMS

America goes mad, and to war with itself

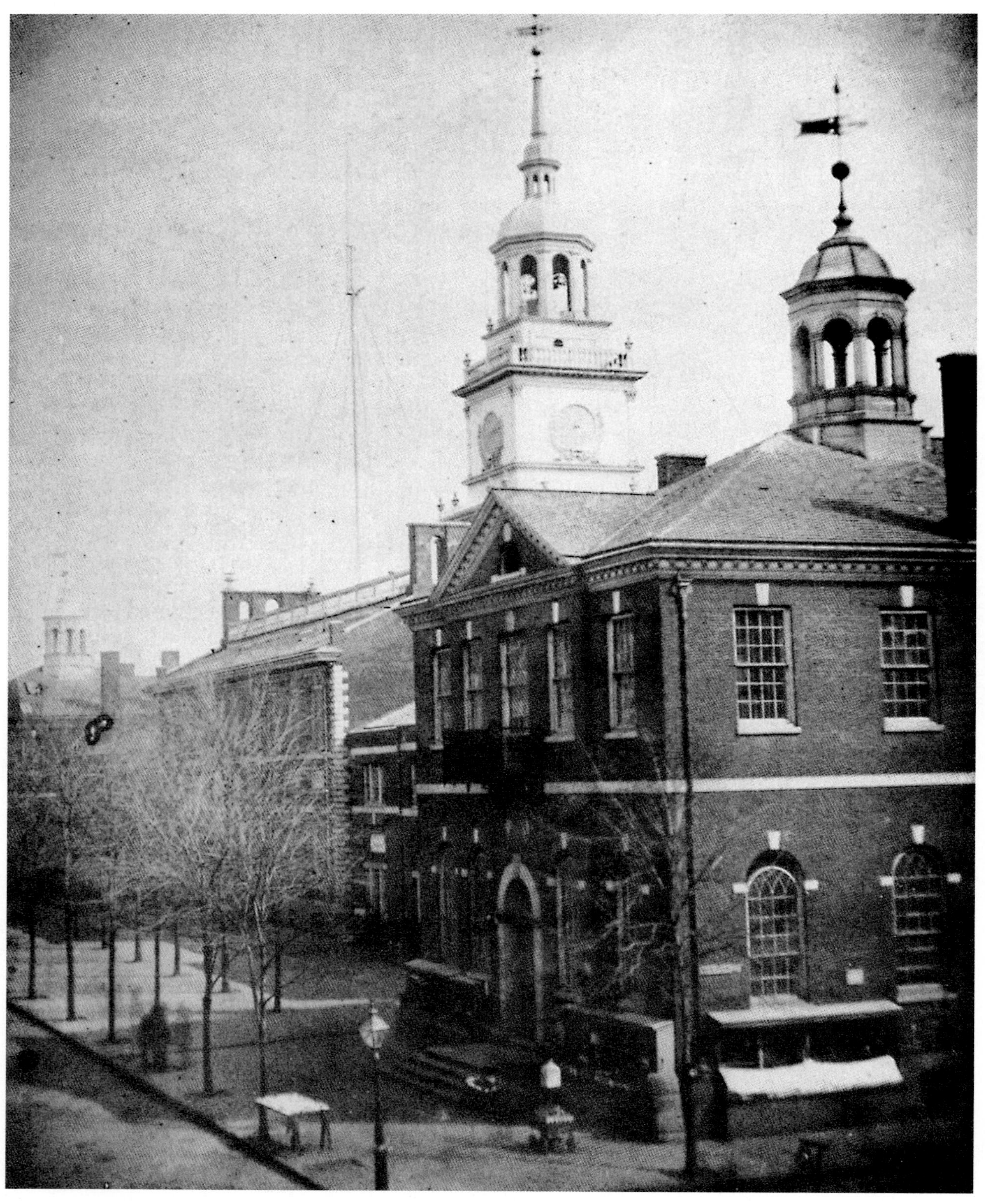

"Let Freedom Ring." Symbols of American independence—Congress Hall, the Pennsylvania State House, and Philadelphia's old City Hall, in 1855. Here began the epic of American nationhood. Here, too, the Founding Fathers planted unknowingly the seeds of dissolution. (FREE LIBRARY OF PHILADELPHIA)

THE MOST SENSATIONAL NEWS in the big city newspapers of the United States in 1855 and 1856 concerned events in far-off Kansas Territory. There, according to reports of correspondents, settlers were committing widespread acts of violence on other settlers, burning and destroying property and engaging in wholesale murder. A certain amount of violence occurred in every frontier area undergoing settlement, and although this was duly recorded in the press, it did not attract special attention. What set the disorders in Kansas apart was that they resulted from, or seemed to result from, a difference in ideology between contesting individuals and groups. Kansans were not killing each other in a spirit of passion or lawlessness but in a mood of crusading zeal. They were fighting to make Kansas a free state—or a slave state. As the turmoil mounted and the deaths increased, the term "Bleeding Kansas" became a national by word.

The question of whether slavery should be permitted to enter the territories was an old one in American politics. It had first arisen in 1819 when Missouri applied for admission as a state with a constitution establishing slavery, and northern opponents of slavery and southern influence in the federal government had attempted to block admission. Although Missouri won entrance in the following year, the bulk of the then existing national domain was declared closed to slavery in the Missouri Compromise. The issue slumbered for years thereafter, but criticism of slavery continued; in deed, beginning in the 1830s more and more persons in the North began to say that slavery must be eradicated, be either abolished immediately or phased out gradually. The territorial issue reappeared in 1848 at the close of the Mexican War. As a result of that conflict, the United States had acquired a huge region to the southwest of the existing boundary, and hardly was the ink dry on the peace treaty when men in the North and the South began to argue about the status of slavery in the new possession.

As the dispute deepened, three proposals to solve the situation were advanced. Most Southerners contended that slaveholders had a constitutional right to take their human property into the recently acquired territory, or for that matter, into any part of the national domain, and to be protected in holding their property by the federal government. The most confirmed anti-slavery Northerners held that Congress had a constitutional power and a moral duty to exclude the institution from the new territory, or from any other territory; they believed that if slavery was prevented from expanding, it would ultimately die a forced death. In between these diametrically opposed views was a third formula that drew its strongest support from Democrats in the north-western states. Known as popular sovereignty, it recommended that Congress should make no pronouncement on the status of slavery in the Mexican cession territory nor, by implication, in any other territory. Slave holders should be permitted to enter, and the position of the institution would be determined by the territorial legislature, or, as advocates of the doctrine liked to say, by the people themselves. Although popular sovereignty did not formally exclude slavery, it was actually a subtle exclusion prescription—the majority of settlers in a territory would undoubtedly come from the more populous North.

Popular sovereignty found enough support to be enacted into law as a part of the Compromise of 1850, which attempted to settle the territorial dispute and other issues which had arisen between the sections. Comparative calm prevailed for several years after passage of the compromise act. But in 1854 Senator Stephen A. Douglas of Illinois offered a measure that stirred fresh and even more bitter controversy. The leader of the northwestern Democrats, Douglas was a believer in popular sovereignty and in the future of the West. Both principles influenced the provisions that he put into his bill. To speed settlement of the western region, he proposed to organize two new territories, Kansas and Nebraska, which lay north of the line proscribing slavery in the Missouri Compromise. But to get southern support for the bill, he had to insert a section that repealed the exclusion clause of the old and revered Missouri law, leaving the determination of the condition of slavery in the proposed territories to their legislatures. The whole North seemed to blaze with fury at passage of the Kansas Nebraska Act. Antislavery leaders cried that the South had used its malign influence to extend its immoral institution and that this latest threat to freedom must be checked—Kansas, the southernmost of the two territories, must be settled by people from the North who would vote to make it a free state. Southern leaders responded to the challenge by urging their people to immigrate to the territory to vote for slavery. Kansas was about to become a prize to be contended for by the sections.

Many of the settlers who went to Kansas did so for the reasons that usually impelled families to move to a new area—they were looking only for a better life. But others entered to support a cause— dedicated enemies of slavery from the northeastern states and dedicated adherents of the institution from the neighboring state of Missouri who were willing to become transitory and illegal voters. Some men on both sides were not content to rely on voting to decide the issue, and soon the intimidation and the shooting started. Violence was superseding the normal democratic process.

The Kansas question stirred men to passion everywhere, including on the floors of Congress. In May 1856 antislavery senator Charles Sumner of Massachusetts delivered a bitter speech attacking various southern colleagues for supporting what he called "The Crime Against Kansas." Representative Preston Brooks of South Carolina, a younger kinsman of one of the senators attacked, was so enraged at the speech that he armed himself with a cane and went over to the other chamber and beat Sumner into bloody unconsciousness. The episode was but one of many examples of actual or threatened violence in Congress. Some members came to sessions wearing thinly concealed pistols, several fist-swinging brawls occurred between individual Northerners and Southerners or between groups, and challenges to duels were freely passed. The violence in halls dedicated to debate, like the violence in Kansas, was a symbol dark with portent for the future. Americans were becoming so aroused about the question of slavery in any of its manifestations that they were not satisfied to discuss it or to vote on it. They could relieve their feelings only by committing physical harm on those who disagreed

Left: It is a thriving, bustling nation, full of itself and its ever-stretching power and prosperity. Already in 1860, Broadway in New York City is one of the busiest streets in the world. (U.S. ARMY MILITARY HISTORY INSTITUTE, CARLISLE BARRACKS, PA.)

Above: On Saturday, October 13, 1860, J. W. Black of the firm of Black & Batchelder loaded his camera into a balloon operated by Professor Samuel A. King, and up they went, several hundred feet above Boston. There below them they captured the image of one of the principal trading cities of the world. Washington Street runs diagonally from lower right, Old South Meeting House at its other end. (U.S. AIR FORCE)

Below: To St. Joseph, Missouri, where immigrant trains jumped off into the Great Plains for the trek to Oregon and California. Albert Bierstadt took this 1859 view of the "Pike's Peak Passenger & Freight Express Co." (KANSAS STATE HISTORICAL SOCIETY, TOPEKA)

Right: It is a nation moving west, leaving in train thousands of rural still lifes such as this unidentified scene. (JOE M. BAUMAN)

Above: West to Nebraska spread the tentacles of a voracious America, taking root in the rich farmlands that produced abundant grain for sale in the East. Steamboats like the Colorado here at Omaha brought the produce to the railhead for the Hannibal & St. Joe and other new railroads to move speedily to market. (NEBRASKA STATE HISTORICAL SOCIETY, LINCOLN)

Below: To the mining camps and burgeoning cities of the mountains like Central City, Colorado. (DENVER Pu,BLIC LIBRARY, WESTERN HISTORY DEPARTMENT)

Left: To Illinois expansion spread, to Galena, and a leather store run by Grant Perkins. Ulysses S. Grant. (CHICAGO HISTORICAL SOCIETY)

with them. Their anger flowed in part from the contradictions in American society, a society that was homogeneous but also diverse, that was experiencing an expansion of wealth and power but was being torn apart by ideological division.

The United States in 1860 was a land of imposing physical dimensions. The writ of American authority ran from the Atlantic Ocean to the Pacific Ocean, from the Canadian border to the Mexican border. A large part of the expanse west of the Mississippi River was as yet unpeopled except by Indian tribes. A tier of states just beyond the river marked the farthest line of settlement, and beyond them was wilderness stretching to California and Oregon on the Pacific coast. But already emigrants were pushing into the distant areas—the movement to Kansas was one example—and a constant increase in the population of the older regions gave promise that the eruptions would continue and that more states would soon be added to what popular orators liked to call "the galaxy of the Union."

The population of the thirty-three states then in the Union was approximately 31,000,000 persons, almost double the number of inhabitants in 1840. Nearly half of these lived west of the Appalachian mountain chain, a distribution that revealed the newer states were growing in influence at the expense of the older ones. Another demographic development, and at the moment a more ominous one, was the disparity in population between the free states and the slave states. The former numbered about 22,000,000 persons and the latter 9,000,000 persons of whom one third were black slaves. The South was becoming a minority, losing strength in the House of Representatives and the Electoral College every decade.

Most Americans lived, as their fathers and grandfathers had lived, in rural surroundings, on farms or in small towns. But beginning in the 1840s a significant shift of population toward cities occurred. New York City, the largest urban center, counted over 800,000 persons in 1860; Philadelphia, 565,000 persons; and Boston, 165,000. The most sensational growth was experienced by Chicago, which in little more than twenty years grew from 250 to over 100,000 inhabitants. Not participating in the trend toward urbanism was the South. If Baltimore, with its 200,000 people, is excepted as a border town, the region could boast of but one large city, New Orleans, whose 165,000 population was small in comparison with the teeming northern centers. Richmond and Charleston, next greatest in numbers, had only 40,000 each.

An increasing population was but one manifestation of national growth. Also expanding was the economy, the most dramatic and significant inflation occurring in industry. Textile, iron, and other plants dotted the Northeast, and manufacturies were beginning to spread into the Northwest and, although to a lesser extent, into the South. Accompanying the revolution in production was a revolution in transportation and communication. Railroads, superseding other means of conveyance, laced the eastern half of the country, the greatest concentration of lines being in the Northeast and the Northwest. The effect of the coming of the railroads on American life was like that of the great technological innovations of the twentieth century—a conquest of time and space had occurred. In the 1830s a traveler required three weeks to go from New York to Chicago or St. Louis; by 1860 he could complete the trip in two to three days. The transportation revolution bound the various parts of the country into a greater if uncomfortable unity.

The section least affected by the transforming changes of the time was the South. The region below the Potomac and the Ohio stood apart, or wanted to stand apart, from the mainstream of progress. The South was still distinctive—rural, agricultural, conservative, maintaining an ordered and orderly social structure, and boasting in its plantation lords the closest approach to an American aristocracy. Above all other differences, the South was the only part of the country that contained in large numbers a race of another color than white, a race held in slavery. Southerners of all classes stood determined to uphold slavery and the system of race relations based on it against all outside attacks. Their peculiar culture, they proclaimed, was superior to that of the North. One spokesman, denouncing free society as a "monstrous abortion," described his own society as a "healthy, beautiful and natural being." The refusal of Southerners to consider any modification of their system was a key to the conflicts that rent the nation during the last half of the 1850s.

The presidential election of 1856 took place against this backdrop of continuing violence in Kansas and continuing debate over the status of slavery in the territories. The Democrats nominated James Buchanan of Pennsylvania as their candidate and offered popular sovereignty as a formula to settle the territorial question. Their opposition was a new party, the Republicans, just two years of age. The Republican organization had been formed in the anger that swept the North after the enactment of the Kansas-Nebraska Act and had absorbed most northern members of the former Whig party and some antislavery northern Democrats. The Republicans nominated as their candidate John C. Fremont of California, famous as an explorer of the Far West, and submitted as their platform congressional exclusion of slavery from all national territories. A one-idea party, they were also a sectional party, having their main strength in the North with only a smattering of support in the border slave states.

The Democrats, although troubled by sectional division, were still a national party, and they elected Buchanan and a majority to Congress. However, the young Republican party had made a surprising showing. Fremont carried eleven of the sixteen northern states and rolled up a large popular vote. A slight shift of votes in a few states would have made the sectional party the majority party.

James Buchanan was a dignified "elder statesman," almost sixty-six years of age at the time of his inauguration, and an amiable and well-meaning public servant. But he lacked resolution of character and flinched from taking strong action in a crisis. Enjoying the company of Southerners, he was inclined to let himself be guided by southern leaders. Cast into office in a period of storm, he could not have controlled all events; he rarely tried to control any of them.

Most of the crises of his administration were concerned with the issues in controversy

Right: To Minnesota's Castle Rock it spread. (MINNESOTA HISTORICAL SOCIETY)

Below: And with "California or Bust," they completed the conquest of a continent, drawn by land, adventure, and gold. This early daguerreotype by Shaw & Johnson shows a gold claim in the early 18505. (CALIFORNIA HISTORICAL SOCIETY LIBRARY)

Below: To the once barren wastes of Utah, where Salt Lake City sprang from the desert and Brigham Young s dream. (UTAH STATE HISTORICAL SOCIETY)

Right: Northwest to Oregon went America, to Table Rock City, on stirring stories of the Oregon Trail. (SOUTHERN OREGON HISTORICAL SOCIETY)

Left: It was a nation thriving on commerce, whose fast clipper ships traded with the world and turned the docks at the end of New York's Wall Street into a forest of masts. (NEW-YORK HISTORICAL SOCIETY)

Below: Yet there were two Americas. While the northern states and their people pushed and built and traded and manufactured, another America took a slower pace. The South, too, had its major trading cities like Charleston, South Carolina, and to be sure, its skyline evidences a few factory smokestacks.

between the sections and every outcome exacerbated sectional bitterness and moved the nation closer to dissolution. In Kansas the turmoil between the contesting factions continued unabated, with efforts now concentrated on electing a convention to write a state constitution. Buchanan used his influence to aid the proslavery side, which was clearly a minority. His action enraged Republicans and disgusted popular sovereignty members of his own party, and Congress refused to accept the constitution presented by the slavery adherents. Kansas remained a territory, and an issue of discord.

At the height of the Kansas dispute the Supreme Court handed down a pronouncement on the question of whether slavery could enter a territory in Dred Scott v. Sanford. The case had a complicated background, but in the broadest meaning it involved the exclusion clause in the Missouri Compromise. The majority opinion (seven of the nine justices were Democrats) held that this clause was in violation of the constitutional provision that forbade Congress to take property without "due process of law." The Congress of 1820 had acted illegally in barring slavery, and no Congress could exclude the institution. Translated into the language of current politics, the decision declared the platform of the Republican party to he unconstitutional. By implication it also disallowed popular sovereignty,

Above: And the factory came to America, the sweatshop, the women and child labor, the endless days at machines producing textiles. There was great prosperity, but it cost great toil. (USAMHI)

Right: Trade between the states flourished, borne on iron rails and man-made waterways like the Chesapeake & Ohio Canal. (NATIONAL ARCHIVES, WASHINGTON, D.C.)

for if Congress could not prohibit slavery in the territories neither could a territorial legislature that was created by Congress. The voice of the highest tribunal did not calm but rather excited sectional passions. A typical Republican effusion denounced the Court as the "last resort behind which despotism is sheltered," and Republican leaders proclaimed that when their party gained control of the government they would reconstitute the Court and retry the case.

Northern anger at the Dred Scott decision was more than matched by southern rage at an event occurring in 1859. John Brown, a fierce foe of slavery who had migrated to Kansas and participated in the killings there, reappeared in the East full of a plan to strike at slavery in the South itself. With encouragement and monetary support from certain abolitionists, who realized his general purpose, he proposed to seize the Federal arsenal at Harpers Ferry in western Virginia, and from this base to incite an armed slave insurrection. In October he and eighteen followers descended on the town and captured the arsenal. No slaves came in to join him, and he was pinned down in his position by attacking citizens and local militia. News of the raid alarmed official Washington, and President Buchanan, reacting with unusual vigor, dispatched a contingent of marines under Robert E. Lee of the Regular Army to Harpers Ferry to

Above: But Southerners preferred to think of themselves in a different way, as the last outpost of a more graceful, pastoral mode of life that existed more in myth than in actual memory. They thought of the beauty of Wade Hampton's garden at his plantation in Columbia, South Carolina. (USAMHI)

Right: The barons of industrial expansion discovered the riches beneath the earth, and profits came to be measured in barrels. Oil Creek Valley, near Rouseville, Pennsylvania already the scars of industry blotted the landscape. (DRAKE WELL MUSEUM, TITUSVILLE, PA.)

Below:. . . of their river cities like Vicksburg on the mighty Mississippi. H. J. Herrick took this view from the Louisiana side of the river, Vicksburg's courthouse towering over all. (OLD COU,RT HOUSE MUSEUM, VICKSBURG, MISS.)

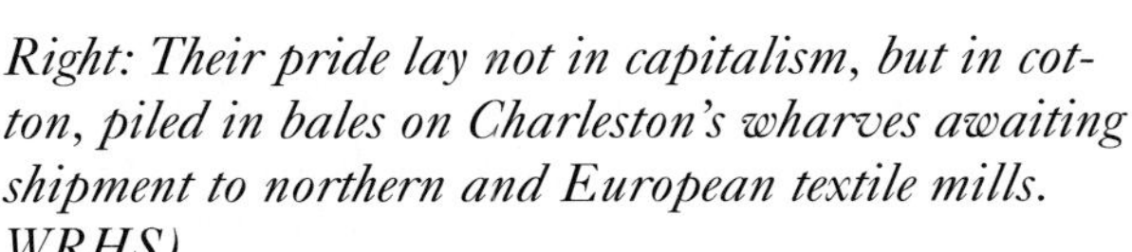

Right: Their pride lay not in capitalism, but in cotton, piled in bales on Charleston's wharves awaiting shipment to northern and European textile mills. WRHS)

Below: Despite differences in their economies and ways of life, North and South still managed to accommodate each other peaceably enough in the first half of the century. Both rejoiced in the young nation's expanding horizons, and celebrated their common heroes on days like the July 4, 1859, celebration at New York Harbor. (USAMHI)

Above and right: Slaves were bought and sold, and between transactions were often kept in pens like this one at Alexandria, Virginia, almost within sight of the Capitol in Washington City. (USAMHI)

Above: Whitney made only part of the work easy. The rest, the picking, must be done by hand, by slaves, the captive labor force of the South, the legacy of a problem the Founding Fathers chose not to solve. Timothy O'Sullivan photographed this slave family on a South Carolina cotton plantation in 1862. (LIBRARY OF CONGRESS, WASHINGTON, D.C.)

deal with the crisis. Brown resisted the onslaught of Lee's force, but with ten of his men killed he finally had to surrender. The national government handed him over to Virginia to be tried for treason against the state.

Brown's raid aroused fury in the South, and also horror. The whites lived in constant fear of a slave uprising, and now it seemed that outside agitators, abolitionists or Republicans, had attempted to incite an insurrection. Southern suspicions were heightened by the praise heaped upon Brown by abolitionist leaders who hailed him as a saint, an "angel of light" in the words of New England writer Henry David Thoreau. Thoreau and others hoped that Brown would not escape hanging and would become a martyr to the cause of freedom. They need not have feared. Brown was duly tried and executed. In his last message to the world he wrote that he was certain the crimes of "this, guilty land" would never be purged away "but with Blood." The stage was set for the fateful presidential election of 1860.

All the boiling tensions in the country came to a head in 1860. The election in that year marked the apogee of sectionalism. Parties represented largely sectional interests, and the result prompted the South to withdraw from the Union. It is the only contest in American history in which the losing side felt that it could not live with the consequence of defeat.

The Democrats were the first to meet in convention. Gathering in historic Charleston in April, they plunged into angry debate on the issue of slavery in the territories. Southern delegates demanded that the platform affirm the right of slaveholders to take their chattels into any part of the national domain, and northern delegates held out for a popular sovereignty plank. When the latter triumphed, a number of southern delegations walked out of the hall. The managers thereupon adjourned the convention to meet again in Baltimore in June, hoping that time would cool the passions of the opposing factions. However, at Baltimore anger was even more intense, and another southern exodus occurred. The remaining delegates nominated Stephen A. Douglas to run on a popular sovereignty platform. The bolters nominated John C. Breckinridge of Kentucky to stand for the rights of slavery in the territories. There were now two Democratic parties in the field, and although each had adherents in the other section, one was a northern party and one was a southern party. The only national political organization in the country had at last split on

Above: They grudgingly gave credit to Yankee Eli Whitney's invention of the cotton gin for making possible the large-scale production and harvest of the fiber. Gin houses like this one on Edisto Island in South Carolina hummed with activity throughout the 18505. (WRHS)

Above: They planted the fields on Pope's Plantation at Hilton Head, South Carolina.

Below: Over the nation loomed the haunting specter of sectionalism, of slavery, of southern pretensions for a nationhood of its own. South Carolina's John C. Calhoun, ardent champion of states' rights and secession, might lie dead in his tomb in Charleston, but what he stood for still lived. (USAMHI)

Left: Slaves became not only a work force, but a measure of wealth as well. These blacks of all ages and sex are gathered in Baton Rouge, Louisiana. (OCHM)

Below: And they brought their day's pickings in every evening to put it through Mr.Whitney's machine. George N. Barnard's postwar photograph was taken near Charleston, South Carolina. (NYHS)

the rock of sectionalism.

The Republicans met in bustling Chicago in May in a huge building, the Wigwam, built by the Republicans of the city to house the convention.

Elated at the promise of victory held out by Democratic division, the party managers were determined to present a platform and a candidate that would appeal to the broadest spectrum of northern opinion. They were especially concerned that the party should not appear to be a collection of wild eyed crusaders who had no other objective but to attack slavery. Now the Republicans were to stand before the voters as men of moderation whose vision embraced many issues. The platform embodied the new strategy. Although reaffirming their opposition to slavery's expansion into the territories, the Republicans declared that they had no intention of interfering with the institution in the states where it already existed. Other planks emphasized economic

Below: Sectional schism was seemingly averted in 1856 when the contest for the presidency First saw a young Republican party, northern for the most part and antislavery in character, defeated at the polls. Democrats in the South paraded horse-drawn "ships of state" in their streets. They elected their candidate, routed Republicanism, and, so they thought, ensured peace. (JMB)

Above: Of all the men ever to hold presidential office, tile people chose the one least suited. ,james Buchanan lacked almost everything, necessary in a President, most of all a firm will and resolution. The collapse of the Union began almost at once. (NA)

issues. The party endorsed a high protective tariff, internal improvements (national financial support to transportation projects), and a homestead bill (free land to settlers in the West). In a shrewd bid for victory the Republicans had combined the idealism of the antislavery impulse and the aspirations of the principal economic groups in the North.

The party showed the same sense of practicality in choosing a candidate. Passing over the best known leaders who had records that might alienate some voters, the convention nominated Abraham Lincoln of Illinois. Lincoln was, in the language of politics, an "available" candidate. He had a national reputation, but he had not been on the national scene long enough to accumulate a list of enemies. He had spoken out against the Kansas Nebraska Act, but he was not thought to be a "radical" antislavery man. His views on slavery squared with those of the mass of Republicans. He believed that the institution was wrong and that it should persistently be labeled as wrong. He would not interfere with the institution where it existed, but he would uncompromisingly oppose its expansion with the purpose of bringing about its demise. The opponents of slavery, he said, must "place it where the public mind shall rest in the belief that it is in the course of ultimate extinction."

The appearance of three major parties indicated an unusual splintering of popular opinion. And this was not the end of it. Still a fourth party entered the lists, the new and hastily formed Constitutional Union party. Composed of former Whigs, it nominated John Bell of Tennessee as its candidate and presented as a platform only support of the Constitution and the Union. The apparent softness in its position was a deliberate strategy. The leaders thought that with so many candidates dividing the vote no one of them would gain a majority of the electoral vote and that the election would be thrown into the House of Representatives. There their conserva-

Above: They picked the cotton under the eye of their white overseers, as in this postwar image. (NA, WOMEN S BUREAU)

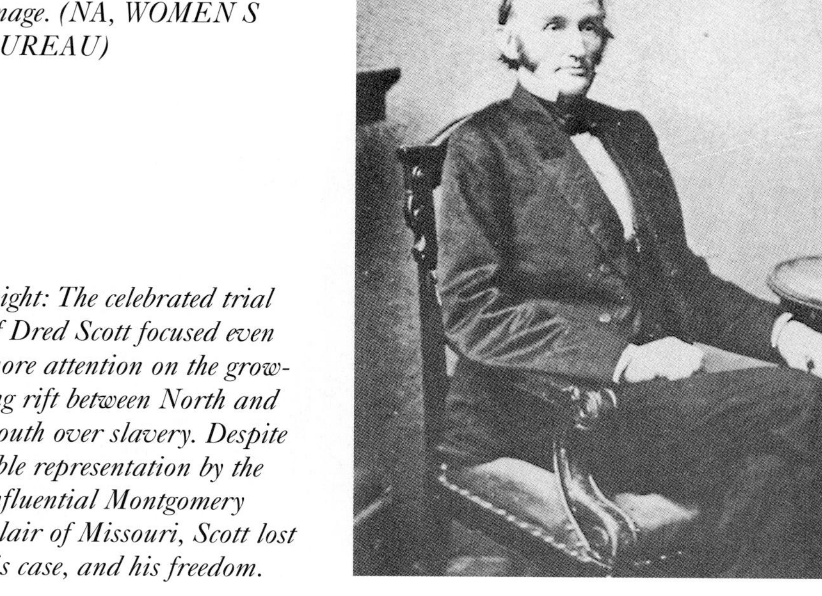

Right: The celebrated trial of Dred Scott focused even more attention on the growing rift between North and South over slavery. Despite able representation by the influential Montgomery Blair of Missouri, Scott lost his case, and his freedom.

Right: Violent men like James Lane led bands of marauders who proved little better than ruffians in the quest to wrest control of Kansas from their o pposition . (u SAM Hi)

tive nominee might emerge as the victor.

The result of the election in November reflected the division of parties and populace. Although Lincoln had a minority of the popular vote, about 40 percent of the total, he rolled up a clear electoral majority, 180 votes. His margin was the consequence of success in the northern states with large electoral votes; he carried every free state except New Jersey, which he divided with Douglas. (The Republican sweep did not, however, bring in a majority in Congress.) Breckinridge carried the Lower South and three border slave states and stood second in the electoral vote. Bell took three border states and came in third. Douglas won only one state, Missouri, and divided New Jersey with Lincoln. However, his popular vote was second to Lincoln's, about 30 percent of the total. If it is assumed that his popular sovereignty followers were voting against the expansion of slavery, 70 percent of the voters had registered a verdict to pen up slavery where it was.

During the campaign, extremist leaders in the Lower South had tried to impress upon their people that if the Republicans won the contest, the interests of the South would not be safe in the Union. The "Black Republicans" would sooner or later be driven to attack slavery, that is, to interfere with the prevailing racial patterns, and to prevent this dire eventuality southern states should secede from the Union. One of the loudest sounders of the cry to get out was Robert Toombs of Georgia, and he became even more strident after the election. Addressing the Georgia legislature in November, he urged secession before the Republicans, "your enemies," took office on March 4, 1861. "Then strike," he thundered, "strike while it is yet time." Leaders in other states reechoed his demand.

The threats of secession were heard in the North with mixed feelings. Many persons refused to believe that the danger was serious,

Right: Then violence erupted at Harpers Ferry, Virginia, and the North and South were so polarized that there seemed no cementing them back together. John Brown of Ossawatomie, a free-state fighter from Kansas, led a band of men across this bridge on the Potomac, turned right, and . . . (USAMHI)

Right: The conflict reached the floor of the United States Senate when Charles Sumner of Massachusetts, decrying the "Crime Against Kansas" in a violent antislave speech, was attacked and caned senseless by Preston Brooks of South Carolina. For three years Sumner's chair remained empty, itself a powerful symbol for the abolitionist forces.

Below: Kansas came to be "Bloody Kansas" as it sought statehood. Antislave men flocked to the territory while proslave interests, fearing that the slave states would soon become a minority in Congress, did likewise. Each hoped to provide a majority to bring Kansas into statehood. The conflict between them led to open warfare on the plains, fought by units like this Free-State Battery at Topeka in 1856. (KANSAS STATE HISTORICAL SOCIETY, TOPEKA)

Right: In 1858 the battle continued in Illinois, where Stephen A. Douglas and Abraham Lincoln vied for a Senate seat. Douglas won the election, but Lincoln won nationwide prominence thanks to their celebrated series of debates. Photograph by Calvin Jackson of Pittsfield, October 1, 1858. (USAMHI)

Above: . . swarmed down this street to the United States Arsenal. Here they hoped to capture arms to lead a slave uprising in the South that would end slavery forever. Instead, the townspeople quickly organized against them, and Brown and his men found themselves cornered across the street . . . (CHESAPEAKE & OHIO RAILROAD CO.)

Left, right and below: In Richmond, Virginia's governor issued the call for troops to suppress this outrage, and many stepped forward. The 1st Virginia Militia, the "Richmond Grays," answered the call. They did not take part in the final capture of brown, but they did arrive in Charles Town, Virginia, in time to form a hollow square a7round a gallows where old John Brown was hanged after his trial. One of their number p7esent was john Wilkes Booth, an actor, who rather pitied Brown, 'na brave old man," he said. These four views, two of them not previously published, show the Richmond Grays at the time of Brown's trial and hanging.

Right: . . . in an engine house. (CHESAPEAKE & OHIO RAILROAD CO.)

thinking that the South was only bluffing to wring concessions from the national government. Other men were acutely alarmed, realizing that the Union was threatened with dissolution. One who was especially concerned was lame-duck President Buchanan.

In his message to Congress in early December, Buchanan took note of the gathering sentiment behind secession in the Lower South. He denied that a state could constitutionally leave the Union, but he also denied that the federal government could force a state that had left to return, or, as he put it, could "make war against a state." To avert secession, he urged Congress to frame an amendment to the Constitution that would guarantee the existence of slavery, ensure the right of slaveholders to enter the territories, and guarantee the privilege of owners to recover fugitive slaves. In pleading for compromise Buchanan thought that he was acting the part of a patriot. He did not seem to realize that his idea of compromise was weighted heavily in favor of the South.

Both houses of Congress took Buchanan's advice, appointing separate committees to frame an amendment. The House committee was never able to come up with a complete plan; it agreed on an amendment guaranteeing the existence of slavery, but arrived at no accord on the question of slavery in the territories. The Senate committee gave earnest consideration to a proposal submitted by Senator John J. Crittenden of Kentucky and known therefore as the Crittenden Compromise. This measure also ensured the existence of slavery and contained a provision to satisfy southern demands as to fugitive slaves. Most important, Crittenden attempted to deal with the troublesome territorial problem. His solution was to establish the demarcation line of the Missouri Compromise, the thirty sixth parallel, in all of the territory of the United States then held or thereafter acquired—slavery would be prohibited north of the line and permitted south of it. Southern members of the committee

Above: Here the old man, who had grown a beard since this 1856 photograph was made, fought desperately, even while his sons were being killed beside him. (KANSAS STATE HISTORICAL. SOCIETY, TOPEKA)

indicated that they would accept this division if the Republicans as a party would support it. Before returning an answer, Republican leaders sought the reaction of President-elect Lincoln, waiting in Springfield to come to Washington. Lincoln returned a negative answer. There could be "no compromise" on the question of extending slavery, he said. "The tug has to come & better now than later," he wrote in one letter. The Senate committee had to abandon its labors.

The attempts at compromise failed for various reasons. Many men on both sides felt that they could not yield their beliefs, either out of devotion to principle or to party. Some men on both sides would have been willing to give way if they had thought war would follow, but they convinced themselves that they could have their desires without war. And there were some in each section who did not care if war came, who, in fact, welcomed it, if for no other reason than to relieve tensions that were becoming unbearable.

While the efforts to compromise were drag-

Right: L.eadership from the Executive Mansion, the "White House," was nonexistent. Here Montgomery C. Meigs, the engineer supervising the expansion of the Capitol building, used his stereo camera to provide a deceptively peaceful image.

Below: Many in the North refused to abide by the Fugitive Slave Law, part of the Compromise of 1850. When this slave, "Old Peter," nearly one hundred years old, escaped to the home of Slater Brown in Lancaster, Pennsylvania, the Quaker refused to return him to his former master.

Left: The man who led the capture of brown, Colonel Robert E. Lee—a photo taken in 1851. (CHS)

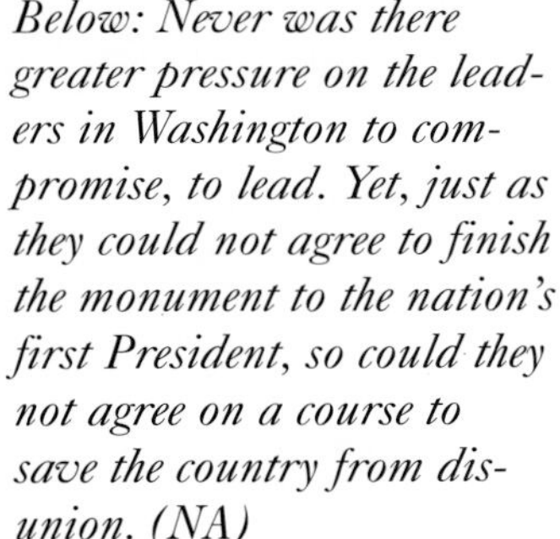

Below: Never was there greater pressure on the leaders in Washington to compromise, to lead. Yet, just as they could not agree to finish the monument to the nation's first President, so could they not agree on a course to save the country from disunion. (NA)

Left: The situation was worse at the opposite end of Pennsylvania avenue. The Congress, like the building in which it met, seemed to be in pieces. Montgomery Meigs's photog;raph shows the old Capitol dome, which he would soon replace, and the partially completed new Senate wing. (LC)

Above: Buchanan and his Cabinet proved hopelessly ineb'ectual. The two members seated at left, Jacob Thompson and John B. Floyd, were suspected of financial malfeasance. Both would become secessionists. Secretary of State Lewis Cass, behind them, had long since ceased to be a potent force in public affairs. Ilowell Cobb of Georgia, standing just right of Buchanan, would support secession as well. Only Jo.seph Holt, standing at far right, and Jeremiah Black, seated far right, were rnen of real force and strong, Union sentiment. Isaac T oucey, seated to the left of Black, remained an unknown quantity. A divided administration could hardly unite a country. (LC)

ging to a sad conclusion in Washington, in the deep South states the adventure in secession got off in a mood of gaiety and exultation. South Carolina, long the leader of southern separatism, acted first. A convention elected to consider the course the state should take proved unanimously secessionist. Meeting in Charleston, the convention voted on December 20 to take the state out of the Union. The news of its action was greeted in the city with wild rejoicing. An English newspaper correspondent visiting in Charleston a short time later caught the spirit of the citizens. "Secession is the fashion here," he wrote. "Young ladies sing for it; old ladies pray for it; young men are dying to fight for it; old men are ready to demonstrate it."

Six other states soon followed the example of South Carolina. They were, in the order of their leaving, Mississippi, Florida, Alabama, Georgia, Louisiana, and Texas. Not all of them went out rejoicing as South Carolina had done. In some conventions there were men who opposed secession, not the right but the need to secede; they counseled delay and cooperative sectional action rather than individual state action. And there were other men who accepted secession reluctantly, and with heavy hearts voted to sever relations with the Union. But the seceders were in

Below: Here compromise failed. The old House of Representatives chamber about 1861. (LC)

Below: There the once powerful voice of Henry Clay had managed compromise from discord. But Clay's voice was stilled, and none stepped forward to take his place. (I\'YH S)

Above: The Capitol from Pennsylvania Avenue in 1860. There is still much work to be done—on the building and the Union. (LC)

Above: Instead the hot-bloods took the floor, the "fire-eaters" like Senator William L. Yancey of Alabama. Dazzled by the idea of a southern nation, and perhaps their own political ambitions within it, they spurned compromise. (NYHS)

Above: Meigs's camera captures Secretary of State Cass standing at a table, and his own image in the mirror in the background. (LC)

Above: Buchanan's Secretary of the Treasury Howell Cobb gaze the secessionists tacit support. (LC)

Below: The fiery W. G. "Parson" Brownlow of Tennessee made strident exclamations for the Union, and published his newspaper called the Rebel Ventilator. (USAMHI)

Above: Alexander H. Stephens, cong,ressman from Georgia, one-time friend of Lincoln, spoke for those who interpreted the Constitution so strictly that secession seemed justified, if not actually legal.

control in every convention and carried their will. The process was completed by February 1.

The secession leaders realized that their states could not exist separately. Their intention from the first had been to create a new and a southern Union. Accordingly, representatives of the seven states met in February at the little city of Montgomery, Alabama (population, 8,800), to write a provisional constitution and form a provisional government. They called their nation the Confederate States of America and chose as its president Jefferson Davis of Mississippi. Davis came to Montgomery to be inaugurated on February 18. In his address he affirmed unrelenting devotion to the cause of southern independence.

Less than a month later Abraham Lincoln was inaugurated President of what had been the United States in a Washington tense with rumors of impending civil conflict. Although in his address he pled with the seceded states to return, he made it clear that he would not offer any concessions to induce them to come back. He denied that any state could lawfully leave the Union, repudiating secession as the "essense of anarchy." The portion of his remarks that most angered Southerners was the announcement that he would "hold, occupy, and possess" Federal properties within the confines of the Confederacy. He did not have to identify the places that he was referring to, offshore forts that the seceding states and the Confederate government had not been able to seize. Two of these forts particularly occupied public attention, Sumter in Charleston harbor and Pickens near the coast at Pensacola, Florida. The Davis government was mounting military preparations to assault them if this was necessary to secure them, and Lincoln was letting Davis know that they would be defended.

Lincoln's policy, although stated subtly, was nevertheless plain—he hoped that the Union could bc restored peaceably but if this was not

Above: Not all Southerners were fire-eaters, though. The old hero of the Texas Revolution, Sam Houston, spoke out against secession and for the Union, even at personal risk. (NA)

Right: Virginia's governor Henry A. Wise, from his experience with John Brown's raid in his own state, felt more keenly than most the fear of slave uprising and northel-n aggressions against slavery. (JACK MCGUIRE)

Left and above: A bitter reminder to the southern cadets were the cannon captured during the war with Mexico a decade before. Southern soldiers contributed considerably to that war, and they had hoped to bring much of the conquered territory into the Union as slave states.

possible, he was willing to employ force, to resort to war. Davis's policy was also clear—the seceded states would not voluntarily return to the Union and the Confederacy would maintain its independence by force if it had to. The policies of both men and both governments accorded with the feelings of the northern and the southern people. Most Northerners valued the Union and would fight to keep it inviolate. Most Southerners valued the political and social system represented by the Confederacy and would fight to defend that. A martial spirit was rising in both sections. It could be seen in the bellicose declarations of leaders, in the cry for action from ordinary people, and, in a picturesque but dangerous manifestation, in the many volunteer and militia groups of young men that were springing into being throughout the once united land and that were loudly eager to demonstrate their manhood.

Only an incident was needed to touch off war.

Left: In the midst of the sectional agitation, and largely stimulated by it, a martial spirit grew rapidly North and South. Cadets at the United States Military Academy at West Point, New York, found themselves divided, often in heated argument. From their practice batteries overlooking the Hudson . . .

Right: . . . to their field exercises at Camp Walker, they argued and took their sides.

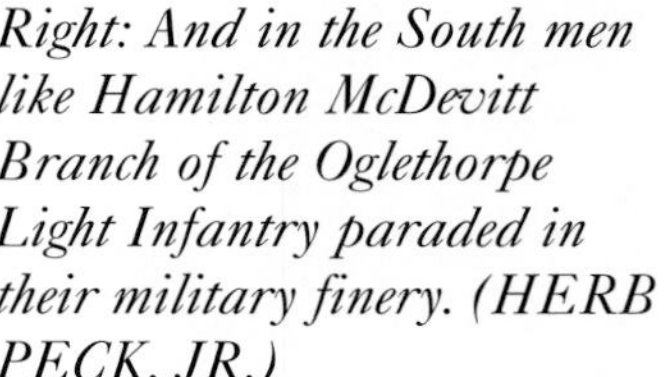

Right: And in the South men like Hamilton McDevitt Branch of the Oglethorpe Light Infantry paraded in their military finery. (HERB PECK, JR.)

Below: Now young men, like these members of the class of 1864, pondered just what their budding militaly careers held for them, and who their first battles would bring against them. Standing at left is Ranald MacKenzie, soon to be a general, and in years to come a noted Indian fighter in the West. (USAMHI)

Right: Even less experienced were the volunteer and militia units springing up everywhere. What they lacked in field knowledge, they made up for in natty attire and precision at drill. Here officers of the 6th New York State Militia and, standing second from the left, E. Elmer Ellsworth, in July 1860. A favorite of Abraham Lincoln, Ellsworth led one of the North's finest drilled units, his "Fire zouaves." (CHS)

Above: The old Regular Army was undermanned, ill equipped, and officered largely by men with no real combat experience, and those that did know battle were acquainted with a kind of war that would never be fought again. Colonel Joseph Plympton and his black orderly. (PEARL KORN)

Left and below: And in Louisville, Kentucky, in August 1860, the State Guard held a much publicized encampment. The holiday atmosphere of it all, with a refreshment stand and ice cream, barely concealed the rattling sabers. (KENTUCKY HISTORICAL SOCIETY,]CENTUCKY MILITARY HISTORY MUSEUM, FRANKFORT, KY.)

Below: By 1860, the last remaining hope of maintaining the Union was the Democratic party. Friendly to southern interest.s, it could keep the South in the nation if it stayed united and defeated the Republicans in November. Instead, the party fragmented. The chiefly northern wing nominated Stephen A. Douglas, the "Little Giant" of Illinois. Immensely popular, he still came in last in the electoral ballot. (USAMHI)

Above: Cincinnati, Ohio's "Guthrie Grays," ready for the foe, whoever it might be. (CINCINNATI HISTORICAL SOCIETY)

Left: The Mobile Cadets from Alabama refined their marksmanship. (HP)

Left: Shortly after his nomination for the Presidency, a still beardless Lincoln unbends his lanky frame for a full-length portrait in his home town of Springfield, Illinois. (LC)

Above: Their election brought jubilation in much of the North, as in Mohawk, NewYork, where the "Mohawk Wide Awakes" and their band paraded in honor of the victory. (LLOYD OSTENDORF COLLECTION)

Left: Animated by years of heated rhetoric, exaggerated fears and hatreds, irresponsible politicians, and an impulse for southern nationalism, South Carolina called a convention here in Secession Hall. The outcome was never in doubt. In December 1860 they adopted here an ordinance of secession. The broadsides on the streets the next day read "The Union Is Dissolved. (USAMHI)

Below: . . . Abraham Lincoln. In June 1860 photographer Alexander Hesler of Chicago captured Lincoln just after his nomination. Friends regarded it as the best portrait of Lincoln ever made. In November he became the sixteenth President of the United States. (KEAN ARCHIVES, PHILADELPHIA)

Above: The more conservative Northerners and the southern rights men nominated Buchanan's Vice-President, John C. Breckinridge of Kentucky. The only candidate with nationwide appeal, his popular vote was evenly divided between North and South, but he placed second in the Electoral College. (LC)

Above: Elected with him, as Vice-President, was Hannibal Hamlin of Maine. (USAMHI)

Above: But there was no rejoicing in Charleston, South Carolina. Despite Lincoln's earnest promises not to interfere with slavery where it already existed, Southerners saw in his election a dagger poised at their labor system, their way of life, and their honor. (NYHS)

Left: Six other states did the same in the weeks to follow, and on February 18, 1861, in Montgomery, Alabama, new capital of the Confederate States of America, they inaugurated their first President, Jefferson Davis of Mississippi. A. C. McIntyre of Mont-gomery sensed something historic taking place, and set his camera to capture the scene. The Alabama statehouse clock says 1 P.M. Davis and Howell Cobb stand at the doorway between the center columns. The Confederacy is begun. (NA)

Left: In the Nor-th, four days after Davis's inauguration, President-elect Lincoln arrived in Philadelphia. Here, on Washington's birthday, he symbolically raised the flag at Independence Hall. The Union, he promised, would be preserved. Frederick D. Richards caught the scene with his camera while the dignitar-ies stood at prayer. Lincoln is visible directly above the star on the left of the lqag, while men view the scene from trees. (LO)

Above: And on March 4, 1861, a crozud gathered before the stands on the Capitol steps in Washington. Meigs set his camera to record the scene. (LC)

Below: Then Lincoln took the oath of office and told the nation that the Union must be preserved. "We are not enemies, but friends," he told the South. "We must not be enemies." "In your hands, my dissatisfied fellow-countrymen, and not in mine, is the momentous issue of civil war." Meigs certainly could not have heard the President, but his camera caught the moment forever. (LC)

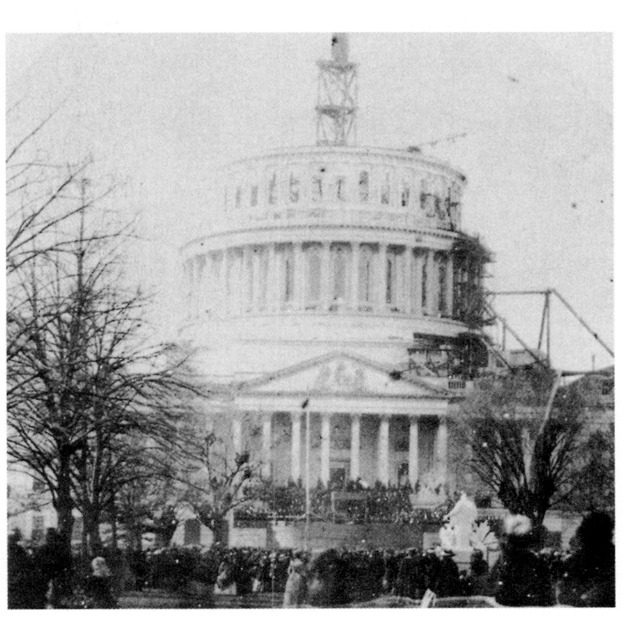

Above: Jefferson Davis, photographed in 1859 by Montgomery Meigs. An unpublished portrait which shows him with a hint of a smile. After 1860 he would rarely smile again. (LC)

Above: The Republicans, in the face of a Democratic split, were ensured of success. New York's William H. Seward, standing at left, had hoped for the nomination, but he lost it to Douglas's old foe from Illinois . . . (NYHS)

Below: The word spread across the nation, to a host of men then little known and not likely to be remembered. In Cairo, Illinois, to a man standing just left of the post office pillar, Ulysses S. Grant . . . (CHS)

Right: . . . to three friends from West Point days, Philip H. Sheridan in the center, and George Crook at left. (u. s. MILITARY ACADEMY ARCHIVES)

Left: . . . to a firebrand Unionist in Missouri, Nathaniel Lyon. (USAMHI)

Above: . . to a captain in the United States Topographi cal Engineers, George G. Meade. (USAMHI)

Below: . . . to an adjutant general in the Army, Lieuten ant Colonel Don Carlos Buell. (USAMHI)

Below: . . . to a professor at the Virginia Military Institute, seen here in Mexican War uniform,Thomas Jonathan Jackson. (USAMHI)

Above: . . . to a young southern officer, Ambrose Powell Hill. (MUSEUM OF THE CONFEDERACY)

Below: . . to a dashing Virginian who had helped Lee corner John Brown, James Ewell Brown Stuart.

Right: And to Chnlleston went the word. It was in their hands, said Lincoln. (LC)

Above: . . . to men like Captain A. W. Reynolds.

Left: In the hands of Brigadier General Pierre G. T. Beauregard, commanding the Confederates gathered in Charleston. (OCHM)

Above: . . . to a sour, humorless, Mexican War veteran, Braxton Bragg. (SOUTHERN HISTORICAL COLLECTION, UNIVERSITY OF NORTH CAROLINA, CHAPEL HILL)

The Guns at Fort Sumter

W.A. SWANBERG

A Charlston April shatters America's innocence

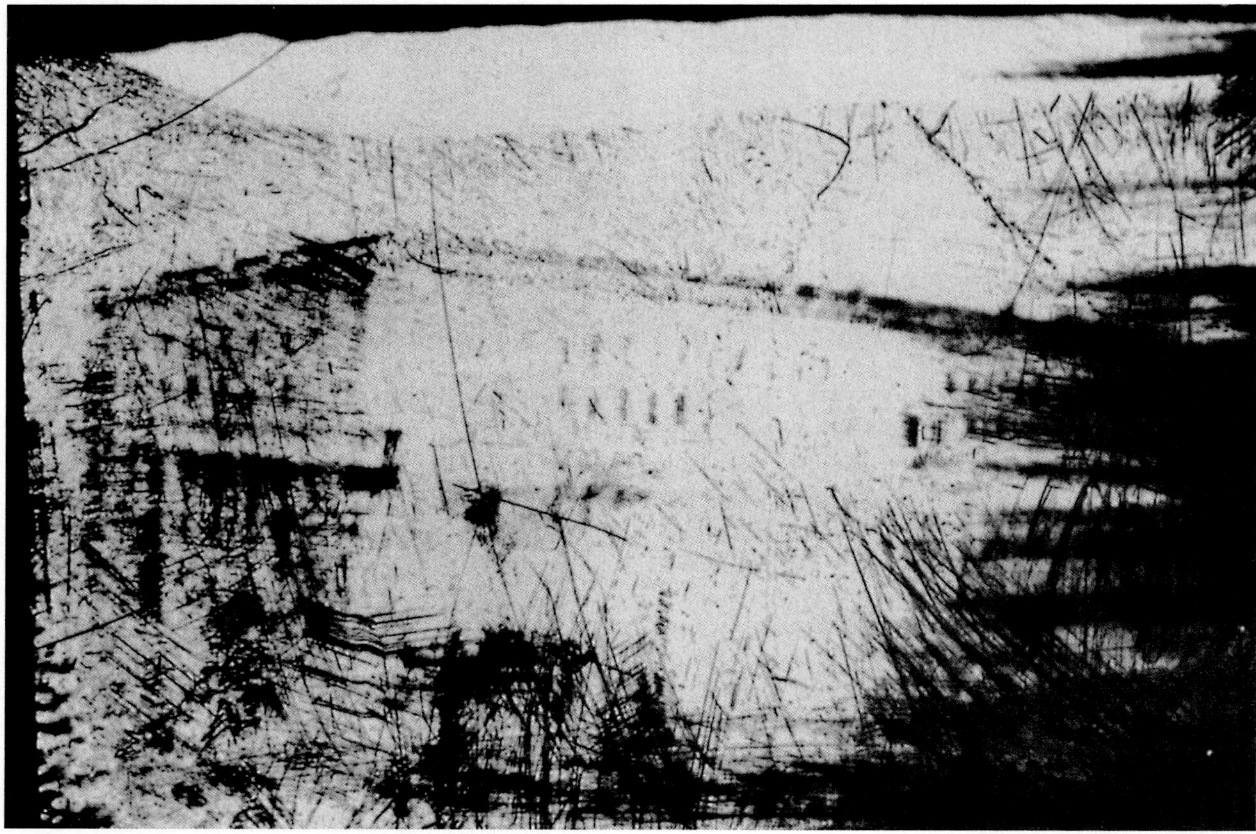

Above: The ghostly face of Fort Sumter in Charleston Harbor, almost lost in this scratched and faded ambrotype. It is the only known photo of the fortress before its bombardment. (VM)

Left: Brigadier General Pierre G. T. Beauregard, commanding Confederate forces in and around Charleston. He appears in his uniform as colonel of engineers in the Provisional Army of Louisiana, shortly after the time he served briefly as superintendent of the Military Academy at West Point. Filled with grand ideas of warfare—and his potential part in it—this Creole officer looked forward to firing on Fort Sumter as soon as the authorities gave him the word. (USAMHI)

"I HAVE THE HONOR TO REPORT," Major Robert Anderson wrote on December 26, 1860, after his night-shrouded move across a mile of water to Fort Sumter, "that I have just completed, by the blessing of God, the removal to this fort of all my garrison." The anger which this clandestine shift of a mere seventy-odd men caused in the South, and the joy it aroused in the North, bespoke the sectional strife of which the major and the Charleston forts had become a symbol.

President Buchanan saw in it none of God's work. "Are calamities never to come singly!" he lamented. Yearning to finish his nine remaining weeks in office and to leave the secession crisis in the lap of the man who had caused it, Lincoln, he had said that there would be no "hostile act" in the harbor. Three South Carolina commissioners, just arrived in Washington to parley about the forts, said Anderson's move was a hostile act. Mississippi Senator Jefferson Davis, soon to be Confederate President, told the President, ". . . you are surrounded with blood and dishonor on all sides." Exultant headlines in the North and outraged ones in the South told the real significance of the major's action. Secretary of War John B. Floyd telegraphed Anderson in anger:

> Intelligence has reached here this morning that you have abandoned Fort Moultrie, spiked your guns, burned the carriages, and gone to Fort Sumter.... Explain the meaning of this report.

But Floyd was a Virginian who had been implicated first in a financial scandal and then in an effort to ship cannon from Pittsburgh to southern points, where they would be useful to the new Confederacy if it came to war. Buchanan had asked him to resign. Floyd had not yet got around to it. His continued presence in the Cabinet was one of the errors of a lame-duck President whose power to govern had virtually become paralyzed. Floyd had sent Anderson to Charleston in the first place because of the major's background as a Kentuckian who had married a Georgia girl, had until recently owned a few slaves, and expressed a sympathy for the South equaled only by his reverence for the Union. At Moultrie he had been deserted by the secretary—left in an untenable fort without reinforcements, his requests for instructions usually ignored. Moultrie, in the midst of extensive repairs, had gaps in its walls entered by neighborhood dogs, children, or secessionist leaders who watched, took notes and photographs, and called the Union presence there "coercion." From secessionist homesoverlooking the fort it would be possible for snipers to pick off cannoneers. A well-armed force could overpower the garrison. Anderson's father, Major Richard Clough Anderson, had defended Moultrie against the British in 1779 and been captured—one particular footstep the son preferred not to follow in. He was aroused by Charlestonian threats and insistence that the forts be handed over, noting, "They are making every preparation (drilling nightly, &c) for the fight which they say must take place and insist on our not doing anything."

Indeed, few outsiders could gauge the Carolinian intensity. Francis W. Pickens had learned this when he returned from a recent tour as minister to Russia, talked with his good Democratic friend Buchanan in the White House, agreed that the Palmetto people were being hasty, and said he would quiet them when he got home. But Pickens, immediately running for governor of the state, found his moderating speeches so disdained that he quickly became a hotspur and was elected. Now, with Anderson in Sumter, the governor seized Moultrie, the United States arsenal (with 22,000 muskets), the customs house, and post office.

That was an error, for the chances were good that if Pickens had only protested, Buchanan would have ordered Anderson back to Moultrie. Now, if the President did such a thing, he would be hanged in effigy in a hundred northern cities and probably impeached. And now he was confronted by Secretary Floyd, whom he considered already fired, coming to him and resigning because of the President's "dishonorable" acceptance of the move to Sumter—a wily exit indeed. And when the South Carolina commissioners left after calling Buchanan lying and deceitful, he seemed more affected by this insult to his person than by the various discourtesies to the Union. Anderson, he said heavily, would have to be reinforced.

At Sumter, Chaplain Mathias Harris led a prayer of thanksgiving. Major Anderson raised Old Glory with slow dignity. The band played "Hail, Columbia" as the battery presented arms, then the men broke into spontaneous cheers, both in enthusiasm for their leader and in relief at escaping Moultrie. Yet, while it was true that Sumter was entirely surrounded by water, four times as big as Moultrie, and planned for three tiers of 146 guns served by 650 men, it was anything but impregnable in its present condition. Work on the fort had been impeded by the current quarrels. The barracks were unfinished, only fifteen guns had been mounted, many embrasures were wide open, the parade was choked with building materials as well as 5,600 shot and shell and sixty-six unmounted guns. The place could have been taken by a few hundred men with scaling ladders. Luckily, this was not known in town. "Twenty-five well-drilled men could hold it against all Charleston," said the Charleston Courier in dismay.

The garrison began mounting more guns. Abolitionist officers such as Captain Abner Doubleday and Captain John G. Foster, who had suspected Anderson of excessive southern sympathies, praised the skillful move to Sumter, and morale was high until the Star of the West arrived from New York on January 9 with two hundred men and supplies for the garrison. It was typical of the confusion and irresolution in government that the men were sent in a rented, unarmed merchantman rather than a Navy warship, and that Major Anderson had not been informed of its dispatch whereas the Charlestonians had. Buchanan's secessionist Secretary of the Interior, Jacob Thompson of Mississippi, had telegraphed the news to Governor Pickens and then resigned his post. Anderson was utterly perplexed when the vessel hove into view and was fired on by one of the Carolina batteries— arguably the first shot of the War Between the States, fired by a young cadet named George E. Haynsworth. Other batteries let fly, with aim mostly poor. Anderson, whose orders had been to act "strictly on the defensive," had his gunners ready but so longed for an

Right: His antagonist, Major Robert Anderson, commanding in Fort Sumter. A native of Kentucky, Anderson's sympathies were severely torn by the sectional crisis, but he saw his duty to the Union as paramount. (USAMHI)

Below: Castle Pinckney in Charleston. Here and at other works like this, the Confederate volunteers gathered during the early months of 1861, to train and await the time of their taking the Yankee fort that taunted them in their own harbor. (VM)

Left: Probably Confederates lounging inside Castle Pinckney, ready to fill its cannon with the shot stacked all about them and send the missiles on their way to Sumter. (SOUTH CAROLINA HISTORICAL SOCIETY)

The Charleston Zouave Cadets in Castle Pinckney, smart, well equipped, and anxious. (USAMHI)

Lieutenant R. C. Gilchrist, standing second from the left, carries a sword more like a scimitar than a saber, but the cadets in their pipe-clayed crossbelts dare not smile. Neither do their black orderlies at the rear. A year before most southern states had statutes on their books preventing slaves from reading or gathering together. Now they were uniformed and sometimes even trusted with arms as they came to the front to see to life's amenities while their masters met the enemy. (VM)

Right: Simon Cameron, Lincoln's Secretary of War, was slow in appreciating Anderson's helpless situation at Sumter, and slower still in doing anything about it. (USAMHI)

Below: Some military organizations that existed before the war, as much fraternal groups as real armed units, readied for the coming fight. Prominent were the men of Charleston's own Washington Light Infantry. They bivouacked in Camp Truesdale on the east end of Sullivan's Island. This faded old print shows their officers before their tent, equipped in a manner that two years hence would be only a fond memory. (WASHINGTON LIGHT INFANTRY)

amicable settlement between the states that he was loath to give the order to fire. As he pondered, the Star took two minor hits and fled. Doubleday and others were incensed at this failure to defend the flag, whereas soldiers with southern sympathies, such as Lieutenant R. K. Meade, thought Anderson's restraint wise. As for the fire-eating Robert Barnwell Rhett's Charleston Mercury, it hailed the striking of the first blow, saying, "It has wiped out a half century of scorn and outrage."

Governor Pickens was in the odd position of heading a self-styled South Carolina republic that still used United States stamps. Its congressmen were using their franking privileges to propagandize for the new Confederacy, and Pickens himself was asking for a $3,000 balance due him as minister to Russia, although he had forbidden the U.S. Subtreasury in Charleston to cash any more drafts from Washington. That cost him dearly when Washington, with intentional irony, sent him a $3,000 draft on the Subtreasury whose payments he had stopped. Pickens sent out his secretaries of state and war, Judge A.G. Magrath and General D.F. Jamison, under a flag of truce to urge Anderson to look to his own safety and evacuate Sumter peacefully since, they said, the United States government itself was crumbling. The major declined, urged diplomacy with Washington, and kept his men at the task of mounting more guns. Meanwhile, Colonel Samuel Colt of Hartford was shipping thousands of firearms south and building himself a mansion, and a Connecticut munitions firm sold 300,000 pounds of powder to Governor Pickens. Treason? Not at all. Did not the President himself declare that the seceded states were still part of the Union?

"The people of the South are mad," old Lewis Cass said; "the people of the North are asleep. The President is pale with fear.... God only knows what is to be the fate of my country!"

With South Carolina spending $20,000 daily for defense, and shipping now avoiding its greatest harbor, bankruptcy became a threat. Yet other southern leaders urged Pickens to go slowly, arguing that northern Democrats would sustain Buchanan whereas if a confrontation could be delayed until Lincoln took office, the Democrats would oppose him and the North would be divided. A new voice in Washington was that of William Henry Seward, Secretary of State-designate for Lincoln, who let it be known that he had plans (as yet unspecified) to resolve the whole quarrel and save the Union too. Other voices rumored that secessionists plotted to seize the capital on February 13, when the electoral votes would be officially counted and Lincoln formally declared the winner. They inspired the aged, Virginia-born General Winfield Scott, head of the Army, to colorful utterance:

> I have said that any [such person] should be lashed to the muzzle of a 12-pounder and fired out of a window of the Capitol. I would manure the hills of Arlington with fragments of his body.... It is my duty to suppress insurrection—my duty!

The day passed without incident. Buchanan's severity had given way once more to caution. He had swallowed the Star of the West affront. He wavered about reinforcing Anderson at all. He hoped that the new Confederate government would be less demanding than Pickens, that the crisis could be put off for his remaining days in the White House. On the complaint of Southerners that it was "warlike," he was ready to cancel a Washington's Birthday parade of six hundred soldiers until the spirited New York Congressman Daniel Sickles exploded that Washington was a Virginian, a national hero. The President was, critics said, ready to "give up part or even the whole of the Constitution to save the remainder."

Lincoln arrived quietly next day, having taken an earlier train to foil a rumored plot to assassinate him. The delegates from the seceded states had already met in Montgomery, elected Jefferson Davis president, and taken pains to remove the question of the forts from the excitable Pickens, who was now only a governor again. The men at Sumter froze in a heatless fort and ran low on tobacco while the aristocratic Carolinians enjoyed madeira, champagne, Spanish cigars and spoiled for a fight. Major Pierre Beauregard, U.S.A., recently deprived of his post as commander at West Point because of his southern allegiance, arrived in Charleston to take charge as Brigadier General Beauregard, C.S.A. He had been Anderson's pupil when the latter taught gunnery at West Point. He respected his one-time teacher but soon realized that he could overpower or starve out the meager Sumter garrison if he could prevent its reinforcement. Anderson, the man of honor, was wrestling also with the problem of what he should do in case his own state of Kentucky seceded, in which event it seemed to him that no matter what course he took there would be dishonor involved. A popular ditty in the North ran:

James is in his Cabinet
  Doubting and debating;
Anderson's in Sumter,
  Very tired of waiting.

Pickens is in Charleston,
  Blustering of blows;
Thank goodness March the Fourth is near,
  To nip Secession's nose.

On the fourth, Lincoln gave his inaugural in a city bristling with police and soldiers against a threatened secessionist coup, saying among other things, "...no state, upon its own mere notion, can lawfully get out of the Union," and "The power confided in me will be used to hold, occupy and possess the property and places belonging to the government." He had earlier said more colorfully that the Union was not a "free love arrangement" which any state could repudiate at will. The new Confederate commissioners arrived in Washington to parley with Lincoln through an intermediary, since the President would not recognize the C.S.A. Secretary Seward launched into an irresponsible and unauthorized course, letting the commissioners know that Lincoln was untutored in national affairs but that he, Seward, would soon bring him around and that Sumter would be peacefully evacuated. Seward's policy was based on his certainty that there was great innate love for the Union in the South and that if the states were permitted to secede, this love

Above Left:Another group of Confederates in Charleston, fully equipped for the field, their knapsacks on their backs, their Harpers Ferry rifles on their shoulders. (VM)

Above Right:Secretary of State William Seward played several ends against the middle in attempting to avoid the outbreak of hostilities in Charleston. In so doing he lied, overstepped his authority, and severely tried the patience of Lincoln. (USAMHI)

Right: Reminder of an earlier brave, now buried at Fort Moultrie. Osceola, the Seminole leader, effectively defeated the U. S. Army's attempt to subdue his people until the government admitted that it had lost the contest. His example was hardly lost on the high-spirited Southrons gathered at Charleston. (VM)

Above Left:Hurt most by Seward's interference was septuagenarian Lieutenant General Winfield Scott. Once the foremost soldier of the young republic, he was now an obese old man, a picture of ruined magnificence. Yet his mind was as active as ever, and he appreciated at once the hopelessness of reinforcing Anderson in Sumter without precipitating war. He advised that the fort be evacuated. Lincoln would not have it. (KA)

And that left Major Robert Anderson caught squarely in a trap. Charleston photographer George Cook took his camera out to Sumter in February 1861 and persuaded Anderson and his officers to sit for him. A tongue-in-cheek broadside soon appeared describing how "Col. George S. Cook, of the Charleston Photographic Light Artillery," stormed Sumter, "heroically penetrated to the presence of Maj. Anderson, and levelling a double barrelled Camera, demanded his unconditional surrender." The broadside appeared under the headline, MAJOR ANDERSON TAKEN! It looked like war was going to be fun. (VM)

Above: Anderson and his officers "captured" by Cook. Most of them would be heard from in the war to come. Seated from the left are Captain Abner Doubleday, Anderson, Surgeon Samuel W. Crawford, and Captain John G. Foster. Standing from the left are Captain Truman Seymour, Lieutenant G. W. Snyder, Lieutenant Jefferson C. Davis, Lieutenant R. K. Meade, and Captain T. Talbot. All but Snyder, Meade, and Talbot will become generals. (USAMHI)

Right: Talbot, Crawford, and Seymour posed separately, enjoying the distinction of being "captured" twice. (USAMHI)

Above: There were those who would help Anderson, and finally a relief expedition was sent, led by Gustavus V. Fox, Assistant Secretary of the Navy. But it could not dare Charleston's guns, and so it sat on the horizon, within sight but not reach of Anderson's exhausted command. (NAVAL PHOTOGRAPHIC CENTER)

Below: The Confederates, from their lookout tower at Fort Washington, expected Fox's coming. Several of them are here waving their caps in celebration, perhaps at the Union fleet's failure to test their batteries. (WASHINGTON LIGHT INFANTRY)

would combine with loss of trade and internal bickering to make them clamor to rejoin the Union within a year or so.

A message from Major Anderson staggered the new administration, for it told of the steady buildup of Confederate forces, the fact that Sumter had supplies for less than forty days, and gave an estimate (in which Anderson's officers substantially agreed) that it would take reinforcements of 20,000 men to hold the fort.

Twenty thousand men! No such force was available, nor were there enough Navy men-of-war to carry them if there had been. General Scott, much under Seward's influence, agreed with Anderson's estimate and told Lincoln, "Evacuation seems almost inevitable."

The idea was repugnant to the President. It would violate his "hold, occupy and possess" promise in his inaugural. It would begin his administration with a surrender which not even the irresolute Buchanan had contemplated. It would outrage the North and subject him to the contempt of the South—indeed, the whole watching world. Seward pressed him with the evacuation idea and the theory of an affectionate South which, if given its way, would spring back into the Union as if on a rubber band—a theory Lincoln deeply suspected. Determined to get the facts, he sent Gustavus Vasa Fox, a former Navy captain who yearned to lead an expedition to reinforce Anderson, to Charleston to confer with the major and find the actual condition of the fort and garrison. He dispatched Ward Lamon and Stephen Hurlbut separately to Charleston to sound officials and private citizens and see if they were, as Seward supposed, affectionate Unionists in a temporary fit of bad temper.

There were signs of spring in Charleston, ladies and gentlemen were promenading on the Battery, and the rumor that Sumter would soon be evacuated—which had appeared in the local papers— added spice to the air. The Army in South Carolina now numbered ten regiments of 8,835 men. Local photographers did a large business perpetuating the likenesses of these young men in their new uniforms. One photographer, George Cook, went to Sumter and persuaded the officers to sit for a group portrait despite Doubleday's conviction that he was a spy. In the city there was a magnificent St. Patrick's Day parade, and the feeling toward Anderson and his tobaccoless and short-rationed men softened enough so that cigars and several cases of claret were sent out for the officers. Captain Fox was permitted to visit Anderson and to observe, without mentioning it to the major, that reinforcement of the fort appeared feasible if done skillfully in darkness. Ward Lamon, Lincoln's close friend, apparently believed that there was now no choice but to quit Sumter, for he clearly gave Governor Pickens that impression and, on visiting Anderson at the fort, left him with the conviction that he would be withdrawn. Hurlbut, a native of Charleston who was now an Illinois lawyer, devoted himself to a survey of relatives and friends he had in the city. He decided that Seward's theory was absurd, that "there is a unanimity of sentiment" against the Union that was deep and unrelenting.

It is doubtful that there was ever so important an issue on which there was so much disagreement, so many misinterpretations and errors, so many men at cross purposes, often utterly mistaken and snarled in confusion.

Anderson was relieved that the issue, as he now believed, was to be settled by his withdrawal and that war would be averted. But as the days passed in Charleston (where there were rumors that the major had resigned his commission and that Captain Doubleday had gone insane and was in irons), impatience grew at the failure of the garrison to decamp. General Beauregard, hearing talk that demolition charges might be left in Sumter, wrote Anderson to suggest discreetly that the fort be left undamaged when he departed. The Confederacy in Montgomery was angry at the delay. In Sumter, the garrison was ready to pack and go north where pork chops, apple pie, and beautiful women were realities instead of dreams. Sumter was down to its last barrel of flour, as Anderson reported on April 3 to the new Secretary of War, Simon Cameron, urgently asking instructions. No instructions came.

The Confederate commissioners in Washington now found through an intermediary that Seward was no longer certain that Sumter would be evacuated. The secretary had done his best to impose his policy on the new President and, in failing, had caused misunderstanding and provoked accusations of bad faith. On April 8, a messenger from Lincoln handed Governor Pickens a paper whose single sentence exuded blunt honesty:

> I am directed by the President of the United States to notify you to expect an attempt will be made to supply Fort Sumter with provisions only, and that if such attempt be not resisted, no effort to throw in men, arms or ammunition, will be made, without further notice, or in case of an attack upon the Fort.

At the same time, Anderson received his first instructions from the new administration: an expedition would attempt to supply him "and, in case the effort is resisted, will endeavor also to reinforce you." He had reconciled himself to his mortifying failure to defend the Star of the West on the ground that he had saved the peace. Now he had mortification and war too. As for Sumter's men, to whom their fort had become a prison, they reacted with a kind of glorious cussedness and cheered lustily at the news that they would have a chance to throw iron at the Carolinians who had made their lives so difficult.

Anderson declined a last offer by Beauregard permitting him to salute his flag if he would leave peacefully. With food left for perhaps sixty hours, he put his men on stern rations. The Carolinians now had at least thirty guns and eighteen mortars bearing on Sumter from six widely separated emplacements, some of which Sumter could not touch. To save his men, the major ordered them to serve only the guns in the more protected casemate tier, which limited them to twenty-one guns, most of them only 32-pounders, and not a single mortar.

The first shot on Fort Sumter was fired from Fort Johnson on James Island at 4:30 A.M. April 12, 1861. It woke up Doubleday, who commented, "[It] seemed to bury itself in the masonry about a foot from my head." He stayed in bed as the firing became an intermittent roar. Sumter did not answer until after 6 o'clock reveille and a

Right: And finally came war. At 4:30 A.M., or shortly after, April 12, 1861, a signal gun was fired from Fort Johnson. Seconds later Edmund Ruffin, fire-eating secessionist from South Carolina, jerked a lanyard . . . (NA, BRADY COLLECTION)

Below:. . . on one of these eight-inch columbiads in the Iron Clad Battery moored off Morris Island, and launched one of the first hostile shots of the war against Sumter's parapet.

A rare, previously unpublished photograph by Osborn & Durbec of Charleston showing the interior of the Iron Clad Battery, taken April 17, 186 just five days after the firing. One of these guns, or a third not shown, fired Ruffin's hostile shot. (CHS)

Left: The first answering Federal shot of the war was fired by Captain Doubleday, who gladly sent a ball toward the Iron Clad Battery, though it bounced harmlessly off its roof. (USAMHI)

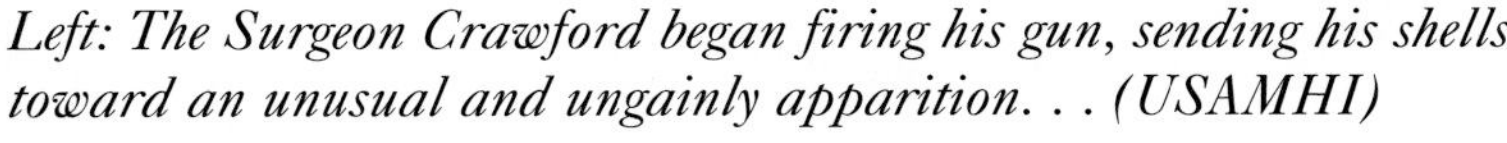

Left: The Surgeon Crawford began firing his gun, sending his shells toward an unusual and ungainly apparition. . . (USAMHI)

Above: The iron-sheathed Floating Battery at Sullivan's Island mounted two 42-pounder cannon and two 32-pounders, and proudly flew the flag of the new Confederacy overhead. A photograph taken on April 16, 1861, by an unidentified photographer, shows the Floating Battery in position off the island. This print has not been published in nearly seventy years. (VM)

Left: After thirty-three hours of bombardment, former Senator Louis T. Wigfall of Texas, aide to Beauregard and an ardent secessionist, carried a truce flag to Sumter and asked Anderson to surrender. Seeing the hopelessness of further resistance, the major gave up. (CIVIL WAR TIMES ILLUSTRATED)

Below: On April 14, Anderson and his command left the fort to its conquerors. The flag of the Confederate States of America went up a makeshift staff, and the next day photographer F. K. Houston of 307 King Street in Charleston became the first to bring a camera into Fort Sumter. Elated soldiers feigned action poses while he made his slow exposure, but the proud new flag would not stay still. (USAMHI)

Below: That day and in those following, several cameramen came to the fort. The names of some are now lost, but thankfully not their photographs. One of them, probably Osborn & Durbec, made a panorama from three separate images of Sumter that shows vividly the damage done by Beauregard's batteries. They claimed to have made these shots the very day of the surrender. (USAMHI)

breakfast consisting of fat pork and water. "Be careful of your lives," Anderson cautioned, ordering his men to stay in the casemates as much as possible. Doubleday, his second in command, was given the honor of firing the first shot against the rebellion—one he accepted with zest, reflecting, "To me it was simply a contest, politically speaking, as to whether virtue or vice should rule." Private John Carmody, knowing that the bigger barbette guns above were loaded and aimed at Moultrie, disobeyed orders, stole up there, and fired them one by one, making a great noise but with little effect on the well-protected Confederate batteries. It was an unequal battle, what with Sumter's lack of mortars and inability to fire shell (there were no fuses), not to mention the poor provender. Enemy fire, gaining in accuracy, cleared the parapet and started fires in the wooden barracks inside, which took smart work to extinguish. Sumter's most visible achievement was a ball that crashed into the large frame Moultrie House hotel, which sent dozens of battle-watchers scurrying.

Early in the afternoon a Sumter watchman saw a United States man-of-war far out beyond the bar. Reinforcements and food! A shout of joy went up from the exhausted gunners—all in vain. The expedition led by Captain Fox had been broken up by confusion in New York and by a storm that drove two of its fighting ships and its tugs off course. The tugs were the heart of Fox's careful plan for reaching the fort, and the guns were essential to protect the tugs. Fox was waiting for help that never came.

The Sumtermen loosed curses the next morning when they saw the "rescue" vessels still waiting in the distance. Cartridges got so low that they restricted their firing to one gun every ten minutes. The barracks took fire again so that there was no putting it out. Flames crept slowly toward the magazine where 275 barrels of powder were stored. The magazine was banked with earth for protection, but flying embers touched off stockpiles of shells and grenades that had been placed at strategic spots along the gorge wall, sending down showers of sparks and broken masonry. The main gates were now ablaze. Smoke poured into the casemates, choking the men serving the guns. From the shore the smoke and flame made it seem impossible that Sumter could continue the battle, and there was Carolinian admiration when its guns kept firing. Texas Senator Louis Wigfall, now a Confederate colonel, who had damned the Union and cheered the attack, marveled at this display of courage but thought it had gone far enough. He got a boat and was rowed to the fort, unseen by the smoke-blinded defenders. He entered an open embrasure, carrying a white flag on his sword, and came upon a sooty-faced Major

Anderson, whose coolness astonished him.

"You have defended your flag nobly, sir," Wig fall shouted. "It's madness to persevere.... General Beauregard wishes to stop this, and to ask upon what terms you will evacuate this work."

Anderson at length agreed to parley. Only three cartridges remained. His men were spent. The larder was all but empty. There was danger of explosions in the fort. The effort to reinforce him had somehow collapsed. It would indeed be madness to persevere.

After thirty-three hours of bombardment, the Sumter flag went down at 1:30 P.M. April 13. A few men on each side had been injured by flying debris, but the only fatality of battle was a horse killed on Morris Island by a Sumter ball. Charleston was in transports over the victory. Headlines in the North used the word "WAR." Young men, North and South, began flocking to the banners. It was, as Horace Greeley said later, a comparatively bloodless beginning for the bloodiest conflict America ever knew.

Sumter's eastern terreplein and parapet, April 15, 1861. Just over the wall can be seen a steam sidewheeler that transported more and more Confederates into the captured fort, and sightseers from Charleston as well. One such is the top-hatted man standing at right. The man at left is Major Nathan G. Evans, who will shortly be a brigadier general at Bull Run. The man in the middle is Lieutenant Robert Pringle. (CHARLESTON LIBRARY SOCIETY)

Top Right: But Anderson's men did some damage, too, and the camera artists were not loath to show it. Here on April 16 the soldiers' barracks at Fort Moultrie showed the effect of Sumter's fire. (CHARLESTON POST-COURIER)

Below Right: So, too, did Moultrie's northwest angle. (CHARLESTON MUSEUM)

Bottom Left: April 15, the interior of Sumter, showing the destroyed western barracks and, in the right foreground, columbiads that Anderson had mounted in the ground to use as mortars. (VM)

Bottom Right: April 15, another view of the southwest angle showing officers' quarters and soldiers' barracks. Elated Confederates stand in groups retelling their experiences while watching the bombardment. (VM)

April 15, the southwest angle of the fort, a panorama formed of two separate images. Dressed smartly on parade, the conquering Confederates line up for the camera, while their flag floats gently overhead. Anderson built the earth bank at left to protect the lower tier of soldiers' quarters. The fort's beacon lantern, removed from its place on the parapet, rests in the parade ground. These two images have never before been juxtaposed to give this wide view of the interior of the fort. (VM)

Right: The only known photograph of the interior of Sumter's casemate, and the guns that Doubleday, Crawford, and others manned in defense. (TU)

Below Left: Another view, April 17 or later, showing the effects of the fire from Charleston upon the mortar and masonry of the fort. (USAMHI)

Below Right: The main sally-port into Sumter, showing the confusion of rubble and the damage done by Beauregard's cannon. (NYHS)

On April 17, 1861, and probably for two or three days thereafter, two special photographers visited not only Fort Sumter, but also all of the Confederate installations that fired against it. They were James M. Osborn and F. E. Durbec of "Osborn & Durbec's Photographic Mart" at 223 King Street in Charleston. They operated a rather extensive establishment, advertising their "Cheap Photographs! Cheap Ambrotypes! Cheap Daguerreotypes! Cheap Ivorytypes! Cheap Melainotypes!" and advised that strangers visiting Charleston "would do well to give us a call before going elsewhere." They sold views of Egypt, photo cases in some five thousand different patterns, and even carried cameras for sale. They are today forgotten, but on those days in April 1861 they took a place beside Brady and Gardner and Edwards and the rest of the war's immortal chroniclers.

Their stereo camera captured over forty scenes in Sumter and the Charleston batteries, the most complete record ever made of the site of a Civil War engagement. Apparently they later attempted to market their stereo views, but the war and the Federal blockade probably prevented their ever getting sufficient chemicals and supplies to manufacture the prints. As a result, very few of their images survive in more than one copy, and all but a few have been entirely lost to view until now.

What follows—in addition to the Osborn & Durbec views already presented in this and the previous chapter—is a nearly complete collection of their work. Two thirds of these images have never before been published and are newly discovered.

As for Osborn & Durbec, their partnership did not survive the war. By 1866 they had gone their separate ways. They left behind a priceless record of the first sad evidence of war between the states.

Left: A group of Confederate dignitaries in front of the shot furnace on Sumter's parade ground. Beside them is one of the columbiads that Anderson mounted to use as mortars against Charleston. They were never fired. The tall figure in the center has long been believed to be Wade Hampton. Others probably include Governor Francis Pickens. (TU)

Below: The sally-port at Fort Sumter seen from the wharf. Already the conquering Confederates are at work cleaning out the rubble and rebuilding. (TU)

Below Left: The southwest face of the fort, showing the damage done by Edmund Ruffin and members of his Palmetto Guard as they fired the columbiads in the Iron Clad Battery. (CHS)

Below Right: The southwest corner, and the effects of shots fired from Morris Island and the Floating Battery. The opening at left is an embrasure for one of Sumter's guns. (CHS)

Above Left: Damage done by Confederate guns firing from Cumming's Point. (TU)

Above Right: The southeast side of the parade, the hot-shot furnace, and the soldiers' east barracks. (CHS)

Above Left: The ruins of the sally-port at right, and to its left the officers' quarters. (CHS)

Above Right: Cleaning up the parade ground in front of the sally-port. (MHS)

The ruined officers' quarters on the southwest side, and a row of cannon Anderson did not emplace. (CHS)

The stair tower at an angle in the perimeter, and jaunty Confederates atop their captured guns. (TU)

Above Left: Damage done by the Iron Clad Battery on the interior of Sumter. (CHS)

Above Right: In the left rear, the powder magazine, protected by an earth traverse. It is on the side facing Charleston, since Sumter was built to withstand an attack from the sea, not the land face. (TU)

Left: Behind the makeshift flagstaff can be seen the effects of Fort Moultrie's fire on the officers quarters and sally-port. (NA,BRADY COLLECTION)

Above: The rear of the same parapet, another dismounted gun, and a traverse built of sand bags to protect men from the fire from Sullivan's Island. (CWTI)

Above: More of the cleanup, with two men working while the others watch. (TU)

Left: The shot furnace and, to the right, Anderson's flagstaff, which was shot off during the bombardment. The new flag of the victors flutters overhead. (CHS)

Right: Sumter's parapet. Fort Moultrie is in the distance, while the guns shown are trained on the Iron Clad Battery. The gun in the foreground has been dismounted by Confederate fire. (CHS)

Far Right: Confederates on Morris Island, very probably men of Colonel J. H. Trapier's Mortar Battery. (SOUTH CAROLINA HISTORICAL SOCIETY)

Below: The Trapier Mortar Battery on Morris Island and, in the right background, Osborn & Durbec's pyramidal portable darkroom. (TU)

Above: Another view of the Trapier Battery, this time manned for action. At the very right of the image, behind the dimly seen man at the edge, is a corner of the portable darkroom. (CHS)

Below: A view of the Iron Clad Battery at Morris Island from the rear. The railroad "T" iron cladding has been removed from its wooden beamed roof. One of the columbiads with which Ruffin sent the first shots against Sumter can be seen within. (SOUTH CAROLINA HISTORICAL SOCIETY)

Left: The harbor face of Fort Moultrie, its shot furnace in the foreground. Since it was assumed that any attacker would come from the sea in wooden ships, the U. S. Army, when building these coastal forts, provided for sending red-hot shot like fireballs into attacking vessels. Just above the gun at the right can be seen a long dark object. It is Fort Sumter. These guns no longer bear upon it. (TU)

Left: Another view of Moultrie's shot furnace, with the officers' quarters behind it. Heated shot from here set ablaze the wooden roofs in Sumter and caused fires that threatened the powder magazine. (TU)

Top Left: The eastern angle of Moultrie, on Sullivan's Island. Damage done by Sumter's return fire can be seen in the roof of the right wing of the large house. (TU)

Top Right: Moultrie's northwestern angle. (TU)

Left: Moultrie's western barracks overlooking the parade ground, and the damage done by Captain Doubleday. (TU)

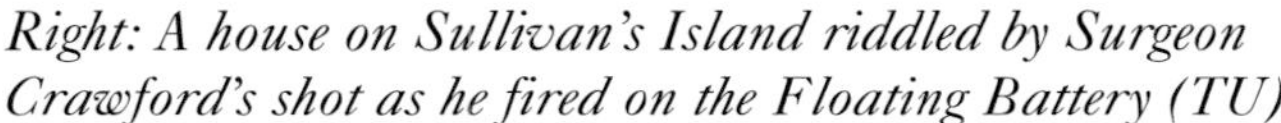

Right: A house on Sullivan's Island riddled by Surgeon Crawford's shot as he fired on the Floating Battery (TU)

Bottom Left: More of Doubleday's handiwork on the western barracks. It was small recompense. (TU)

Bottom Right: Empty gun emplacements on Sullivan's Island and, in the harbor beyond, Fort Sumter. The bloodless beginning to a bloody war. (TU)

The Boys of '61

BELL I. WILEY

Euphoric thousands enlist before they miss "the fun"

Above: As Lincoln and Davis issued their calls for the boys of '61, the first to be ready were those already enrolled in the scores of active militia units in North and South. New York photographer Charles D. Fredericks turned his camera out his own studio window on July 4, 1860, to catch this resplendent unit at parade. The bearskins would soon disappear. (USAMHI)

THE TREMENDOUS WAVE of patriotism that swept over North and South in the wake of Fort Sumter produced an epidemic of volunteering. Very few of the recruits had any prior military experience. Conversion of the hordes of civilians into effective soldiers presented an enormous challenge, but authorities on both sides rose to the occasion and the results proved better than might have been expected.

Since governors usually took the lead in mobilization, most recruits had a brief stint of state service before they were sworn in as Federal or Confederate troops. First came a physical examination, usually a perfunctory test consisting largely of responses to questions put by the doctors concerning the recruits' medical history. Then came formal muster into national service—inspection by the muster officer, pledging allegiance to the United States or the Confederacy, promising to obey orders, swearing to abide by the 101 articles of war to which recruits listened while standing in company formation, and signing the company muster roll.

On both sides recruits chose their officers. As a rule the rank and file elected only their company officers (lieutenants and captains), who in turn chose the field grade officers (majors, lieutenant colonels, and colonels), but in some units soldiers elected all officers, from corporals to colonels. Those who took the lead in raising units were generally chosen to command them, but when, as was sometimes the case, more than one candidate vied for a position, lively campaigns ensued. Victors in these contests sometimes celebrated their success by hosting drinking parties.

During the first weeks in camp, recruits within the various companies organized themselves into informal groups known as messes. These varied in size from six to a dozen men, drawn together by similarity of inclination and interest. Members took turns in drawing rations, gathering wood, and cooking. Ties became very close with continuing association. An Illinois soldier wrote early in 1862: "Cap wanted to take some more men in our mess but we told him we would rather not, we wanted mess No. one to remain as it was....Ours...is the most intelligent mess in this Reg[iment], the best fellows, the bravest boys, can kill more Secesh & Eat more hard Crackers & stand more hard marching, waid deeper mud & do less grumbling than any other mess in the Northern army."

As the time approached for departure from home for "the seat of war," volunteers took part in a series of farewell activities. One of these was the presentation of a flag by one of the feminine patriots who had helped to make it. As the pretty donor made the presentation, she delivered a flowery speech, extolling cause and country and calling on the recipients to protect the emblem from the vile creatures who sought to defile it. The officer receiving the colors, usually a colonel, responded in words glowing with patriotism and pledging himself and his associates to defend the banner with their lives.

On the day of departure friends and neighbors gathered at the railway station or steamboat wharf or some other place of rendezvous to bid the soldiers farewell. After a prayer by a local minister, the recruits took their leave amid a chorus of good-byes and best wishes. The volunteers joked and laughed to mask their sadness, and loved ones left behind did their best to fight back the tears that filled their eyes.

The trip to the fighting zone, made sometimes by train and sometimes by boat, was a boisterous experience. Troops traveling by rail sometimes obtained better ventilation and visibility by knocking holes in the sides of boxcars; many rode on top of the cars, despite the admonitions of the officers. Escape from home restraints and the prospect of new and exciting experiences brought a holiday attitude. So did the hearty cheering of pretty girls who greeted them along the way. Many volunteers added to their joviality by taking generous swigs from liquor bottles which they had slipped into their baggage before taking leave of their loved ones. The first casualties experienced by some units came not from hostile bullets but from tipsy soldiers falling from trains. The congestion and filth of some of the trains and boats that transported soldiers were enough to provoke excessive drinking. In March 1862 an Illinois Yank wrote home from West Tennessee: "We was aboard the steamer Memphis 8 or 9 days. We was in dirt, lice, shit, grease & Hard crackers."

Arrival at the front, whether in Tennessee, Kentucky, Missouri, Maryland, or Virginia, brought a change in the character of soldiering. During the initial period of service when the men were near their homes, discipline was lax and duties relatively light. Recruits frequently called their superiors by their first names or addressed them as "sarge" or "cap." Leaves were easy to obtain, and officers and men spent much of their time in nearby towns or cities. But the proximity of the enemy and the certainty of combat gave serious and urgent purpose to training. Recruits and their officers came under the control of hard-bitten professionals like Joseph E. Johnston, Braxton Bragg, U.S. Grant, and George B. McClellan. These commanders knew that the novices flowing in from farms, shops, and factories had to undergo a swift and drastic transformation before they could win battles. And they set themselves to effecting the change with determination and vigor. Men who previously treated soldiering as a lark now complained of the hardness of their lot. "I don't believe God ever intended for one man to pen up another and keep him in this manner," wrote a Reb to his homefolks; he added, "Dam Old Abe and Old Jeff Davis. Dam the day I 'listed." Another Reb wrote from a camp near Richmond in May 1861, "A man may come here with as much devil in him as they please, but they will soon tame him." A Georgian, after his transfer to Virginia in the fall of 1861, wrote his father: "I love my country as well as any one but I don't believe in the plan of making myself a slave.... A private soldier is nothing more than a slave and is often treated worse. I have during the past six months gone through more hardships than anyone of ours or Grandma's negroes; their life is a luxury to what mine is sometimes." But this soldier came to realize the value of discipline, and while he never completely gave up the cherished practice of grumbling, he eventually accepted and approved the new order. The same was true of most of his comrades and of the men they fought.

In the fighting zones, platoons, companies, and regiments had to be fitted into larger organizations. Two platoons, each commanded by a

Above: The Kentucky State Guard encampment at Louisville in August 1860 proved a training ground for several future Confederate companies. Commander of the Guard was Brigadier General Simon Bolivar Buckner, soon to be a trusted commander of the Confederacy. This group, the Lexington Rilqes, was raised and captained by John Hunt Morgan. In the fall of 1861 he would lead them into the rebellion, to become a part of his famed cavalry. For now they are content to pose and drink and feast on watermelon. (KHS)

Above: Buckner's own unit, the Citizen Guard, and more bearskins. (KHS)

Left: But militia were not enough. New volunteer armies must be raised. Though defeated by Lincoln in 1860, Stephen A. Douglas stood firmly behind his antagonist's administration, and now took to the stump in speaking to raise support and volunteers. He wore himself out in the process, and died that summer. The last words of his final public address declared his stand for the Union: "United, firm, determined, never to permit the Government to be destroyed. (USAMHI)

Right: Lincoln's old friend Senator Edward Baker of Oregon helped raise a regiment. He would lead it to destruction, and his own death, at Ball's Bluff in October. (RICHARD C. OSTERHOUT)

Right: Colonel E. Elmer Ellsworth, once a denizen of Lincoln's Illinois law office, brought his New York Fire Zouaves, composed chiefly of New York City firemen, to Washington soon after the crisis came to shots at Sumter. (NYHS)

Below: To the War Department in Washington fell the task of organizing, equipping, training, and assigning the largest army ever raised in the hemisphere. No one had any experience in dealing with such numbers. (CHS)

Left: Officers like Brigadier General George Cadwallader did their best to hold precarious states like Maryland and Kentucky in the Union when Lincoln's call for volunteers to put down the rebellion aroused their southern sympathies. Cadwallader defied Chief Justice Roger B. Taney himself in carrying out Lincoln's suspension of the writ of habeas corpus in Maryland, for fear of seeing it secede. (USAMHI)

Below: The courthouse at Natchez, Mississippi, long thought to show Confederates enlisting in 1861. The photo, by Henry Gurney, more likely depicts Federal soldiers sometime after 1862, but the scene would be much the same if they were wearers of the gray. (JOAN AND THOMAS CANDY)

lieutenant, comprised a company, led by a captain; ten companies formed a regiment, commanded by a colonel; two or more regiments comprised a brigade, led by a brigadier general; two or more brigades combined to make a division, commanded by a major general; two or more divisions comprised a corps, commanded by a lieutenant general on the Confederate side and a major general on the Union side; and two or more corps made an army, commanded by a full general on the Confederate side and a major general on the Union side. In the artillery, the battalion, consisting of four batteries, each containing four to six guns, was a standard organization. The squadron (known also as the troop and the equivalent roughly of the infantry company) consisting of two or more platoons was a distinctive feature of the cavalry organization. Combination of arms normally began with the attachment of artillery (usually a battery) and cavalry to an infantry brigade. Engineer, signal, and other supporting elements were added on the corps or army level.

The basic unit on both sides was the infantry company, which at full strength numbered some thing over one hundred officers and men. But, after the first few months of service, companies commonly dwindled to about half their authorized strength and subsequently some experienced even greater attrition. Long and intimate association and the sharing of perils and hardships of soldiering promoted a relationship among company officers and their men very much like that of a family. The captain was the father who supervised daily routine, saw that his men were equipped, fed, clothed, and sheltered, heard their complaints, administered punishment for minor offenses, looked after their health, and led them in combat. He knew every man by name and had some acquaintance with the soldier's home circumstances. He sometimes mediated domestic squabbles, wrote letters for illiterates, supervised religious worship, buried the dead, and wrote letters of sympathy to bereaved wives and mothers. The lieutenants and noncommissioned officers were the captain's helpers and their role was very much like that of the elder children in a large family. A key member of the group was the company's first or orderly sergeant, who called the roll, kept the records, and translated the captain's wishes into orders.

On the Confederate side, and to an increasing extent among the Federals, blacks were obtained to help clean quarters, launder clothing, clean boots and shoes, cook, and perform other menial chores. Early in the war some enlisted men even had one or more Negroes, usually body servants, to lighten the burdens of camp life, even to the extent of standing guard under the supervision of their masters. But after a few months most of these servants went home; those who remained were usually the personal aides of officers, or blacks assigned to companies and regiments as hostlers or teamsters. The blacks encountered in northern camps were ex-slaves hired for a pittance to relieve officers and men of some of the more burdensome aspects of army service. Home letters of many Yanks in 1861 and later told of the writer's good fortune in having obtained the service of black menials. Private Andrew Rose of an Ohio regiment stationed in middle Tennessee wrote his parents in

1863: "The captain got two nigers for our company; every company has got them; all we do when we want nigers is to send a company after them." In 1862 a Maine captain wrote from Louisiana: "Officers & men are having an easy time. We have Negroes to do all fatigue work, cooking and washing clothes." In both armies black servants were often called on to dance and provide music for the entertainment of officers and soldiers. The Negroes sometimes sought diversion for them selves by gambling and drinking. During the last two years of the war, about 200,000 blacks were recruited by the Federals for service as soldiers. Inspection reports show that colored troops were often required to do more than their share of labor and that sometimes their white commander treated them more like menials than as fighters.

The training received by Johnny Reb and Billy Yank was very much alike. Hardee's Tactics—written by William J. Hardee, a Confederate general—was the most widely used infantry manual on both sides. In accordance with rules prescribed by Hardee for "the school of the soldier" recruits mastered such fundamentals as saluting or standing erect; facing left and right; marching forward, to the rear, by the flank, and obliquely; shifting arms to the various positions; parrying and thrusting with the bayonet; and loading and firing their guns standing, kneeling, and lying down. Most Yanks and Rebs were armed either with the Springfield or the Enfield rifled musket. Since both were muzzle loaders, much time and patience were required for their effective use. For loading the gun Hardee specified nine movements, each initiated by the instructor's command. At the order "Load!" the soldier dropped the butt of his gun to the ground, grasped the barrel with his left hand and with his right hand reached for the cartridge box hanging from his belt. In response to subsequent commands he bit the end from the paper cartridge; poured the powder into the barrel; inserted the bullet, with hollow base down, into the muzzle and with a ramrod pushed it to the other end of the barrel; returned the ramrod to its place beneath the barrel; took a percussion cap from a leather pouch on his belt and placed it on the nipple of the tube extending from beneath the hammer into the barrel; and shifted the gun to his right shoulder. Firing was then accomplished by movements executed at the commands "Ready," "Aim," "Fire." Despite the complexity of the procedure, a well-trained infantryman could load and fire his gun twice a minute.

After obtaining proficiency in the use of their rifles, soldiers were taught progressively to march and maneuver in squads, companies, regiments, brigades, and divisions. However, drills by units larger than brigades were infrequent and "sham battles," with infantry, artillery, and cavalry functioning together, were almost unknown until after the first year of the war, and even then they were rare.

Other branches followed a training routine com parable to that of the infantry. In the artillery much practice was required for each member of the gun crew to become proficient in his duties; the most widely used field piece on both sides was the 12-pounder smoothbore called the Napoleon. Functioning by numbers, from 1 to 10, each crew man not only had to

Right: A recruiting scene in an unidentified town. These men, perhaps, are Confederates. Certainly they have the rugged look of those rough-edged, tough men of the trans-Appalachian west who, North and South, proved to be the fiercest fighters—and worst disciplined—of the war. (JMB)

Left: They came in whole families, like these four brothers in blue with their target rifles. (LO)

Below: They spoke in strange tongues, like men of this all-German artillery unit. Tens of thousands of Germans marched behind the Federal banners, often induced to volunteer by high rank being given—sometimes unwisely—to prominent Germans. (AMERICANA IMAGE GALLERY)

Left: They came in baggy pants, the uniform of the French Chasseur. (USAMHI)

Right: They came magnificently equipped, like Sergeant Dore of the 7th New York State Militia. (USAMHI)

Right: They came, like Lieutenant A. Kintzing Post of the 45th Massachusetts, enlisting for and expecting a nine-month war. (USAMHI)

Below: They came like these two brothers of Company I, 2d New Hampshire Volunteers, with their deceptively light colored blouses and rather distinctive headgear. (HP)

Right: And they came young. This unknown boy wears the fatigue blouse and cap, common dress for most Federal infantry. (ROBERT MCDONALD)

Below: And younger still they came. A photograph taken in 1861 by Lieutenant Henry Digby of Ohio, of drummer boys William Ambrose and Jimmy Carvill. (AMERICANA IMAGE GALLERY)

make the specific movement associated with his number, such as removing the shell from the ammunition chest, passing it on to another, placing it in the muzzle, and ramming it down, but he also had to learn the movements as signed to all the other numbers so that when casualties were experienced shifts could be made with out loss of efficiency.

While learning to drill and to use their weapons, recruits had to adjust to the regimented routine of army life. The soldier's day was ordered by drum or bugle calls, which ordinarily ran to about a dozen. First came reveille, sounded about dawn, to wake the soldiers and summon them to roll call. After lining up and responding to their names, they were dismissed until a second call a half-hour later ordered them to breakfast. The third call sent the ailing to the regimental surgeon and the well to such duties as cleaning quarters, tidying company grounds, and cutting wood. About eight o'clock, the musicians sounded the call for guard mounting, at which the first sergeant of each company turned out his guard detail for the next twenty-four hours' duty, inspected them, and marched them to the regimental parade ground. There the guards were formed into line, inspected by the adjutant, and sent to their respective posts. Details were so arranged that each member stood guard only two hours out of every six.

Next came the call for drill, which ordinarily lasted until drummer or bugler signaled "roast beef," which was the call for lunch. Following a brief post-luncheon period of relaxation, soldiers were summoned to another drill which normally lasted from one to two hours. Then the men returned to their quarters, brushed their uniforms, blacked their leather, polished buckles and buttons, and cleaned their weapons in preparation for retreat, which consisted of roll call, inspection, and dress parade. Both officers and men took pride in the dress parade, held sometimes by regiment and sometimes by brigade, and always to the accompaniment of music. Dress parades were the occasion for reading orders and making official announcements.

Supper call came shortly after retreat, followed not long after dark by tattoo, which brought an other roll call, after which the men returned to their quarters. The final call of the day required the cessation of noise and the extinguishing of lights. In the course of the war this call became "taps."

This was the typical routine of an infantry regiment in camp during a season of quiet. Practices varied to some extent in different camps and with changing situations. Sunday routine differed from that of other days. The major event on the Sabbath was a general inspection of quarters, grounds, personnel, and equipment. After a preliminary check by the units' own officers, the regiment or battalion formed by companies. The inspector, usually the brigade commander or one of his staff, proceeded up and down the open ranks, carefully observing clothing, weapons, and other equipment. The soldiers were then required to stack arms, unsling and open their knapsacks, and lay them on the ground for examination. The inspector checked the contents of the knapsacks, and if he found a dirty garment he rebuked the offender. Further reproof for this and any other faults discovered by the inspector was given by the unit commander after the men returned to their quarters. The inspecting officer made the rounds of guardhouse, hospital, sutler's shop, kitchen, and such other facilities as he chose to examine. He concluded the inspection shortly before noon by going through the company quarters and checking floors, bunks, and walls. Soldiers usually spent Sunday afternoons writing letters, playing games, reading, or gambling. Those of religious inclination might attend prayer meetings or listen to sermons delivered by the regimental chaplain or by one of their comrades.

Every other month soldiers were mustered for pay. Standing in company formation, each soldier certified his presence by responding "here" when his name was called. After the mustering officer had accounted for every man listed on the roster, he forwarded a copy of the muster roll to the adjutant general in Washington, or Richmond. At the beginning of the war the monthly pay on both sides was $11 for infantry and artillery privates and $12 for cavalry. Early in the conflict the Union government increased the pay of privates in all three branches to $13 a month and in May 1864 to $16. Confederates received only one raise and that was on June 9, 1864, when the monthly stipend of infantry and artillery privates was increased to $20 and that of cavalry privates to $21; by that time the gold value of the Confederate dollar had shrunk to about five cents. Pay was often in arrears, sometimes as much as four months on the Union side and six to twelve months among Confederates.

An essential part of the transition from civilian to soldier was getting accustomed to military clothing. On both sides the first uniforms worn by some soldiers were those in which they had paraded as militiamen. These varied considerably in color and design. Concerning troops whom he observed in Washington in the early summer of 1861, General William T. Sherman stated: "Their uniforms were as various as the cities and states from which they came." When Northerners wore gray militia uniforms into battle and Southerners wore blue, as was the case in some of the early engagements, they had the unhappy experience of being fired on by their comrades. In 1861 and later, both sides had some Zouave units that wore fezzes, red bloomers, gaily colored vests and sashes, and white gaiters. Considerable variation in dress persisted throughout the war, but a fair degree of standardization was achieved in both armies before the end of 1861.

The usual outfit of a Federal infantryman was a long woolen dress coat of dark blue with a high stiff collar; a dark blue jacket or blouse which for field service was much preferred to the dress coat; light blue trousers; black brogan shoes; a flannel shirt; long flannel drawers; socks; blue cap with black visor; and a long blue overcoat with cape. Artillery and cavalry dress was the same as for the infantry except the coats were shorter and boots were normally worn instead of shoes. In both armies each branch had distinctive trimmings (red for artillery, blue for infantry, and yellow for cavalry). Branch was also indicated by insignia worn on the front of the headgear; Union officers below the grade of generals wore crossed cannons for artillery, a bugle for infantry, crossed sabers for cavalry, turreted

Left: And still younger. David Wood, aged ten. The children came to be drummers, but many, the larger ones, often passed for beyond their years and took their place in the battle. The veterans sometimes sang nursery songs in camp when they spied these boys of '61. But it was a young man's war. Some "boys" would be generals before they were old enough to vote. (RICHARD E. WOOD)

Below: C. C. Taylor, J. D. Jackson, and a man named Porter, all from Georgia, enlisted in the 3d Georgia Infantry, but did not leave for war before posing for this ambrotype. The numbers were against them. In this war, nearly one of every three Confederates would die. (MC)

Right: The Southrons flocked to their country's call, too. At Fredericksburg, Virginia, in June 1861, these confident young Virginians posed in a mixture of military and civilian dress. For many it was the best they would ever get. (JOHN A. HESS)

Right: They came to photographers who supplied them with props like Roman short swords and sometimes ungrammatical patriotic expressions. (PRIVATE COLLECTION)

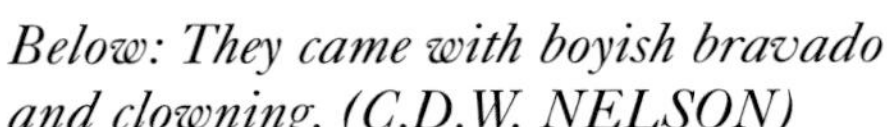

Below: They came with boyish bravado and clowning. (C.D.W. NELSON)

Above: They came with double-barreled shotguns, huge bowie knives, and a look of wild determination. (HP)

Left: Some looked rather bemused by it all. (WILLIAM A. ALBAUGH)

castle for engineers, and flaming shell for ordnance, along with a brass numeral designating regiment and, when applicable, a brass letter specifying company. Union privates wore brass letters and numerals on their caps to indicate company and regiment; on the Confederate side, branch was designated by the color of the cap crown.

Confederate Army regulations specified a double-breasted coat for both officers and enlisted men, but among enlisted men this garment was rarely seen after the first few months of the conflict. In its stead a short, gray single-breasted jacket was worn, thus giving to Johnny Rebs the nickname "gray jackets." Confederate Army regulations also specified trousers of dark blue, but from the beginning, until the use of homemade dyes produced a yellowish brown or "butternut" hue, trousers, like coats, were of gray. Confederate shoes and socks at first were very much like those worn by Yanks, but after the northern blockade became effective, inferior shoes made of home-tanned leather had to be used, though many Rebs equipped themselves with sturdier footwear by appropriating the shoes of Yankee battle casualties. Some Confederates, especially those of rural background, regarded drawers as superfluous. Regulations of both armies listed leather stocks or ties as standard items of issue, but these were rarely worn. Many soldiers in both armies wore soft hats instead of caps. Well-meaning relatives North and South frequently loaded the soldiers down with "extras" such as havelocks to protect necks from sun and rain, sleeping caps, scarfs, and mittens, but these were usually discarded soon after the recruits arrived in camp, if not before.

The soldier's prescribed equipment included a haversack for his food, a canteen, a knapsack for extra items of clothing, stationery, toilet articles, and other personal items, a leather cartridge box, and a small leather pouch for percussion caps. But comfort, convenience, and other considerations led to a shedding of some of this equipment. Knapsacks were frequently discarded and the contents rolled in a blanket which the soldier threw over his left shoulder and tied at the ends above his right hip. Many Rebs and Yanks regarded tin cups and small skillets as essential items of equipment. These they suspended from their belts. The cups some times were used for boiling coffee over the coals of the campfire.

During their period of breaking in as soldiers, Yanks and Rebs frequently had to sleep on the ground under the open skies. Those fortunate enough to have shelter usually were occupants of either Sibley or "A" tents. The Sibley tent, shaped like a bell or wigwam and supported by a vertical center pole, was eighteen feet in diameter and twelve feet high. Its twelve or more occupants slept with their feet to the center and heads near the outer edge, like spokes in a wheel. Guns were stacked around the center pole and other equipment arranged according to comfort and convenience. "A" tents, known also as wedge tents, consisted of a large sheet of canvas draped over a long horizontal bar supported by upright poles, placed at each end. Front and rear were covered by two other pieces of canvas which, when tied together, had the shape of an "A." Each tent housed from four to six men;

occupants could stand up right only when directly beneath the center ridge pole, and in sleeping they found maximum comfort when arranged in spoon fashion; but this meant that when one turned over, all had to do likewise. Officers normally were housed in wall tents, which, in effect, were "A" tents elevated two to four feet from the ground and walled with canvas. They were much more commodious and comfortable for their one or two occupants than were the Sibley and wedge tents.

After 1861 Sibley and "A" tents generally were replaced by lighter and less expensive dwellings known as shelter tents, or dog tents. These were two-man habitations made by buttoning together the rectangular pieces of canvas known as half shelters which each soldier carried as a part of his equipment. These halves, when combined, were made into a miniature wedge, with both ends open. Sometimes four soldiers would combine their half shelters to make a larger covering. Lacking a partner, a soldier could stretch his half shelter horizontally over a framework of four horizontal sticks, one placed at each corner. Ingenious Rebs and Yanks arranged their shelters in various other ways to satisfy their tastes and comforts.

In seasons of cold, when the military situation was quiescent, soldiers winterized their tents or built log cabins. A winterized tent was a rectangular log pen, about four feet high, roofed with sloping canvas and with the interior dug out perhaps to a depth of two feet to provide more standing room and warmth. Log cabins were one-room huts, chinked and daubed like frontier dwellings. Roofs were of boards, grass, or canvas. Spaciousness of the huts was sometimes increased by digging out the interiors. Both huts and winterized tents were heated by fireplaces with chimneys built of logs and chinked and lined with clay. Often chimneys were topped with barrels or kegs to in crease the draft, provide better combustion, and keep the dwellings free of smoke. Sometimes chimneys would catch fire and cause a great commotion in the soldier community.

Many soldiers laid wooden floors to increase the comfort of their winter residences. They drove nails or pegs around the walls for the hanging of hats, haversacks, and cartridge boxes. They made stoves and tables of boxes or barrels obtained from the commissary or of boards taken from nearby barns or residences. Some built double or triple-deck bunks along the walls to conserve space. Bayonets were stuck into floors or walls and candles inserted in the sockets to provide illumination. Photographs, books, and writing materials were conveniently arranged on shelves and tables. Some soldiers added a humorous touch by placarding the entrance of their huts with designations such as "Buzzard Roost," "Astor House," "Howlers," and "Growlers." Many Yanks and Rebs boasted to their womenfolk about the comfort and attractiveness of their winter quarters. A Texan stationed in Virginia wrote his mother on January 14, 1862: "Our house is about 12 feet square... Our guns are in racks on the walls; our utensils consist of one skillet, a stew kettle, a bread pan, a frying pan, & a large kettle. Our china ware is a half dozen plates and the same number of forks & spoons (silver of course), our cups are of tin, 4 quart cups and two pint cups.

Above Right: They came looking ready and alert, like Henry Kelley of the 1st Virginia, with his Colt revolving rifle. (RONN PALM)

Above Left: And they came without spit or polish or posture. (LES JENSEN)

Left: They came with poise and dignity, obviously the sons of the first families. (WENDELL W. LANG, JR.)

Right: And they, too, came young. Brother privates, William E. Spach and Bennett Spach, of the 1st Battalion of North Carolina Sharpshooters. (JOHN T. SPACH)

Above: North and South, the departure of the volunteers for the front was a major occasion. With great ceremony the town fathers or state officials presented the regiments with their colors. Here the 1st Michigan Infantry receive their flags in Detroit on May 1, 1861. (BURTON HISTORICAL COLLECTION, DETROIT PUBLIC LIBRARY)

Below: Then it was off to the war. In April 1861, the 1st Rhode Island Infantry marched to the railroad depot in Providence to ride to the South, their governor, William Sprague, at their head. (RHODE ISLAND HISTORICAL SOCIETY)

Just above the fireplace you will see something which we call a mantle piece.... There are only four of us in this house." A member of the 1 6th Maine Regiment wrote from near Fredericksburg, Virginia, in January 1863: "Max and I built generously, and inside our finished house, in the warmth of a roaring blaze, we set up bedsteads and overlaid them with pine boughs for mattresses, and covered the boughs with blankets for counterpanes. How proudly we gazed upon those beds!"

Members of some regiments, after completing their huts, built ornate entrances to their camping area. A New Englander stationed near Falls Church, Virginia, wrote his homefolks in January 1862: "The 2nd Maine have erected arches and other fancy works over the entrance to each avenue. These are made of cedar boughs and trees set in and around their camps. Nor has the 17th N.Y. been behind in beautifying their grounds. Over the entrance is placed the name of 'McClellan'—below and on the right is 'Porter' (commanding division), on the left Butterfield (commanding brigade) ." Because of the comfort of their winter dwellings, and the respite from marching and fighting that came with cold weather, most soldiers came to regard winter as the most tolerable of their wartime seasons.

For many recruits the most undesirable feature of breaking in to army life was being "put through the measles." Troops from rural areas, largely be cause they had not been exposed to this malady in childhood, were more susceptible to it than were those from towns and cities. Measles usually struck during the first few months of military service and with devastating consequences. In the summer of 1861, one out of every seven Confederates of the Army of Northern Virginia had measles, and in one camp of 10,000 recruits, 4,000 men were stricken with the disease. Early in 1863 a soldier of Grant's army wrote from near Vicksburg: "Mesles... is what kilde the most of our boys—thay would take the measels and haf to lay out in the rain and storm and thay wod only laste abot 2 days." Comparatively few men died from measles alone, but the tendency to get up too soon often led to complications which proved fatal. A soldier of the Army of Northern Virginia wrote in August 1861: "We have some 5 or 6 that is very sick ones in our company.... They all had the measles, & were getting well & they turn out to drill too soon after it and they all have relapsed." Recruits of 1861 also had dysentery, malaria, typhoid, pneumonia, and other diseases that plagued Civil War armies, but the incidence of measles was much greater among new soldiers than among veterans.

Yet sickness, discomfort, drill, and discipline paled in comparison to the real business of soldiering, and all too soon these boys of '61 would mature in fire and blood to become the men of Bull Run.

Left: Camps of instruction like Camp Chase outside Columbus, Ohio, appeared all over the divided nation, as volunteers poured in to be made into soldiers. (OHIO HISTORICAL SOCIETY)

Left: Hasty makeshift bivouacs sprang forth in most major cities, crowding even major public buildings and filling the square in front of Philadelphia's Independence Hall. (LO)

Above: The 7th New York State Militia on review in 1861 at Camp Cameron. The drill and review were all too new to the recruits of 1861. It would become all too familiar in the years to come. (MHS)

Left: "I have seen Him in the watch-fires of a hundred circling camps," wrote Julia Ward Howe. The camp of the 1st Connecticut Artillery, near Washington. (CHS)

Above: The 9th Mississippi on parade near Pensacola, caught by J. D. Edwards in April 1861. They, too, however rustic in appearance, learned the intricacies of the drill manual, though it often baffled them. They fought back by giving to the evolutions their own peculiar appellations. A right wheel soon became a "stauchendicilar to the right." (MC)

Above: Exposed for the first time to large numbers of their fellow countrymen in close quarters, the boys of '61 were as well exposed to their germs. Hospitals and camps went in tandem all across the land. Here a tent hospital at Kendal Green, near Washington. (LC)

Right: The best respite from the drill and fatigue duty attendant to training came at meal times. Everyone took a hand, though early in the war tasting the soup could be as dangerous as an enemy bullet. At least there were women in camp to do the laundry. And others followed the camps, tending the men's needs of the flesh. (USAMHI)

Left: The officers dined together and fought in imagination the battles and triumphs they would visit upon the enemy. Here the officers of Company F, 8th Massachusetts Infantry, at Camp Brightwood in the District of Columbia. (USAMHI)

Right: The men in the ranks looked forward to their boxes from home, the letters and liquor and delicacies sent by mothers and sweethearts. Men of the 8th Massachusetts. (USAMHI)

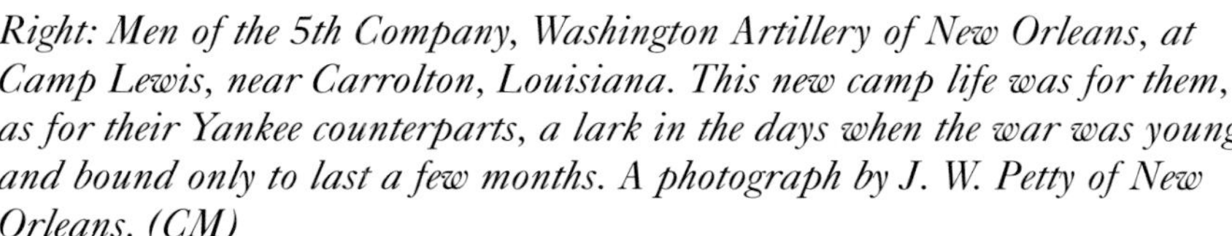

Right: Men of the 5th Company, Washington Artillery of New Orleans, at Camp Lewis, near Carrolton, Louisiana. This new camp life was for them, as for their Yankee counterparts, a lark in the days when the war was young and bound only to last a few months. A photograph by J. W. Petty of New Orleans. (CM)

Left: The soldiers read, relaxed, played cards, tickled each other in the ear with feathers, and even stacked the deck for the camera. The gambler to the left holds a "full house," kings and twos. Even a passing bird stops to perch on the cannon's sponge for the photographer. The 1st Massachusetts Light Artillery. (USAMHI)

Above Left: Swords and pistols must be polished bright. The man seated burnishes and cleans his Starr revolver, while his mates of the 1st Massachusetts Light Artillery squint at the camera. (USAMHI)

Above Right: For some in these first days of the war, campaigning was no reason to dispense with the luxuries of home life. The Washington Light Infantry of Charleston, South Carolina, lounge contentedly before their tent, awaiting baskets of food and wine served in glass goblets by their black servants (WASHINGTON LIGHT INFANTRY)

Left: Many Confederates, even private soldiers, appeared for muster with their bodyservants in tow. Andrew Chandler brought his slave Silas Chandler with him, and both armed for a fight. Men who once feared arms in the hands of slaves now thought little of handing them knives and shotguns. (STERLING CHANDLER AND RICHARD S. YOUNG)

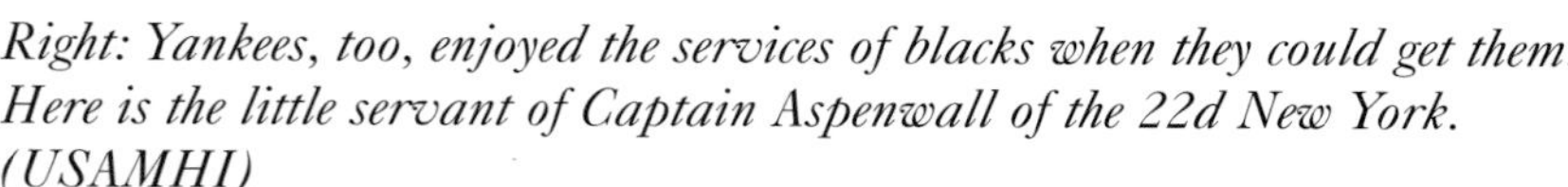

Right: Yankees, too, enjoyed the services of blacks when they could get them. Here is the little servant of Captain Aspenwall of the 22d New York. (USAMHI)

Above: Most of all the men North and South did as American soldiers have done in all wars, make the best of it. Confederates of the Washington Artillery relaxed, indifferent to what lay ahead. When they left New Orleans they were told, "May the Lord of Hosts be round about you as a wall of fire, and shield your heads in the day of battle! (JAN P. REIFENBERG)

Above Right: They and their foes to the north, like the 7th New York, will be ready, or think they will. None of them, in their bright uniforms. . . (USAMHI)

Right: . . . their gaily festooned quarters for Phunny Fellows . . . (USAMHI)

Above: . . . their striped trousers, their blouses decorated with flannel badges and galloping horses . . . (USAMHI)

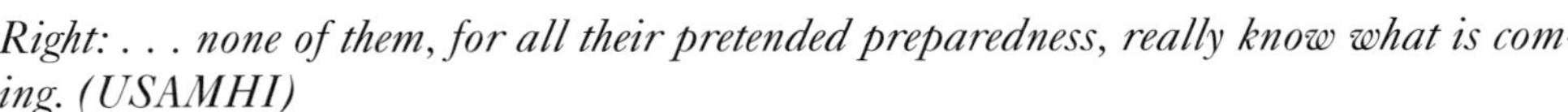

Right: . . . none of them, for all their pretended preparedness, really know what is coming. (USAMHI)

Above Left:Instead, they smile and pose. The 23d New York Infantry. (USAMHI)

Above Right: They pose in little groups. The 33d New York Infantry, the man at right armed with a "Volcanic" repeating pistol in his belt. (USAMHI)

Above: They pose by companies, their lady friends often with them. The 22d New York State Militia. (USAMHI)

Above: They gather around the colors they expect to lead to glory, and defend with their lives if need be. The colors of the 7th New York State Militia, at right and left the general guides, at left center the regimental banner, and right center the national colors. (NA)

Left: The officers and men join together for the camera. Colonel William Wilson, center, and men of his 6th New York Infantry, "Wilson's Zouaves." (USAMHI)

Left: They clowned indoors at mock battle. (LO)

Left: With bread and cider and camaraderie, they passed the summer days of soldiering. But it would not last. These militiamen are guarding the Chain Bridge over the Potomac at Washington in 1861. (RINHART GALLERIES INC.)

Right: Washington was a threatened capital. With Virginia across the Potomac hostile, and Maryland filled with southern sympathizers who attempted to block Federal communications and reinforcement from the North, Lincoln and his city were almost blockaded. Then Benjamin F. Butler, a Massachusetts Democrat and now an ardent supporter of the war, acted under his major general's commission and led an expedition to secure . . . (MICHAEL J. MCAFEE)

. . . the Baltimore & Ohio Railroad junction at Relay House, Maryland, thereby holding open a rail route for troops to reach Washington. From May 6, 1861, onward, troops like these flowed through Relay House and on to the capital. (MHS)

The First Bull Run

JOSEPH P. CULLEN

Reality at last in the heat and dust and blood of Manassas

Above: In the wake of Fort Sumter, the pressure on Lieutenant General Winfield Scottóshown here with his staffóbecame intense. The Union must strike back, put down the Rebellion. (NA)

Left: First Washington must be made secure and troops brought in from the North Benjamin F. Butler's occupation of Relay House on the vital Baltimore & Ohio ensured that. (USAMHI)

IT WAS ALREADY HOT that morning of July 16, 1861, when they marched out of the camps around Washington to fight the first major battle in what has been called the last of the old wars and the first of the new. And the camera would be there, or not far behind, to record for posterity the men of the armies and the scenes of battle—a hill, a stream, a field, a copse of woods; a bridge, a church, a house, a barn. Ordinary everyday things in ordinary, everyday life, but these simple things assumed importance beyond their functional purposes. They became landmarks to show where men fought and died; landmarks to be photographed and recorded for future generations.

Since April, when the guns of Fort Sumter roared out their message that North and South were at war, troops had poured into the Washington area until the surrounding heights blossomed white with tents in a care-free, carnival atmosphere. And the untrained, undisciplined citizen-soldiers, with their gaudy, multicolored uniforms—the flamboyant 11th New York Zouaves in their blue and scarlet shirts and jackets and white turbans; the checked flannels of Michigan lumberjacks; the colorful Garibaldi Guards—added a picturesque touch. A few were army regulars, some state militia, but most were three-month volunteers with romantic ideas about wars in general and battles in particular, who fully expected to end the war with one battle and be home at the end of their brief enlistment.

Many tried to bring the comforts of home with them into the field. One volunteer admitted that his knapsack held "a pair of trousers, two pairs of drawers, a pair of thick boots, four pairs of stockings, four flannel shirts, a blouse, a looking glass, a can of peaches, a bottle of cough-mixture, a button-stick, chalk, razor and strop, a Bible, a small volume of Shakespeare, and writing utensils," in addition to a "tailor's shop," usually made of leather or cloth and "containing needles, pins, thread, buttons, and scissors." He also carried a rubber blanket and a woolen blanket and "a belt bout the body, which held a cartridge-box and bayonet, a cross belt, also a haversack and tin drinking cup, a canteen." The cartridge-box held forty rounds of ammunition and the haversack three days' rations of "salt junk, hardtack, sugar and coffee." Altogether a load to challenge a mule.

There was an air of excitement, a feeling akin to a sudden unexpected holiday, a welcome break in the humdrum monotony of everyday living. And that feeling was very much in evidence that morning as 35,000 men in their colorful uniforms, carrying the stiff new flags clinging to their shiny staffs, marched off to battle with bands blaring and drums rolling. They knew nothing of wars or battles or any of the realities of actual combat. They expected to march for a few days and then line up somewhere in formation and shoot at the enemy from afar. Then when the Southerners ran back to Richmond it would be over and they could all go home as heroes. So they went to war as if to a picnic.

After a few days of marching in the brutal heat and choking dust, however, many of these civilian soldiers began to have second thoughts about the glorious adventure ahead of them. "My canteen banged against my bayonet," one recruit noted, "both tin cup and bayonet badly interfered with the butt of my musket, while my cartridge-box and haversack were constantly flopping up and down." Blistered feet and aching muscles soon dictated that loads had to be lightened, so various pieces of equipment were surreptitiously dropped along the way. Thus would they learn the hard way—by experience.

In command of this ragged mass of men marching out of Washington was Irvin McDowell, a native of Ohio recently promoted to brigadier general of volunteers. A graduate of the U. S. Military Academy, McDowell was forty-three years old, a robust, heavy-set man with dark cropped hair and an iron-gray beard. He had served creditably in the Mexican War in staff positions, but had never commanded a large body of troops in the field. A quiet, introverted person who neither smoked nor drank, he was too reserved to be popular with his fellow officers, and definitely not the type to inspire men. Still he was a professional and as such recognized the weaknesses of his raw recruits. He did not want to fight until the men had been trained sufficiently to at least act like soldiers rather than civilians. "This is not an army," he told his superiors. "It will take a long time to make an army." But the times were against McDowell. The enlistments of most of the three-month volunteers was about up and the people of the North became impatient. "Forward to Richmond" screamed the newspaper headlines. And the government listened to the voice of the people. McDowell was ordered to move against a lesser Confederate force at Manassas, Virginia, about twenty-five miles southwest of Washington. To be sure, there was another Confederate force to the west in the Shenandoah Valley, but it was to be pinned down by other Federal troops and thus prevented from reinforcing the Confederates at Manassas. "You are green, it is true," President Lincoln told the reluctant McDowell, "but they are green also."

And green they were. A few days after the firing at Fort Sumter, Virginia seceded from the Union. In Richmond there was dancing in the streets and bonfires burned to celebrate the historic event. Cannon were dragged by hand from the state arsenal to Capitol Square to fire a salute. The new Confederate flag fluttered proudly atop the capitol building. Virginians by the thousands flocked to the newly opened recruiting stations, fearful the fighting would end before they could play a part in it. Then in May the Confederate Congress, in session at Montgomery, Alabama, voted to move the Confederate capital to Richmond. Now the city underwent a dramatic change. When hundreds of regiments from farther south streamed in, Richmond took on the appearance of a vast military camp. At night the glow from thousands of campfires lit the sky. One observer noted, "One of the remarkable features of the times is that men of all classes and conditions, of all occupations and professions, are of one mind."

Although a Richmond newspaper could bluster, "There is one wild shout of fierce resolve to capture Washington City, at all and every human hazard," that was not the immediate objective of the new government. If the South could not secede from the Union peacefully, then it was determined to defend every acre of territory and maintain its independence to the last. As Confederate President Davis proclaimed: "All

Below: With men of the 7th New York and other regiments garrisoning the camps around Washington, the capital was safe. That done, it was time to press the war and end the Rebellion. Within weeks these boys of '61 would become men in battle. (WRHS)

Above: The first move was to occupy Alexandria, Virginia, just across the Potomac from Washington. Confederate flags flying over the city taunted Lincoln, and on May 24 Colonel Elmer Ellsworth led his Fire Zouaves, now the 11th New York, across the Potomac. (USAMHI)

Left: There Ellsworth saw a Rebel banner flying above the Marshall House. He personally went to the roof and removed it from the staff still visible. On his way to the ground floor, he was met by the house's proprietor, who murdered him on the spot. Ellsworth became the nation's first great martyr, and Lincoln grieved sorely for his dead young friend. (USAMHI)

Left: With Winfield Scott too old to take active field command, a member of his staff, Irvin McDowell, was elevated to brigadier general and given the unenviable task of molding an army and advancing to meet the enemy in Virginia. (USAMHI)

Above: Men of the 1st Rhode Island at Camp Sprague, outside Washington, well trained and ready (LC)

Above: The engineer company of the 8th New York in Arlington, Virginia, in June 1861. Photograph by Brady or an assistant. (LC)

Above: Colonel Ambrose Burnside and officers of the 1st Rhode Island Infantry formed a part of McDowell's developing army. (USAMHI)

we ask is to be left alone." With this philosophy there was nothing to be gained by invading the North. Rather, the South wanted to exploit the advantages of a defensive posture, which would require fewer men and allow it to use its interior, or shorter, lines of communications and supply to best advantage. In addition, all the various government departments, as well as an army, had to be created, organized, and staffed to carry on a war, while at the same time a government had to be set up to pass laws governing what was hoped would be a new nation.

So thousands of young men streamed into Richmond to prepare to defend their independence, and like their counterparts in Washington, their uniforms exhibited an amazing variety. The various state militia colors mixed with fancy home made uniforms, while some regiments had nothing but civilian clothes. Some of the higher ranking officers still wore the dress of the United States Army. And like the Northerners, the new recruits posed stiffly for portraits, followed the bands down the springtime streets, waved to the cheering girls, and set about, they thought, getting the war over with in a hurry. As one lady recorded in her diary, "There was much music and mustering and marching, much cheering and flying of flags, much firing of guns and all that sort of thing."

With Richmond now the Confederate capital, the area of Manassas, about seventy-five miles to the north, became strategically important to the defense of the city. The central point was Manassas Junction, a small railroad settlement consisting of a handful of decrepit buildings scattered carelessly about the railroad crossing. Here two railroads joined. The Orange & Alexandria, running north and south, connected with both Washington and Richmond; and the Manassas Gap Railroad, which extended westward through the Blue Ridge mountains to the rich, fertile valley of the Shenandoah. There were many good roads also, east and west, north and south, the main one being the Warrenton Turnpike, which led through the town of Centreville to Alexandria and Washington. The surrounding area was a gently rolling country of soft ridges, small farms, rail fences, crooked creeks, and quiet woods. About midway between Manassas and Centreville, Bull Run Creek meandered peacefully through the plains, the trees along its banks forming a leafy tunnel with the sun sifting through to form lacy gold patterns on the water, while picturesque arched bridges spanned it.

In June the South moved to protect this vital point. In command was Brigadier General P. G. T. Beauregard, hero of the firing on Fort Sumter. A classmate of McDowell's, his last United States Army assignment had been as Superintendent of the Military Academy at West Point, New York. A small, graceful man in his early forties, Beauregard was a proud Creole from Louisiana who had distinguished himself in the Mexican War as a staff officer but, like McDowell, had never commanded a large body of troops in the field. Outspoken and critical of others, yet sensitive to criticism himself, he generally found it easier to make enemies than friends. But he too was a professional, and now with about 22,000 raw civilian-soldiers he set his line of defense along Bull Run. Although the creek itself was a formidable obstacle to any attacking force with its steep wooded banks,

Left: The 2d Michigan came a long way to be in on the one battle that would surely end the war. (THE BURTON HISTORICAL COLLECTION, DETROIT PUBLIC LIBRARY)

there were many fords and two bridges to be defended. On his right flank he destroyed the railroad bridge at Union Mills; built fortifications at McLean's, Blackburn's, and Mitchell's fords; and stationed other forces at Ball's Ford, Lewis Ford, and the Stone Bridge on the Warrenton Turnpike, his extreme left flank. At Manassas Junction itself massive fortifications were erected running out in different directions from the little station. And across Bull Run he established advance guard posts at Centreville and Fairfax Court House and several strategic crossroads to warn of the approach of the enemy. Sixty miles away to the west across the mountains sat another force under Brigadier General Joseph E. Johnston. If Beauregard was outnumbered and attacked, he hoped to be reinforced by Johnston's troops. They would come on the cars of the Manassas Gap Rail road.

While these preparations were being made, the recruits were constantly marshaled and drilled in a desperate attempt to give them some training before the battle they knew must come. Yet the camps, like the ones in the North, had a gay, festive atmosphere about them, with constant visitors at all hours of the day and night. In them could be found well-prepared meals, "caddies of tea, barrels of sugar, and many articles better suited for a picnic or a party in a summer house than to soldiers in the field." A young lady visitor wrote that they "were able during those rallying days of June to drive frequently to visit 'the boys' in camp, timing the expeditions to include battalion drill and dress parade, and taking tea afterward in the different tents. Then were the gala days of war, and our proud hosts hastened to produce home dainties dispatched from far-away plantations."

Such was life in the Confederate camps when McDowell left Washington that July 16. Beauregard received word at once that he was coming from a female spy in Washington. Not that it was any secret anyway—everyone in Washington and in the Army knew where they were going. Beauregard immediately requested that Johnston's troops in the valley be sent to him. Two days later the Union Army concentrated on the heights of Centreville overlooking the plains of Manassas as the Confederate outposts fell back to their main line behind Bull Run. McDowell spent the next two days probing for a weak spot in the Confederate line. A reconnaissance in force was repulsed in the center at

Left: The camp of the 1st Minnesota, near Edwards Ferry, Maryland. They were eager to march south and put down the Rebellion. (MHS)

Left: McDowell marched his arriving regiments across the Long Bridge and others leading from Washington to the Virginia side, and trained and organized his army in and around Arlington. (USAMHI)

Left: He made his headquarters in the stately mansion, Arlington House, that, until a few weeks before, had been the home of Robert E. Lee. Mrs. Lee was still there when he moved in, and he took great care not to discomfort her. Here he planned his campaign. (USAMHI)

Above: Old General Robert Patterson was to keep the Confederate Army of Joseph E. Johnston occupied in the Shenandoah Valley so that it could not reinforce Confederates around Manassas when McDowell attacked them. If Patterson failed, McDowell could be in grave danger. (USAMHI)

Above: On July 16, 1861, McDowell's army moved out of its camps on the road toward Manassas and the Rebel Army. This image of the 8th New York was taken that same day as they prepared for the march. (MJM)

Above: Charles P. Stone, inspector general of the District of Columbia militia, would command one of Patterson's brigades. (USAMHI)

Above: As they marched they passed historic Falls Church, where George Washington had worshipped. (USAMHI)

Mitchell's and Blackburn's fords, and no suitable terrain for attack appeared on the right. On the Confederate left, however, two unguarded fords, Popular and Sudley, were discovered. A crossing here would put the troops on the Sudley road, which led to the Warrenton Turnpike near the Stone House, and behind the Confederate left.

So on the afternoon of July 20, McDowell issued his battle order for the attack the next morning. His plan was simple but sound. Realizing the center of the Confederate line was too strong for a frontal attack by inexperienced troops, he ordered just a feint there, and then a long flanking march to the right to Sudley and Popular fords to circle and crumple the enemy left. Although McDowell could not know it, the two-day delay in preparing his plan was to prove fatal. Even as he issued his orders the first of Johnston's troops from the valley arrived on the railroad cars at the Junction. When they all got there the Confederates would have about 32,000 men.

Word that the battle would be fought the next day, a Sunday, quickly reached Washington and hundreds of people made frantic preparations to get there to see it. "Every carriage, gig, wagon, and hack has been engaged by people going out to see the fight," wrote an English newspaper reporter. "The French cooks and hotelkeepers, by some occult process of reasoning, have arrived at the conclusion that they must treble the prices of their wines and of the hampers of provisions" the people were ordering to take with them. "Before the battle," wrote a congressman from Ohio, "the hopes of the people and of their representatives are very elated and almost jocosely festive."

The next morning the road to Centreville jammed with nervous horses and handsome carriages, pretty ladies in bright crinoline dresses carrying picnic baskets filled with cool wines and tasty snacks. Senators and congressmen, foreign dignitaries, bureaucrats, and reporters, dressed in their light summer clothing and carrying spyglasses and revolvers and flasks of Bourbon,

Above: They passed by Taylor's Tavern, outside Falls Church, Virginia. (WRHS)

Above: On July 17 the Federals skirmished with the enemy around Fairfax Court House. (NA)

Above: And the next day McDowell occupied Centreville, until that morning a fortified Confederate camp. (USAMHI)

Right: From Centreville, McDowell sent Colonel Daniel Tyler forward with his division to reconnoiter the enemy positions along Bull Run. He was ordered not to bring on an engagement. (USAMHI)

Above: Instead Tyler and his chief lieutenant, Colonel Israel B. Richardson, became engaged in a hot fight at Blackburn's Ford, and were repulsed. (PENNSYLVANIA—MOLLUS COLLECTION, WAR LIBRARY AND MUSEUM, PHILADELPHIA)

Above: Three days later, McDowell launched his battle plan, sending his marching columns toward Bull Run, shown here in a July 1862 image by Timothy O'Sullivan. (LC)

Above: McDowell's coming was detected well in advance by men in signal towers built and supervised by Beauregard's signal officer, Captain Edward Porter Alexander, a Georgian who graduated from West Point four years before. He appears here in his cadet uniform, probably in 1857. (LSU)

Above: By contrast, McDowell's signal officer, Captain A. J. Myer, spent most of the day unsuccessfully attempting to launch an observation balloon from which to spy enemy movements. (LC)

Above: July 21, 1861, was Brigadier General David Hunter's fifty-ninth birthday. As he led McDowell's flanking column that was to assail the Confederate left via Sudley Ford, he received a birthday present in the form of a serious wound that put him out of the battle. (USAMHI)

rushed to Virginia to watch the great event, greeting friends, laughing and joking.

To the men in the Union ranks the occasion was not so festive, however. Since two-thirty that morning the flanking march had been taking place under bright moonlight. Across the Turnpike, over Cub Run Creek, through the woods and fields, heading for the Sudley fords. About three hours later, as the first gray streaks of dawn turned the landscape from brown to green, they heard the roar of a Union cannon near the Stone Bridge shatter the early quiet. The first major battle of the Civil War had begun. By seven o'clock they should have been crossing Bull Run at the fords, but these civilians in uniform could not march that fast. They were still more than two hours away, and already the heat was oppressive. Now they were hot and tired, the fancy uniforms covered with choking dust. Even though the maneuver was already several hours behind schedule, the recruits still straggled after ripe blackberries, stopped for a refreshing drink, or just rested in the shade of the trees. It was about nine-thirty before they reached the fords, and then a Confederate officer high atop a signal tower spotted the glint of the sun on a brass cannon. The surprise was lost.

Quickly the Confederates swung their left flank back to Chinn Ridge behind the Stone House and rushed up reinforcements to counter the threat. Shortly after ten o'clock the Union troops came charging out of the woods into the fields on either side of the Sudley road and drove the Confederates back across the Turnpike to a new position on the plateau around the Henry and Robinson houses. The battle had opened

Above: Hunter's men passed the Thornton House, shown here in a March 1862 image by George N. Barnard. (LC)

Above: Then they passed the Sudley Springs Ford and crossed over Bull Run to move toward Beauregard. Photograph by Barnard, March 1862. (USAMHI)

Above: Sudley Church, above Bull Run. The Federals swarmed past it on their way to the first major engagement of the war. (WRHS)

Above: Burnside led his brigade in the initial assaults against Confederate defenders on Mathews' Hill. (USAMHI)

Above: One of Burnside's regiments, the 2d Rhode Island Infantry, was the first of Hunter's column to engage the enemy. They fought bravely, even after their colonel was killed and many of their officers put out of the fight. They are shown at drill here in a photograph taken several months following the battle. (USAMHI)

Right: Colonel Andrew Porter was next into the fray with his brigade. He felt that Burnside had attacked with "perhaps, too hasty vigor," but he immediately moved to Burnside's support and took command of the division after Hunter's wound. Porter stands at center in this image taken prior to the battle. (P-M)

Above: The 8th New York, perhaps the most resplendent of regiments in McDowell's army, went into battle with Porter. (TERENCE P. O LEARY)

Above: William Weir's house Liberia was not far from the home of Wilmer McLean, where Beauregard made his headquarters. McLean himself was so disturbed by the war's coming to his very doorstep that he moved where he thought it would never find him again. Appomattox. (WRHS)

Above: George Barnard's March 1862 photograph of the battlefield at Bull Run, looking over the Warrenton Turnpike. (USAMHI)

Above: They were fighting an army led by the hero of Fort Sumter, P. G. T. Beauregard, now a brigadier general in the Confederate Army. (LC)

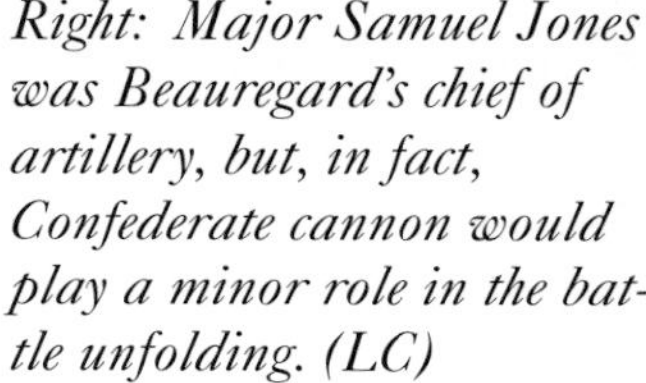

Right: Major Samuel Jones was Beauregard's chief of artillery, but, in fact, Confederate cannon would play a minor role in the battle unfolding. (LC)

Right: The man who stopped the initial assault by Hunter's column, and several succeeding attacks, thus buying time for Beauregard to rush troops to the threatened left, was another veteran of Fort Sumter. Brigadier General Nathan G. Evans, called "Shanks" by friends, was a rough, uncouth braggart whose orderly always stood behind him with a "barrelita" of whiskey. He would later claim that he alone, with the aid of the Almighty "and a few private gentlemen, won the battle. (SOUTH CAROLINIANA LIBRARY)

with frightening reality. Yellow sheets of flame flashed along both lines as regiment after regiment exploded into action with a metallic roar. Gigantic crashes of artillery split the air. Shells screamed overhead, exploding in clouds of earth, horses, and men. The noise roared to a crescendo that left men dazed and confused, as the fighting surged back and forth, the issue in doubt, into the afternoon.

On a hill just below Centreville overlooking the plains of Manassas, the carriages from Washington were drawn up as if at a country horse race. Surprisingly, their presence did not seem to bother the troops who saw them. "Near Cub Run we saw carriages and barouches which contained civilians who had driven out from Washington to witness the operation," one soldier remembered. "We thought it wasn't bad idea to have the great men from Washington come out to see us thrash the Rebs." The visitors had a panoramic view of the lovely wooded

Above: A few of those "private gentlemen" who held the line with Evans. Major Roberdeau Wheat's battalion of Louisiana Zouaves, commonly called Wheat's Tigers. They are photographed here in New Orleans in 1861. (LC)

Above: As the battle between Hunter's and Evans's troops developed, Brigadier General Samuel P. Heintzelman's division came into the fight. He, too, would be wounded, but acted heroically in attempting to hold his command together in the confusion of its first fight. (USAMHI)

Above: Soldiers like this rugged-looking woodsman from the 4th Michigan went into the action in Orlando Willcox's brigade of Heintzelman's division. The Michiganders fought like demons, the first Westerners to do battle in the East. (HP)

Above: While the battle raged on the Confederate left, Colonel William T. Sherman led his brigade across a ford near the Stone Bridge in the center of the line and assailed Evans's depleted command. Sherman is shown here as a major general in an 1865 photo. (NYHS)

Above: Colonel Michael Corcoran, center, and officers of the 69th New York crossed with Sherman. (MJM)

Above: So did Colonel James Cameron of the 79th New York. The son of Secretary of War Simon Cameron, he would not recross Bull Run. He died in battle. (USAMHI)

Below: Battery E, 3d United States Artillery, commanded by Captain Romeyn B. Ayres. Called Sherman's Battery because it was formerly led by Thomas W. Sherman, this unit was greatly feared by the Confederates because of its mighty Parrot rifles. This image shows the battery on July 24, 1861, in Washington, three days after the battle. (BRUCE GIMELSON)

Above: Erasmus D. Keyes, like Sherman, a colonel of a brigade in Tyler's division, also crossed Bull Run, but played a lesser role in the fighting along the Warrenton Road. (USAMHI)

Above: The 3d Connecticut of Keyes's brigade. Their gallantry, he believed, "was never surpassed." (LC)

Above: The fighting raged first around the Matthews' House on Matthews' Hill, where the advancing Federals slowly forced Evans and his outnumbered command back to the Warrenton Turnpike. (USAMHI)

Above: Evans's command retreated past the Stone House on the Warrenton Road, shown in this March 1862 photo by Barnard and James F. Gibson, and up the slopes of Henry Hill. (USAMHI)

Above: And on Henry Hill the fighting raged for most of the rest of the day. Soon after Evans's arrival, sharp fighting took place on the right of the hill near the Robinson House, where Sherman attacked the line held by yet another veteran of Fort Sumter... (USAMHI)

country, dotted with green fields and cleared lands. According to one observer, "undulating lines of forest marked the course of the streams which intersected it and gave by their variety of color and shading an additional charm to the landscape which, enclosed in a framework of blue and purple hills, softened into violet in the extreme distance, presented one of the most agreeable displays of simple pastoral woodland scenery that could be conceived." Somehow it was difficult to believe that men would actually shoot at and kill each other across this beautiful scene. But then the woods echoed to the roar of cannon, thin lines of dirty gray haze marked the angry muttering of musketry, white puffs of smoke burst high above the treetops, bayonets flashed in the glaring sun, and clouds of dust shifted constantly back and forth across the landscape. One lady spectator with an opera glass "was quite beside herself when an unusually heavy discharge roused the current of her blood—"That is splendid. Oh, my! Is not that first-rate? I guess we will be in Richmond this time tomorrow."

All afternoon the battle lines surged back and forth across the plateau, around the Henry House and the Robinson House, on Chinn Ridge, and along the Turnpike as men died by the hundreds in the woods, in the fields, on the banks of Bull Run, in a nightmare battle of mistakes fought by untrained volunteers led by inexperienced officers. Then when the last of Johnston's fresh Confederate troops reached the field late in the afternoon, because the Federal force had failed to hold them in the Shenandoah Valley as planned, McDowell realized any chance of victory was gone and ordered a withdrawal. The exhausted troops started an orderly retreat from the field. The battle was over. "There was no confusion or panic then," one soldier remembered, but the men cursed their generals because they did not have fresh reinforcements as the enemy did. The orderly retreat quickly turned to confusion and then panic when the Confederates pursued, while the civilian spectators and their carriages and buggies created a frenzied jam among the army wagons, caissons, guns, and ambulances. "Infantry soldiers on mules and draft horses with the harness clinging to their heels, as much frightened as their riders," wrote a reporter. "Negro servants on their masters' chargers; ambulances crowded with unwounded soldiers; wagons swarming with men who threw out the contents in the road to make room, grinding through a shouting, screaming mass of men on foot who were literally yelling with rage at every halt." No longer under any effective control, many of the soldiers headed for Washington, a confused mob with little semblance of order or discipline. By sundown it was a question of whether or not they should try to make a stand at Centreville. McDowell decided against it. "The condition of our artillery and its ammunition," he reported, "the want of food for the men, and the utter disorganization and demoralization of the mass of the army seemed to admit of no alternative but to fall back."

For miles the roads leading into Washington be came strewn with the paraphernalia of waró-caps, coats, blankets, rifles, canteens, haversacks. "I saw the beaten, foot-sore, spongy-looking soldiers," a reporter wrote, "officers and all the

Above: ... Colonel Wade Hampton, commanding Hampton's Legion. Hampton himself was wounded, but he held his line. (VM)

Above: Lieutenant Thomas M. Logan of Hampton's Legion played a conspicuous part in the fighting around the Robinson House. In February 1865 he would become a brigadier general.

Above: Colonel Francis S. Bartow of Georgia exposed himself recklessly on the battlefield in leading his brigade against the Federals. It cost him his life. (VM)

Above: The fighting became even more fierce in the center of the Confederate line on Henry Hill. There Brigadier General Barnard E. Bee of South Carolina fought desperately against several enemy assaults. His very presence on the field was a harbinger of victory, for he and his brigade had been sent to Beauregard from the Shenandoah. Johnston had eluded Patterson, and even as the battle raged, more of his regiments were on their way. Bee would fall with a mortal wound, but not before bestowing on another of Johnston's brigade commanders an immortal sobriquet. Attempting to rally his men after a charge, he pointed to a brigade of Virginians behind them and said... (VM)

Above, right: ... "There stands Jackson like a stone wall." It was the brigade of General Thomas J. Jackson, shown here in a 1855 daguerreotype. A man of inordinate peculiarities, he would become the greatest legend of the war. (NATIONAL PORTRAIT GALLERY, SMITHSONIAN INSTITUTION, WASHINGTON, D.C.)

Right: Officers of the Washington Artillery of New Orleans, who helped Jackson stand like a wall. They are brothers, Miles Taylor Squires, Samuel Smith Squires, and Charles W. Squires. (W. H. T. SQUIRES, JR.)

Right: The battle raged for hours on Henry Hill, often around the Henry House itself, where poor old widow Henry, who refused to leave, was blown out of her bed by a shell that severed her foot and mortally wounded her. An 1862 view by Barnard . (USAMHI)

debris of the army filing through mud and rain, forming in crowds in front of the spirit stores." Muddy, hungry, and scared, they staggered through the streets begging food and buying liquor, dropping in exhaustion on porches, lawns, and sidewalks. Many of the younger officers, completely demoralized, filled the hotel barrooms and cheap saloons. One of the civilian casualties who walked forlornly back to Washington was a photographer, already noted for his portraits, who would later become famous, Mathew Brady. He and his assistants had lost the wagon with his camera and all his equipment in the panic, or so he claimed.

And on the plains of Manassas the soul-searing moans of the wounded and dying echoed through the still night air. Motionless forms covered the ground in grotesque positions, as if someone had carelessly heaved them from a wagon. The Federals suffered almost 3,000 casualties in killed, wounded, and missing; the Confederates almost 2,000. All through the night the stretcher-bearers, doctors, friends, and even relatives worked tirelessly among the dead and wounded, the flickering flames from the candles and lanterns casting weird shadows among the dark, silent trees.

"The capture of Washington seems now to be inevitable," a frightened government official declared. "The rout, overthrow, and utter demoralization of the whole army is complete." This, of course, was an exaggeration. A more sober, realistic view of the situation was made by another close observer of the events. "We have undertaken to make war without in the least knowing how," he wrote. "We have made a false start and we have discovered it. It only remains to start afresh." A lesson had been learned—a hard lesson. It was not going to be a short, easy war. The politicians now realized that all the powerful resources of the North would have to be organized and directed in preparation for a long, bitter struggle. And the war was not going to be won by the theatrical heroics of untrained three-

Left: Nearly as badly used up as Ricketts's battery was Battery D, 5th United States Artillery. Captain Charles Griffin obeyed orders to take it nearly to the brow of the left of Henry Hill. Once there, Griffin mistook an enemy regiment dressed in blue for his own troops, and discovered the mistake too late. All of his cannoneers were shot down and only three of his six guns escaped, and two of them had to be abandoned later. (P-M)

Above: In desperate fighting on the forward slope of Henry Hill, Captain James B. Ricketts of Battery I, 1st United States Artillery, was wounded four times and captured along with all six of his cannon and forty-nine horses. He would recover to become a brigadier general in less than a year. (USAMHI)

Above: Former Governor of Virginia William "Extra Billy" Smith, now colonel of the 49th Virginia, took a place in the Confederate line just in time to assist in the destruction of Ricketts's and Griffin's batteries. He is shown here in the uniform of a brigadier general, probably in 1863. (USAMHI)

Above: Patterson's failure in the Shenandoah allowed Brigadier General Joseph E. Johnston to bring almost his entire army to assist Beauregard. Johnston arrived on the field and took overall command of operations the day before the battle. This rare photo of Johnston has never before been published. (VM)

Above: The unexpected arrival of Johnston's last brigade to reach the field, led by Colonel Arnold Elzey, threw McDowell's right flank into a panic. (VM)

Above: Colonel Oliver 0. Howard, commanding a brigade of Heintzelman's division, was at the right flank when Elzey arrived. Heroic efforts by him brought few results, and before he received orders to retire, his men were doing it on their own. He stands at left here, shortly after his promotion to brigadier general. (WRHS)

Left: While his right crumbled into a disorganized retreat, McDowell found his left threatened when Confederates like Colonel Micah Jenkins led the 5th South Carolina across Bull Run. There was little left for McDowell but a general retreat. For Jenkins there would be a brigadier's promotion a year and a day later. (LC)

Left: Colonel Joseph B. Kershaw spearheaded the pursuit with his 2d South Carolina and, along with old Edmund Ruffin, helped turn retreat into rout when they managed to disable the main bridge over Cub Run that led to safety for the Federals. (SHC)

Above: With the enemy on the run, Brigadier General Milledge L. Bonham's South Carolina brigade took over the pursuit. He would leave the Army in a few months to go to the Confederate Congress, then serve as governor of his state, then don his uniform again in the war's last days. (VM)

Below: McDowell's chief of staff, Colonel James B. Fry, made extraordinary efforts to control the retreat, but to no avail. Most of the army did not stop until it reached Centreville, and many soldiers fled all the way to Washington. (P-M)

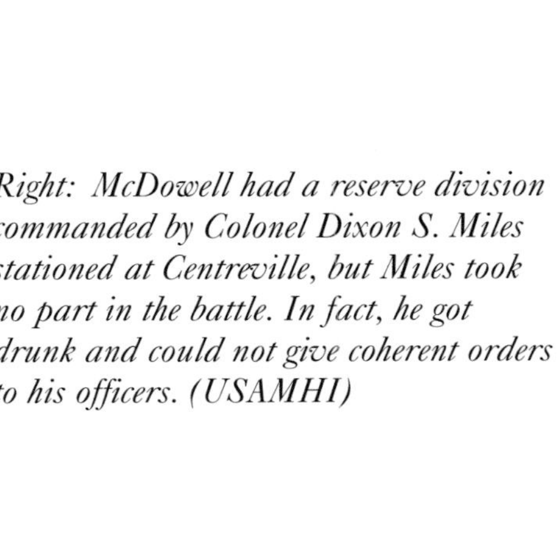

Right: McDowell had a reserve division commanded by Colonel Dixon S. Miles stationed at Centreville, but Miles took no part in the battle. In fact, he got drunk and could not give coherent orders to his officers. (USAMHI)

Above: Miles's soldiers, like flamboyant Colonel Louis Blenker, shown here with men of the 8th New York, chafed at being left out of the battle. Standing just left of Blenker is Lieutenant Colonel Julius Stahel. In two weeks Blenker will be a brigadier... (NA)

Left: ... and Stahel will get his first star in November. These German and Hungarian officers were enormously popular, and the Lincoln Administration hoped that giving them high command would encourage the thousands of their nationality in the North to enlist. It also put great responsibility in the hands of men with little ability. (USAMHI)

Above: Another popular foreigner, Colonel Frederick G. D'Utassy (third from the right) and the staff of his 39th New York, the "Garibaldi Guard." They, too, sat out the battle at Centreville. (MJM)

Above: And for some who missed the fight, the war was already over. The 4th New Jersey and its officers shown here mustered out of service ten days after the battle . (USAMHI)

Above: Still, there were many heroes of the battle. One was the son of amateur photographer—and now quartermaster general of the Union Army—Montgomery C. Meigs. John R. Meigs served as a volunteer aide to Colonel Israel Richardson. "A braver and more gallant young man was never in any service," said Richardson. Here his father photographed him and his sister on his return from the battle, perhaps looking at the elder Meigs's own stereo photographs. Three years later, in the Shenandoah, Confederate guerrillas would kill him. (LC)

Above: The famous "Sherman Battery" came through the battle with all of its guns, and was the object of much curiosity afterward. Here, again, it was photographed in Washington. (MHS)

month volunteers and comic opera officers. Large armies would have to be raised, trained, and equipped, with the enlistments for three years or the duration, not three months. Washington would have to be adequately protected against the slightest chance of capture, for if the capital fell there would be no United States as such.

While the North thus learned a vital lesson from this first major defeat, the South seemingly was lulled into a false sense of security by the victory. "We are resting on our oars after the victory at Manassas," a clerk in the War Department in Richmond recorded in his diary. The articulate and observant wife of an aide to President Davis put it more succinctly. "That victory did nothing but send us off into a fool's paradise of conceit, and it roused the manhood of the Northern people." Indeed, there was much indignant criticism of the generals because they did not immediately follow up the victory by marching into Washington right then and there to end the war. But the fact was, as General Johnston tried patiently to explain, that "the Confederate army was more disorganized by victory than that of the United States by defeat." In addition, the men were near exhaustion, they were short on rations and ammunition, the raw troops lacked proper discipline and training, stragglers were numerous, the Federals had erected powerful fortifications around Washington, and the broad Potomac River would have had to be crossed. Also, many of the soldiers now believed the war was just about over anyway. "Exaggerated ideas of the victory among our troops cost us more men than the Federal army lost by defeat," Johnston reported. "Many left the army—not to return." Despite this premature complacency, the South was determined to resist to the bitter end, thus assuring the nation of a long, bloody struggle.

A young lady from Virginia wrote after Manassas:

> A few days later we rode over the field. The trampled grass had begun to spring again, and wild flowers were blooming around carelessly made graves. From one of these imperfect mounds of clay I saw a hand extended....Fences were everywhere thrown down; the undergrowth of the woods was riddled with shot; here and there we came upon spiked guns, disabled gun-carriages, cannon balls, blood-stained blankets, and dead horses. We were glad enough to turn away and gallop homeward.

For the men in the armies, however, that home ward turn lay distant years ahead in the uncertain future.

Above: For many of the Bull Run regiments, defeat or not, there was a triumphal welcome when they returned home to muster out of service. Many of these were three- and nine-month regiments. They will be replaced by regiments enlisted for three years or the war. The North now knew that it would not be over quickly. The return of the 1st Michigan for mustering out in Detroit, August 7, 1861. (BURTON HISTORICAL COLLECTION, DETROIT PUBLIC LIBRARY)

Left: For many of the men of Bull Run, however, there was no welcome home. Hundreds were captured and sent south to makeshift prisons. Many, like these men of Corcoran's 69th New York, were placed in Castle Pinckney at Charleston. They kept their spirits high, lightheartedly decorating their quarters with a sign reading "Music Hall 444 Broadway." (USAMHI)

Left: Men of Cameron's 79th New York suffer the same fate. (VM)

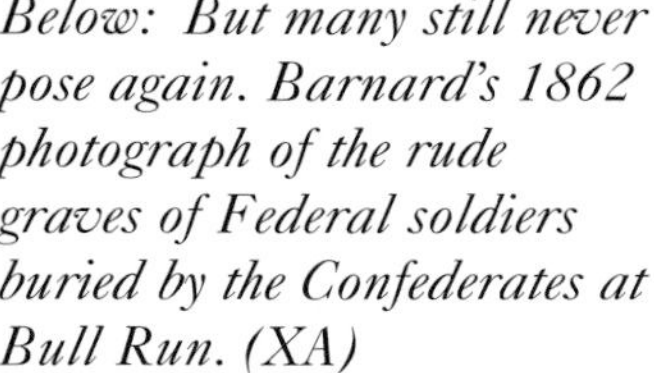

Below: But many still never pose again. Barnard's 1862 photograph of the rude graves of Federal soldiers buried by the Confederates at Bull Run. (XA)

Above: And Irvin McDowell will not go unscathed. Not entirely to blame for his loss, still he must be replaced. A new general from the west comes to take over, a man with Napoleonic pretensions and the nickname "Little Mac," Major General George B. McClellan. For the next year the war in the East will be his war. He stands at center here, hand in blouse, with the principal generals of the Army in August 1861. From the left they are Brigadier General William F. Smith, Brigadier General William B. Franklin, Heintzelman, Porter, McDowell, McClellan, Major General George McCall, Brigadier General Don Carlos Buell, Blenker, Brigadier General Silas Casey, and Brigadier General Fitz John Porter. They pose with hats on… (LC)

Below: … and with hats off. (AMERICANA IMAGE GALLERY)

Above: Barnard's 1862 image of a "hecatomb" where 100 Union soldiers sleep below the Sudley Church. For them the war was over. (KA)

The Navies Begin

VIRGIL CARRINGTON JONES

Improvisation and innovative technology clash on the water

Above: The U.S.S. Constitution, *symbol of past naval glory, and of an out-of-date United States fleet in 1861. (LC)*

EVEN BEFORE the Confederate triumph at Bull Run, the Civil War enhanced the stature of Stephen Russell Mallory, Confederate Secretary of the Navy. He took office and accepted the seemingly impossible task of sending against the enemy a fleet that did not exist. At the end of 1861, however, he had things so well organized that he was posing a threat which caused the Union to try to find effective ways to stop him.

Little about Mallory as an individual explained why the President of the new-born Confederate States of America, Jefferson Davis, so quickly singled him out for the job he held. He was rather naive and had dabbled at various occupations—town marshal, real estate dealer, admiralty lawyer, county judge, customs collector, newspaper correspondent, political leader. At age twenty-four he had had a touch of soldiery in the Seminole War. And then, in 1851, he was elected to the United States Senate from Florida, serving in that capacity for ten years, and rising in time to the chairmanship of the important Naval Affairs Committee, a responsibility that unquestionably drew Davis's attention to him.

As his record shows, he was in no sense a quitter. This was demonstrated in his wooing of a Spanish beauty who was bored by his manners at first, but later accepted his proposal of marriage. It was a trait that stood him in good stead when the burden of creating a navy was placed upon his shoulders. While participating in a losing cause, he strove so diligently to succeed that he helped revolutionize the field of naval science. Under his guidance, the Confederacy took part in history's first battle between ironclads, produced the first submarine to sink a ship, and developed the underwater mine or torpedo as an effective weapon of defense.

The war still was nearly two months away when Mallory took office, but the threat was strong. Ominously, the widely scattered ships of the Union began sailing homeward, some of them steering for southern ports. At the mouth of the Mississippi River, vessels passing up or downstream were searched. Floridians surprised and captured the United States Coast Survey schooner Dana.

Some of the seceded states demanded that Union ships within their ports be turned over to them. Among the commanders who refused to do so and fled with their vessels were John Newland Maffitt, later an outstanding Confederate naval officer, and David D. Porter, equally as staunch a Unionist.

Leaders who formed the nucleus of the Confederacy gathered in early February at Montgomery, Alabama. Even before the government was organized, a committee was named to summon "all such persons versed in naval affairs as they may deem advisable to consult with." Only a few United States Navy officers of high rank—five captains and four commanders—had "gone South" at this time, their action hinging on the secession of their respective states. Nevertheless, telegrams were immediately sent to all officers thought to be southern in their sympathy. The response was favorable. By June, a fifth of the officers so contacted had resigned, among them sixteen captains, thirty-four commanders, and seventy-six lieutenants.

One of these officers was Commander Raphael Semmes, a member of the Lighthouse

Board at Washington and only a short period away from one of the most outstanding privateering careers in history. Another was John M. Brooke, already recognized for the banded guns of his own design he was having manufactured at the Tredegar Iron Works in Richmond. Still another was John Taylor Wood, Naval Academy instructor and grandson of President Zachary Taylor.

When the Confederate Navy was created by formal act, it was soon announced that it was to be headed by chubby-faced, side-whiskered Mallory. He took office immediately, heading a fleet that existed only on paper. He had little to draw from. The South possessed virtually no merchant bottoms, no large force of skilled mechanics, and only a few seamen, for seafaring pursuits were not a favorite among its people. It had only two navy yards, one at Pensacola, Florida, and one at Norfolk, Virginia; only three rolling mills, two in Tennessee and one in Georgia, the latter unfitted for heavy work; and no machine shops of superior workmanship. Its sole foundry capable of casting heavy guns was at Richmond, soon to replace Montgomery as the capital of the Confederacy. The only raw material available was standing timber. All else, including iron, would have to be acquired. Only seven steam war vessels had ever been built in the South, and the engines of only two of these had been contracted for in the states involved.

Confronting Mallory as Union Secretary of the Navy was Gideon Welles, described as a small town politician. His task would be one of organization, for the fleet at his disposal was recognized as third in world power. It consisted of eighty-nine vessels, forty-two in commission, twenty-six available but not in commission, and twenty-one rated unserviceable. Although considered very slow, Welles took immediate action for the purchase of 136 vessels, to be altered and commissioned, and the construction of fifty-two others.

Abraham Lincoln's inauguration on March 4 added to the burden Mallory faced, for the new President announced a policy of reoccupying and holding the forts in the South. As the approach to the most important of these was by water, it meant the Confederacy must do something promptly about its deficiency in naval armament. Water mines were settled upon as the answer.

Along with the South's plans for a navy also came the original move for the training of personnel. At Montgomery on March 16, the Congress passed an act providing for a Confederate States Naval Academy, but it would be 1863 before steps actually were taken to bring such a facility into service. At this later period, an academy was actually set up in Richmond and the steamer Patrick Henry, formerly of the James River squadron, was used as a schoolship. The Union in the meantime took action to protect its important Naval Academy at Annapolis, Maryland. Because of its proximity to southern soil, it was transferred, along with its training ship, to Newport, Rhode Island.

On April 1, Commander Semmes, who had been sent North on a buying tour, detrained at Montgomery. He had had little success, finding no ships available which were suitable for service on the high seas. The only purchase he had made was a large amount of ordnance stores.

Above: The Navy Department in Washington, faced with the herculean task of building quickly a new navy to blockade the southern coast and conquer its rivers. To organize and run this mammoth undertaking, Lincoln selected... (LC)

Right: ... a Connecticut newspaperman, Gideon Welles. He wore an ill-fitting wig, lacked humor, and proved to be one of the most capable and loyal members of Lincoln's Cabinet. (NA)

Above and below: War of 1812 frigates like the Santee *and* Constitution *were still in service and totally unsuited for the war to come. They are shown here at Annapolis, Maryland, at the United States Naval Academy. (USAMHI)*

Left: Many of the personnel were even older and more out of date. Captain William B. Shubrick had been in the Navy since 1806 and served aboard the Constitution *in the War of 1812. (USAMHI)*

Below: Flag Officer Charles Stewart, senior officer in the Navy, had been born in 1778, and commanded the Constitution *when Shubrick served aboard her. He was eighty-three years old when war broke out and still on the active list. (NYHS)*

Left: And promising younger officers like David D. Porter, son of an earlier naval hero and brother of "Dirty Bill" Porter, who would serve on the Mississippi. *(USAMHI)*

Meanwhile, James D. Bullock, captain of the United States mail steamer *Bienville*, and another who had resigned to side with the South were dispatched to England to make arrangements for the construction of ships.

The fall of Fort Sumter was simultaneous with one of Lincoln's most important decisions, for on this same date, April 14, 1861, the sailing frigate *Sabine*, equipped with forty-four guns, began a blockade at Pensacola. Soon it would be extended along the entire southern coast—more than 3,500 miles, the longest ever attempted by any nation—and eventually would rank as one of the North's most effective steps of offense.

Two days later, Lincoln issued a call for 75,000 troops. A counter proclamation came from President Davis on April 17, an offer of letters of marque under the seal of the Confederate States against ships and property of the United States. This was a direct strike against the Union's extensive merchant fleet.

The seventeenth brought other important action. Virginia seceded, affording an answer as to what was to be done with the Gosport Navy Yard at Norfolk, one of the largest in the nation. For weeks, the North had been undecided, withholding action in the hope that Virginia would remain in the Union. When the state seceded, officials at Washington decided to abandon the yard. This was one of the greatest strokes of luck that Mallory would have in his efforts to build a navy.

While ships and buildings at the yard were set afire before they were abandoned, Southerners moved in time to salvage much of what was at hand. Six ships, among them the *Merrimack*, the drydock, large supplies of ammunition and food, and more than a thousand guns were recovered. Without these guns, the Confederacy would have had to wait for months to arm some of its posts. And on April 18, the *Sumter*, a passenger ship converted into a raider, slipped out of the port of New Orleans. At its helm was Raphael Semmes, commencing the career that would afford him his place in history.

Right: But there was new blood, and wood, in the Navy as well. The U.S.S. Hartford *was a powerful 24-gun sloop launched in 1858, shown here after her commissioning at the Boston Navy Yard in 1859. (LC)*

Before the end of the war, he would capture 305 ships, bond ten of them and burn fifty-five, making a contribution in money and destruction valued at more than $5,000,000.

By May, the South had the nucleus of a navy—ten vessels carrying fifteen guns. Some had been seized, some purchased, and some were captured slavers. The Confederacy was not alone in its quest for additional craft. The United States was just as persistent and soon acquired every available steamer in Canada.

Mallory became more and more convinced that ironclad ships would help substantially in offsetting the South's fleet discrepancy. On May 8, he wrote: "I regard the possession of an iron-armored ship as a matter of the first necessity. Such a vessel at this time could traverse the entire coast of the United States, prevent all blockades, and encounter, with a fair prospect of success, their entire navy."

His reference to the blockade was at the moment no exaggeration. All along the Atlantic coast it was mostly a matter of bluff. Lincoln realized this and appointed an overall commander to strengthen it. The assignment went to Commodore Silas H. Stringham, a born seaman and experienced officer. Almost at the same time, the North took steps to block the Mississippi River. They were encouraged by James B. Eads, a veteran shipbuilder thoroughly familiar with the western rivers, who came to Washington to propose blocking the Mississippi to commerce, thereby shutting off a main artery by which the Confederacy could get food, as well as an important route by which it could move cotton to sea. Commander John Rodgers, capable and efficient, was assigned the task of developing a naval force along that major stream.

By July, Mallory was able to report:

> The frigate *Merrimack* has been raised and docked at an expense of $6,000, and the necessary repairs to hull and machinery to place her in her former condition is estimated by experts at $450,000. The vessel would then be in the river, and by the blockade of the enemy's fleets and batteries rendered comparatively useless. It has, therefore, been determined to shield her completely with three inch iron, placed at such angles as to render her ball-proof, to complete her at the earliest moment, to arm her with the heaviest ordnance, and to send her at once against the enemy's fleet. It is believed that thus prepared she will be able to contend successfully against the heaviest of the enemy's ships, and to drive them from Hampton Roads and the ports of Virginia.

The *Merrimack* was only one phase of the Confederacy's program to provide its navy with iron clad ships. As it was considered impracticable to purchase these in Europe, plans were pursued to build them in the waters of the South. Contracts were let for a supply of all classes of iron. In this connection, it was learned that the Union was preparing an ironclad fleet of gunboats at St. Louis, Missouri. The Navy Department at Richmond sent reliable mechanics to that city to obtain employment on the vessels and to report on their strength and fighting character, as well as the progress made on them. In time, this information was made available to Mallory, influencing him to concentrate on the

Above: As in all navies in all times, Welles would find more than enough eager young officers hoping to see action after he retired the men now too old to command. (NAVAL HISTORICAL CENTER)

Below: Sailors must be enlisted to crew the growing fleet. A naval recruiting station at the Battery in New York City. They advertised a bounty of $400 to those who would enlist. (WENDELL W. LANG, JR.)

Left: Time did not allow the building of a complete fleet. To have a Union naval presence in the South's waters as soon as possible, Welles bought merchant steamers and even New York ferry boats like the Commodore Perry *and converted them quickly into river gunboats. (USAMHI)*

Right: There was also the safety of the Naval Academy to consider. At Annapolis it was too exposed and vulnerable to Confederate sympathizers in Maryland. (USAMHI)

Above: Welles moved it temporarily to Newport, Rhode Island, where it continued to produce officers for the Union, as this class in 1863. (RP)

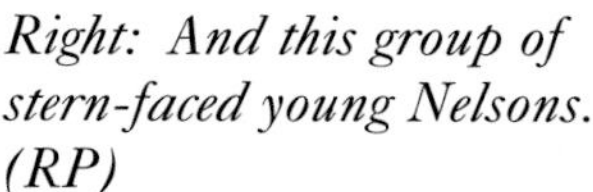

Right: And this group of stern-faced young Nelsons. (RP)

Left: The midshipman of 1861 could affect a jaunty air, but many felt grave fears that there would not be enough action for them in this war. (USAMHI)

defense of New Orleans against an at tack from above rather than from the Gulf of Mexico.

The first attack would come elsewhere, however. By August, the North was ready to launch a naval blow against the South. So far as the blockade was concerned, the seat of troubles was at Hatteras on the North Carolina coast. Since May, it had developed into a haven for both runners and privateers, creating such a threat to northern commerce that newspapers referred to it as "a nest for pirates." Hampered by a succession of gales, a fleet for an expedition against Hatteras slowly assembled in Hampton Roads under the direction of Major General John E. Wool, commanding at Fort Monroe. Foremost among the vessels it consisted of were the flagship *Minnesota*, the *Wabash*, *Cumberland*, *Monticello*, *Pawnee*, and *Harriet Lane*, as well as three troop carriers, the steamers *Adelaide* and *George Peabody*, and the tug *Fanny*. The frigate *Susquehanna* would join it at its destination. On August 26, the ships started moving southward. At four o'clock the next afternoon, they were sighted off Hatteras.

Early on the morning of the twenty-eighth, the signal for a landing was given. The South had nothing on hand with which to combat such a fleet, and Forts Clark and Hatteras, defending the point, lowered their flags within a matter of hours. The surrender gave the North a foothold along the southern coast and put it in possession of the main passage to the North Carolina sounds. It was the first sizable victory for the Union since its troops had suffered defeat in the Battle of Bull Run. Prisoners included 670 officers and men. Guns found in the forts had been a part of the armament made available to the Confederates on the abandonment of the Gosport Navy Yard.

The moral effect of the victory was most important, for there were indications that the South was moving ahead in its efforts to build a navy, as well as to arm its troops. The United States consul at London reported the Rebel agents, with more funds at their control than previously, were buying at random. He revealed that the ship *Bermuda* had sailed from England with a million-dollar cargo made up of cannon, rifles, powder, cartridges, and other munitions of war. Her destination was Savannah, Georgia.

Also, the South's shipbuilding program had been stepped up considerably. Construction of two war ships, the *Arkansas* and the *Tennessee*, had been started at Memphis, while two others, the *Mississippi* and the *Louisiana*, were under way at New Orleans. Lieutenant Bullock, meanwhile, was meeting with success in England. He had arranged for the building of two vessels, the *Florida* and the *Alabama*, that would eventually become grave threats to the North's ocean-going commerce. In addition, individual states were forming their own navies, later to be turned over to the Confederacy. South Carolina in March had prepared for sea the first ship she had launched since the Revolution.

As Mallory hurriedly pressed forward, October found the North ready for its second naval expedition. This time the destination was Port Royal Sound, a body of water on the coast of South Carolina. Early in the war, the Union Navy Department listed it as one of three points that would serve as bases from which to combat blockade running. So easily could it be defended that the Federals feared the Confederates would make it impregnable before it could be taken over.

Again the starting point was Hampton Roads. There, under the command of Commodore Samuel Francis du Pont, head of Lincoln's Naval Advisory Board, a fleet of fifty ships assembled. The expedition sailed on October 29 amid much secrecy. But within a matter of hours after the fleet started moving, the Confederacy's Acting Secretary of War, Judah P. Benjamin, was able to wire military authorities at Savannah that the destination was Port Royal. This warning did little good. The Confederates again had nothing to stop a powerful fleet. The forts at Port Royal quickly fell.

While the North now had two naval victories to its credit, it still aimed no decisive blow at the South. By November, the blockade runners were nearing the peak of their activity. Eight out of every nine were getting into port, picking their destinations at random and using every trick to avoid the blockaders. It was not long before lanterns went out of style among the Union vessels standing guard off the southern coast, for it was found these lights at night were like buoys to the ships trying to make shore. Meanwhile Mallory, by December, had a fleet he no longer could count on his fingers. Thirty-five ships and sailing craft of various classes and armaments had been equipped by the Confederacy. Twenty-one of these were steam vessels, most of them small and built for speed rather than power. A majority had fewer than five guns. Some were protected by bales of cotton. He had entered into thirty-two contracts for the construction of forty gunboats, floating batteries, and vessels of war. In addition, the Navy Department had vessels under construction at its own direction. Progress was made in other quarters. A powder mill, engine mill, boiler mill, machine shops, and ordnance workshops were erected. Also completed was a ropewalk capable of making all kinds of cordage, from a rope yard to a nine-inch cable, with a capacity of 8,000 yards a month.

At Washington, Navy Secretary Welles also had been busy. By December, the Union fleet consisted of 264 vessels, carrying 2,557 guns and manned by 22,000 seamen. But the imbalance between the two navies was not the point of interest at this stage of the war. Rather, attention focused on the blockade runners. They brought the guns and ammunition, the vital items needed to make the Confederacy's armies more formidable, more able to repeat their early victories. The runners would have to continue to bear this responsibility until the South could further expand its facilities. Mallory had started office with appropriations of only $17,300. In the first eighteen months of operations, he would have available $14,605,777.

In the offing, he gained a reputation of doing much with nothing. But time would bring a kaleidoscopic pattern as the Union armies marched southward and the Union fleets gave them much needed support in times of desperation. And after the initial Union successes at Hatteras and Port Royal, the focus of attention, land and water, turned to the West.

Left: They learned the art of naval gunnery... (NA)

Below: And practiced aboard the old Constitution, *which moved to Newport as well. (USAMHI)*

Above: One hundred miles to the south of Washington, another naval secretary grappled with the problems of creating a navy. Stephen R. Mallory of Florida displayed a talent for innovation which left his personal stamp on the whole course of Confederate naval operations. It was he who would implement the building of the first ironclad. (SHC)

Below: A stroke of good fortune was the seizure of the Gosport Navy Yard at Norfolk, shown here in Timothy O'Sullivan's image taken in the spring of 1862 after its recapture. Battlefield artist Alfred R. Waud sits in the foreground. (USAMHI)

Above: Commander George N. Hollins, in prewar uniform, made the Confederate Navy's first capture, the St. Nicholas, *on the Potomac in June 1861. The next month Mallory sent him to oversee naval defenses at New Orleans. (OCHM)*

Below: Lieutenant John Mercer Brooke, shown here in United States uniform around 1852, went to work for Mallory developing the strong and powerful naval guns that would be a major addition to the new navy. He, too, was responsible for much of the concept for the new ironclad Virginia, *converted from the* Merrimack *found at Norfolk. (GEORGE M. BROOKE)*

Above: Raphael Semmes, another former officer in the United States Navy, went to the North before Sumter and actually purchased naval supplies for Mallory. Soon he would outfit and command the C.S.S. Sumter, *first of the South's great commerce raiders. This photograph was probably taken in England in 1864. Semmes rests his arm on an early Confederate flag. (NAVAL PHOTOGRAPHIC CENTER)*

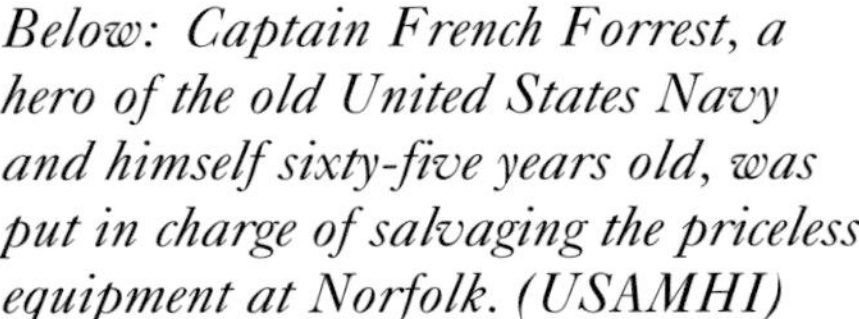

Below: Captain French Forrest, a hero of the old United States Navy and himself sixty-five years old, was put in charge of salvaging the priceless equipment at Norfolk. (USAMHI)

Below: Mallory depended on what was captured at United States installations at the war's outset. The Warrington Navy Yard at Pensacola yielded much, as well. This superb J. D. Edwards photograph, taken in April 1861, hints at what the Confederates seized. Row upon endless row of solid shot, ship's parts; and being refitted, the sidewheeler Fulton. *A previously unpublished image recently discovered. (SHC)*

Below: The Confederacy, too, needed a naval academy for training new officers. Hubbard T. Minor was one of its cadets, shown here in an 1864 photo by Howell & Brown of Savannah, Georgia. (KENNETH HATHAWAY)

Below: The sons of the South's notables attended the new academy, located aboard the C.S.S. Patrick Henry. *General John C. Breckinridge's son attended, and here, at left, is Daniel M. Lee, nephew of Robert E. Lee. (TU)*

Left: Welles quickly put as many ships as possible at sea to implement Lincoln's declared blockade. The U.S.S. Pensacola *had to pass Confederate batteries on the lower Potomac to reach Alexandria in early 1861, but she helped open the river. (USAMHI)*

Above: Soon the wharves at Alexandria saw all manner of vessels coming and going, on all kinds of missions. The mail steamer State of Maine. *(USAMHI)*

Above: The U.S.S. Sabine, *a frigate that took thirty-three years in the building, was one of the first to go on station in the Atlantic blockade. She also carried relief to the garrison at Fort Pickens at Pensacola in April 1861. (NA, U. S. BUREAU OF SHIPS)*

Above: One of Welles's first captures, the Confederate steamer Thomas Collyer, *taken at Alexandria on May 25, 1861, by the U.S.S.* Pawnee. *(USAMHI)*

Above: The deck of the Hudson, *the first blockade runner captured in what would be a four-year game of cat and mouse. (NA)*

Above: The tiny Marine Corps was also the Navy's responsibility, and Welles augmented that arm somewhat. Here a battalion of Marines drill at the Philadelphia Navy Yard. (USAMHI)

Right: They will play a minor role in this conflict, and chafe at their inactivity. (USAMHI)

Above: And here at the Washington Navy Yard. An 1864 image. (NYES)

Below: The Naval Observatory in Washington. Every branch of the Navy's operations was enhanced during Welles's tenure. (USAMHI)

Above: The sail loft at the Boston Navy Yard. Though this was the era of steam, many of the Union's lesser ships still relied on the wind, and even steam vessels were equipped with sails to augment their speed. (USAMHI)

Left: The Washington Navy Yard, launching and refitting site for much of the burgeoning Union fleet. (LC)

Above: Captain Joseph Smith, chief of the Bureau of Navy Yards and Docks, ran the commission which made the commitment to go ahead with ironclad design and building. (USAMHI)

Left: The officers of the Bureau of Steam Engineering, and seated at center, Chief Engineer Benjamin F. Isherwood. They supervised the Union's construction program for steam war vessels. They designed and built the engines that drove the Federal Navy. (USAMHI)

Left: Captain Samuel Barron, the unsuccessful Confederate defender at Hatteras, spent eleven months in prison after his capture. (CHS)

Left: September 17, 1864, the launch of the frigate U.S.S. Franklin *at the Portsmouth, New Hampshire, Navy Yard—a common scene in the years after Welles took command. This screw frigate itself never saw action. (NA)*

Above: Then came the time for offensive action. Commodore Silas A. Stringham, one of Welles's most trusted confidants, commanded the Atlantic blockading squadron and planned and led the successful attack on Fort Hatteras. (USAMHI)

Left: The steam frigate Minnesota, *Stringham's flagship in the attack on Forts Clark and Hatteras. (NA)*

Above: The U.S.S. Wabash, *flagship of Captain Samuel F. I. du Pont, standing in the center of the group of three officers. In it he led the attack on Port Royal. (USAMHI)*

Above: Captain Charles H. Davis, fleet captain of Du Pont's seventeen ships as they attacked Forts Walker and Beauregard. (USAMHI)

Above: Port Royal, South Carolina, the next scene of Union naval victory. A Timothy O'Sullivan photograph, probably taken in early 1862. (USAMHI)

Above: O'Sullivan's photograph of the Coosaw Ferry to Port Royal Island. (USAMHI)

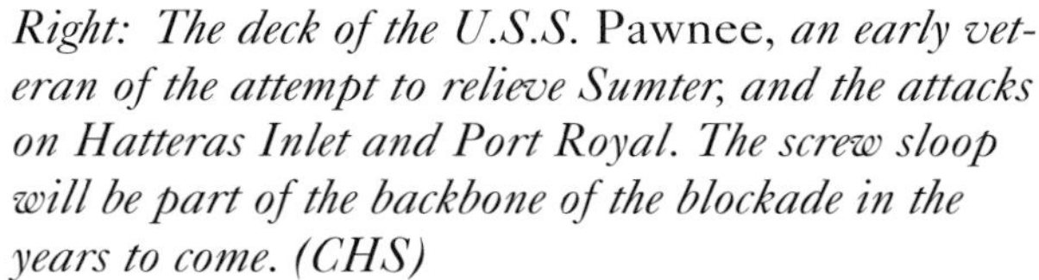

Right: The deck of the U.S.S. Pawnee, *an early veteran of the attempt to relieve Sumter, and the attacks on Hatteras Inlet and Port Royal. The screw sloop will be part of the backbone of the blockade in the years to come. (CHS)*

Above: A Federal pontoon wharf at Coosaw Ferry after the capture of Port Royal. (NYHS)

Right: Confederate Fort Walker on Hilton Head, seen from the rear, by O'Sullivan. (USAMHI)

Below: Fort Beauregard, showing ten heavy guns within its earthworks. From its commanding position on Bay Point, it still could not deter Du Pont's fleet. (USAMHI)

Left: The interior of Fort Beauregard, the Union's first strong foothold in South Carolina. (USAMHI)

Left: O'Sullivan's 1862 photograph of one of the Confederate guns inside Fort Beauregard. (USAMHI)

Right: Members of the 79th New York, veterans of Bull Run, could be happy about a victory for a change. After the battle they built this mock battery at Seabrooke Point on Port Royal Island. (USAMHI)

Left: The Mills Plantation on Port Royal Island, where life went on much as usual. (USAMHI)

Right: Quickly the Union took advantage of its capture, and enhanced it. The wharf at Hilton Head that fed a constant stream of supplies to the South Carolina Federals. (USAMHI)

Right: The boat landing at Beaufort began to bustle with Federal craft. (USAMHI)

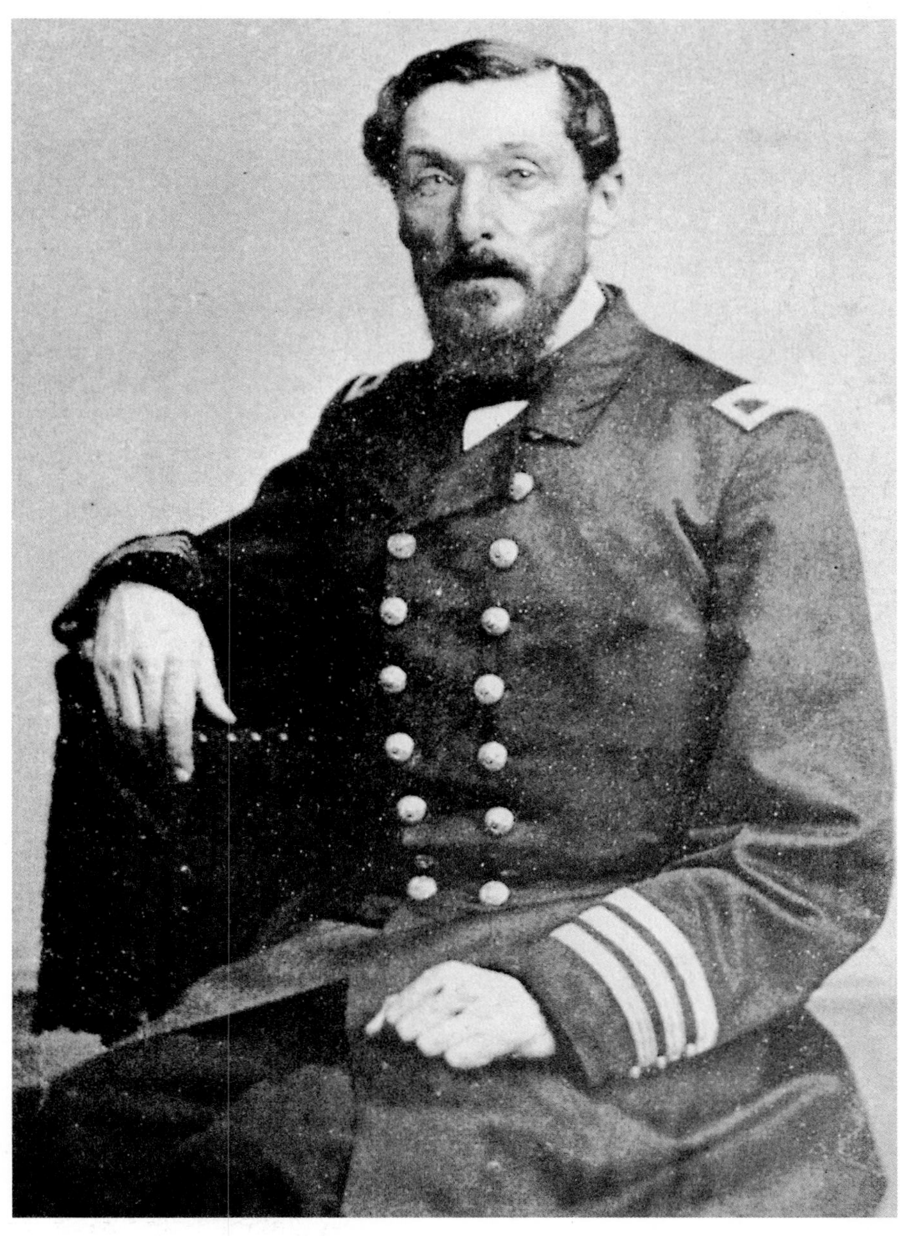

Above: A man torn by conflicting loyalties. Commander Percival Drayton was a native of South Carolina, yet he stayed with the Union. He commanded the U.S.S. Pocahontas *in the attack on Hilton Head. The commander of the Confederates defending Hilton Head was… (USAMHI)*

Above: … his brother, Brigadier General Thomas F. Drayton. (USAMHI)

Above: Private homes like the Fuller House became officers' headquarters. (USAMHI)

Right: The generals, like Isaac I. Stevens seated here for O'Sullivan, were a commonplace sight. (SOUTH CAROLINA HISTORICAL SOCIETY)

Above: Workshops and barracks sprang up on the sand. (USAMHI)

Above: Guns came aboard ships, ready to renew the offensive against the enemy. (USAMHI)

Left: Hilton Head would soon become an area of great importance for repair of the Navy's blockade fleet. The chief engineer's quarters at Bay Point. (USAMHI)

Below: And the photographer could once again look for scenic beauty rather than the scars of war. (USAMHI)

Right: And the price of any great gain in this war, the graves of the dead. Eight men were killed aboard Du Pont's ships. They are buried here on Hilton Head. Photograph by O'Sullivan. (USAMHI)

Right: By November 16, 1861, with two significant successes to its credit, the Union Navy could justifiably preen for its President. The men of the U.S.S. Pensacola *man the yards in honor of a visit in Alexandria by Abraham Lincoln. (WRHS)*

The War Moves West

ALBERT CASTEL

Names like Grant and Sherman and Shiloh emerge in battle

Above: The broad Tennessee River cut through the South like a crooked knife, from Paducah, Kentucky, to Knoxville. (WRHS)

IN THE PREDOMINANTLY RURAL WEST the camera, like the war itself, was still a novelty in 1861. Moreover, just as more words were printed about military operations in the East, so were more photos taken. The majority of western photographers remained in their studios. Only a few ventured forth to the battlefields.

Perhaps this was because of the different character of the war in the West. In the East combat took place in a small area and it was comparatively easy for Brady and Gardner and others to haul their cumbersome paraphernalia to the scene. Out West, on the other hand, the fighting sprawled from the Appalachians to the Mississippi, from the banks of the Ohio to the Gulf of Mexico. Furthermore, it was hard to predict where or when a battle would occur. In fact, for a long time after the bombardment of Fort Sumter there were no battles of consequence at all.

The western soldiers, Union and Confederate alike, were eager enough. Brandishing flintlocks, butcher knives, and a hodge-podge of other impractical weapons, they looked most bellicose. However, they had to wait awhile to hear the bullets buzz and the cannons roar. First of all both North and South at the outset concentrated most of their forces near Washington in expectation that one big battle there would decide the war. Then, when the western armies did begin building up after Bull Run, they could not get at each other because of Kentucky.

As with other slave-holding border states, public opinion in Kentucky was fragmented. Many Kentuckians favored the Confederacy. Many more adhered to the Union—more or less. But in 1861 the majority preferred neutrality. Realizing this, both Lincoln and Davis refrained from sending troops into their native state for fear of pushing it into the enemy's camp. As Lincoln commented, for the Union to lose Kentucky would be to "lose the whole game." On the other hand, should the North secure control of the state, it would be in a position to penetrate the southern heartland.

Hence during the summer of 1861, increasingly strong Federal and Confederate forces stood poised on Kentucky's borders, neither daring to be the first to cross them. Meanwhile Kentucky Unionists and Secessionists formed military units which sometimes drilled simultaneously in different parts of the same town! Also at Camp Andrew Johnson, Lieutenant Samuel P. Carter of the United States Navy, acting on Lincoln's orders, organized regiments of Unionist refugees from East Tennessee. Lincoln was anxious to liberate that region from Confederate rule.

Sooner or later the Bluegrass impasse had to end. It did so on September 3 when Confederate General Leonidas Polk seized Columbus on the Mississippi River. He claimed that the Yankees had planned to do the same thing, but his real purpose was to obtain a stronger position from which to resist a Union thrust down the Mississippi.

In any event he made the first and greatest of his numerous contributions to southern defeat. His incursion outraged most Kentuckians and transformed hosts of neutralists into Unionists. At the same time it provided the Federals with a legitimate excuse to invade Kentucky also. On September 6, Brigadier General Ulysses S. Grant

Above: For over two years the course of the war in the West would follow its meanderings, its water stained red with the blood of America. (USAMHI)

Left: Simple places with names like Shiloh and Chickamauga would, in years to come, assume a symbolic importance, as would rude churches, and humble dwellings marked by the war. Here in Washington, Kentucky, is the birthplace of Albert Sidney Johnston, a romantic figure who became a general in the Texas revolution of 1836, fought in the Mexican War, and on the plains as colonel of the 2d United States Cavalry. (WRHS)

Right: With war coming to the West, troops must be raised. Existing units, like the Kentucky State Guard, provided many companies already trained and equipped for the Confederacy. Standing at center, in the top hat, is Kentucky's governor, Beriah Magoffin, in this August 1860 photograph. When called on to furnish volunteers to suppress the Rebellion, he refused to aid "the wicked purpose" with Kentucky soldiers. (KHS)

countered Polk's move by occupying Paducah. Other Union forces soon took control of the northern two thirds of the state. General Albert Sidney Johnston, top Confederate commander in the West, sent troops up from Tennessee to block their further advance.

Still, no serious fighting occurred. Each side grossly overestimated the other's strength and so held back from a confrontation. Brigadier General William Tecumseh Sherman, commanding the center of the Union line south of Louisville, was so sure that the Rebel army at Bowling Green would overwhelm him that he nearly suffered a nervous breakdown.

It was Grant who struck the first blow. Earlier in the war, while chasing guerrillas in Missouri, he learned that the enemy was just as scared as he was, and that the secret of military success was to make his foe more scared. Applying that lesson, on November 7 he loaded 3,000 troops onto transports at Cairo, Illinois, steamed down the Mississippi, and attacked an outpost Polk had established at Belmont, Missouri, across the river from Columbus. Superior Confederate numbers finally drove him away, but he gave the Southerners a jolt and strengthened their belief that the main Union offensive would be down the Mississippi.

On the night of the day after the fight at Belmont, bands of Unionists burned five railroad bridges in East Tennessee. This strike had been approved by Lincoln, who hoped thereby to cut a vital southern supply line and at the same time set the stage for the liberation of East Tennessee. The Confederate authorities rushed troops into the area, declared martial law, jailed scores of "Tories," and hanged suspected bridge burners. Hundreds of Unionists fled northward to escape persecution; others remained to wage a ruthless guerrilla war against their persecutors.

The movement of a Federal army commanded by Brigadier General George H. Thomas toward East Tennessee led to the next important battle in the West a little over two

Above: Officers of the Kentucky State Guard at Louisville in August 1860. Almost all of them will become Confederates. The officer at right shaking hands with a civilian is Colonel Thomas H. Hunt, who would later command the 9th Kentucky Infantry in the celebrated Orphan Brigade. (KHS)

Above: The Federals flocked to the banners in even greater numbers; here a group of Iowa volunteers pose in their training camp. (MISSOURI HISTORICAL SOCIETY)

Right: The status of Kentucky, key to Union and Confederate war plans, was precarious. Declared neutral, she had to depend on both sides to honor that stance. Neither did. Major General George B. McClellan, commanding Ohio state forces in April and May, refused to recognize that neutrality, and thereby helped hold Kentucky in the Union. An 1861 photograph by the Brady studio. (USAMHI)

Right: "We are coming, Father Abraham," they sang. The 28th Wisconsin, bound for Kentucky. (NA)

Below: Officers of the 1st Minnesota gather at the home of the commandant at Fort Snelling in May 1861, ready to go to war. (MHS)

months later. This time the scene was eastern Kentucky and the Confederates were the aggressors. Early on the morning of January 19, 1862, at Logan's Crossroads near Mill Springs, some 5,000 of them under Major General George B. Crittenden made a surprise attack on Thomas's somewhat smaller force. At first driven back, Thomas's troops rallied, then routed the ill armed Southerners who were demoralized by the death of their popular second-in-command, Brigadier General Felix Zollicoffer. The ragged, famished remnants of Crittenden's army retreated into East Tennessee, which now lay open to northern occupation. However, much to Lincoln's frustration, supply problems prevented the Federals from pushing further southward.

Thomas's victory wrecked the right wing of Johnston's long line across Kentucky. The following month Grant and the United States Navy smashed the left wing. First, on February 6, Commodore Andrew H. Foote's gunboats captured Fort Henry on the Tennessee River. Five days later Grant marched his army to the Cumberland River, where on February 13 he invested the large Confederate garrison at Fort Donelson. An attack by Foote, who had steamed back down the Tennessee to the Ohio and then up the Cumberland, failed on February 14. The following day the Confederates almost broke out to the south—indeed, probably would have had not their commander, Brigadier General John Floyd, lost his nerve. On the other hand, Grant, again applying the lesson he had learned in Missouri, promptly counterattacked and drove the Rebels back into their fortifications.

On February 16 Brigadier General Simon Bolivar Buckner, who had succeeded Floyd as commander, asked Grant for terms. Grant replied: "No terms except unconditional and immediate surrender.... I propose to move immediately upon your works." Buckner had no choice except to comply. Close to 12,000 Confederates became prisoners of war.

It was the biggest Union victory so far in the war. Along with the fall of Fort Henry it opened middle Tennessee to Federal invasion via the Cumberland and Tennessee rivers, made Polk's position at Columbus untenable, and forced Johnston to retreat hastily from Kentucky all the way to Corinth, Mississippi.

There he began concentrating his hitherto scattered forces. By April he had 40,000 troops organized into four divisions commanded by generals Polk, Braxton Bragg, William J. Hardee, and John C. Breckinridge. On April 3 he set out to attack Grant at Pittsburg Landing on the Tennessee. His plan, which had been devised by General P. G. T. Beauregard, who had been posted from Virginia to serve as second-in-command in the West, was to surprise and destroy Grant's 42,000-man army before it was joined by another large Union force under Major General Don Carlos Buell heading down from Nashville. If successful, central Tennessee would be redeemed and the tide of the war in the West reversed.

It was only twenty miles from Corinth to Pittsburg Landing. But the roads were bad and the march discipline of the raw Rebel troops worse. Hence, instead of striking Grant on the morning of April 5 as planned, the Confederates found them selves on the evening of that day still several miles from their objective. Beauregard, despairing of achieving surprise, advised returning to Corinth. However, Johnston, believing that a retreat would be more demoralizing than a defeat, ordered the attack to be made at dawn on April 6.

And so it was—and with great success. Despite the fact that some of their patrols had heard, seen, and even clashed with advance units of Johnston's army, most of the Federals were taken by surprise. Grant, who had been promoted to major general for Fort Donelson, simply had not expected Johnston to bring the battle to him. Furthermore, he had posted his troops with a view to drilling rather than defense—nor, as usual during the early period of the war, had they bothered to entrench. Consequently the Confederates, charging with a ferocity that henceforth would be their trademark, drove back Grant's men, thousands of whom fled in wild eyed panic. It seemed that Johnston's prediction to his staff as the battle got under way, "Tonight we will water our horses in the Tennessee River," would come true.

However, most of the Northerners fought with a stubbornness equal to the Southerners' dash. In particular several thousand of them under Brigadier General Benjamin Prentiss, stationed in a sunken road which soon and ever after was called The Hornets' Nest, repulsed assault after assault. Nearby, scores of wounded from both sides mingled as they sought to quench their thirst in "The Bloody Pond." At 2:30 P.M., Johnston, while urging his men on against the Yankee strongpoint, bled to death when a bullet severed an artery in his right leg. Not until late in the afternoon, after surrounding him, did the Confederates force Prentiss to surrender. By then Grant had been able to form a compact defense line around Pittsburg Landing with his 7,000 remaining effectives, who were bolstered by massed artillery, gunboats, and several regiments from the vanguard of Buell's army. When at twilight a few thousand exhausted Rebels—the most Beauregard, who had replaced Johnston, could muster—made a last desperate effort to drive the Federals into the river, withering fire flung them back.

It was a hideous night of torrential rain falling on thousands of untended, moaning, screaming wounded. During the night 5,000 Union troops under Brigadier General Lew Wallace, who had been encamped to the north of Pittsburg Landing, belatedly joined Grant's army. More importantly, 20,000 of Buell's men also arrived. In the morning Grant counterattacked. Beauregard, who had no more than 20,000 muskets in his firing line, slowly gave way. Finally, late in the afternoon, seeing that victory was impossible and defeat inevitable, he ordered a retreat back to Corinth. The Federals, happy to see the Confederates leave, did not pursue.

Pittsburg Landing, as the North called it, or Shiloh, as the South named it after a log church around which much of the fighting centered, was the biggest and bloodiest battle of the war to that time. Nearly 11,000 Confederates and over 13,000 Federals were killed, wounded, captured, or missing—a loss for each army of 25 percent of the troops actually engaged. Strategically it clinched the Union gains resulting from Forts Henry and Donelson. Psychologically it was a tremendous blow to Confederate morale and

Above: By the fall, Federal recruiting and training camps appeared in the Bluegrass, at places like Camp Nelson, complete with bakeries... (NA, U.S. WAR DEPT. GENERAL STAFF)

Above: ... well-supplied workshops... (NA, U. S. SIGNAL CORPS)

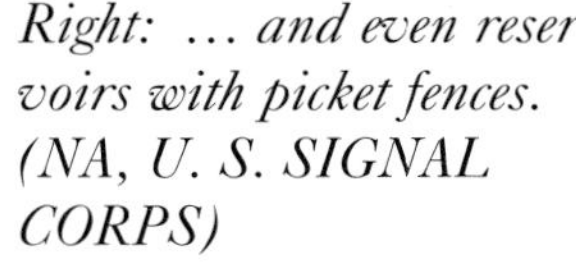

Right: ... and even reservoirs with picket fences. (NA, U. S. SIGNAL CORPS)

Left: Even larger camps of instruction like Camp Butler, near Cairo, Illinois, began to produce the regiments that would fight the western war. (ILLINOIS STATE HISTORICAL LIBRARY)

Left: And in came the volunteers. The 52d Illinois paraded through Elgin, Illinois, on its way to put down rebellion. (ILLINOIS STATE HISTORICAL LIBRARY)

Above: Members of the 9th Missouri try to look their best on the street in St. Joseph, but these western soldiers will ever appear unkempt... and rugged as hell itself. (STATE HISTORICAL SOCIETY OF MISSOURI)

Left: Friends and families saw them off to war in front of their courthouses, as here at Paris, Illinois, in April 1862. While the speeches were made and the colors presented, the wagons loaded with their gear awaited the march to Dixie. (EDWARD STEERS)

Right: From farther west they came by river steamer, like these Nebraska soldiers aboard the Henderson at Bellview, Iowa, in 1861. (NEBRASKA STATE HISTORICAL SOCIETY)

gave the northern soldiers of the West something of the same sense of superiority that the Southerners in Virginia derived from Bull Run. Yet if Johnston had been able to attack on the day planned, probably he would have destroyed Grant, although it is unlikely that his army would have been in condition to follow up the victory.

As it was, the Federals failed to exploit fully their success. After the battle Major General Henry W. Halleck, overall Union commander in the West, took personal charge of operations. He soon revealed himself to be more at home at a desk than in the saddle. Although he accumulated over 120,000 men, he moved with excessive slowness and caution on Corinth, where Beauregard, despite reinforcements from the Trans-Mississippi under Major Generals Earl Van Dorn and Sterling Price, mustered barely 50,000. Then, when he finally forced Beauregard to evacuate Corinth on June 7, he neither pursued nor struck for Vicksburg, which as a result of the Union captures of Island No. 10, Fort Pillow, and Memphis during the spring was the last remaining major Confederate stronghold on the Mississippi north of Baton Rouge. Instead he broke up his host into a number of separate armies spread between Memphis and the approaches to Chattanooga. By so doing he gave the Confederates, now commanded by Bragg, a breathing spell which they put to good use.

Kentucky and Tennessee were not the only western states to witness a Confederate rollback during the early months of 1862. The same occurred from the opposite direction in Louisiana and Mississippi. On the night of April 24, in a daring surprise move, Flag Officer David Farragut, United States Navy, ran his wooden warships past Forts St. Philip and Jackson guarding the mouth of the Mississippi. A Confederate attempt to stop him with gunboats, rams, and fire rafts failed, and on the afternoon of April 25 he seized New Orleans, the South's largest city and main port. He then proceeded up the river to capture Baton Rouge on May 12 and Natchez six days later.

However, strong fortifications and the powerful ironclad *Arkansas* foiled him at Vicksburg during June and July.

Meanwhile, Union troops commanded by Ben Butler, a political general from Massachusetts, garrisoned New Orleans. There some of the women expressed their resentment of the Yankee presence by spitting on blue-clad soldiers. In retaliation Butler on May 15 issued an order declaring that "hereafter when any female shall by word, gesture, or movement insult... any officer or soldier of the United States she shall be regarded and held liable to be treated as woman of the town plying her vocation." This order enraged Southerners, who denounced Butler as a "beast." But it stopped the spitting.

Numerous male Louisianans expressed their opposition to northern rule by forming guerrilla bands which harassed Federal outposts and shipping. On May 28 forty of these bushwhackers fired on a boat from Farragut's flagship *Hartford*, which was putting ashore at Baton Rouge. Outraged, Farragut promptly opened up with his heavy cannons, wrecking the state capitol along with many other buildings.

Not all Louisianans resisted Yankee domination. Hundreds of free blacks—many of whom were in fact white-skinned—joined the 1st Louisiana Native Guards, the formation of which had been authorized by Butler on August 22, a full month before Lincoln issued the Preliminary Emancipation Proclamation. Mustered in at New Orleans on September 27, it was one of the first Negro regiments to serve in the Union Army.

Baton Rouge suffered further devastation on August 5 when 2,600 Confederates under Breckinridge tried to retake it. At first they drove the 2,500-man Union garrison toward the river. But then they came under heavy fire from gunboats and eventually retreated. Plans had called for the ironclad *Arkansas* to assist Breckinridge's assault, but owing to engine trouble she failed to arrive in time and on the following day her crew blew her up in order to prevent her capture by Federal warships. Both sides lost heavily at Baton Rouge, with the northern commander, Brigadier General Thomas Williams, being among the slain.

Six days after the battle the Federals evacuated the town, which was given over to pillaging and burning by Negroes and convicts released from the state prison. As for Breckinridge, he withdrew to Port Hudson, where he fortified the bluff overlooking the Mississippi. The approximately 150-mile stretch between that point and Vicksburg constituted the last link between the eastern and western halves of the Confederacy.

In northern Mississippi Bragg spent the early part of the summer reorganizing and training the army he had taken over from Beauregard. His men hated his harsh discipline and him for it, but they became better soldiers and, perhaps, even better fighters. By late July he was ready to launch an offensive which had as its object nothing less than the liberation of Tennessee and the occupation of Kentucky. Leaving behind 15,000 men under Sterling Price to keep an eye on Grant in West Tennessee and another small army under Van Dorn to guard Vicksburg, he transferred his remaining 35,000 troops by rail from Tupelo through Mobile and Atlanta to Chattanooga. By this maneuver, the most brilliant of its kind during the war, he outflanked the entire Federal front in the West. In addition, raids by the hard-riding gray troopers of Frank Armstrong, Nathan Bedford Forrest, and John Hunt Morgan caused Buell's army, which had been slowly advancing on Chattanooga, to fall back to Nashville, thus opening a path into Kentucky.

On August 28 Bragg began marching north. "Fighting Joe" Wheeler's cavalry led the way; the infantry jubilantly sang "Dixie." Two days later another Confederate army, 7,000 men under Major General Edmund Kirby Smith, who had moved up from Knoxville, routed 6,500 Federals at Richmond, Kentucky, then occupied Lexington. Expecting to be attacked next, the people of Cincinnati frantically constructed fortifications as thousands of Ohio and Kentucky militia hastened to their aid. But Kirby Smith neither advanced northward against Cincinnati nor moved westward to reinforce Bragg: He was too cautious to do the former and too reluctant to give up his quasi-independent command to do the latter.

Above: A troop transport loaded with soldiers lands at Cairo, Illinois, where the men will train for the war. These men come aboard the Aleck Scott, *unaware that before the war she was piloted briefly by a writer who will take his pen name from the cry of a steamboat leadsman, "Mark Twain." At the moment, he is still Samuel L. Clemens, and now a young and very scared Confederate soldier. (LO)*

Above: Southerners who remained loyal to the Union enjoyed wide popularity in the North, and often obtained high rank. Samuel P. Carter of East Tennessee outdid them all. A graduate of the United States Naval Academy, he was commissioned a brigadier general in the Army in 1862, simultaneously holding that rank and a commander's commission in the Navy. He was invaluable in stirring Union sentiment in Tennessee, and in 1862 was leading loyal Tennesseans in raids against their enemies. (NA)

Above: But these Confederates are not at all frightened. Officers all, their cigars and miniature flags proclaiming their bravado, they look forward to the coming fray. (LSU)

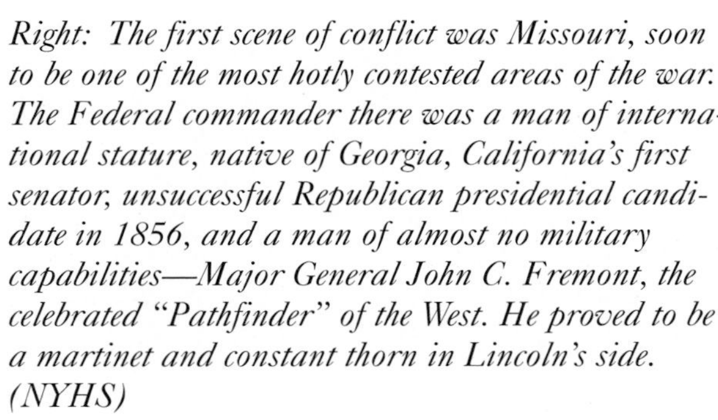

Right: The first scene of conflict was Missouri, soon to be one of the most hotly contested areas of the war. The Federal commander there was a man of international stature, native of Georgia, California's first senator, unsuccessful Republican presidential candidate in 1856, and a man of almost no military capabilities—Major General John C. Fremont, the celebrated "Pathfinder" of the West. He proved to be a martinet and constant thorn in Lincoln's side. (NYHS)

Above: The first action came bloodlessly on May 10 when a body of secessionist Missouri militia training at Camp Jackson near St. Louis was seized by the man who almost single-handedly saved Missouri for the Union. (MISSOURI HISTORICAL SOCIETY)

Above: Captain Nathaniel Lyon. A Unionist firebrand who brooked no obstacle to his single purpose of keeping Missouri out of the hands of the secessionists. When meetings with Missouri Confederates looking toward compromise produced nothing, he stated to them laconically, "This means war." A previously unpublished portrait probably taken after his promotion to brigadier. (NA)

Above: Missouri Confederates did not give in peacefully. The flamboyant Colonel M. Jefferson Thompson, in 1860 mayor of St. Joseph, marched on Cape Girardeau with nearly 5,000 men when Fremont took command in the state. Later, after the general issued an ill-advised and unauthorized proclamation of emancipation, Thompson promulgated his own proclamation countermanding Fremont's. He would remain throughout the war one of the most colorful figures of the western Confederates. (JM)

Above: Lyon's foe was a Tennessean commanding Arkansas troops, Brigadier General Ben McCulloch, a man who disdained a uniform and went into battle attired, as here, in a black velvet suit. In 1835 he went to Texas with Davy Crockett. In March 1862 he would die in battle at Pea Ridge, Arkansas. (VM)

Below: Lyon was right when he said there must be war. In attempting to rid the state of Confederates, he led his little army against that of General Benjamin McCulloch at Wilson's Creek, near Springfield, on August 10, 1861. It was war, and here, where the numeral "2" rests on the horizon, Lyon fell in battle. Probably an early postwar photo. (WRHS)

Above: Mosby Monroe Parsons, former Missouri attorney general and a commander of Confederate Missouri state guardsmen at Wilson's Creek. (LSU)

Above: Men of Missouri's Union State Guard. No other state, even Kentucky, would suffer as much from divided loyalties and families. (MISSOURI HISTORICAL SOCIETY)

Above: The next month Confederates led by Sterling Price besieged and captured Lexington, Missouri, defended by Colonel James A. Mulligan and his 23d Illinois Irish Brigade." (USAMHI)

Above: By early 1862, Missouri still had not been firmly taken by either side. On March 7-8, the largest battle west of the Mississippi took place at Pea Ridge, Arkansas, its outcome deciding the fate of Missouri. Ben McCulloch would die in the battle. Brigadier General Alexander S. Asboth, leading a Union division, would be wounded. (USAMHI)

Left: Confederate Brigadier General Albert Pike was a native of Boston, Massachusetts, but raised Indian troops for the South in Arkansas and led them ingloriously at Pea Ridge. A fellow general said he was "either insane or untrue to the South." He resigned soon thereafter, and spent much of the rest of his life writing the ritual and dogma for Masonry. (NYHS)

Below: Brigadier General Daniel M. Frost, a native of New York who sided with the South, was offered command of a brigade at Pea Ridge, but refused to accept such a small command and instead watched the battle "from a convenient height." (LSU)

All the while Buell, believing that Bragg was aiming for Nashville, remained at the Tennessee capital with his 50,000 troops. Not until September 7 did he realize that the Confederate objective was Kentucky and so set out in pursuit.

Given his long lead, Bragg by rapid marching might have taken Louisville—a stroke which would have panicked the Northwest. However, Davis had instructed him not to take unnecessary risks, and he feared being caught between the forces protecting that city and Buell's army moving up from Tennessee. Therefore, after capturing a 4,000-man Federal garrison at Munfordville, Kentucky, on September 17, 1862 (the same day as the Battle of Antietam), he swerved eastward to link up with Kirby Smith. Ten days later Buell reached Louisville, where he began readying a counteroffensive. His preparations were somewhat disrupted when on September 29 Brigadier General Jefferson C. Davis murdered Brigadier General William "Bull" Nelson after the three-hundred-pound Nelson slapped him during an altercation at a hotel.

Back to the south: Price, having been instructed by Bragg to enter middle Tennessee, advanced to Iuka, in northeastern Mississippi, on September 14. Grant countered by sending a column under Major General William S. Rosecrans to strike Price from the south while Major General E. O. C. Ord's army hit him from the north. However, owing to an atmospheric freak condition, neither Ord nor Grant (who accompanied him) heard the sound of battle when Rosecrans assaulted Price on September 19. Consequently they did not attack, and Price, after beating off Rosecrans, slipped out of the trap that night.

Late in September Van Dorn came up from Vicksburg to join Price at Ripley, Mississippi. Taking command of their combined force of 22,000, he marched for Corinth, which was held by 23,000 Federals under Rosecrans. On October 3 he drove Rosecrans from his outer for-

Above: Brigadier General William Y. Slack was mortally wounded on the first day at Pea Ridge and died two weeks later. It was nearly a month later that the Confederate Senate promoted him to brigadier, the news of his death not having reached them. The uniform in this photograph has been painted on. (VM)

Right: A Confederate commander whose capabilities were as grand as his name, John Sappington Marmaduke. Educated at Yale and Harvard, he graduated from West Point in 1857, when this photograph was taken. Colonel of Missouri and Arkansas troops, he fought gallantly at Prairie Grove, Arkansas, in December 1862, and rose steadily in ability. He was the last Confederate to win promotion to major general, on March 18, 1865, and was later governor of Missouri. (LSU)

Above: Native of Kentucky, Brigadier General James F. Fagan also distinguished himself in the Confederate defeat at Prairie Grove. (JM)

Left: While the war west of the Mississippi dragged on in its bloody and tragic course, one of the Union's first victories came in January 1862 at Mill Springs, Kentucky. Brigadier General George H. Thomas, a native of Virginia, led part of his division against the Confederate command in southeast Kentucky. (USAMHI)

Above: The Confederates Thomas faced were led by Major General George B. Crittenden. His father was Senator John J. Crittenden, who unsuccessfully attempted a last-minute compromise between North and South in 1861. His brother was a major general in the Union Army; so were Kentucky families divided. This previously unpublished photograph shows him probably in 1862. He was forced to give battle to Thomas at Mill Springs, thanks in part to disobedience to his orders from a subordinate... (LSU)

Above: ... Brigadier General Felix Zollicoffer of Tennessee, who was killed when he accidentally rode into Union troops during the battle. (JM)

Right: Mill Springs destroyed the right of the Confederate defensive line in Kentucky. Now a new general, Ulysses S. Grant, went to work on the left of the line. (USAMHI)

Above: Assisted by Federal gunboats under the command of Flag Officer Andrew H. Foote, Grant moved against Confederate bastions on the Tennessee and Cumberland rivers. (LC)

tifications but the next day suffered hideous losses in an attempt to storm the town. A column sent by Grant blocked his retreat, but thanks to Armstrong's cavalry he managed to escape. Shortly after the battle a photographer took pictures of Texans killed assaulting a Union redoubt known as Battery Robinette. They are among the most grim photos of the war. Any civilian viewing them would immediately realize that real-life—or rather real-death—battlefields bore little resemblance to the scenes depicted in Currier and Ives prints.

Bragg and Kirby Smith had expected swarms of recruits in Kentucky—indeed without them they could not hope to hold the state. Instead only about 2,500 joined their ragged legions. Disgusted, Bragg decided to resort to conscription. To that end he arranged for the installation of Richard C. Hawes as Confederate Governor of Kentucky. But the inauguration ceremonies, held at Frankfort, the state capital, on October 4, were abruptly terminated by Union shellfire. Buell had launched his counteroffensive—and sooner than Bragg had anticipated, with the result that he caught the Confederates badly scattered.

Bragg fell back, planning as he did so to regroup his units for a stand west of Lexington. However, on October 8, being pressed by advancing Federals near Perryville, he lashed back at them. Charging through sheets of cannon and rifle fire, 15,000 of Polk's and Hardee's veterans hurled back the Union line, which was held by 14,000 troops, many of them raw. Then, after being reinforced, the Northerners rallied,

Above: Foote had four new river ironclads, among them the U.S.S. Cincinnati, *one of the powerful "city class" gunboats. (NHC)*

Above: Another was the U.S.S. Carondelet, *heavily armed and armored, and here tied at the bank on one of the western rivers. (NHC)*

counterattacked, and regained much ground. Ferocious but indecisive fighting continued until nightfall. The Confederates lost 3,400 and the Federals 4,200 of the 22,000 men they had engaged.

Bragg thought that he faced at Perryville only a portion of Buell's army, most of which he believed heading for Lexington by way of Frankfort. In actuality Buell had threatened Frankfort with a small column of 7,000 while his main force, 54,000 strong, had advanced on Perryville. Furthermore, Bragg's assault fell on Buell's left wing alone. Fortunately for the Confederates, Buell was so far to the rear that he did not even know a battle was taking place until two hours after it started! And then, again through ignorance plus poor staff work, he failed to exploit a splendid opportunity to crush Polk's and Hardee's divisions by striking them in the flank and rear with his virtually unopposed center and right. In brief, both Bragg and Buell were lost in the fog of war.

That night Bragg, belatedly but in time, realized that he faced Buell's concentrated power at Perryville, whereas his and Kirby Smith's forces still were dispersed. He also learned of Van Dorn's debacle at Corinth, which meant that he could not expect any help from him but that Grant was free to aid Buell—or else sweep southward. Consequently he at once retreated, first to Harrodsburg, then to Bryantsville. There on October 12 he and Kirby Smith decided to return to Tennessee before the Federals cut them off from Cumberland Gap.

Twelve days later the last of the foot-sore Confederates trudged through Cumberland Gap on the way to Knoxville. Their invasion of Kentucky, like Lee's of Maryland the month before, had ended in failure after a brilliant beginning. Many Southerners then and afterward denounced Bragg for abandoning Kentucky without an all-out battle. Bragg, however, saw no point in risking his army fighting for the Confederate cause in the Bluegrass State when so few of the Kentuckians themselves were willing to fight for it.

Lincoln urged, indeed expected, Buell to follow the Confederates to Knoxville, defeat them, and liberate East Tennessee. Instead Buell headed for Nashville. Lincoln thereupon

Above: A markedly different ironclad was the U.S.S. Essex, *a converted centerwheel steamboat whose arming was personally overseeen by her commander… (USAMHI)*

Above: … William David Porter. Called "Dirty Bill" because of his unlikable manner and sometimes less-than-honest methods, he was the son of Commodore David Porter of the original Essex. *His brother was Admiral David D. Porter, his half-brother Admiral David Farragut. He would be badly scalded by steam when a shot from Confederate Fort Henry penetrated the* Essex's *boiler. (USAMHI)*

Above: One of Foote's three wooden gunboats, the U.S.S. Tyler. *It would do workhorse duty on the western waters, though even great warships still had to dry their laundry now and then. (USAMHI)*

Right: Grant and Foote first moved against Fort Henry on the Tennessee River. They set the attack for February 6, 1862, but mud slowed Grant's soldiers and it was all Foote's affair. He soon forced Confederate Brigadier General Lloyd Tilghman to lower his flag, after sending most of his garrison to Fort Donelson. (SHC)

Right: Donelson would be a different matter entirely. Commanding there was General John B. Floyd, who a year before was Buchanan's Secretary of War. On February 13, Grant launched his land attack with the division of Brigadier General Charles F. Smith, his one-time teacher at West Point. (NA)

Above: Unidentified western Confederates, probably from Louisiana, men of the stamp of those who gallantly defended Donelson until it was hopeless. (CM)

Right: Two days later, facing a hopeless situation, Floyd decided to escape, abandoning his command to General Gideon J. Pillow. A man of reprehensible character, Pillow, too, chose to flee rather than share the fate of his soldiers. In January 1863, at the Battle of Stones River, he would be seen hiding behind a tree while his brigade went into battle. Thereafter he gave perjured testimony against fellow generals in the political infighting that would always plague the Confederate Army of Tennessee. (VM)

Below: Men of the 2d Kentucky Infantry almost cut a way out of Grant's trap, but they were called back before they could take advantage of it. Some of these members of the National Blues, Kentucky State Guard, made up the 2d Kentucky. (KHS)

Below: Refusing to abandon his men as did Floyd and Pillow, the dashing Brigadier General Simon B. Buckner, formerly commander of the Kentucky State Guard, stayed with them and finally asked his old friend Grant for terms. (SHC)

replaced him with Rosecrans—who completed the move to Nashville, then remained there through November and most of December despite repeated orders and even pleas from Washington to advance. Like Buell he believed that a winter invasion of mountainous, thinly populated East Tennessee would be logistically impractical and strategically barren. He pre ferred instead to accumulate a large stockpile of supplies before doing battle with Bragg, who in the meantime had shifted his forces—now and thereafter known as The Army of Tennessee—to Murfreesboro, thirty miles southeast of Nashville.

Both Buell and Rosecrans were not without justification in their concern about supplies. Late in December cavalry raids by Van Dorn and Forrest caused Grant to abandon an attempt to capture Vicksburg by marching south through Mississippi. Similarly Morgan and Wheeler snipped away at Rosecrans's communication lines in Tennessee and Kentucky, delaying thereby his preparations.

Finally, on the day after Christmas, Rosecrans moved out from Nashville with 45,000 troops and an immense wagon train containing twenty days' rations. Bragg waited for him west of Murfreesboro, his 40,000 men straddling easily fordable Stones River. The Federals arrived in front of the Confederate position on December 29, having been slowed by Wheeler's cavalry. Each commander made preparations to attack with his left. The only difference was that Bragg struck first. On the morning of December 31 the redoubtable southern infantry, spearheaded by Irish-born Patrick Cleburne's division, rolled back Rosecrans's right wing until it was at a 90-degree angle to his left. However, the Federals, whose defense was anchored by Irish-descended Phil Sheridan's division, managed to hold just short of the Nashville Pike, their lifeline to the north. A gallant but foolish Confederate attempt to break the Union center at the "Round Forest" failed and the mutual slaughter—for such it was—ceased with the coming of darkness.

That night Rosecrans asked his generals if he should order a retreat. Bearlike George H. Thomas, awakened from a doze, said, "This army doesn't retreat," then went back to sleep. The army stood.

Both sides spent the first day of 1863 (the date the Emancipation Proclamation went into effect) recuperating and redeploying. Then on January 2 Bragg threw Breckinridge's division at Rosecrans's left. The blue infantry broke, but massed Federal artillery tore Breckinridge's ranks to pieces. During the night of January 3 Bragg, who had lost 10,000 men, retreated. Rosecrans did not pursue beyond Murfreesboro. He had suffered 13,000 casualties and Wheeler had destroyed many of his precious wagons. Although actually a draw, the battle was hailed as a victory in the North, where it revived morale that was flagging badly after Burnside's bloody fiasco at Fredericksburg.

Thus ended the first year of fighting in the West. Clearly the North had gained much, the South lost much. Indeed, it would scarcely be an exaggeration to say that while the South had been winning *battles* in the East, in the West the North had been winning the *war*.

But the western Confederates remained undaunted and dangerous. Union Colonel Abel

Above: Gallant defenders of Donelson like Colonel Adolphus Heiman and his 10th Tennessee were downcast at the prospect of going to a northern prison. Heiman would die as a result of his confinement. (HP)

Left: Major George B. Cosby of Kentucky carried Buckner's request for surrender terms to Grant. He would later become a brigadier. A previously unpublished portrait. (SHC)

Above: Bushrod R. Johnson of Ohio was one general who would not stay captured. After the surrender he escaped. (VM)

Left: And there was another Confederate who would not accept surrender. A lieutenant colonel of the 7th Tennessee Cavalry, a rich man before the war, Nathan Bedford Forrest would be heard from in this conflict. (LC)

Above: Then came Albert Sidney Johnston and his surprising attack on Grant's army at Pittsburg Landing on April 6. It was Johnston's first and last battle of the war. Shot in the leg, he bled to death, dying in the arms of his brother-in-law... (USAMHI)

Above: ... Colonel William Preston, former Kentucky congressman and Buchanan's minister to Spain. He would become a general in another week. (VM)

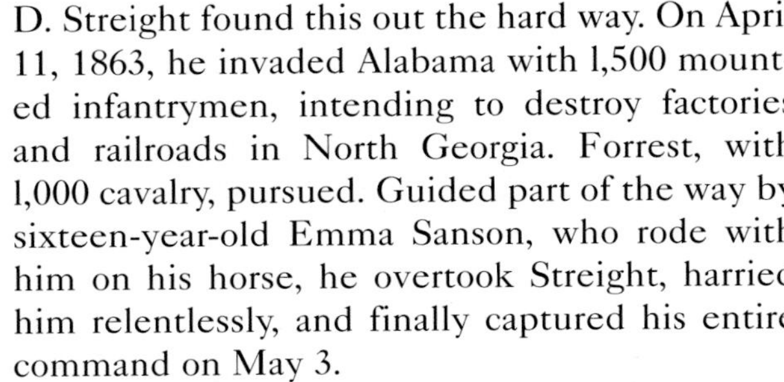

D. Streight found this out the hard way. On April 11, 1863, he invaded Alabama with 1,500 mounted infantrymen, intending to destroy factories and railroads in North Georgia. Forrest, with 1,000 cavalry, pursued. Guided part of the way by sixteen-year-old Emma Sanson, who rode with him on his horse, he overtook Streight, harried him relentlessly, and finally captured his entire command on May 3.

Meanwhile Rosecrans's Army of the Cumberland, as it was now called, and Bragg's Army of Tennessee, lay motionless throughout the winter and spring, recuperating, skirmishing with cavalry, and steeling themselves for the fighting to come. That there would be more fighting—a great deal more—was obvious to all. It was just that no one knew when it would be, or where—although probably some general, gazing at the map, had already noted a stream, not far away in Georgia, with a strange name: Chickamauga, an Indian word meaning "River of Death."

Above: Upon Johnston's death, command of the Confederates at Shiloh passed to the seemingly ubiquitous hero of Sumter and Bull Run, General P. G. T. Beauregard. He consolidated the gains of the first day's fighting, aided largely by his confidant and adjutant… (NA, U. S. SIGNAL CORPS, BRADY COLLECTION)

Below: … Thomas Jordan, who will be made brigadier for his gallantry in this battle. (LC)

Above: Colonel James B. Walton ably commanded his… (THE HISTORIC NEW ORLEANS COLLECTION)

Below: … Washington Artillery of New Orleans in the fight, the first for this branch of the famed organization that also sent several companies to the Virginia front. (CM)

Above: Private John Rulle of the 2d Tennessee Infantry came to Shiloh ready for a fight, from the look of him. His unit were mostly Irishmen from Memphis. (HP)

Left: Others, too, won laurels. Benjamin Franklin Cheatham a brigadier from Tennessee, will be promoted to major general in recognition of his service at Shiloh. (MC)

Left: A magnificent photograph, taken May 10, 1861, of the "Clinch Rifles," men of the 5th Georgia. The variety of clothing and pose, with their black servant in the background, are among the most interesting to be found in Confederate images. They were to be far less relaxed at Shiloh. (JOSEPH CANOLE, JR.)

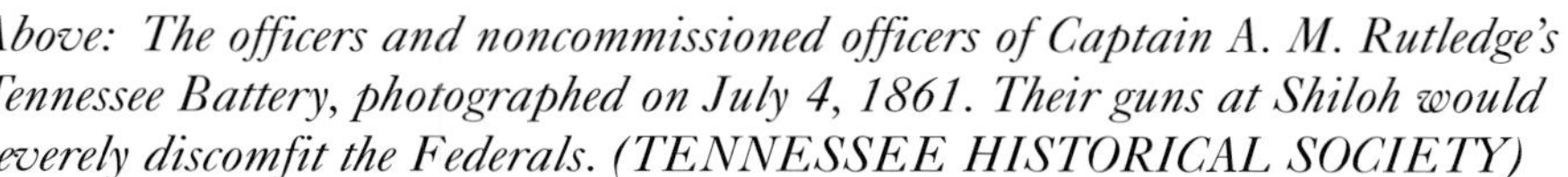

Above: The officers and noncommissioned officers of Captain A. M. Rutledge's Tennessee Battery, photographed on July 4, 1861. Their guns at Shiloh would severely discomfit the Federals. (TENNESSEE HISTORICAL SOCIETY)

Left: The peach orchard at Shiloh. Through here swarmed the Confederate corps of Brigadier General… (CHS)

Right: … John C. Breckinridge, formerly Vice President and a presidential contender. No believer in secession, and almost certain that the Confederacy could not win, he was forced out of the Union and nevertheless took a command from President Davis. (NA)

Left: Breckinridge's corps and others were bottling up the Federal division of Brigadier General Benjamin M. Prentiss in a place called… (USAMHI)

Right: … the Hornets' Nest. It was in one of their attacks that A. S. Johnston fell mortally wounded . (CHS)

Above: It was a bitter fight. Westerners like these used their Colt revolving rifles to deliver heavy fire power against the Confederates. (RP)

Above: Brigadier General Daniel Ruggles, a native of Massachusetts, retaliated by massing some sixty-two cannon against the Hornets' Nest. (USAMHI)

Above: In the final encirclement of Prentiss, Kentuckians of the Orphan Brigade closed the final trap. Colonel Thomas Hunt, standing eighth from the left here, commanded one of the Kentucky regiments that sealed the Federals' fate. (KHS)

Below: More of the Kentuckians, photographed in August 1860, who would eventually man the Orphan Brigade. (KHS)

Left: Meanwhile dour Major General Braxton Bragg continually pushed the Federals back toward the Tennessee River.

Above: Finally Prentiss could not hold out longer, and beneath this tree he surrendered. An early postwar photo. (CHS)

Above: On the Federal right, Brigadier General William T. Sherman, like Beauregard a veteran of Bull Run, fell back under heavy Confederate attacks. (USAMHI)

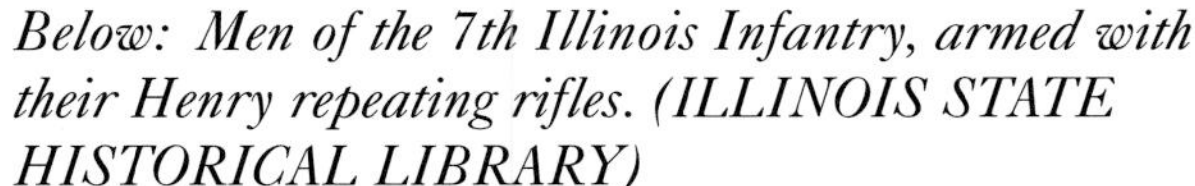

Below: Men of the 7th Illinois Infantry, armed with their Henry repeating rifles. (ILLINOIS STATE HISTORICAL LIBRARY)

Above: Finally, as evening approached, a last line was established by Grant and Sherman. These 24-pounder siege guns were a part of it, and here the Federals stood . (USAMHI)

Right: They held on stubbornly, men like Colonel Madison Miller of the 18th Missouri. (LC)

Left: And boys like Johnny Clem, the "drummer boy of Shiloh," acted like men. (LC)

Left: Even bandsmen, usually noncombatants, took arms in holding the last line. (CHICAGO PUBLIC LIBRARY, SPECIAL COLLECTIONS)

Above: The arrival of a relief column under Brigadier General Don Carlos Buell late that evening finally ensured that Grant would not be pushed into the Tennessee. (USAMHI)

Above: The next day, April 7, thanks to Buell's troops arriving here at Pittsburg Landing, and the exhaustion of the Confederates, Grant forced Beauregard to retire from the field. This photograph was taken a few days after the battle. The steamer at right is the Tycoon, *sent by the Cincinnati Sanitary Commission with stores and medical supplies for the wounded. Next to it is Grant's headquarters boat, the* Tigress. *(USAMHI)*

Above: At right, the Universe unloads more supplies for Grant's command. The Tigress *is at the center, and across the stream stands the woooden gunboat* Tyler. *The guns from Foote's fleet played a large part in halting the Confederate drive on April 6. Shiloh was not exactly a victory for Grant, but not a defeat either, and in the aftermath of several Union disasters, that was more important. (USAMHI)*

Above: Four days after Shiloh, Major General Henry W. Halleck took command from Grant. Called variously "Old Brains" and "Old Wooden Head," he was an able administrator, and a miserable general. Outnumbering Beauregard two to one, he still could not catch the Confederates at Corinth. (MJM)

Left: Brigadier General Daniel Tyler, of Bull Run and Blackburn's Ford fame—or ill repute—was sent west to command a brigade in the "siege" that Halleck laid to Corinth. The Federals finally moved into the town the day after the enemy escaped them. (LC)

Above: Later in the year, with a Federal command under Major General William S. Rosecrans stationed in and around Corinth, the Confederates were not so slow. Major General Sterling Price led his little army to Iuka on the way to Corinth, and was there attacked by Rosecrans on September 19. A previously unpublished portrait of Price in 1862. (TU)

Above: Price's most trusted subordinate, Brigadier General Lewis Henry Little, was killed at Iuka while talking with Price by a bullet that first passed under Price's arm. (CHS)

Above: Two weeks after Iuka, the armies collided again at Corinth, on October 3-4, 1862. (CHS)

Left: It was an important railroad depot and supply center for Rosecrans and his growing army of 21,000 men. A Howard & Hall photograph taken before the battle. Their tent studio appears just left of the Tishomingo Hotel. (USAMHI)

Left: Rosecrans's army were western men, men of the 47th Illinois… (WILLIAM M. ANDERSON)

Below: … and the 2d Minnesota, which bore much of the brunt of the fighting. (MHS)

Left: His opponent was the colorful Major General Earl Van Dorn of Mississippi, the loser at Pea Ridge. (MISSISSIPPI DEPARTMENT OF ARCHIVES & HISTORY)

Right: Their commander, Major General William S. Rosecrans, was himself a western man, born in Ohio. He is seen here, with a hint of a smile, taken by Corinth photographer George Armistead of Armistead & White, sometime prior to the battle. (LC)

Right: For two days they fought. The 8th Indiana Artillery was heavily engaged for the Union. (RP)

Left: Fifty-two-year-old Brigadier General Thomas J. McKean led one of Rosecrans's divisions, even though he was considered too old for active command. He is seated here with members of his staff. (NYHS)

Right: Samuel Jones, like many of these men in Mississippi in 1862, was another veteran of Bull Run. He commanded a division under Van Dorn, and was also in the process of making himself the second most photographed general of the Confederacy. (VM)

Above: Major General Mansfield Lovell, a native of Washington, D.C., joined Van Dorn after he lost New Orleans to Farragut, and skillfully commanded the Confederate retreat from Corinth. (CHS)

Above: It was a costly battle. Here in front of Federal Battery Robinette, the Confederate dead and their horses were piled deep. This photograph, taken the day after the battle, shows the horse of Colonel William P. Rogers in the center, and to the left of it, the body of Rogers himself. (WRHS)

Above: Several of the Confederate dead in front of Robinette. Colonel William P. Rogers of the 2d Texas lies at left, and to his right, leaning on his shoulder, is the body of Colonel W. H. Moore, who led a brigade of Missouri and Mississippi troops in futile assaults against Robinette. (ALABAMA STATE DEPARTMENT OF ARCHIVES AND HISTORY)

Left: The Confederate threat gone, Corinth became undisputedly a Union town, and the men of Rosecrans's army enjoyed it as they could. Supplies came in regularly, and Howard & Hall expanded their gallery next to the Tishomingo. (CHS)

Above: Officers like Brigadier General Grenville Dodge established their headquarters in the better homes of the city. (CHS)

Left: Life returned to normal for the inhabitants. (CHS)

Left: The soldiers patronized the local business establishments. (CHS)

Above: They built their winter quarters like Camp Davis, home for the 66th Illinois, south of the city. (ROBERT YOUNGER)

Above: But it would not be a peaceful winter in Mississippi and Tennessee, nor in Kentucky. Brigadier General Jefferson C. Davis, once an officer in Fort Sumter, in late September shot and killed his superior, William Nelson, after an altercation. It could not have come at a worse time, for after a year of seeming security, Kentucky was being invaded by the Confederate Army of Tennessee, commanded now by Beauregard's successor… (LC)

Above: Their bands tuned for the season's demands for entertainments. Here the 97th Indiana musicians. (CHS)

Above: And their earthworks and tents dotted the landscape for the winter ahead, while the firms of Armistead & White and Howard & Hall kept busy with their captive clientele. Winter quarters could mean a small fortune to a photographer. (CHS)

Above: … General Braxton Bragg. This previously unpublished image of Bragg was made by McIntyre of Montgomery, Alabama, just a few weeks prior to his launching of the Kentucky campaign. (CM)

Above: Commanding the Federals who would resist Bragg was Major General Don Carlos Buell, of Shiloh. (USAMHI)

Above: Bragg's offensive was spearheaded by a Floridian, Major General Kirby Smith, who had been wounded leading a brigade at Bull Run. At Richmond, Kentucky, he defeated Nelson in the only real Confederate battle victory of the campaign,

Above: Leading Bragg's cavalry was a young brigadier who turned twenty-six during the campain, Joseph Wheeler. He would become one of the war's premier cavalrymen. (LC)

Below: Bragg and Buell finally met at Perryville, Kentucky, along Doctor's Creek. Probably an early postwar view. (USAMHI)

Above: Rousseau aligned his command beside a 100-year-old tree that, miraculously, survived the battle.

Below: Federal artillery placed on this high ground, plus numerical superiority, finally gave the battle to Buell. (USAMHI)

Above: The H. P. Bottoms House near the position of Brigadier General Lovell Rousseau, who gallantly led a division against repeated enemy attacks. (USAMHI)

Above: Brigadier General J. Patton Anderson of Tennessee led one of Bragg's divisions to no avail . (USAMHI)

Above: Losses were heavy. General S. A. M. Wood took a serious wound from Federal fire . (VM)

Above: Union Brigadier General William R. Terrill of Virginia was struck in the side by a piece of shell and died that night. His brother was a general in the Confederate Army, and would die in the war as well. (USAMHI)

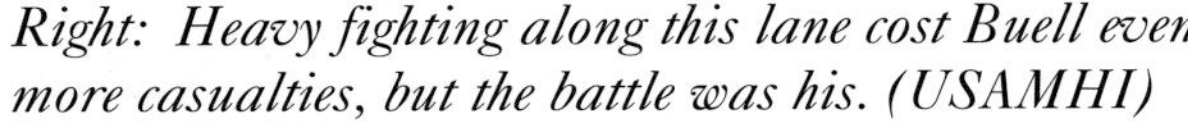

Right: Heavy fighting along this lane cost Buell even more casualties, but the battle was his. (USAMHI)

Below: Brigadier General James S. Jackson was a native of Kentucky, and at Perryville he died on his home soil. (USAMHI)

Right: Bragg watered his army at this spring, and retreated into Tennessee, his dream of conquering Kentucky gone in smoke. (USAMHI)

Left: In December the armies meet again, this time at Murfreesboro, Tennessee, and the Federals are once again commanded by Major General William S. Rosecrans. He is seated fourth from the left in this pose with his staff. The man sitting next to him on the right is Brigadier General James A. Garfield, who will become his chief of staff after the battle and, years later, President of the United States. To the far right sits Philip H. Sheridan who, as a brigadier, commands a division at Murfreesboro, and wins promotion. (USAMHI)

Above: The courthouse in Murfreesboro. The town remained in Confederate hands during the battle. (USAMHI)

Above: Rosecrans fought a largely defensive battle, letting Bragg hurl his divisions against tough fighters like the 38th Indiana, shown here in Murfreesboro in April 1863. (JMB)

Above: The telegraph office from which Bragg boastfully—and prematurely—wired President Davis that he had won a great victory. (USAMHI)

Left: Those attacks were overseen by Bragg's corps commanders. Lieutenant General William J. Hardee of Georgia was known widely in both armies, thanks to his authorship of Hardee's Tactics, a standard manual North and South. (LC)

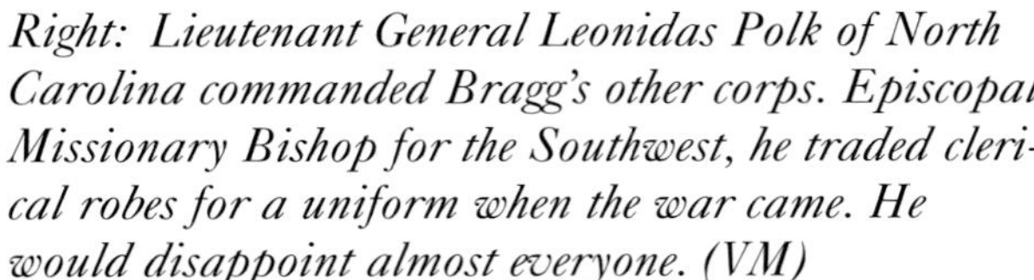

Right: Lieutenant General Leonidas Polk of North Carolina commanded Bragg's other corps. Episcopal Missionary Bishop for the Southwest, he traded clerical robes for a uniform when the war came. He would disappoint almost everyone. (VM)

Above: Some of the greatest infantry assaults of the war took place at Murfreesboro, and they were terribly bloody. Brigadier General Roger Hanson of Kentucky, commander of the Orphan Brigade, fell mortally wounded when the fuse from an exploding shell struck his leg. While being carried from the field he cheered his men, telling them that it was a glorious cause to die for. (JM)

Right: Brigadier General James E. Rains was killed leading his division of Hardee's corps into a charge. His last word was "Forward!" (USAMHI)

Below: Determined resistance by Sheridan and others finally forced Bragg to abandon the field and retreat into the interior, leaving the Federals the field and the victory. (USAMHI)

Above: The Federals occupied Murfreesboro for most of the rest of the war. Here the headquarters from which Rosecrans sent Lincoln the good news of a victory for the New Year, 1863. (USAMHI)

Photographer of the Confederacy: J. D. Edwards

LESLIE D. JENSEN

Prolific yet unknown chronicler of rustics in rebellion

Above: The ever-frowning brow of General Braxton Bragg. He commanded the regiments of rustics forming at Pensacola when Edwards made his historic visit in April 1861. (CHS)

With only four exceptions, all of the J. D. Edwards photographs reproduced here are published for the first time. Several others were published in 1911, but the originals from which they were reproduced have since disappeared. The images that follow are all taken from surviving original prints newly unearthed.

BEFORE the war guns really roared, East or West, on May 14, 1861, the citizens of New Orleans, reading the military columns of their newspapers, came across the following advertisement:

> THE WAR !
> Views of Pensacola, Forts Barancas, McRae and Pickens; of the Companies there—"Orleans Cadets" "Crescent Rifles" "Chausseurs a Pied," Mississippi and Alabama Regiments and of the U.S. Fleet—39 different Photographic Views, taken by an accomplished artist on the spot, will be on sale tomorrow at the Book Stores, Picture and Looking Glass Stores. They are very large and taken superbly. Price $1 per copy.

The "accomplished artist" was J. D. Edwards, a shadowy figure who remains obscure to this day, yet a man who had accomplished a feat that would not be repeated in the Confederacy. Edwards had produced a comprehensive photographic panorama of the forts, guns, barracks, shipyards, and most importantly, the men who comprised the Confederate Army. Were it not for Edwards, photographic coverage of Confederate military events would be limited to a mere handful of isolated pictures, many of them taken in northern prison camps.

Little is known about Edwards personally or of his life before his Pensacola views went on sale, and practically nothing is known of him afterward. In 1860, he was working in New Orleans. Edwards was twenty-nine years old at the time, had been born in New Hampshire, and gave his occupation as "Ambrotype Portrait." His wife, Mary, a Missourian by birth, was twenty. The Edwardses could not have been in New Orleans long, for their son Edouard had been born in Massachusetts only eight months before. The remainder of the household consisted of Eliza Zeigler, a nineteen-year-old German servant, and Edwards's two assistants, B. Barker, a twenty-nine-year-old native of Massachusetts, and a twenty-four-year old Canadian named Johnson. Edwards valued his personal estate at $3,000.

Yet, though a newcomer to New Orleans, Edwards must have made an impression of being innovative and willing to take on unusual business assignments. When the U. S. Treasury Department and Custom House and the Marine Hospital were under construction in June 1860, Edwards took twenty-three views of the former and twelve views of the latter for the U. S. Army Engineer in charge of the work, a native Louisianan named P. G. T. Beauregard. This assignment may well have started a tradition for both men, outdoor photography for Edwards, and the inclusion of photographs with reports for Beauregard, a practice he continued during the 1861 and 1863 Charleston operations.

By 1861, Edwards operated a studio at 23 Royal Street, yet, though he was listed in the alphabetical section of a city directory, he was still not established enough to be included in the separate section devoted to photographers. Later in the year he moved to 19 Royal Street, occupied when the directory was put out by a photographer named E. J. Newton, Jr. It is not known whether Edwards bought out Newton's operation or went into business with him.

After the firing on Fort Sumter, only one

Right: Fort Pickens photographed from Fort Barrancas, across Pensacola Harbor. The ship is probably the Federal flag-of-truce boat U.S.S. Wyandotte. *(SHC)*

Above: First Lieutenant Adam J. Slemmer of the 1st United States Artillery, the thorn in Bragg's side who refused to give up Fort Pickens, thus ensuring the mighty bastion for the Union as a base deep in Confederate territory. Edwards never captured Slemmer as Cook did Major Anderson and his men at Fort Sumter, but more than once he turned his camera toward the low, brooding profile of Pickens, a constant reminder of Federal power and determination. (USAMHI)

Left: Guns in the old Spanish part of Fort Barrancas, trained on Fort Pickens in the distance. "I was rather interested with Fort Barrancas," wrote William H. Russell, "built by the Spaniards long ago—an old work on the old plan, weakly armed, but possessing a tolerable command from the face of fire." (SHC)

Above: The rear of Fort Barrancas and a Confederate regiment camped beyond, probably the 1st Alabama. The variety of tents, the makeshift nature of the camp, and lack of uniformity in the dress of the Confederates drawn up in line, all attest to the informal and inexperienced nature of the Southrons who flocked to Pensacola in 1861. (GULF ISLANDS NATIONAL SEASHORE)

Left: A side view of part of Fort Barrancas as Bragg's men move yet another cannon into place. (SHC)

major U.S. bastion remained in the Confederacy: Fort Pickens, guarding the harbor of Pensacola Bay, Florida. The importance of Fort Pickens has often been overshadowed by other events, and particularly because no major battles were fought to control it. Yet, in April 1861, it was one of the most important areas of potential trouble. As the last Union stronghold on Confederate soil, it was not only irritating to southern pride, but it blocked the bay to southern shipping and restricted the use of the splendid former U. S. Navy Yard at Warrington, just across the bay from the fort. Moreover, it could, and in time did, become a base for operations against the Confederacy. Whoever controlled Fort Pickens controlled the use of one of the best anchorages on the Gulf Coast.

Theoretically, the Confederates, vastly outnumbering the Union troops in the area, should have had little trouble taking control of the bay, but the unexpected stubbornness of Lieutenant Adam Slemmer's tiny Union command, supported by an ever growing Union fleet, kept the Confederates at bay until Union reinforcements arrived. By late April, Confederate volunteers poured into the area, preparing for what every-

Above: The sand battery at Fort Barrancas, and a stand of the ill-formed shot. Despite the seemingly strong positions of these guns, Russell believed that if Bragg opened fire on Slemmer, Fort Pickens "ought certainly to knock his works about his ears." (SHC)

Above: Edwards captioned this a "View of two Sand Batteries, showing subterranean passages connecting them together, with Fort Pickens in the distance." Pickens has now disappeared from this faded print, but the crude board shoring of the tunnels is visible in the foreground. Much work remains to be done, but Russell did not find the summer soldiers anxious about it. "The working parties, as they were called—volunteers from Mississippi and Alabama, great long-bearded fellows in flannel shirts and slouched hats, uniformless in all save brightly burnished arms and resolute purpose—were lying about among the works, or contributing languidly to their completion." (TU)

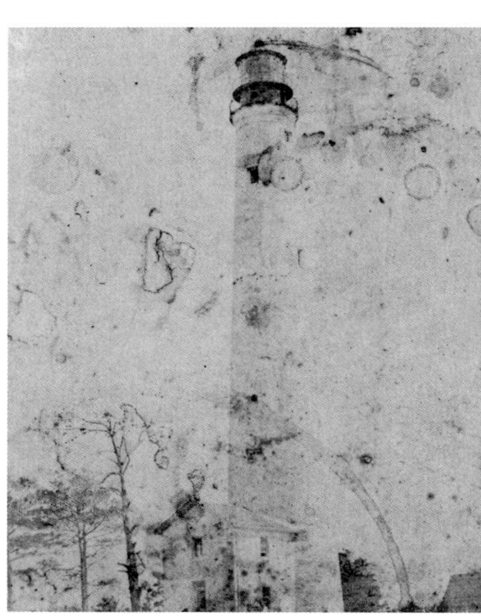

Above: The lighthouse west of Fort Barrancas. Built in 1859, it quickly attracted Edwards's eye, and he and his camera were soon at its top taking the first aerial photos of the war. (PENSACOLA HISTORICAL SOCIETY, PENSACOLA, FLORIDA)

Below: Looking east from the lighthouse. Barely visible on the shore in the right center is a two-gun sand battery. Just above the right-hand row of tents is another. And just above the tents at left, distinguishable by the straight horizontal line of its parapet, is Fort Barrancas. The buildings to its left are the Barrancas Barracks, while the tall building with cupola in the distance to the right of the barracks is the Marine Hospital. This is, arguably, the first "aerial" photograph in military history. (SHC)

Below: A water battery at Warrington. In the distance to the right is the lighthouse. Bragg did not wish to open fire on Pickens, and the Englishman Russell believed him right. "The magazines. of the batteries I visited did not contain ammunition for more than one day's ordinary firing," he wrote. "The shots were badly cast, with projecting flanges from the mould, which would be very injurious to soft metal guns in firing." One of these rustics, standing at the wheel of the front gun, holds a shot in his hand, while his mates sham preparing to fire. The poor man at the second gun, seeing his chance for immortality about to be blocked by a cold iron cannon, had to stoop to present his face to the camera. In the right center is a hot-shot furnace for heating incendiary projectiles. (NA, OFFICE OF THE CHIEF OF ENGINEERS)

one thought would be the next big showdown of the war. Many of the Confederates headed for Pensacola were from New Orleans, and J. D. Edwards apparently saw in this an opportunity to create a pictorial record of the war, make a reputation for himself, and turn a profit by selling his products to the soldiers and the folks back home. Accordingly, sometime in late April, he too headed for the scene of the war's next big battle.

Happily, because Edwards numbered at least some of his negatives in the order he took them, it is possible to follow his work pattern in the Pensacola area with a fair degree of certainty. He seems to have started at the Navy Yard itself, where General Braxton Bragg had his head quarters and where Edwards probably had to go to get permission to take his photographs. He took pictures looking across the bay toward Fort Pickens and photographed the steamer Fulton in dry dock, surrounded by the vast quantities of shells the Confederates had both captured and were making in the yard's foundry. From there, he moved west, photographing Coppens's Louisiana Zouave Battalion at drill on the grounds of the Marine Barracks. He spent a great deal of time at Fort Barrancas, photographing it inside and out, including its old Spanish half-moon battery. From there, Edwards photographed some of the sand batteries and then found himself drawn to the lighthouse. Its 165-foot height provided a perfect view of the coast, and Edwards took his camera to the top, photographing the forts and camps below. He spent considerable time in the camps themselves, mostly in those of the 1st Alabama and 9th Mississippi regiments, before moving on to the Confederate bastion on the right flank, Fort McRee. On the way back, Edwards may have

Right: Confederate camps and a four-gun sand battery immediately below the lighthouse. The "subterranean passages" connecting the guns are clearly visible, as are several Confederates lounging in the vicinity. These are Alabama troops. In the distance on the low spit of sand dune is Fort McRee, "weak and badly built," thought Russell, and "quite under the command of Pickens." (GULF ISLANDS NATIONAL SEASHORE)

Above: A Confederate encampment just south of Bayou Grande, near Pensacola, probably the Orleans Cadets. This may be the finest Confederate camp scene to survive, excellent not only for its clarity, but for what it shows as well. Almost every aspect of camp life is depicted. A bugler with his instrument to his lips, a soldier with fishing pole in hand, men reading letters and newspapers, others cleaning their rifles, a fatigue detail with shovel on shoulder, two Johnnies feigning a spar, and at right, pipe in mouth, a company officer handing orders to a saluting corporal. To the left are piled boxes of fresh rations. In this image Edwards outdid himself. (STATE PHOTOGRAPHIC ARCHIVES, STROZIER LIBRARY, FLORIDA STATE UNIVERSITY)

taken additional camp scenes, and at some point, probably toward the end of his stay, he went to Bayou Grand, just north of Warrington, where he photographed the camp of the Orleans Cadets. Exactly how long Edwards stayed in the Pensacola area is unknown, but given the volume of work that he did and the probable work and travel time, he may have been there a week or more.

The photographs went on sale in New Orleans on May 15, but curiously, Edwards only ran his notice for three days. The various newspapers made some editorial comment on the photographs, but beyond confirming that the advertisement indeed refers to the work of J. D. Edwards, they tell us little. The New Orleans Bee, however, suggested that the photographs would "make an interesting souvenir for the parlor, particularly in the event, considered now so near at hand, of the capture of Fort Pickens."

Some of the photographs made their way north with surprising speed. On June 15, a woodcut appeared in Harper's Weekly entitled "INTERIOR OF A SAND-BAC BATTERY BEARING ON FORT PICKENS.

Harper's claimed that it was the work of their special artist, Theodore Davis, but close comparison with Edwards's photograph No. 33, "Perote Sand Batteries 10 inch Columbiads," reveals the wood cut to have been pirated from Edwards. It is entirely possible that Davis, who had been in Pensacola with William Howard Russell at about the time Edwards was photographing, knew Edwards's work and either made a sketch from the photograph or simply sent the photograph on to Harper's, who incorrectly captioned it. A week later, Harper's ran another woodcut with the caption BIVOUAC OF REBEL TROOPS AT GENERAL BRAGGíS CAMP AT WARRINGTON, FLORIDA, and this time admitted that it was from a photograph, although they did not identify the photographer. The scene was the well-known one of men cooking around a campfire in the 9th Mississippi's camp, but Harper's, not content with the original photograph, rearranged the figures.

Edwards's photographs seem to have been rather widely distributed at the time. Some ended up in the hands of S. H. Lockett, an officer in the 1st Alabama, and somehow Charles Allgower, a member of the 6th New York and an occasional artist for Harper's, also acquired some,

Above: The encampment of the Louisville Blues, the 1st Alabama, near the lighthouse. There is a definite lack of order in this camp, blankets and clothing and equipment hanging wherever convenient. These men would learn a lot about soldiering in the years ahead, and about sanitation, too. A trench, perhaps a latrine, is just a few feet to the left of their tents and mess area. Disease, in this war, will kill far more men than bullets. (RP)

Left: Camps of Mississippi regiments behind the lighthouse. (TU)

Left: Edwards did not move his camera after capturing the Mississippi camps. Instead, he moved the Mississippians. Here they parade in all their sartorial chaos. Top hats, stovepipes, slouch and military caps, hunting shirts, bow ties, flannel checks, and their captain in front in a decidedly unmilitary vest. Yet they all have rifles, and an unshakable determination. Nowhere in the world was there another soldiery like them. (PHS)

The 9th Mississippi in camp, and for an Edwards photo, an unusually clear surviving print. Rarely can one see such a brilliant representation of the Confederate soldier of 1861. Especially eye-catching is the soldier crouching to the left of the stand of rifles at left. The significance of the numeral "4" on his shirt is unknown, but his resplendence is unarguable. They all have the lean, hardened look of the American backwoods. Such men could be unbeatable. (RP)

One of Bragg's five big siege guns, a 10-inch columbiad, and, to its right, a tunnel passage to the next gun. There are more uniforms here, more of a military look, but the same posturing for the camera of all these Southrons of 1861. The war was still a lark to them. Most had never been this far from home in their lives. They expected to be home again before the fall. (TU)

The second 10-inch columbiad in this Perote sand battery. It is manned by more Mississippians, the Quitman Rifles. (PHS)

A quiet moment in camp for men of Company B, 9th Mississippi, the Quitman Rifles. These are men from Holly Springs, Mississippi, and at least one of them is probably writing home. His tent mate reads a book, while their friend in the shadows behind their rifles appears to be peeling potatoes. Three years from now the Confederate soldier will regard this simple tent and its furnishings as unimaginable luxury. (PHS)

Company B of the 9th Mississippi again. The man stooping over the frying pan is Kinlock Falconer. One day he will serve on Bragg's staff. For the moment, he is about to serve some fried pork. The closest thing to a uniform for this company would appear to be checkered pants. (LC)

probably while his regiment was stationed in the Pensacola area. Despite Edwards's claim that he produced thirty-nine views, it is now clear that the actual total was much higher. Known views, many of them published in 1911 but since lost, total forty-four. However, Edwards's negative numbers run as high as sixty-eight, and there is at least one photograph numbered "2B." Thus, despite the large number of Edwards photographs which are presented here for the first time, there may be as many as twenty or more yet unaccounted for, including at least two, those of the Crescent Rifles and the Chausseurs a Pied, referred to in the ad.

One wonders whether the appearance of the woodcuts in Harper's Weekly may have been a spur to another photographer, the nation's finest, Mathew B. Brady. The Confederates had already scooped him in the early coverage of the war, and the fact that their photographs were appearing in northern papers, competing with his own portrait work, may well have helped to inspire Brady to take his camera teams into the field.

The fact that the Pensacola front never produced any major battles and was eventually abandoned by the Confederates may have hurt the long-term sales of Edwards's work, but in any case, after the appearance of the photographs, he slipped once more into obscurity. Two of his negatives were seized by U.S. authorities after the fall of New Orleans, and prints from them were turned over to the U. S. Engineers office in Washington in 1863. Unfortunately, we do not know the circumstances of the seizure, and while the prints survive, the negatives have disappeared. Francis Trevelyan Miller claimed that Edwards later worked for the Confederate secret service, but no hard evidence to support the claim has come to light. Yet, there is one tantalizing clue which may indicate that Edwards was an even more important photographer than his Pensacola series indicates. Roy M. Mason, one of the searchers sent by Miller to locate Confederate photographs for the 1911 Photographic History of the Civil War, recalled his experiences in the armory of the Washington Artillery in New Orleans. He noted that the one-armed armorer, Sergeant Dan Kelly, "said that there were no photographs, but consented to look in the long rows of dusty shelves which line the sides of the huge, dark armory. From almost the last he drew forth a pile of soggy, limp cardboard, covered with the grime of years. He passed his sleeve carelessly over the first, and there spread into view a picture of his father sitting reading among his comrades in Camp Louisiana forty-nine years before. The photographs were those of J. D. Edwards, who had also worked at Pensacola and Mobile. Here were Confederate volunteers of '61 and the boys of the Washington Artillery which became so famous in the service of the Army of Northern Virginia." Some Washington Artillery photos were by J. W. Petty of New Orleans, but if

Mason's implication is correct, Edwards may have continued to photograph Confederate troops at least as late as early 1862, when the 5th Company, Washington Artillery was photographed just before Shiloh. If so, Edwards may be responsible for a larger body of Confederate photographs than he has been given credit for.

Yet, if early 1862 was the last time that Edwards may have been at work, it is also the end of any documentation on his Civil War work. The man simply disappears for the next two decades. In the late 1880s he reemerges, working his trade in Atlanta, and there he dies in 1900. How much more wartime work he did, if any, and how much more of it survives, is a mystery.

Miller called Edwards a "pioneer camera man," but apparently even Miller was not aware of just how much of a pioneer Edwards was. In this country there was virtually no tradition of war photography, and while the Crimean War photographs of Roger Fenton and others were known, there was no one who could set the pace in this new art. While enterprising Confederates in Charleston were the first on the scene of America's bloodiest war, their job was made easier by the fact that they were photographing local events. The established photographers remained in their studios, content to take the portraits of the generals and soldiers who would fight the war. Into this scene stepped J. D. Edwards, packing his equipment over miles of swamps and bayous and into a war zone, taking pictures at least as good as Brady's and then marketing them with little apparent financial backing other than his own. At the time Edwards's work was of a far wider scope than anything any other photographer was producing, and while he was eclipsed by the superior resources of Brady, Gardner, and hundreds of others, it was J. D. Edwards, whether known by name to these other photographers or not, who showed the way a war could be photographed. In the Confederacy, no one else would match his work for innovation and sheer importance. If there was anyone who could claim the title Photographer of the Confederacy, it was the obscure Yankee from New Orleans, J. D. Edwards.

Above: A mortar in the water battery just west of the lighthouse, which can be seen above the trees at left. Some of the projecting flanges William H. Russell mentioned can be seen on the shot stacked at right. There is much evidence of work, but apparently it was not necessarily done with perfect harmony. "Considerable improvements were in the course of execution," found Russell, "but the officers were not always agreed as to the work to be done. Captain A., at the wheelbarrows: 'Now then, you men, wheel up these sandbags, and range them just at this corner.' Major B.: 'My good Captain A., what do you want the bags there for? Did I not tell you, these merlons were not to be finished till we had completed the parapet on the front?' Captain A.: 'Well, Major, so you did, and your order made me think you know darned little about your business; so I am going to do a little engineering of my own.'" Such was American democracy in action. (NA, OFFICE OF THE CHIEF OF ENGINEERS)

Above: The Orleans Cadets and their leader, Captain Dreux, a well-uniformed unit for a change. New Orleans was particularly anxious to know the doings of her native sons at Pensacola, and Edwards was aware of the commercial possibilities of selling photographs of them at home. "Any of them will form an interesting souvenir for the parlor," read his advertisement for the prints in New Orleans, "particularly in the event, considered now so near at hand, of the capture of Fort Pickens." (TU)

Above: But the only Confederate who would capture Fort Pickens would be Edwards himself, and here he takes not only the fort, but a Federal ship as well, the U.S.S. Macedonian. *His epic task done, J. D. Edwards, truly the "Photographer of the Confederacy," would take back with him to New Orleans a priceless record of Southerners in the early days of their bid for nationhood. Yet his images would be all but lost, and Edwards a forgotten man. He and they deserved better. He was truly a man with vision. (USAMHI)*

The North at War

MAURY KLEIN

Life in a country in conflict, yet still growing

The North at war was a bustling place. The great cities grew greater, frontiers moved farther west, business and industry expanded. An early postwar view of New York and, in the foreground, its city hall. (USAMHI)

UNLIKE THE SOUTHERNERS captured by J. D. Edwards and others, for most Northerners the Civil War was a distant event. They did not witness its carnage firsthand, and their cities and farms escaped the devastation that blighted large areas of the South. Seldom did the din of combat reach their ears or the menace of invading troops disturb their daily routines. Life went on, if not as usual, at least with a minimum of disruption.

But distance from the battlefield could not protect Northerners from the effects of a long and bloody war. The ordeal of sustaining so massive a struggle intruded upon people's lives in countless ways. The most obvious of these was, of course, the absence of friends and kinfolk in the service. Every town and hamlet watched its young men depart for the front, some to die and others to return home with bodies maimed or spirits broken. Concern for the safety of loved ones permeated house holds throughout the North, aggravated by the slowness with which accurate details or casualty lists reached home after a major battle. Thus did distance from the seat of war breed anxiety as well as security.

The presence of men in uniform, whether home on leave or forming into newly organized units, also served as constant reminders to civilians. Soldiers could be found on the streets of cities and villages everywhere. Returning wounded brought home stark evidence of their ordeal in combat. Rare was the town that did not welcome home a veteran minus an arm or leg or worse. Army camps and prisoner-of-war compounds were opened in many towns, and by 1862 conscription officers had begun to replace recruitment drives and became objects of loathing wherever they appeared. Through all these agents the war came home to every northern community. Those who did not join the army found their lives affected in other ways. The northern war effort depended not only upon its advantage in men and guns but also upon its superior industrial and agricultural might. In terms of productivity the war was fought as much at home as on the battlefield, and the fight enlisted men, women, and children alike. The drain of manpower for military service, coupled with increased demand for goods, meant simply that there were fewer people to do more work. Farm and factory alike responded to this need in two ways: by increasing their use of machinery to replace human labor and by putting more women and children to work.

The North relied upon its staple crops both to feed its people and army and to produce surpluses which could be sold abroad for sorely needed gold. As thousands of men left the farms to fight the war, women, children, and older men took up the heavy field work. At the same time the use of agricultural machinery spread rapidly, a fact which delighted manufacturers who sniffed bonanza profits. As Cyrus McCormick reminded one of his salesmen in Illinois, "Don't be so blue over the prospects. Remember 20,000 militia have to leave this state… and these men will have to come, many or a large share of them, from the farms."

Mowers and reapers were still relatively new machines in 1860; by 1864 production of them exceeded 70,000, or twice the output of 1862. These wondrous devices saved human labor and could be operated even by women and children. Other machines, including the horse-rake, cultivators, new harrows, corn planters, steam threshers, and grain drills were also devised and marketed. The use of machinery increased the scale of agriculture and enabled farmers to bring more land under cultivation, especially in the West.

The results of this effort were impressive. Northern farmers produced large enough corn, oat, and wheat crops during the war years—including record crops in 1862—to fill domestic needs and still sell large quantities to England, which experienced three straight years of crop failures. Hog and cattle output also increased dramatically, and wool production jumped from 60 million pounds in 1860 to 140 million pounds in 1865. During that same period the number of sheep in the North doubled, an important gain since wool offered the most common substitute for the cotton supply diminished by the South's secession.

Apparently photographers, like other Northerners, took great pride in this record of productivity; at least they delighted in capturing scenes showing the new machines at work. But when they turned their attention to the factories, something more than productivity caught the eye. Pictures of giant machines sweeping across fields, or of fishing boats plying the waters of Nantucket, conveyed a sense of majesty, even charm. However, scenes of women and small children toiling in a factory, although they might suggest the sacrifice and productivity so vital to the war effort, were utterly lacking in beauty or nobility. Unlike the sight of a man or woman astride a reaper, no charm attached to the spectacle of people young and old harnessed to machines inside dingy mills.

But the mills and factories played a major role in carrying the North to victory. From their bustling, clanging interiors came a swelling stream of muskets, cannon, equipment, locomotives, rails, wagons, tools, uniforms, shoes, and thousands of other items. Wartime needs spurred the development of other industries besides agricultural implements and armaments. The demand for uniforms and shoes prompted increased use of sewing machines. One by-product of this work was the discovery that uniforms and shoes manufactured in a few basic sizes would fit most men. This standardization simplified the production of uniforms and shoes in quantity and after the war stimulated the rise of the ready-made clothing industry. Military needs also lent a strong impetus to the canned food industry, including Gail Borden's canned milk. The desire to produce canned food quickly and in quantity led to improvements in canning techniques and machinery.

As its farms and factories responded to the war effort, an aura of prosperity settled across the North. Newspapers and politicians alike waxed eloquent over the nation's material well-being. The New York Times noted in 1864 that Northerners were better housed, clothed, and fed than ever be fore "in the midst of the most gigantic civil war... yet seen." Wholesale farm prices doubled during the war years while nonagricultural wages rose 43 percent. Farm land values soared, as did real estate values in general.

For most Northerners, however, this prosperity proved more apparent than real. As always, war time brought a sharp inflationary trend which in many cases erased gains in wages or income. Wholesale prices more than doubled

Left: Fifth Avenue, looking north from the southeast corner of Twenty-eighth Street, New York, 1865. (NYHS)

Left: Away from the eastern coast, the market towns and county seats continued to thrive as before the conflict. Indeed, the presence of large-scale armies boosted business in many communities. The market square in Carlisle, Pennsylvania, in 1862. (LC)

Left: Chestnut Street in Philadelphia just before the war. Hotels, booksellers, typesetters, engravers—the North bustled with the work of tradesmen and artisans. (FREE LIBRARY OF PHILADELPHIA)

Right: Hanover Junction, Pennsylvania, around November 1863. Like hundreds of minor railroad towns, its townspeople saw little of the war and felt its effects even less, except when the trains came through loaded with soldiers going to the front. (USAMHI)

Above: An apple seller in Cincinnati, Ohio, typical of the street vendors that every large city spawned. (LO)

Right: St. Paul, Minnesota, a city that grew largely from the speculations in the 1850s of Washington politicians and bankers, several of them now Confederates. (MHS)

Right: Travel and sightseeing increased, even among the notables, and especially among the soldiers and foreign observers and dignitaries. Here Secretary of State William Seward entertains a host of diplomats in a pastoral setting. Those seated are, from the left, Molena, Nicaraguan minister; Seward; Baron de Stoeckel, Russian minister; and Mr. Sheffield, the British legation attache'. Standing from the left are Donaldson of Seward's State Department, a man unidentified, Secretary Bodesco of the Russian legation, Swedish minister Count Piper, Italian minister Bertenattie, Hanseatic minister Schleider, French minister Henri Mercier, and Lord Lyons, minister from Britain. (NA)

Above: Main Street in Salt Lake City, Utah, October 24, 1861. Western Union, impelled largely by the war, completes the first transcontinental telegraph. Beneath the backdrop of the mighty mountains, a simple ceremony marks the occasion. With great good fortune, Western Union's "Telegraph Office" is right next to a combination liquor store and "Ambrotype Gallery." The result was this ambrotype of an historic moment. (LO)

while the consumer price index increased from 102 to 177. According to one recent calculation, the real wage index actually declined from 102 in January 1861 to 67 in January 1865.

Wage earners suffered most from the ravages of inflation, but attempts to improve their lot through organization made little headway during the war. Most wartime trade unions began at the local level, primarily in New York, Pennsylvania, and Massachusetts, and boasted some 300 locals with an estimated 200,000 members by 1865. City federations, begun in Rochester in March 1863, soon sprang up in most major industrial centers. Intended only as advisory bodies, the federations assumed such tasks as organizing trades and boycotts, generating publicity during strikes, and opposing the importation of strikebreakers. They also founded labor newspapers and in thirty-six cities and towns helped establish cooperative stores.

Attempts to revive national trade associations made some gains, but the national organizations were loose bodies with little effective power over their locals. In general the labor movement remained weak during the war. Unskilled workers, especially women, children, and blacks, endured starvation wages and sweatshop conditions with little hope of improving their lot.

Wartime conditions imposed unusual hardships upon workers. According to a Senate report, industrial workers provided the Union Army with about one third of its troops. The Conscription Act of 1863, with its provision that service might be evaded by hiring a substitute or paying a three hundred-dollar commutation fee, especially rankled laborers. On several occasions resentment against the draft boiled into bloody riots. The most spectacular of these occurred in New York City in July 1863 when a mob wrecked the recruiting station, demolished rail and streetcar lines and ship yards, closed factories, attacked the homes of leading Republicans, and killed several blacks. Similar riots engulfed other cities in turmoil but brought no relief to workers.

Strikes proved equally futile in wartime. The public regarded them as disloyal and the government sometimes responded with troops. On several occasions President Lincoln felt obliged to intervene in an attempt to salve the feelings of workers and preserve their loyalty to the war effort. At the same time the government took

Left: The people of the Union played, and baseball became more and more a pasttme. The New York Knickerbocker Nine in 1864. (NATIONAL BASEBALL LIBRARY)

Below: Of course, there was no escape from the war entirely. Guns were everywhere. A mammoth Rodman smoothebore, photographed by Montgomery C. Meigs. (LC)

Above: Russian sailors like these were a new sight in New York and San Francisco, where the czar's fleet made showings of support for the Union. (WRHS)

steps to increase the labor supply diminished by military service and a decline in immigration. In both 1861 and 1862 immigration, which had averaged 281,455 people a year during the 1850s, fell off to slightly less than 92,000. The figure rose to 176,282 in 1863, but the following year Congress, prodded by Lincoln and concerned industrialists, passed a law which permitted the importation of contract laborers. What ever the effect of this act, immigration rose to 193,418 in 1864 and 248,120 in 1865.

But if workers found prosperity elusive, many businessmen reaped fat profits from wartime opportunities. Alert contractors were quick to take advantage of the government's needs. Some were content to earn legitimate fortunes while others resorted to dishonest means to make their killings. Never had the nation created so large an army or required armaments and equipment on so vast a scale. The scale of operations, as well as the urgency of purchasing so much so quickly, invited corruption of unprecedented dimensions. Revelation after revelation rocked the public, prompting the New York Herald in June 1864 to denounce the "gross corruption prevailing in nearly every department of the government." Large commissions went to men whose only service was to procure lucrative government contracts for firms.

On the stock and gold exchanges, speculators thrived on the uncertainties of wartime. Good news from the front boosted the prices of gold and stocks; bad news sent them crashing downward. Hordes of speculators, including some women braving ridicule in a traditionally male arena, plunged into the treacherous currents of Wall Street seeking a quick fortune. One crafty manipulator, Daniel Drew, recalled that "Along with ordinary happenings, we fellows in Wall Street had the fortunes of war to speculate about.... It's good fishing in troubled waters."

Right: The mode of transporting a Rodman by rail, suspended from a bridge truss. (LC)

Below: Federal commanders did rule over certain threatened parts of the country. Major General John A. Dix exercised considerable authority over largely secessionist Maryland. (USAMHI)

Left: Governors like Andrew Curtin of Pennsylvania initiated calls for volunteers for the Army, Curtin calling for 50,000 in 1862 and 60,000 the next year. Unlike most northern governors, he also faced the trauma of Confederate invasion of his state at Gettysburg. (CHICACO PUBLIC LIBRARY, SPECIAL COLLECTIONS)

Right: Even on Broadway in New York the recruiters worked, and at right, behind the flag, stands the evidence of their success, an army barracks in the heart of the city. No wonder an enterprising vendor selected this spot to sell his sarsaparilla and beer at 3 cents per glass. (USAMHI)

Above: Recruiting offices appeared in every city of any size, as here on New York's State Street. The three main buildings house the United States Quartermaster's office, but the partially obscured house on the far right has a flag in front, and a broadside offering a three-hundred-dollar bounty to men who enlist. (USAMHI)

Right: Photographer Fuller of Madison, Wisconsin, visited his local recruiter, not to enlist, but to shoot. "Enlist—Veteran Regiment" reads the broadside. Perhaps more than a few boys were induced to join after sampling the bottles and jugs, but the significance of the fencing match is, alas, lost. (USAMHI)

Above: All through the war the United States Military Academy at West Point continued to produce officers for the armies. (NA, U. S. SIGNAL CORPS)

Young Jay Gould went one step further: he devised an ingenious system whereby he obtained by telegraph advance information on Union victories or defeats and shifted his speculations accordingly.

Not all northern businessmen were corrupt or dishonest, and not all made fortunes. But the war created a free-wheeling, opportunistic atmosphere that proved irresistible to many people. It is important to remember that not all Northerners bothered to fight the war or even tender it active support. Some people lacked strong interest in the conflict and either ignored it as best they could or resented it as an intrusion into their private affairs.

Among this group were men who found the wartime situation a golden opportunity for self-advancement. Their activities escaped the camera's eye, as did those of the plungers on Wall Street and the hustlers of government contracts, but their ultimate importance rivaled anything that took place on the battlefield. These ambitious young entrepreneurs used the war years to establish themselves in business while their peers were caught up in the clash of arms. Some made their fortunes even before the war ended, while others planted the roots of what were to be long and prosperous careers.

Within this group could be found a surprising number of the business titans who were to dominate the economy, and therefore much of American life, during the half century between the Civil War and World War I: Andrew Carnegie, J. P. Morgan, John D. Rockefeller, George F. Baker, James J. Hill, Gustavus Swift, Charles A. Pillsbury, George M. Pullman, Mark Hanna, Marshall Field, Jay Gould, John Wanamaker, and Peter Widener, to name but a few. Each of these men, and others like them, ignored the call to arms and concentrated instead upon the windfall business opportunities bred by wartime conditions. Few of them even tried to enlist, fewer still stayed home because of disability, and several (Carnegie, Gould, Morgan, Rockefeller, and Philip D. Armour among them) hired substitutes.

In later years some of these men grew defensive about their failure to enter the service. "I was represented in the army," Rockefeller insisted. "I sent more than twenty men, yes, nearly thirty. That is, I made such arrangements for them that they were able to go." The majority, however, seemed content to concentrate on the business at hand. One son of banker Thomas Mellon begged his father for money to speculate in wheat. Writing from Wisconsin, he observed that people "continue growing richer and don't care when the war closes." Mindful of the educational value afforded by prevailing conditions, the elder Mellon flatly for bade another son from enlisting:

> I had hoped my boy was going to make a smart intelligent businessman and was not such a goose as to be seduced from duty by the declamations of buncombe speeches. It is only greenhorns who enlist. You can learn nothing in the army.... In time you will come to understand and believe that a man may be a patriot without risking his own life or sacrificing his health. There are plenty of other lives less valuable or ready to serve for the love of serving.

To most of these men, wartime opportunities

brought financial nest eggs from which huge fortunes later hatched. For them, and for many others who advanced their prospects during those turbulent years, prosperity was anything but illusory.

Social activities reflected this mood of rising affluence, especially in the cities. As the war dragged on through month after weary month of bloody battles that produced defeat or indecision, Northerners sought diversions to dispel the gloom of uncertainty that clouded the future. So frenetic did the quest for amusement and gaiety become that stern observers periodically denounced the populace for their indifference to the suffering and hardships endured by soldiers at the front.

In rural areas, where the workday was always long and sources of amusement few, life went on much as it had before the war. There were church socials, husking bees, country fairs, and occasional barn dances. Young men played baseball or competed in foot races, wrestling, and shooting matches. A religious revival or camp meeting, accompanied by picnics and other festivities, might enliven a farm community for a week or more. Many a small town possessed an "opry house" that never saw an opera but welcomed touring lectures, dramatic companies, or minstrel shows. Occasionally too a traveling circus might wend its way through the countryside, thrilling farm folk with its menagerie of strange animals and exotic freaks. No event rivaled the celebration of national holidays like the Fourth of July, for which families gathered from miles around to enjoy barbeques, games, fireworks, oratory, and dancing, usually accompanied by liberal swigs from jugs of whiskey or hard cider.

City life offered far more varied and sophisticated amusements. As always the upper class set the standards and indulged themselves most freely. Dinners, receptions, and elegant parties occupied the fashionable in every city, especially Washington and New York. Roller-skating made its appearance in 1863 and New York's social denizens seized upon it as a pleasure which they hoped to confine to "the educated and refined classes." Ice-skating parties lightened the tedium of winter while periodic visits to fashionable resorts in Newport, Narragansett Pier, or upstate New York helped pass the summer months. Every major city had its lyceums and lecture halls, and in New York the Academy of Music offered the cultured elite a sampling of grand opera imported from Europe.

Crowds flocked to the theaters of every city in unprecedented numbers. Comedies were the staple fare, both in the high-tone playhouses and in lower-class theaters like those in New York's Bowery, where huge crowds gathered to yell and whistle, cheer and hiss, chew peanuts and spit tobacco juice. Although the emphasis upon comedy reflected a desire to escape the war, at least for a few hours, dramas based upon recent battles also proved popular. One energetic producer opened a play about Bull Run within a month of the battle, and later engagements were put on the boards by adapting a standard script to each occasion.

Besides theater, northern urbanites patronized minstrel shows, burlesque, dance halls, winter gardens, prizefights, cockfights, and the saloons. In New York, P. T. Barnum's American Museum drew enormous crowds, as did imitation counter parts in other cities. To the rest of

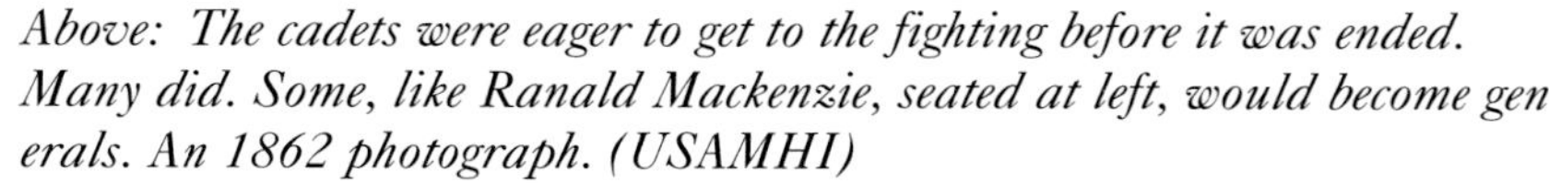

Above: The cadets were eager to get to the fighting before it was ended. Many did. Some, like Ranald Mackenzie, seated at left, would become generals. An 1862 photograph. (USAMHI)

Below: Two cadets of the class of 1864. They will have their chance for glory. (USAMHI)

Left: They, like many of the generals North and South now battling all across the country, learned their military science from Professor Dennis Hart Mahan. His alumni formed a register of nearly all the high command of both armies. (USAMHI)

Left: The Army's military posts in the North continued their functions as before, only now incredibly more busily. The second oldest post in the nation was Carlisle Barracks, Pennsylvania. Here we see guard mounting at the cavalry school of practice in 1861. Portions of the barracks behind them will be sacked by Jeb Stuart's cavalry in 1863. (T. SCOTT SANDERS)

Left: The evidences of a nation at war were not hard to find. Fort Ellsworth in Alexandria, Virginia, named for the Union's first martyr. (USAMHI)

Right: Forrest Hall Military Prison in Georgetown, D.C. Next door a candy store, with jars of peppermint sticks in the window. (USAMHI)

Above: Industry for the war. A Du Pont powder mill near Wilmington, Delaware.(E.I. DU PONT DE NEMOURS & CO.)

Right: The Schuylkill Arsenal in Philadelphia. (KA)

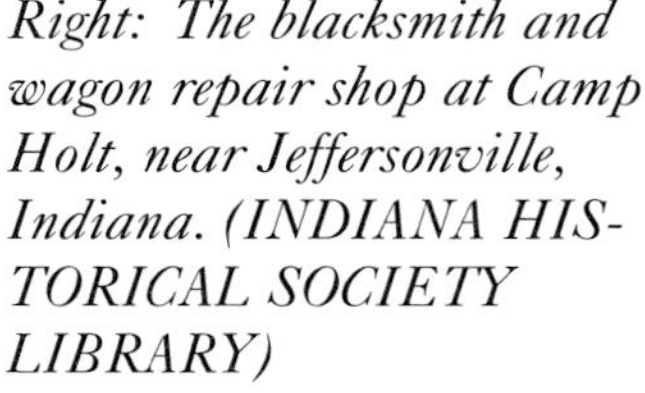

Right: The blacksmith and wagon repair shop at Camp Holt, near Jeffersonville, Indiana. (INDIANA HISTORICAL SOCIETY LIBRARY)

Left: While fighting all along its southern "borders," the Union also had to cast a careful eye to its northern boundaries, should Great Britain decide to aid the Confederacy. Then Canada would be a natural launching place for invasion. Major General John 1- Peck commanded the troops along the North's Canadian frontier in 1864-65. (P-M)

the North Barnum sent his traveling circus, the Grand Colossal Museum and Menagerie, with curiosities borrowed from the American Museum and animals gathered from every corner of the world.

As always in wartime, amusements offered a counterpoint to anxiety and uncertainty. To outward appearance, at least as the photographer captured it, life in the North hewed as closely to its normal patterns as was possible in an era of great duress. The camera recorded with an unblinking eye scenes of a wartime society clinging to its familiar habits while adjusting to changes imposed by the conflict. In so doing it portrayed the landscape of northern society unembellished and often unadorned. This fidelity freed later generations from the illustrator's imagination. Unlike the artist's drawing, the photograph offered viewers not an interpretation of a scene but some raw materials of a scene which one might interpret for himself.

More than this the camera could not do. For one thing the technology of photography was still in its infancy. Photographers still relied upon the wet-plate collodion process, a cumbersome and complicated business which required a wagonload of equipment, including a traveling dark tent for immediate developing, for all work done outside the studio. In effect the photographer could not operate abroad without carrying his laboratory with him. Even then he could not take action pictures with the equipment at his disposal.

In a real sense, then, the camera could capture little more than the bare surface of northern life during the war. On one hand, most of what was important took place beyond the photographer's—or anyone else's—eye; on the other, the technology of photography was unprepared to record the dynamism that was the essence of life in the North during these years.

War is not a still life, either on the battlefield or on the home front. The camera could preserve the residue of battle but not battle itself, the portraits of heroes but not their heroic deeds. Similarly, it might depict the stage, scenery, and characters of northern life, but not the dramatic action or inner moods and conflicts of the play itself. That realm still belonged to the writers, the painters, and the illustrators.

It is not possible to reconstruct the North at

war through photographs or any other artifacts. Through the camera's eye we may look down Broadway in New York or inspect a prison in Chicago or pause at a corner in Hanover Junction. We can feel the heat and drabness of a textile mill or watch track layers at work or fishing boats casting their nets off Narragansett Bay. Each of these pictures represents neither an action nor a scene but a single-frame, a fleeting moment of time frozen and preserved for our imaginations to mull over.

Nothing before the camera had the power to do even that. To those who possess an insatiable appetite for knowledge of the past and of our ancestors, these frozen fragments remain a towering achievement and a precious legacy. Previously it was scarcely possible to preserve intact even the faces, structures, and artifacts of history. In that sense the advent of the camera divides the historical record into two distinct epochs: that about which we have read or heard or viewed the remains of, and that which we have glimpsed with our own eyes, if only fleetingly and in part.

It is fortunate indeed that the Civil War lies, if only barely, upon the latter side of that division. Without these photographs our sense of what life was like in those terrible years would be much the poorer.

Above and Left: In all the major cities and ports, the barracks. Fort Richmond on Staten Island, New York. June 29, 1864. (USAMHI)

Below: Gunboats like the U.S.S. Michigan, *the Navy's first iron-hulled warship, built in 1844, cruised the Great Lakes during the war. (NAVAL PHOTOGRAPHIC CENTER)*

Left and below left: In the larger cities the churches and civic groups operated entertainment centers for the soldiers home on leave or recovering from their wounds. Here the "Union Volunteer Refreshment Saloon" in Philadelphia catered to the soldiers' tastes for food and beverage, if not ladies. (LO)

Below: But for most Northerners, the most common war experience was seeing the ever-present soldiers, either going or coming, in city and country. Hanover Junction, Pennsylvania, in November 1863, saw several, some obviously recuperating from wounds and walking with canes. (USAMHI)

Above: In the larger cities the churches and civic groups operated entertainment centers for the soldiers home on leave or recovering from their wounds. Here the "Union Volunteer Refreshment Saloon" in Philadelphia catered to the soldiers' tastes for food and beverage, if not ladies. (LO)

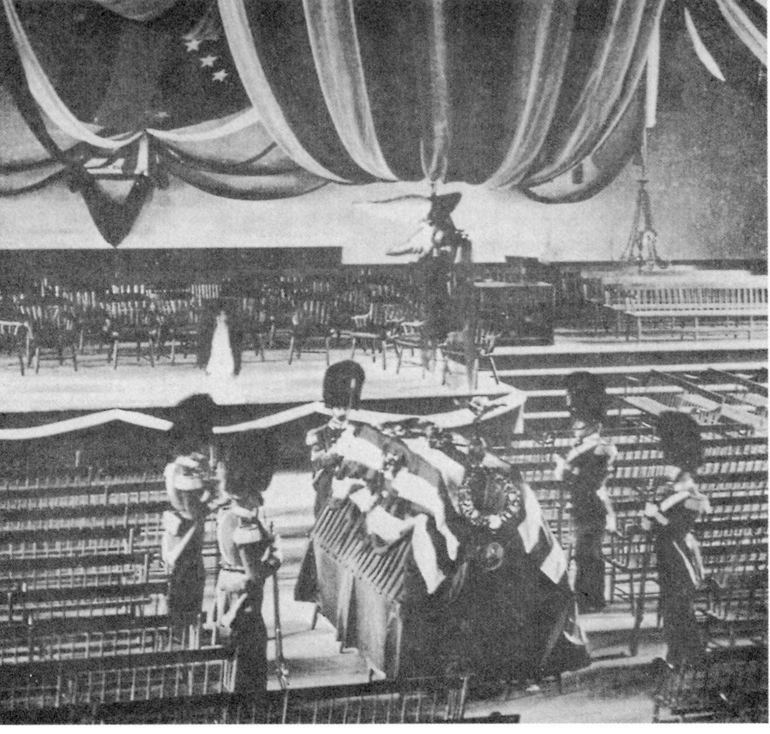

Above: The guard of honor for the funeral of Lieutenant Colonel George E. Marshall of the 40th Massachusetts, killed at Cold Harbor, Virginia, in June 1864. Here at home in Fitchburg, even the eagle above him is draped in mourning. (USAMHI)

Above: Happy were the men of the regiment whose enlistment expired. The 45th Massachusetts, at Readville, July 7, 1863, the day before they muster out. (MICHAEL J. HAMMERSON)

Below: The Ottawa, Illinois, home of Brigadier General W. H. L. Wallace, mortally wounded at Shiloh. His portrait, his riderless horse, the flag for which he died tell the whole story. (CHS)

Left: Homecoming for all too many, however, meant crepe and tears and the cold ground. It was a sight the North would become used to. (NA)

Above: Finally they will come in such numbers that the government must set aside special sanctuaries for its honored dead. A. J. Russell's photograph of the military cemetery at Alexandria. (NEIKRUG PHOTOGRAPHICA, LTD.)

Above: Only on a few occasions will the North actually feel the sting of the enemy's sword, and nowhere more than in Chambersburg, Pennsylvania. In July 1864, Confederates set the torch to the town when it could not raise a ransom. The fire devastated much of the town. This view by the Zacharias brothers looks down Queen Street. (MAURICE MAROTTE, JR.)

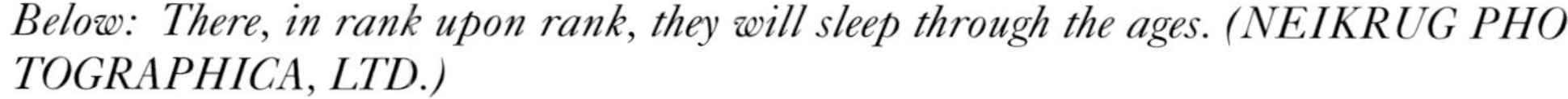

Below: There, in rank upon rank, they will sleep through the ages. (NEIKRUG PHOTOGRAPHICA, LTD.)

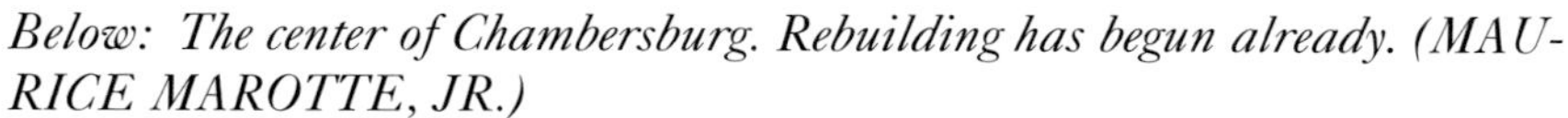

Below: The center of Chambersburg. Rebuilding has begun already. (MAURICE MAROTTE, JR.)

Left: Greater crises faced the nation than enemy raids. The men of the Supreme Court had to deal constantly with the limits of authority in an emergency, with habeas corpus, and the safety of the nation versus the rights of the individual. (NA)

Right: In December 1864, this military commission tried and convicted Indiana dissenter Lambden P. Milligan of treason and sentenced him to death. Two years later, in ex parte Milligan, *the Supreme Court would reverse that conviction. (INDIANA STATE LIBRARY)*

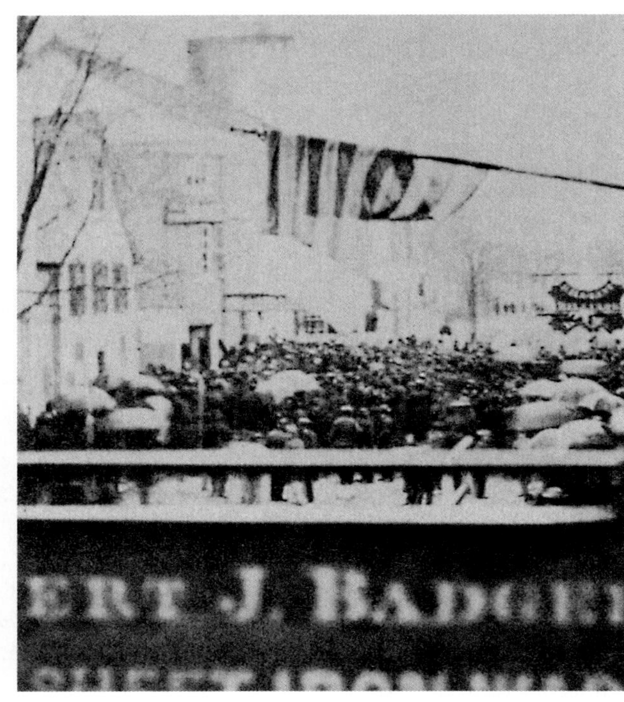

Above: Riots against the military draft in 1863 turned New York City into a bedlam, and left over 100 people dead. Lieutenant Commander Richard W. Meade, Jr., nephew of General George G. Meade, subdued the rioters. (USAMHI)

Above: "Copperhead" newspapers, those seemingly disloyal or opposed to the war on whatever grounds, were often mobbed and destroyed. In Portsmouth, New Hampshire, a mob gathers in front of the States & Union office angrily denouncing its editorial stance. The sudden appearance of rain dampened their ardor, and the newspaper was not molested. (USAMHI)

Right: In the North, war news came chiefly from the press, and the industry capitalized whenever possible on the salability of the most recent news. Here on June 9, 1862, the Pittsburgh Dispatch office advertises LATER FROM RICHMOND & MEMPHIS, Genl McClellan's Report of the Battle, Our loss in killed wounded & missing 5,134." Three days before, thirteen Union and Confederate ships met in the last fleet battle of the war at Memphis. On June 1 the Battle of Fair Oaks in McClellan's Peninsula Campaign concluded. The Dispatch was reporting both, and its billboard sign probably lists Pittsburghers injured in the battles. The editor, Joseph Singerly Lare, appears in top hat seated at the right on the second-floor ledge. (MRS. ALBERT MCBRIDE)

Far right: The Dispatch took offices above J. M. Fulton's Drug Store on Fifth Avenue. Interested citizens gathered outside on the sidewalk for the early edition with the latest news from the fronts. (MRS. ALBERT MCBRIDE)

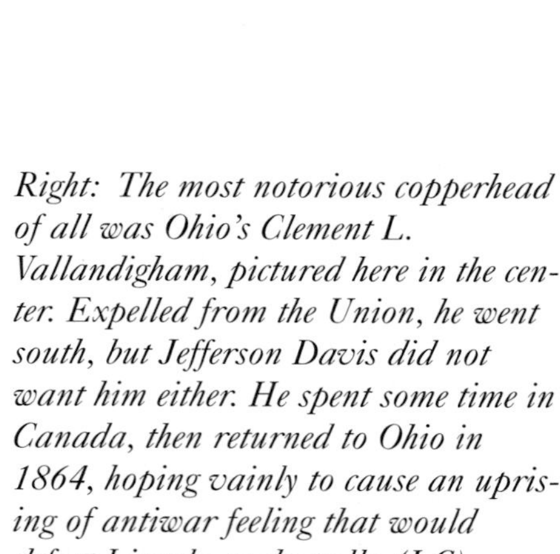

Right: The most notorious copperhead of all was Ohio's Clement L. Vallandigham, pictured here in the center. Expelled from the Union, he went south, but Jefferson Davis did not want him either. He spent some time in Canada, then returned to Ohio in 1864, hoping vainly to cause an uprising of antiwar feeling that would defeat Lincoln at the polls. (LC)

Above: *Running against Lincoln was his one-time general, George B. McClellan. Virtually shelved after Antietam in the fall of 1862, "Little Mac" accepted the Democratic nomination in 1864. There was no beating Lincoln. (USAMHI)*

Left: *Momence, Illinois, like most other towns in the Union, saw large demonstrations for Lincoln. He won handily. (CHS)*

Left: *Meanwhile, the people of the North watched and waited. The ladies sewed mammoth flags for the soldiers. These are the ladies of the Pennsylvania Academy of Fine Arts. (LO)*

Below: *Mammoth exhibitions were held to benefit soldiers' relief organizations, like the Union Avenue fair held in Philadelphia in 1864 by the Sanitary Commission. All manner of war relics were displayed, including ship's wheels from famous vessels, cases of bullets, flags, and even photographs. (RA)*

Below: *Art exhibited at the Sanitary Fair, including Emanuel Leutze's heroic depiction of Washington crossing the Delaware. (NA)*

Right: *New York's great Metropolitan Fair, the largest of its kind, attracted thousands. (NA)*

Above: They saw a wondrous array of relics, displayed in that cluttered fashion so beloved of the Victorians. Here the uniform of the martyr Elmer Ellsworth, stained with his holy blood. (NA)

Below: Captured enemy flags and relics of the battlefields. (NA)

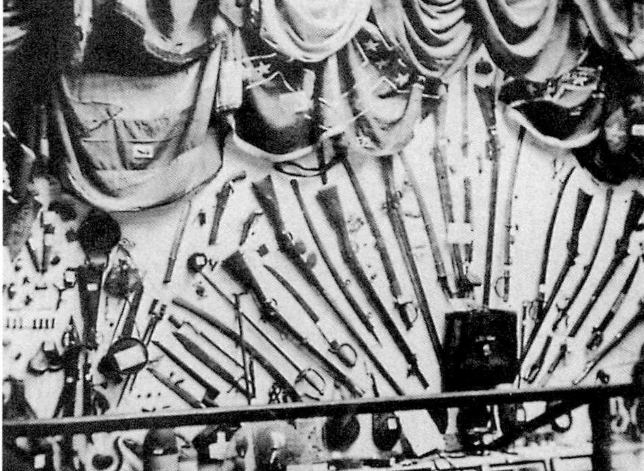

Above: All manner of weapons, and even soldier art works, like miniature churches fashioned during the long hours in winter quarters. (NA)

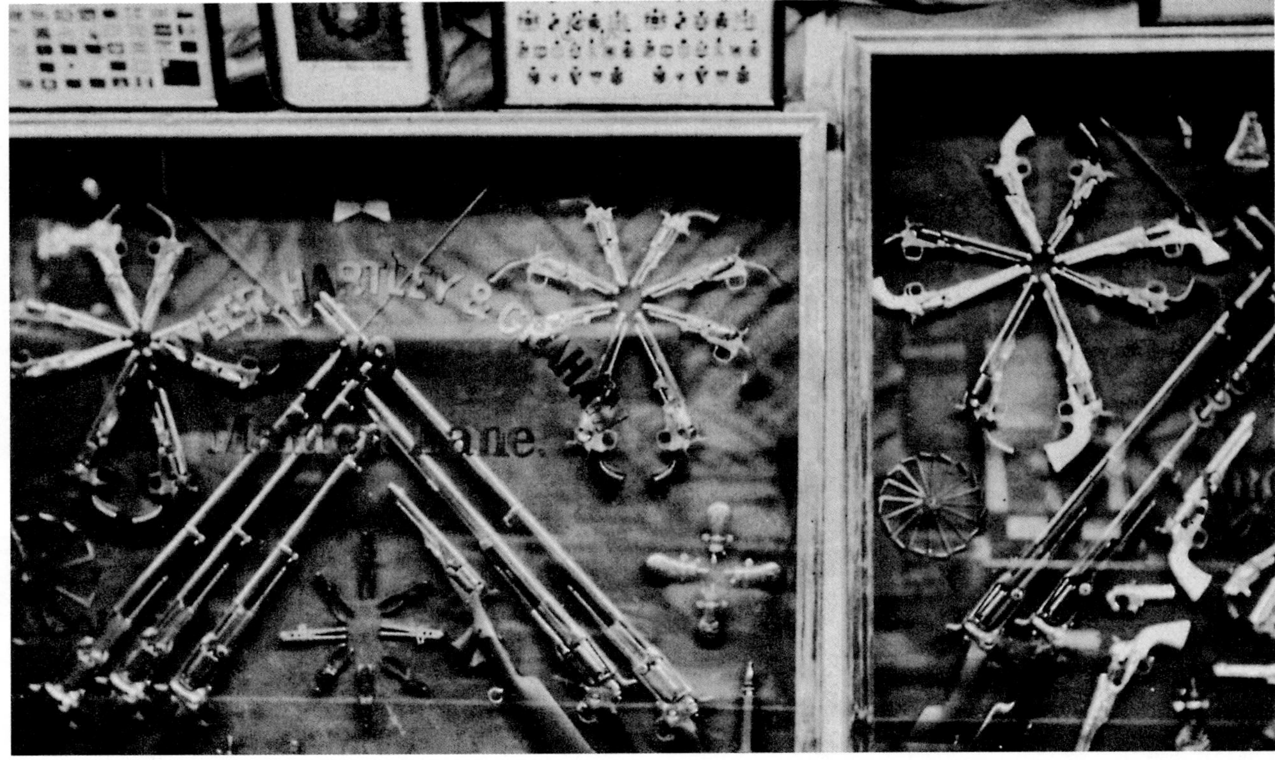

Above: Suppliers of military hardware displayed their stock. Here a complete exhibit of the pistols and accessories made by the Colt firearms company of Connecticut. The war made Samuel Colt a millionaire, and he sold to both sides. (NA)

Right: Giant projectiles, swords, rifles, axes, even items totally unrelated to the war, and much of it for sale to a souvenir-hungry public. "Relics from Vicksburg Sold Here." (NA)

Above: And for those not interested in the current war, a little something from an earlier era. (NA)

Right: Young girls shammed at soldiering for the camera, often to send to boyfriends in the Army. (WENDELL W. LANG, JR.)

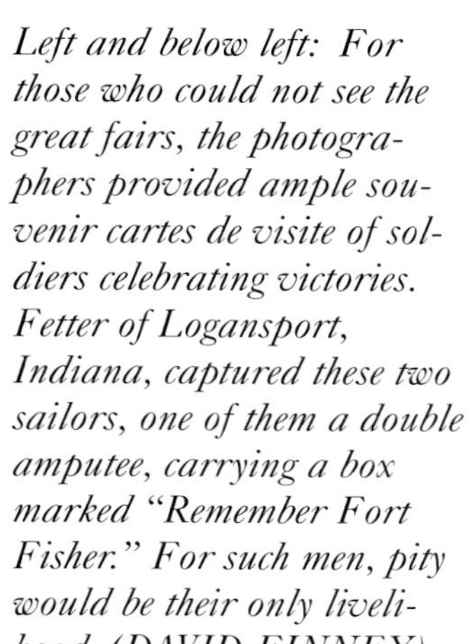

Left and below left: For those who could not see the great fairs, the photographers provided ample souvenir cartes de visite of soldiers celebrating victories. Fetter of Logansport, Indiana, captured these two sailors, one of them a double amputee, carrying a box marked "Remember Fort Fisher." For such men, pity would be their only livelihood. (DAVID FINNEY)

Above: And a few women who actually passed for men or otherwise served the Army, made capital of it at home. Actress Pauline Cushman (not a very good actress) publicized widely her activities as a spy (not a very good one) in Bragg's army. (LO)

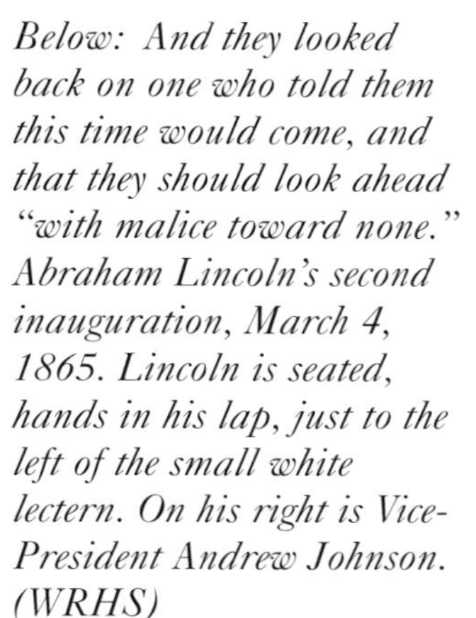

Below: And they looked back on one who told them this time would come, and that they should look ahead "with malice toward none." Abraham Lincoln's second inauguration, March 4, 1865. Lincoln is seated, hands in his lap, just to the left of the small white lectern. On his right is Vice-President Andrew Johnson. (WRHS)

Left: Another popular image, the old bugler and his dog. A Brady gallery photo taken at West Point in 1864. (LO)

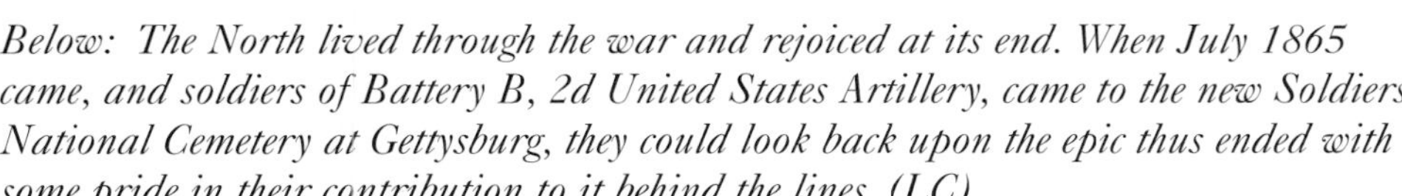

Below: The North lived through the war and rejoiced at its end. When July 1865 came, and soldiers of Battery B, 2d United States Artillery, came to the new Soldiers National Cemetery at Gettysburg, they could look back upon the epic thus ended with some pride in their contribution to it behind the lines. (LC)

The Photographers of the War

FREDERIC E. RAY

Historians with cameras and their journey for posterity

America, even more than Europe, fell in love with the camera. All across the land the photographers and their apparatus set to work. By 1860 there were over three thousand plying the trade, like this dour fellow, lens cap in hand, recording America and Americans. It is noted Oregon artist Peter Britt. (SOUTHERN OREGON HISTORICAL SOCIETY),

WHEN AMERICA WENT TO WAR, the camera went with it, and by 1861 neither was a stranger to the other. Photography, as an art and an industry, had already marked its first quarter century before the guns sounded. It had come a long way.

A Frenchman, Joseph-Nicephore Niepce, experimented with the camera obscura in the 1820S and in 1826 produced probably the first successful photograph on a polished pewter plate. The exposure took eight hours. Nine years later an Englishman, Henry Fox Talbot, developed the first practical imaging process. He called it the calotype and produced it by using paper sensitized with silver salts.

But it remained for another Frenchman, one time partner of Niepce, to make the photograph truly attainable. Louis-Jacques-Mande Daguerre announced his "Daguerreotype" in 1839. He used a sensitized, silver-coated copper plate to capture light images in less than one half hour. Unlike Talbot, Daguerre made his methods public and the daguerreotype quickly found enthusiastic acceptance in Europe.

Thanks to two remarkable men of genius, it also found its way to America almost from the moment of creation. Samuel F. B. Morse, inventor of the telegraph, visited Daguerre in Paris in 1839 and brought back with him the process. The next year he and John W. Draper, a noted New York physicist, began experiments which led shortly to a reduction in exposure time from half an hour to half a minute. At once a lucrative portrait business mushroomed in the country, and one of the principal proponents of this new process was upstate New Yorker Mathew B. Brady, whose fashionable New York and Washington studios would soon attract the notables of the day. Before long a "Brady" became the commonplace term for a portrait.

In 1851, seven years after Brady went into business, another Englishman, Frederick Scott Archer, developed the collodion or wet-plate process. By recording his image on a glass plate, thus producing a negative, he and his revolutionary invention enabled the multiple duplication of photographs printed on salt-or albumen-treated paper, whereas the daguerreotypist could make one image, and one only. Archer's soon became the accepted process for portrait photographers, and their profession spread throughout America. By 1860 there were 3,154 photographers, ambrotypists, daguerreotypists, calotypists, melainotypists, and practitioners of other varieties of the art, spread from New York to San Francisco, from Chicago to New Orleans. The image took America by storm.

By the early 1860s almost every middle-class family owned an album, filled not only with portraits of their own, but also with copies of mass produced images of their presidents, public figures, even actors and actresses. The carte de visite, a calling card-sized photograph ideally suited for albums—and for calling cards—became a rage. And for those wanting more realism, there was the stereoscopic view. The camera made two images simultaneously from two different lenses. They were mounted side by side on a card which, when viewed through a hand-held stereoscope, produced a three-dimensional picture. Thousands were sold to the parlors of America in the late 1850s.

With this market burgeoning just as the

Left: A burgeoning industry begins. In the years immediately prior to the Civil War, the homes of Europe and America discovered the photograph. Here, in an English shop, workers cut and mount stereoscopic views for home consumption, and the public's appetite was voracious. The raw prints hang in the background. The man in the white vest seated at the center is cutting them. Ladies at the table prepare the mounting boards and glue the prints to them, while the two boys standing at the left run the finished pieces through a press. And even here the camera captures not just a scene, but history. Times are starting to change. Men and women are working together in the same shop. Yet some things have not changed, for children are working with them, too, and the clock in the background shows it is nearly 6 P.M., with the day's work not yet done. (NYHS)

Right: Alexander Gardner's own 1863 image of his gallery on 7th and D streets, N.W., in Washington, D.C. Here one of the foremost photographers of the war made his headquarters when not in the field with the armies. Here he thumbed his nose at his one-time employer, Mathew B. Brady, whose own gallery stood nearby. While proclaiming his magnificent "Views of the War" being available on one side of his building, Gardner was a good enough businessman to devote even more advertising to the real bread and butter for all cameramen of the era, the portrait work in cartes de visite, ambrotypes, and a variety of other techniques. (LC)

nation went to war in 1861, the economic potential of supplying war scenes to the public became self evident. And others had already led the way in previous conflicts. Fifteen years before, an anonymous daguerreotypist went to Saltillo during the war with Mexico and made at least four outdoor military images that have survived. One shows Major General John E. Wool and his staff astride their horses in the streets of the city and is remarkable for its clarity. Several years later, during the Crimean War, a British artist turned photographer, Roger Fenton, employed the collodion process to capture over 350 images of the war in the Crimea.

And then the Civil War. In fact, the first artists to recognize and attempt to exploit its possibilities were southern photographers, and it is a happy thing for posterity that they did. Just a few months later the blockade so restricted the necessary imported chemicals and supplies that Confederate artists could no longer afford the highly speculative business of taking outdoor war views. After 1861 they almost exclusively used their carefully husbanded materials for the indoor portrait work that made their livelihood.

Simultaneously they descended on Charleston and Pensacola. Within days after the surrender of Fort Sumter, F. K. Houston of 307

Above: Brady and Gardner had the big studios, but hundreds of others like Bowdoin, Taylor & Company's gallery at 204 King Street in Alexandria, Virginia, operated the studios that most Americans saw. Always there was the large opening in the roof to let in the sunlight essential for the camera and always the case of samples displayed outside the front door. (T. SCOTT SANDERS)

Right: And once the war came, the photographers proved nearly as fascinated by themselves at their work as they were with the conflict itself. Just as the Confederates fired the first shots of the war, so, too, did Confederate photographers take the first shots, both of the war and themselves. Even before the pioneering J. D. Edwards went to Pensacola, the remarkable Osborn & Durbec of King Street in Charleston captured Fort Sumter as surely and completely as did Beauregard.

Among their host of images stands this faded stereo print. It is unique, from a photographic viewpoint perhaps the most important Confederate picture from the entire war. The chief focus of attention are the men and two guns of the Trapier Mortar Battery on Morris Island, guns that bombarded Sumter. But what makes this photo so important is what lies hidden in the background. Lost for over a century and here published for the first time, this is the only known view of Confederate photographic apparatus in the field. Behind the mortar on the right stands a large pyramidal object, and just faintly visible on it are the words "Osborn & Durbec 223 King St." This is their portable darkroom, required for the speedy development of the emulsions of the era.

One of the great misfortunes of a tragic war is that the scarcity of chemicals and materials prevented artists of the caliber of Edwards and Osborn & Durbec from doing for their side of the conflict what Brady and others did for his. (TU)

Right: Mathew B. Brady, the entrepreneurial genius who so identified himself with Civil War photography that for over a century afterward almost every Civil War image was just naturally assumed to be a "Brady." This somewhat retouched image purports to show him in field costume on July 22, 1861, the day he returned to Washington from the battlefield at Bull Run. Brady's whole story of his trip to the battle with McDowell's army is highly suspect, but the evidences of his showmanship in this photo are undeniable. Already he had begun to make Americans believe that he was the war photographer. (USAMHI)

Below: Thanks to his failing eyesight, Brady probably spent little if any time behind the camera during the war. But he certainly spent a lot of time in front of it. In top hat he poses next to General Samuel P. Heintzelman and with members of the general's staff on the steps of Arlington House, the former home of Robert E. Lee, in Arlington, Virginia. It is the late summer of 1861, following the debacle at Bull Run. (LC)

Right: At Blackburn's Ford, by the wateis of Bull Run, two photographers pause for a glass in March 1862. (LC)

King Street in Charleston set his camera within the parade ground of the fortress and captured it himself on his wet plates. On April 17 arrived James Osborn and F. E. Durbec of Osborn & Durbec's Southern Stereoscopic & Photographic Depot on 223 King Street, at the "sign of the Big Camera." Their epic coverage of the fort and its environs would not be surpassed during the rest of the war. And at the same time, far away in Pensacola, Florida, J. D. Edwards of New Orleans began his own epic. Others, George S. Cook of Charleston and J. W. Petty of New Orleans, for instance, made less ambitious forays from their studios, but after the first spring of the war, they rarely did so again. Only Cook took one brief sortie in 1863, again to Sumter. For the rest of the war they would not be heard from again.

Then came Brady. "I can only describe the destiny that overruled me by saying that, like Euphorion, I felt that I had to go." So he said, and so he did. Perhaps he was urged by the example of Edwards and the others—for he and the North knew of their work—but more likely he and they had the same idea at the same time. In July 1861, excited by the prospect of capturing scenes of the then three-month-old war, he claimed to have accompanied McDowell's army on the road to Bull Run.

"I went to the first Battle of Bull Run with two wagons," he said. His innovative portable dark room, a wagon hooded in black, was dubbed the "what-is-it" wagon. Clad in linen duster and straw hat, Brady says he "got as far as Blackburne's Ford." "We made pictures and expected to be in Richmond next day, but it was not so, and our apparatus was a good deal damaged on the way back to Washington." So Brady claimed thirty years later. In fact, no verifiable images from the first expedition have survived. Some that Brady later said were taken then, actually date months later, calling into question his entire account of his first trip to the front. Brady was first and foremost a businessman, a promoter, and his stories of many of his war exploits are highly colored by exaggeration.

Brady's eyesight was failing and he relegated the actual camera work to his assistants. He appears frequently in front of the camera in a number of his war views, but it is probable that he did not expose any images in the field himself. Throughout the war years, he only occasionally ventured to the armies, and instead spent his time in New York and Washington, supervising his flourishing portrait business and amassing the collection of views taken by his assistants and others that he would produce as "Brady's Album Gallery" and other series. In addition, his views were widely published by the illustrated weeklies of the day, *Harper's* and *Frank Leslie's*, whose artists rendered the images into woodcuts.

The men actually following the armies for Brady were a remarkable array of artists: Alexander and James Gardner, Timothy O'Sullivan, William Pywell, George N. Barnard, David Woodbury, E. Guy Foux, James F. Gibson, Stanley Morrow, James Reekie, and several others. Some were out standing. O'Sullivan would produce many of the best-known war scenes. Alexander Gardner and O'Sullivan together were unequaled in their coverage of the Army of the Potomac and both captured many scenes which transcended photography to be come genuine art. Gibson would become Brady's partner late in the war. Woodbury and others would journey to Gettysburg in November 1863 to preserve for the future the historic gathering at the dedication of the National Cemetery. Lincoln can be discerned on the speakers' platform from which he would deliver his now famous address. Gardner, too, would capture Lincoln in the field, during his visit to General McClellan at Antietam in 1862. Several, most notably Gardner and O'Sullivan, eventually leave Brady when he refuses them credit for their work.

In fact, there were several varieties of photographers with and around the armies during the Civil War. Very few enjoyed a truly official position. Indeed, probably only one, Captain A. J. Russell, can be called a genuine Army photographer. Working for the U. S. Military Railroad, he operated the War Department's only photographic laboratory. His images are among the best that survive from the war.

Far more common were the artists who occasionally took contracts from the War Department for special assignments. George N. Barnard is the most notable for his series of views of the fortifications around Atlanta following its capture. Samuel A. Cooley was paid to photograph government warehouses and other installations at Hilton Head, South Carolina, in 1864. And several, among them Alexander Gardner, worked at enlarging and photographically copying maps for distribution in the armies.

Yet most of the war photographers, like Brady and his assistants, enjoyed no connection at all with the authorities. Rather, they were businessmen looking for profits. If they could obtain a pass from the generals commanding, they might travel freely among the troops, capturing scenes for their stereo and carte de visite series to sell in the North, and doing a lucrative trade in selling portraits to the soldiers. And many of them simply happened to be in the right place at the right time. The war came to them. When the armies reached Corinth, Mississippi, Howard & Hall and Armistead & White were there ready to take their trade. When the Federals occupied Baton Rouge, McPherson & Oliver and the prolific

Above: At Sudley Springs on the Manassas battlefield, the cameramen left their equipment wagon across the stream, then waded over to capture the scene, and with it their footprints in the mud. (LC)

Left: One of the war's finest young photographers was Timothy O'Sullivan, among the first northern cameramen to return to South Carolina with the invading Federals. At Beaufort, in April 1862, he recorded an outstanding series of images, and this one probably includes himself, seated second from the right, at his 'mess." (USAMHI)

Left: Photographers went with the army of McClellan to Yorktown in May 1862. (LC)

Left: Their portable darkroom intrigued a boatload of soldiers at White House on the Pamunkey River. (WRHS)

Right: Timothy O'Sullivan, "Our Artist at Manassas," the brilliant and energetic cameraman who covered most of the Civil War in the East, and later took his lenses to the West and to Central America. (LARRY J. WEST)

Left: When the armies returned to Manassas in July 1862, so did O'Sullivan, who pauses here for a drink beside his "what's it" wagon on the Fourth of July. (LC)

Above: The equipment box in the front of the wagon says "Brady's Washington." The men are two of his numerous assistants, the one seated at left probably being David B. Woodbury, arguably the best of the artists who stayed with Brady throughout the war. (LC)

Right: Timothy O'Sullivan's wagon stands at the end of a bridge built by McDowell's engineers across Bull Run in August 1862, just before he met defeat for the second time on the same ground. (LC)

Andrew D. Lytle happily accommodated them, doing a brisk business not only in studio portraits, but also in outdoor views. At New Bern, North Carolina, J. L. Dowling gladly obliged the Massachusetts troops occupying the town by accepting their custom. Of those who took their operations where the soldiers were, Samuel Cooley proved the most ambitious. He operated four separate galleries, three in South Carolina and one in Jacksonville, Florida. And surely no one surpassed the flair for scenic back drop of R. M. Linn. Perched atop Lookout Mountain, his "Gallery Point Lookout" offered the grandeur of the valley of Chattanooga as background for the portraits he made. A few northern artists made special trips to the field just to capture the doings of home state boys for civilian consumption. G. H. Houghton of Brattleboro, Vermont, made scores of outstanding images with the Vermont regiments in McClellan's army on the Peninsula, then took them home to sell to friends and loved ones.

By contrast, as already noted, Confederate field photography almost ceased to exist after 1861. Thus, the photographic record of the Confederacy is limited largely to formal studio portraits of its statesmen and military figures. Charles Rees of Richmond did venture outdoors in 1863 or 1864 to capture two images of the infamous Libby Prison, and another of Belle Isle in the James River. A. J. Riddle of Georgia took his camera to Andersonville in 1864 and there made a handful of poignant scenes of the thousands of Union prisoners in captivity. And at Brownsville, Texas, A. G. Wedge of Matamoros, Mexico, took his camera across the Rio Grande to photograph the Confederate evacuation. But these were the exceptions.

As the war stretched on, photographers followed the armies through most major campaigns, capturing nearly everything in sight. The most trivial things seemed to fascinate them, and they dearly loved to catch themselves at their work as well. A time exposure of several seconds was necessary for the successful transmission of light on the collodion plate, and the pictures thus necessarily resulted in somewhat frozen "still life" images. There are no real "action" pictures from the war. Artists deceptively posed many of their views to appear to be action scenes—cannoneers positioned at their guns, troops on parade and drill field. And at times the camera came close to battle, as at Antietam and in front of Petersburg. George Cook actually recorded accidentally the explosion of a Federal shell inside Fort Sumter in 1863. Yet for most practical purposes, the darkroom wagon could only be deployed behind the lines because of the time-consuming procedures required for taking such pictures.

These operations were tedious and exacting. The usual medium for the images was a supply of clear glass plates varying in size, but usually eight by ten inches or about four by ten inches for stereo views, carried in dust-proof boxes. When ready to expose, the artist carefully coated a plate with collodion made of a solution of gun cotton in equal parts of sulphuric ether and 95 proof alcohol. Bromide and iodine of potassium or ammonia were then added, sensitizing the surface of the plate. After letting the ether and alcohol evaporate to the right texture, the plate was immersed for three to five minutes in a bath holder solution of silver nitrate. This must be done in absolute darkness, or at best a dull amber light. The sensitized plate then went into a holder for insertion in the camera, which had already been aimed and focused. Uncapping the lens permitted an exposure of from five to thirty seconds, depending on available sunlight. Then the operator had just a few minutes to remove the plate from the camera, return it to the darkroom wagon, and develop it in a solution of sulfate of iron and acetic acid. Then it was washed to remove surplus silver with a solution of cyanide of potassium, and finally washed again, dried, and varnished.

Considering the conditions under which the war photographers worked, and the attendant chances of spoiling their plates during any one of the thirteen separate steps, the degree of quality and clarity achieved in their images is truly remarkable. A century later the best techniques could hardly do better.

The darkroom wagons in which they worked, and which so often appear in the background of their images, were well described by photographer George Rockwood some years after the war as "an ordinary delivery wagon of the period."

[It] had a strong step attached at the rear and below the level of the wagon floor. A door was put on at the back, carefully hung so as to be light-proof. The door... came down over the step which was boxed in at the sides, making it a sort of well within the body of the wagon rather than a true step. The work of coating or sensitizing the plates and that of developing them was done from this well, in which there was just room enough to work. As the operator stood there the collodion was within reach of his right hand, in a special receptacle. On his left also was the holder of one of the baths. The chief developing bath was in front, with the tanks of various liquids stored in front of it again, and the space between it and the floor filled with plates.

On exceptional occasions in very cold weather the life of a wet plate might be extended to nearly an hour on either side of the exposure, the coating or the development side, but

Left: The men who made the pictures. The first publication of a remarkable image taken at Berlin, Maryland, October 28, 1862. Standing at right is Mathew Brady. David B. Woodbury crouches to the right of him. The other assistants are, left to right, Silas Holmes, a cook named Stephen, E. T. Whitney, Hodges, and a teamster named Jim. No other surviving image from the war shows Brady and his assistants in such detail, and their equipment as well. These are some of the men who did the real work for which Brady took credit. (KA)

Right: Brady surveys the ruins of the United States Arsenal at Harpers Ferry in October 1862. He stands at right in this image by his assistant David B. Woodbury. (USAMHI)

Below: Brady, standing at right, again by Woodbury. He looks across the Potomac River, with the Arsenal ruins in the background. (LC)

Right: Major General Ambrose Burnside had no idea this shot of him was being taken. He just finished posing for Brady's camera operator and had sat down on a sack of oats to read a newspaper. Brady, in the straw hat, instructed his assistant to take another shot and then sat in the chair facing the general. He loved to pose with the generals. (USAMHI)

Above: O'Sullivan's photograph of his winter quarters with telegraphers at Brandy Station, Virginia, in 1863. (LC)

Left: When the armies came to Gettysburg, so did the cameras. William H. Tipton sits aboard the Tyson Brothers' darkroom wagon in front of the house that served Union General George G. Meade as headquarters during the battle. (DONALD TYSON)

Right: The tent of an army photographer in camp along the Rappahannock in 1863. (DON W. MINDEMANN)

Left: At Chattanooga, Tennessee. Morse from Huntsville, Alabama, and his "Gallery of the Cumberland.') (USAMHI)

ordinarily the work had to be done within a very few minutes, and every minute of delay resulted in loss of brilliancy and depth in the negative.

To be sure, other processes were used as well. Most of the portraits of private soldiers that were made in the camps were ambrotypes, or tintypes, cheap processes within reach of the lowly private's pocketbook. The image on a tintype was caught on a small iron sheet plated with tin and coated with black lacquer. The ambrotype was a glass negative mounted against a dark background to produce a positive image. Unlike the true print derived from the collodion negatives, daguerreotypes, ambrotypes, and tintypes, were almost always mirrored copies of the subject. This reverse image called for some simple ingenuity on the part of the photographer in posing his subjects. Accoutrements were often reversed on the person of the sitter to present them correctly in the finished picture. Even belt plates bearing the letters "US" were turned upside down, presenting a perfect "S" to be sure, but a somewhat peculiar "U."

With these hundreds of photographers traveling the country, there was little that they missed, and most of what they caught has survived. Yet, there are still the "might have been's." A Chambersburg, Pennsylvania, photographer named Bishop is supposed to have arranged his camera in a window in anticipation of the arrival of General Lee during 1863's Gettysburg Campaign. The camera attracted the attention of Confederate soldiers and teamsters along the curbstones who arose to get into the image, thereby blocking Bishop's view of their general and robbing posterity of a memorable moment in time. Off Cherbourg, France, in 1864, the photographer Francois Rondin set up his camera and made an exposure of the battle raging at sea between the U.S.S. *Kearsarge* and the dreaded Confederate commerce raider C.S.S. *Alabama*. Seen widely at the time in the window of Rondin's Cherbourg shop, the priceless print has disappeared. A dozen or more wartime images of Abraham Lincoln are known to have been taken, but are now lost. A much rumored photograph taken from aloft in a Federal observation balloon has yet to surface, if indeed it was ever really taken.

Yet what does survive is truly staggering. An enormous debt is owed for the legacy left by those enterprising men with their little wagons, rolling over rutted roads with their fragile contents, hauling their clumsy cameras in camp and battlefield, occasionally risking their lives, and recording history as it had never been done before.

Mathew Brady, as usual, speaks for all of them, and largely it was through his energy and initiative that they all preserved for generations to come the image of the war and its people. "I felt that I had to go," he would say. "A spirit in my feet said 'Go' and I went."

Left: The tent of an army photographer in camp along the Rappahannock in 1863. (DON W. MINDEMANN)

Above: Jefferson Rock at Harpers Ferry, overlooking the Shenandoah River, and the "Jefferson's Rocks Photographs" establishment. A soldier poses on the rock while the artist aims the camera out the window of the "gallery." (RP)

Above: And at Lookout Mountain, near Chattanooga, in 1864. Royan M. Linn was the "Brady" of itinerant portrait photographers. He sold himself almost as well as he sold his carte de visite portraits taken at his "Gallery Point Lookout." Establishing himself on the summit of this scenic promontory, Linn sold thousands of images of generals and soldiers posing on the point. Here "Linn of Lookout" himself sits, cane in hand, beside a stereo camera. Over his shoulder is spread the majesty of the Tennessee River. Here was a man with an eye for grandeur. (NA)

Above: At Chattanooga again. (USAMHI)

Left: Disdaining Brady's taste for notables, when Linn posed with others he selected commonplace people. Brady would never have been seen in a stovepipe hat aboard an ox-drawn wagon. (TERENCE P. O'LEARY)

Above: Linn once again at Pulpit Rock, another favorite posing place for his subjects. (KA)

Left: Linn fascinated himself. Here he or an assistant photographs Brigadier General Thomas Sweeny, standing above the group of soldiers at left. (USAMHI)

Above: Western photographers, though less numerous than those in the East, still made their mark, and put themselves in the picture.

A landmark of the western campaigns was Corinth, Mississippi's Tishomingo Hotel. Usually unnoticed in the war images of the hotel is the rather considerable establishment to its left, "Howard & Hall Photographers." They could boast no less than three sunlights in their roof. (CHS)

Above: Vicksburg's "Washington Photograph Gallery," headquarters of Joslyn & Smith. (JOHN A. HESS)

Above: Competition among these western artists was sometimes stiff When Brigadier General Grenville Dodge and his staff posed beside their campaign maps for Howard and Hall... (MICHAEL J. HAMMERSON)

Above: Little Rock, Arkansas, in 1863 went onto emulsion for posterity in a splendid series of views taken by "White's Photograph Gallery." The studio appears at the lower right, its awninged sunlight extended toward the Arkansas River. Unusual for their striking clarity and quality, White's photographs have never been published before. (NA)

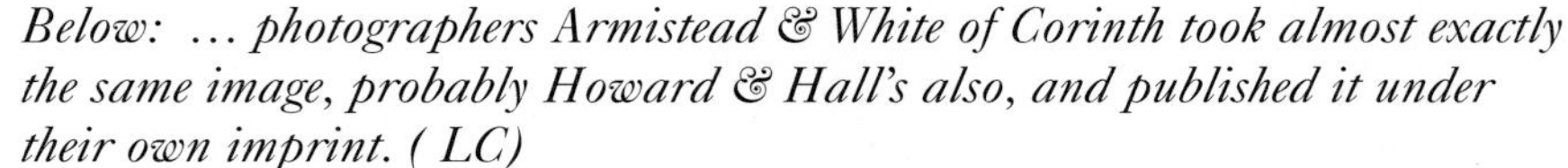

Below: ... photographers Armistead & White of Corinth took almost exactly the same image, probably Howard & Hall's also, and published it under their own imprint. (LC)

Right: A. D. Lytle of Baton Rouge, Louisiana, one of the most prolific of the western artists. Besides extensive portrait work, he took his camera outdoors and captured a remarkably complete record of a southern city under Union occupation. It was erroneously believed after the war that he used his camera to furnish information via photographs to the Confederates. (LSU)

Above: In 1864, with the main focus of the war in the East, so was the chief focus of the cameras. Stanley J. Morrow, a soldier stationed at the Point Lookout, Maryland, prison camp, learned the trade—from Brady himself he would claim—and opened his own studio. If his sunlight cover looks rather makeshift, how much more so is his business sign. Hopefully Morrow planned his darkroom operations better than he did the lettering for his "Picture Ga…" (STANLEY J . MORROW COLLECTION, W. H. OVER MUSEUM)

Above: James Gardner, brother of Alexander, one of the many unsung true photographic artists of the war. (LJW)

Above: Timothy O'Sullivan caught on June 13, 1864, this almost ghostly scene of a photographer and his camera, just beneath the tree at left, about to shoot a private soldier at Charles City Court House, Virginia. (LC)

Above: Timothy O'Sullivan again, like his profession, a little older and experienced in war. (LJW)

Above: "Bergstressers' Photographic Studio." Attaching themselves to the V Corps of the Army of the Potomac, three brothers, A. J., S. L., and J. Bergstresser, took their tintype or "melainotype" establishment to the front and flourished. The Pennsylvanian artists stayed with the Army for two years or more and took, said an observer, "the Lord only knows how many thousand portraits." Operating more than one gallery, and charging one dollar for a portrait, they sometimes took 160 in a day. "If anybody knows an easier and better way of making money than that," said a New York newspaper, "the public should know of it."

The Bergstressers were not only enterprising, but also innovative. Rather than building a permanent sunlight into this rude log studio, they put in a sliding roof. (USAMHI)

Above: The interior of a photographer's winter quarters. On the wall behind him to the right hang several of the brass or copper frames used for cased ambrotypes. (RP)

Above: One of Brady's wagons at Cold Harbor in June 1864. The photographer could develop his negatives at the back of the wagon, under the black hood. (LC)

Above: Soldiers posing for the camera are joined by a one-eyed visitor, the camera on the ground at lower left. (NA)

Right: Sherman's great photographer during the Atlanta Campaign, George N. Barnard, posing for Brady's camera. One of the very few artists to be paid by the United States Army, Barnard was commissioned to record photographically Atlanta and its defenses. (KA)

Above: June 1864, Bermuda Hundred, Virginia. The signal tower built by General Benjamin F. Butler, a flag-holding signalman atop it, seems almost an extension of the Brady wagon and operator. (LC)

Above: A photographer's printing room at Bermuda Hundred. (JOHN A. HESS)

Right: Barnard's portable darkroom, chemicals, and other equipment attract the attention of several of Sherman's "bummers" in abandoned Confederate trenches southeast of Atlanta. (LC)

Above: Henry P. Moore opened his "DAGTYPS" gallery on Hilton Head, South Carolina, in 1862, and concentrated his efforts chiefly on the men of the 3d New Hampshire. Outdoor views like this one, however, were not daguerreotypes but wet-plate photographs. (LC)

Above: "Sam A. Cooley. U.S. Photographer. Department of the South." That is how he billed himself, never hesitant to make capital on his quasi-official position as a contract artist for the Army in South Carolina. Hucksterism aside, he proved to be one of the most talented camera artists of the war. (WRHS)

Above: "Robbers' Row" in Hilton Head. Here the sutlers and camp followers set up their wares to lure the soldiers' money. Moore was one of them, and his gallery stands second building from the left, the simple sign "PHOTOGRAPHS" stating his business. (USAMHI)

Above: "Cooley's," headquarters in Beaufort, South Carolina, for the enterprising Samuel Cooley. (WRHS)

Above: Cooley, Genter, with his associates and his own improved version of the "what's it" wagon. It paid to advertise. (USAMHI)

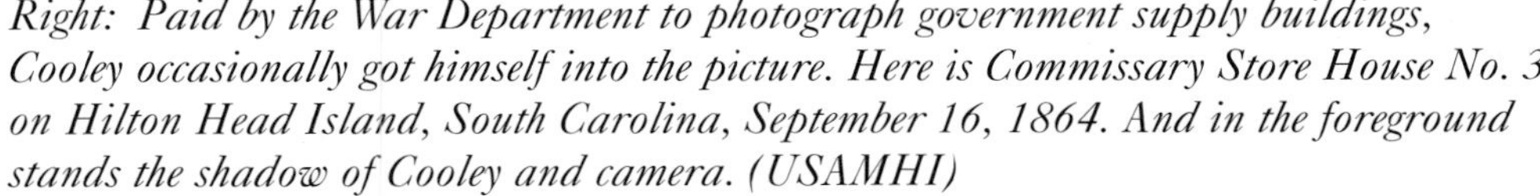

Right: Paid by the War Department to photograph government supply buildings, Cooley occasionally got himself into the picture. Here is Commissary Store House No. 3 on Hilton Head Island, South Carolina, September 16, 1864. And in the foreground stands the shadow of Cooley and camera. (USAMHI)

Left: For many of the war's photographers, their images of themselves at work are all by which we can remember their names. Take J. L. Dowling of New Bern, North Carolina. He made a remarkable series of prints of the Federal troops occupying his town in 1862 and 1863; yet, while they survive, he is totally forgotten. His recognition depends entirely on this one photograph of his "Ambrotype & Daguerreotype Gallery" situated on a second floor above a drug store. The focus may seem to be the men of the 25th Massachusetts lounging below. But the real attraction is in the window above Dowling's sign. There, standing beside his camera, is the artist himself. This was a man with style. (USAMHI)

Above: George S. Cook, the Confederate photographer who, in 1863, braved Federal fire to take his camera out onto Fort Sumter to record the ruin caused by the enemy's bombardment. Two years before, he made the same trip to capture the images of Major Robert Anderson and his officers as they were about to become the targets of the first shots of the war. (VM)

Above: Alexander Gardner established a great reputation in the Civil War, then enhanced it by going to the Far West immediately afterward to record the opening of the new country. (LJW)

Above: One of Brady's photographic wagons at City Point, Virginia, during the Siege of Petersburg. A familiar sight by now, the "what's it" wagons no longer attracted the attention they once enjoyed. (NA, U. S. SIGNAL CORPS PHOTO, BRADY COLLECTION)

Right: Three photographers lie asleep in the shade of their tent near Petersburg, their wagon in the background, while a fourth writes a letter and a Zouave private apparently wanders into the picture. (LC)

Left: Some artists' chief official services for the War Department came in copying maps for the Topographical Engineers Corps. Here in March 1865, in front of Petersburg, a camera is ready to shoot a map for reproduction. (USAMHI)

Above: "Photographic Wagon, Engineer Department." Perhaps part of Gardner's equipment, shown amid the bomb proofs at Petersburg in the fall of 1864. (LC)

Above: The goal of four years at last attained. Richmond, taken from the south side of the James River, in April 1865. In the foreground stands a portable darkroom and operator at work, which explains the blur of the cameraman who is developing his image. Across the river, the large brick building, painted white on its lower stories, is the infamous Libby Prison. An Egbert G. Foux image, an associate of A. J. Russell. (WRHS)

Left: Richmond in Federal hands, and a stereo camera ready to complete the conquest. (THE MESERVE COLLECTION)

Above: A heavily retouched photo of Messrs. Levy & Cohen of 9th and Filbert streets, Philadelphia. Their series of photographs taken in Richmond immediately after its fall are among the best produced by anyone. Levy's untimely death six months later from a heart attack prevented the firm from publishing and distributing their prints. Instead, their negatives were sold, and never presented to the public until now. (KA)

Left: April 8, 1865, while Grant is cornering Lee at Appomattox, Brady is already in Richmond posing for his own cameras. Here at Pratt's Castle on Gambler's Hill, he stands in top hat, the war that made him great almost done. (USAMHI)

Right: Federal artists were quick to make use of captured Confederate photographs, and one of their favorites was southern photographer Charles Rees's print of Libby Prison in Richmond, taken probably in 1863. It was found after Richmond's fall, and several northern operators published it over their own copyright. This print was part of "Levy & Cohen's Views of the Rebel Capital and Its Environs." It is one of the very few photographs showing Confederate men and officers outdoors. Libby's commandant, Richard Turner, stands third from the left in the foreground. (KA)

Below: At the end of the long road, the war and the camera have come full circle. Here at Fort Sumter they meet again in April 1865, four years after the beginning. Samuel Cooley prepares to photograph the remnant of a once mighty parapet. The guns are now stilled. The war's final shots belong to the camera. (LC)

Above: Samuel Cooley photographs a soldier in the ruins of Fort Sumter in April 1865. (LC)

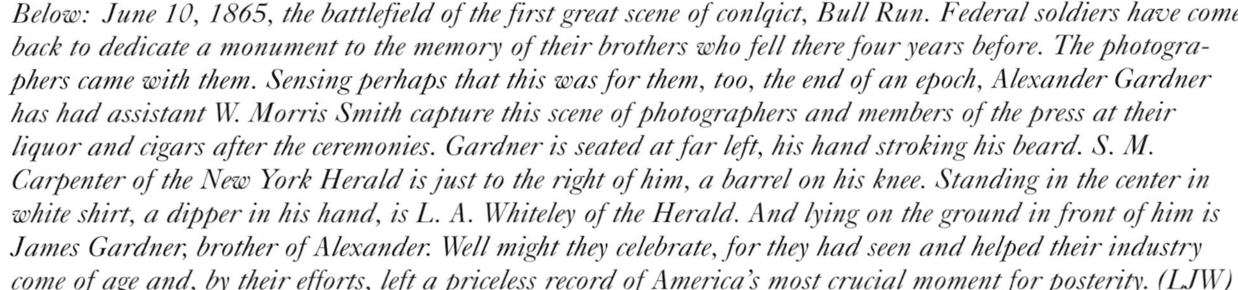

Below: June 10, 1865, the battlefield of the first great scene of conlqict, Bull Run. Federal soldiers have come back to dedicate a monument to the memory of their brothers who fell there four years before. The photographers came with them. Sensing perhaps that this was for them, too, the end of an epoch, Alexander Gardner has had assistant W. Morris Smith capture this scene of photographers and members of the press at their liquor and cigars after the ceremonies. Gardner is seated at far left, his hand stroking his beard. S. M. Carpenter of the New York Herald is just to the right of him, a barrel on his knee. Standing in the center in white shirt, a dipper in his hand, is L. A. Whiteley of the Herald. And lying on the ground in front of him is James Gardner, brother of Alexander. Well might they celebrate, for they had seen and helped their industry come of age and, by their efforts, left a priceless record of America's most crucial moment for posterity. (LJW)

THE GUNS OF '62

Part of the ruin of 1862. Rolling stock of the Orange & Alexandria Railroad, once used to supply a Union Army marching to Manassas, and now destroyed by it to deny it to the victorious Confederates. It, like so many other scenes this year, is indicative of the almost constant defeat suffered by the North. (U.S. ARMY MILITARY HISTORY INSTITUTE, CARLISLE BARRACKS, PENNSYLVANIA)

Yorktown: The First Siege

WARREN W. HASSLER, JR.

A "Napoleon," a "Prince John," and other dignitaries do battle for Richmond

Above: Major General John E. Wool, a hero of the Mexican War, turned seventy-seven just before the outbreak of war. Yet he showed no lack of energy in immediately ensuring the safety of Fort Monroe at Hampton Roads, Virginia, a vital base in Confederate territory, and in the course of the war a staging area for more than one major campaign. In the coming campaign for Yorktown… (U.S. ARMY MILITARY HISTORY INSTITUTE)

YORKTOWN ! Mere mention of the Virginia river port could conjure heroic images of great historical moment to both Northerners and Southerners at the start of the Civil War.

Both sides knew that it was at this quaint town on the south bank of the York River that Lord Cornwallis had surrendered his British Army to General George Washington's Continentals and their French allies, thereby virtually terminating the Revolutionary War with America triumphant. To Abraham Lincoln's Federals, it was well remembered that Washington had been a staunch nationalist, one who had gainsaid the particularism preached by the states' rights doctrinaires. To Jefferson Davis's Confederates—who naturally hoped to be able to retain control of the grass covered redoubts still remaining at Yorktown—there was still fierce pride in the fact that Washington was a native son of the Old Dominion, a stalwart who had been the one indispensable man of the patriots' struggle to establish an independent nation.

And Virginia was destined to be a central battle arena of the Civil War. Even though they had occupied the great National naval base at Norfolk and had emerged victorious over the Union Army at the First Battle of Bull Run on July 21, 1861, the Southerners were well aware of Federal pressure on their seaward littoral. From the start of hostilities, blue-clad soldiers had maintained control of the most powerful Gibraltar in North America—Fort Monroe, located at Old Point Comfort at the tip of the historic Peninsula between the York and James rivers—a stronghold their forces would hold throughout the war.

Yorktown was a charming, staid village of tree lined streets and neat, impressive houses. It was a prize the North coveted. Even though Confederate forces under John Bankhead "Prince John" Magruder and Daniel Harvey Hill had easily repulsed the inept and feeble attacks on June 10, 1861, of Benjamin Franklin Butler's troops at Big Bethel, a few miles from Old Point Comfort, by early 1862 the Union garrison at Fort Monroe under John E. Wool would be enlarged to some 12,500 soldiers. And the strategic offensive would remain with the Federals, now near Washington, D.C., being molded by the "Young Napoleon," George B. McClellan, into the truly superb Army of the Potomac.

"Little Mac," as the latter was called—a West Point graduate, a twice-brevetted hero of the War with Mexico, an official observer in the Crimean War, and a railroad president—argued long and hard with Lincoln and Secretary of War Edwin M. Stanton over what route the Army of the Potomac should take to move against the Confederate capital of Richmond. The administration favored the overland route through Manassas, but McClellan strongly recommended taking advantage of superior National sea power by moving his force down the Chesapeake Bay and landing it at Urbana on the lower Rappahannock River, or, as less desirable but nonetheless viable alternatives, disembarking it at Mobjack Bay or Fort Monroe. A quick move to West Point on the Pamunkey River —a tributary of the York—would bring the Federals to the point where they expected to employ the Richmond & York River Railroad to supply their short land march upon Richmond. After much disputation, McClellan was authorized to move with approximately 150,000 men on his amphibious operation. However, when the immense movement—one of the largest amphibious ones in warfare up to that time—actually unfolded in late March 1862, the Union commander's force was reduced—against his strenuous objections—to some 100,000 men.

The Confederate victor of Bull Run, Joseph E. Johnston, had gotten warning of the Federal plans and pulled his army back from Manassas to Fredericksburg on the Rappanhannock River. This rendered inoperative McClellan's scheme to debark at Urbana, so he determined to go ahead with the plan to land at Fort Monroe and advance up the Peninsula via Yorktown and Williamsburg toward Richmond. Further, and, McClellan would claim later, crippling to his strategy, was Lincoln's sudden insistence at the beginning of the operation on withholding Irvin McDowell's I Corps of some 38,000 men near Washington to assure the safety of the National Capital (although McClellan believed he had left Washington perfectly secure). The Union commander had earmarked McDowell's force as a flying column to move swiftly by water up the York to land on the Peninsula across from West Point so as to outflank and take in the rear the Confederate forces under Magruder on the lower Peninsula near Yorktown, where the Southern general had established his headquarters. Additionally, 10,000 of John E. Wool's troops which had been pledged to McClellan were now withdrawn from his use.

Also hampering the Union commander initially was the presence near Hampton Roads of the Confederate ironclad warship CSS *Virginia* (formerly the *Merrimack)*, which was neutralized by the USS *Monitor* in the classic battle of March 9, 1862. The Federal naval authorities assured McClellan that he could now proceed with his Peninsular campaign, and they even promised naval assistance in reducing and running past the enemy artillery batteries and fortifications being constructed by "Prince John" at Yorktown and across the river, which at that point narrows to less than a mile in width, at Gloucester Point. But Lincoln so lacked faith in McClellan that he not only withheld McDowell's corps but also demoted "Little Mac" from General-in-Chief of all the Union armies, a vote of no-confidence which left him in command of just the Army of the Potomac and not even of his base of supplies and communication. The President did not agree with McClellan's contention that the best defense of Washington was the heavy pressure McClellan was about to apply against Richmond. Lincoln was concerned about Rebel forces under "Stonewall" Jackson lurking in the Shenandoah.

Delays in assembling the vast shipping slowed the movement of the Union amphibious force to Fort Monroe, and once the troops began landing there—in the heaviest rains known to the region in twenty years—a shortage of supply wagons further impeded the advance. Only 42,000 men could be initially landed; several more weeks would be required for the rest of the army of about 100,000 to arrive and disembark. And McClellan was a most circumspect general, seldom one to take chances—especially since he was convinced time and preponderant resources were on the side of the North.

So colossal was the Federal undertaking that a foreign observer hailed it as "the stride of a

Right: ... Fort Monroe would play a significant part. The exterior of the officers' quarters. (USAMHI)

Below: The house at Fairfax Court House where McClellan made his headquarters. Here he planned his campaign for the Virginia Peninsula. A Timothy O'Sullivan image taken in June 1863. (USAMHI)

Above: Secretary of War Simon Cameron, his administration tainted by charges of corruption, resigned his portfolio on January 11, 1862. This left McClellan working with a new war secretary,... (NATIONAL ARCHIVES)

Below: Major General George B. McClellan and his staff in the Yorktown operations. "Little Mac" was well named, standing a full head shorter than the rest. Immediately to his left is his chief of staff, Brigadier General Randolph B. Marcy, who also happened to be McClellan's father-in-law. To the left of Marcy stands Brigadier General Stewart Van Vliet, quartermaster. (CHICAGO HISTORICAL SOCIETY)

Below: ... Edwin M. Stanton, a Democrat who opposed Lincoln's election, but who now became the President's strong right arm. (NA)

Left: Like McDowell before him, McClellan built his army in and around Washington and northern Virginia while he formulated his plan of campaign. Several familiar faces from the Bull Run debacle are with him. General Samuel P. Heintzelman stands bearded in front of the pillar on the right, with his staff. Robert E. Lee's Arlington House was a favorite posing place. (USAMHI)

Right: McDowell, too, was to cooperate with McClellan, but when a threat appeared in the Shenandoah Valley, Lincoln held him back to protect Washington. McDowell and staff at Arlington House. (MINNESOTA HISTORICAL SOCIETY)

Below: The always ready-to-pose Brigadier General Louis Blenker, with hand in coat, at his brigade headquarters near Washington. After being left out of the fight at Bull Run, he, too, would be withheld from McClellan. On his left stands Brigadier General Julius Stahel; on his right Prussian nobleman Prince Felix Salm-Salm. (WESTERN RESERVE HISTORICAL SOCIETY)

giant." But Fort Monroe lacked sufficient wharf facilities for so gigantic a movement; therefore, a secondary landing place was brought into use at Ship Point, nearer Yorktown. Without the flying column of the I Corps sweeping up the York to West Point, McClellan—now informed by the navy that it would not be able to join in attacking the Confederate batteries at Gloucester Point and Yorktown, or to run past them—was obliged to slog through the seas of mud and lay siege to the latter strong hold.

Meantime, the Confederates had not been idle. The local commander, John Magruder—a native Virginian—was a tall, erect, dark-haired general of fifty-one who had won brevets in the Mexican War and who, as a master of bluff and legerdemain, could make his 15,000 defenders look much more numerous than they were. There were few more colorful Civil War figures than "Prince John." A dandy dresser, he was an artillerist who had gained a wide reputation in the old army as a bon vivant and bountiful host at a myriad of social functions. Magruder never wearied of penning entreaties to his superiors for more reinforcements of men and artillery. He would in due time be joined by Johnston's main army which would, with Magruder's own force, total some 56,000 troops. The limited wharf facilities in the old river port of Yorktown made it difficult to enlarge his force rapidly, as there was no railroad down the Peninsula from Richmond or Williamsburg, and the few roads, upon which the Southern troops had to march, were infamous in this unusually heavy rainy season.

For many months, Magruder had been working steadily on the fortifications to defend Yorktown and the lower Peninsula. The earthworks immediately around the town were fairly strong, and Magruder incorporated with his own new ones some of the old Revolutionary War British redoubts. The water batteries, down low near the York River, as well as the field entrenchments, were buttressed by cotton bales, used also as breast works. Similarly, Gloucester Point, across from Yorktown, was fortified, though less strongly so.

Noting that the Warwick River ran across the Peninsula at right angles to McClellan's line of advance from Fort Monroe, Magruder determined to erect defenses behind this stream. To make the Federal advance and expected attacks more difficult, the Confederate commander built five dams which backed up water from the Warwick to such an extent that it inundated the countryside. This flooding allowed for only a few dry crossings at such points as Lee's Mill on the Confederate right and Wynn's Mill toward Yorktown, and where these roads passed, the Southerners erected batteries and rifle-pits.

Even to the experienced McClellan and other Union Army engineers, these enemy fortifications looked stronger than they actually were. Moreover, the Federal maps of the area were inaccurate, showing erroneously that the Warwick ran parallel to the York and James and therefore comprised no military obstacle. A probing attack on April 16 at Lee's Mill on the Federal left was repelled by the grayclads. So the Union commander set up his headquarters a little less than a mile west of the Farnholt House, on the Federal right, and began the slow process of a siege of the Yorktown-Warwick River

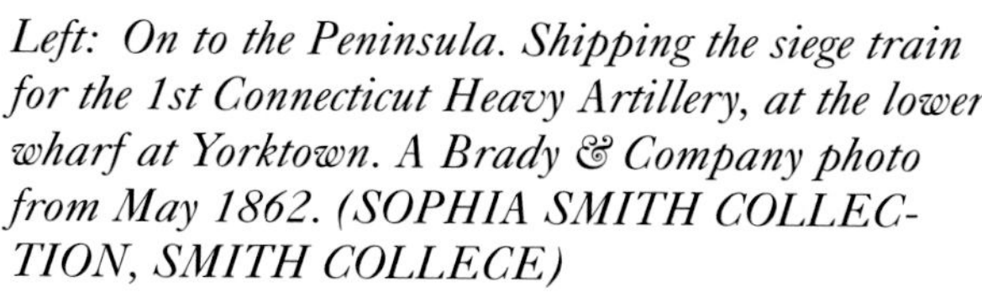

Left: On to the Peninsula. Shipping the siege train for the 1st Connecticut Heavy Artillery, at the lower wharf at Yorktown. A Brady & Company photo from May 1862. (SOPHIA SMITH COLLECTION, SMITH COLLECE)

Right: More of the wealth of ordnance and ammunition shipped to the Peninsula to help subdue Johnston and Magruder. A Brady & Company image taken after the fall of Yorktown. (USAMHI)

defenses by regular approaches. This meant miners and sappers would dig parallels encompassing earthworks and wooden platforms for the cannon, with bombproofs for soldiers and ammunition.

The Federals were assisted by a large captive observation balloon, in the basket of which such high ranking officers as Fitz John Porter ascended to examine the Confederate lines through their field glasses. Aloft almost daily, the Union air force suffered a near-catastrophe on one occasion when it slipped loose from its moorings "and sailed majestically over the enemy's works; but fortunately for its occupants it soon met a counter-current of air which returned it safely" to friendly lines.

Owing to the dearth of experienced engineering officers, McClellan, who in the mid 1850s, had personally witnessed the siege of Sevastopol in the Crimean War, felt obliged to make many personal reconnaissances himself at the front lines of his besieging forces. He was often accompanied by his large and glittering staff, which included several volunteer aides from the French nobility, namely, the Orleans princes, including the Prince de Joinville and the Comte de Paris. On one of these occasions, while observing from a redoubt at the front, McClellan and his aides were spotted by Confederate gunners who opened fire upon them. As an eyewitness described it, when several enemy artillery projectiles struck close by, the startled prince "jumped and glanced nervously around, while McClellan quietly knocked the ashes from his cigar."

The strained relations between the Union commander and the administration in Washington continued during the one-month siege of Yorktown in April 1862. As a petulant McClellan related one such incident in a letter to his wife, "The President very coolly telegraphed me yesterday that he thought I had better break the enemy's lines at once! I was much tempted to reply that he had better come and do it himself." On the Confederate side, when Johnston arrived, his rapport with Davis was not at all good, but the Southern commander was at least blessed in having a general—the masterful

Left: Flattered by the attention from European commanders, the Federal officers delighted in posing with them. Brigadier General William F. Barry with British officers and two French noblemen. (NATIONAL LIBRARY OF MEDICINE)

Right: Several pose here on May 1, 1862, at headquarters in Camp Winfield Scott. Seated in the front row, left to right, are Captain L'Amy of the Royal Army and the Duc de Chartres. In the center row, seated, are Colonel Fletcher of the Royal Army, the Prince de Joinville, and Stewart Van Vliet. Standing from the left are Colonels Beaumont and Neville of the Royal Army, an unidentified man, the Comte de Paris, and another unidentified civilian. (USAMHI)

Above: Louis Philippe Albert d'Orleans, Comte de Paris on the left, and Robert Philippe Louis d'Orleans, Duc de Chartres, on the right. Both wear the Union uniform in their capacity as aides to McClellan. (CHS)

Above: James F. Gibson's May 3, 1862, image of, from the left, the Duc de Chartres, the Prince de Joinville, and the Comte de Paris on the day of Yorktown's fall. (WAR LIBRARY AND MUSEUM, MOLLUS-PENNSYLVANIA)

Above: The Prince de Joinville, a familiar sight in McClellan's army. (USAMHI)

Above: Colonel V. DeChanal, French military observer. (USAMHI)

Robert E. Lee—positioned in Richmond as a buffer between himself and the Confederate President. Lee could and did get along amicably with both Davis and Johnston, and he was responsible in a large degree for amassing the force on the Peninsula that Johnston and Magruder had deployed at the Yorktown-Warwick River line.

As April waned, both sides worked feverishly to strengthen their positions. McClellan—who excelled at this sort of thing—laboriously wheeled into position some 114 big guns, howitzers, and mortars. Some of these were impressive pieces of siege weaponry. For example, close to the Farnholt House near the York River, a Federal battery was established which comprised five 100-pounder Parrotts and one monster 200-pounder Parrott. Others included 10-inch and 13-inch siege mortars. The Confederates, on the other hand, while possessing some large, modern, rifled pieces, also had to make do with older and less effective 32-pounder naval smoothbores and columbiads. After completing a 4,000-yard-long first parallel, McClellan's troops then began a second parallel much closer to the main Confederate defenses. All these activities were slowed by continuing torrential rains, execrable roads, and shortages of supply wagons.

But Joe Johnston saw the writing on the wall. He knew his troops and defenses could not stand up to the greatly superior weight of metal that the mushrooming Union batteries would be able to throw when they were ready to open fire. "We are engaged in a species of warfare," Johnston acknowledged in a message to Davis and Lee on April 30, "at which we can never win. It is plain that General McClellan will adhere to the system adopted by him last summer, and depend for success upon artillery and engineering. We can compete with him in neither." Lee and the Confederate President concurred.

Finally, on May 4, just as the massed Federal artillery was about to open a mammoth bombardment of Yorktown, Johnston wisely withdrew his troops and as many of his guns as he could, blew up some of his powder magazines, and retreated precipitately toward Williamsburg

Above: Gibson's photo of several of the British observers. (LIBRARY OF CONGRESS)

Above: Lieutenant George T. Munroe, Royal Canadian Rifles. (USAMHI)

Above: The commander of Royal Army forces in Canada, Lieutenant General Sir John Michel, K.C.B. (USAMHI)

Above: H. M. Hippisley of the Royal Navy. (USAMHI)

Above: And best known of all, Colonel Arthur Fremantle of the Royal Army, who wrote of and published his experiences with both Union and Confederate armies. (THE NEW-YORK HISTORICAL SOCIETY)

Right: But this campaign was for the Americans. McClellan's topographical engineers, photographed by Gibson on May 2, 1862. The use of the pistols to hold the corners of the map was a bit melodramatic of the engineers, but their services were invaluable in an area for which reliable maps were not available. (LC)

and Richmond. "Yorktown is in our possession," McClellan telegraphed Washington triumphantly. So was Gloucester Point. Only then could the Union commander speed troops up the York River to Eltham's Landing, near Brick House Point, opposite West Point, to speed the Confederate retreat—a retreat that was made possible by a partially successful rearguard stand made by the graycoats on May 5 at Williamsburg. As McClellan's Army of the Potomac moved into the evacuated Warwick River and Yorktown fortifications, they captured some seventy-seven heavy guns that Johnston had been unable to remove in his hasty retrograde movement—a loss the Confederates could ill afford. But the Federals also discovered, at the cost of some fatalities, a new engine of destruction in the form of primitive but effective land mines, then called "torpedoes." These were apparently innovated and ordered to be placed in positions around wells, springs, and elsewhere by Gabriel J. Rains. These land mines were regular 8-inch and 10-inch columbiad shells buried a few inches in the ground, and rigged with the ordinary cannon friction primer, or fulminate of mercury, so that they detonated when moved or stepped upon. So angered was McClellan at these devices that he ordered Confederate prisoners to discover the torpedoes and remove them. Some Southerners also considered the use of the "torpedoes" unethical, and James Longstreet directed Rains to halt the practice. But later in the war both sides employed land mines efficaciously.

Following the capture of Yorktown, McClellan moved up the Peninsula via Yorktown

Below: A special feature of McClellan's army was Colonel Hiram Berdan and his United States Sharpshooters, men selected and trained for their marksmanship and equipped with special rifles. (USAMHI)

Above: McClellan's antagonist looked every inch a great general. The resplendent Major General John Bankhead Magruder—"Prince John." He managed to completely mislead McClellan about his strength in the works at Yorktown, thereby delaying the Federals for precious days while Richmond forwarded more Confederates to the front. (LOUISIANA STATE UNIVERSITY, DEPARTMENT OF ARCHIVES AND MANUSCRIPTS)

Left: Isaac M. St. John was Magruder's chief engineer at Yorktown, responsible largely for the defenses that so intimidated McClellan. (USAMHI)

Above: Brigadier General Samuel R. Anderson was nearly sixty but still exercised active command of one of Magruder's brigades. Ill health forced him to resign just one week after the evacuation of Yorktown. (USAMHI)

to close in on Richmond. Yorktown was held by the Federals throughout the remainder of the war, its dockage facilities being used, along with those at Fort Monroe and later of City Point, in the final campaigns of the war against Richmond and Petersburg. Yorktown was the first major operation of the initial massive campaign of the Civil War in the eastern theater of operations, and it drew to the scene a number of photographers who were attracted there not only by the large military movements then unfolding, but also because of the historical associations of the place during the final and pivotal campaign of the revolution which had paved the way for the birth of the republic.

The skillful defense of the Yorktown-Warwick River line by first Magruder and then Johnston, combined with McClellan's caution, enabled Lee to take steps to better defend Richmond with fortifications and additional troops so as to hold the capital of the Confederacy through three more years of grim warfare before the final ennobling scene took

Right: At Lee's Mill, soon after McClellan began his investment of Yorktown, Magruder stood off an engagement on April 16. Here is McClellan's uncharacteristically unpretentious headquarters during the battle. Brattleboro, Vermont, photographer G. W. Houghton, who accompanied Vermont troops to the Peninsula, made this image as part of his excellent series of unpublished photographs. (VERMONT HISTORICAL SOCIETY)

Left: Houghton's portrait of Brigadier General William F. Smith, commanding a division that included the Vermonters. It was taken in April 1862, at the Gaines House. Seated at left is Captain Romeyn B. Ayers, later a noted general. (VHS)

Above: Magruder made his headquarters in the large house on the left in this photo of Yorktown made by Brady's company within days of the evacuation. (USAMHI)

Below: The sally port into the defenses around Yorktown, just after McClellan occupied the quiet town. (USAMHI)

Above: George N. Bernard's photograph of Magruder's headquarters in June 1862. "Prince John" not only dressed in style but lived that way as well. (USAMHI)

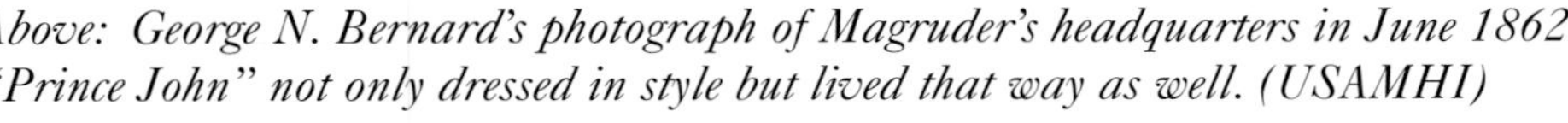

Right: The ravine behind the defenses where the Confederates placed their powder magazine. These huts were occupied by Magruder's command until a few weeks before Barnard caught this scene. (LC)

Above: Both North and South drew inspiration from the American successes in the Revolution, and Yorktown was a storied place indeed. Here on the right the building that served as headquarters for Charles Lord Cornwallis during Washington's siege of Yorktown. Magruder used it as a hospital, as would Dorothea Dix shortly afterward. Brady & Company's May 1862 image. (KEAN ARCHIVES)

Above: The front line of the works Magruder and St. John built to hold back McClellan. (USAMHI)

Above: Making the best use of the materials at hand, St. John sometimes employed bales of cotton along with sandbags in building his earthworks. When hit, the bales really showed what they were made of. (USAMHI)

Above: Barnard's June photo of a Confederate battery, with McClellan's Battery No. 1 in the distance. The Confederates liked to name their cannons for their generals. As seen by the remnant of an ammunition box in the foreground, this gun—now gone—was named after Major General D. H. Hill. (USAMHI)

Above: A naval battery near the Nelson church in Yorktown, shown on George N. Barnard's July 1862 image. At left are arranged loads of canister—tin cans filled with lead or iron balls—and stands of grapeshot, clusters of a dozen or more larger iron projectiles fired like a scatter-load from the cannon. (LC)

Above: Magruder also erected defenses at Gloucester Point, including this large Dahlgren smoothbore. (USAMHI)

Below: The much-touted Water Battery, strongest of the Confederate works preventing McClellan's easy conquest of Yorktown that he expected. (USAMHI)

Below: These Rodman guns in the Water Battery bear Magruder's name on their carriages, probably put there when they were being shipped to him from elsewhere in the Confederacy. (LC)

Right: Magruder took as many of his cannons with him as possible when he evacuated. Others had to be abandoned to the enemy, and this one, at least, he did not mind leaving. An exploded gun at one of the inland batteries. By Barnard . (USAMHI)

Above: The Water Battery became a favorite place for the Federals to pose after Magruder evacuated. Barnard was happy to catch them as they lounged in the works… (USAMHI)

Below: … and walked the parapet overlooking the York. (USAMHI)

Left: Part of Magruder's defenses, with the York River in the background. (USAMHI)

Below: Gloucester Point, with Yorktown in the distance, and more Dahlgren naval guns. (NLM)

Above: Gibson's photo of Battery No. 4, whose eight mortars lobbed shells into Yorktown constantly. The barge holds their powder and shells. Built into the earth itself are the gunners' quarters, a "bombproof" protecting them from enemy fire. (LC)

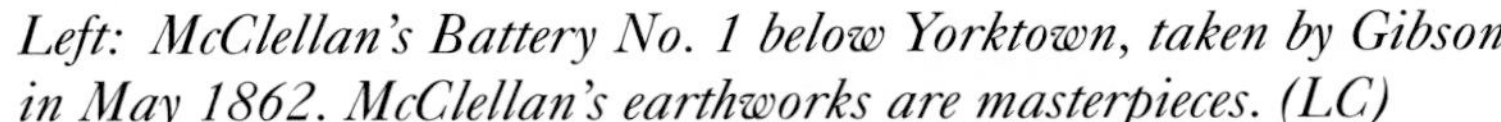

Left: McClellan's Battery No. 1 below Yorktown, taken by Gibson in May 1862. McClellan's earthworks are masterpieces. (LC)

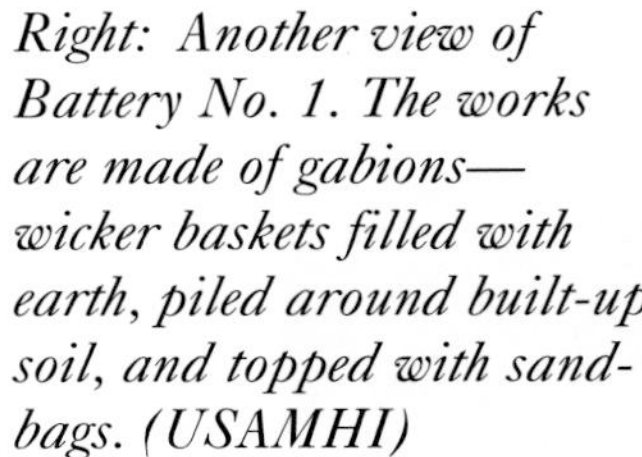

Right: Another view of Battery No. 1. The works are made of gabions—wicker baskets filled with earth, piled around built-up soil, and topped with sand-bags. (USAMHI)

Below: The Farnholt House behind Battery No. 1, seen at left. Gunners used the roof to observe the effect of their shells. (USAMHI)

Right: McClellan's headquarters, Camp Winfield Scott, taken by Gibson on the day Magruder evacuated. (USAMHI)

Right: Always the tourists, Federal soldiers visit "Cornwallis' Cave," the small cavern where the British general reputedly took refuge from Washington's artillery in 1781. (NLM)

Left: "Little Mac's" tent in the center, the day of his "victory" over Magruder. (LC)

Left: And officers of the 1st Connecticut Artillery pulled enemy shells from within the cave for jaunty poses like this one, published by Brady & Company. (LC, FITZ JOHN PORTER PAPERS)

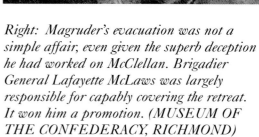

Right: Magruder's evacuation was not a simple affair, even given the superb deception he had worked on McClellan. Brigadier General Lafayette McLaws was largely responsible for capably covering the retreat. It won him a promotion. (MUSEUM OF THE CONFEDERACY, RICHMOND)

Above: Magruder used the cave as a powder magazine. Brady's assistants used it as a backdrop for images like this. (USAMHI)

Above: Major General Gustavus W. Smith attacked McClellan's pursuing Federals at Eltham's Landing on May 7 while he covered the withdrawal of Magruder's army. It was effectively the end of the Yorktown campaign. (TULANE UNIVERSITY)

Above: Brigadier General Gabriel J. Rains also contributed his part. One of D. H. Hill's brigade commanders, he laced the roads out of Yorktown with hidden shells triggered to explode when stepped upon. "Infernal machines" they were called, or "torpedoes." He had just pioneered the antipersonnel mine. Even many Confederates thought it a barbarous concept. (USAMHI)

The New Ironclads

WILLIAM N. STILL

Invention went wild in the race for newer and more powerful iron behemoths

Above: The Union Navy granted contracts for three radically different ironclad vessels at first. Here the USS New Ironsides, *powerful and effective, though largely conventional in design. (SMITHSONIAN INSTITUTION)*

ON MARCH 9, 1862, occurred what has rightly been called one of the most important naval engagements in American history. Two iron-armored warships, the USS *Monitor* and the CSS *Virginia*, met in mortal combat, the first such battle in history. Although not the first ironclad warships completed and battle-tested, they were the first completed in North America and the first that fought against each other. They were responsible for the decision by both Abraham Lincoln's and Jefferson Davis's governments to create a powerful naval force of armored vessels.

The Confederates took the first step. Perhaps this was inevitable considering the fact that the South lacked both a navy and the potential to keep pace with their opponents in building warships. On May 9, 1861, Confederate Secretary of the Navy Stephen R. Mallory wrote in an oft-quoted report, "I regard the possession of an iron-armored ship as a matter of the first necessity.... If we... follow their [the United States Navy's]... example and build wooden ships, we shall have to construct several at one time; for one or two ships would fall easy prey to her comparatively numerous steam frigates. But inequality of numbers may be compensated by invulnerability; and thus not only does economy but naval success dictate the wisdom and expediency of fighting with iron against wood." That same day the Confederate Congress appropriated $2,000,000 for the purchase or construction of ironclads in Europe. Although the Confederacy would contract for several powerful armored vessels in England and France, initial efforts were unsuccessful. Secretary Mallory then determined to construct ironclads within the Confederacy. In the middle of July the decision was made to convert the *Merrimack* into the *Virginia*, and six weeks later contracts were awarded for the construction of two ironclads later named the *Arkansas* and *Tennessee* to be built in Memphis; a fourth one, the *Mississippi*, was to be built in New Orleans. In September the *Louisiana* was also laid down in New Orleans. These five initial armor clads were designed to operate on the open sea as well as on inland waters. They were designed not only to break the blockade, but as Secretary Mallory wrote, to "traverse the entire coast of the United States... and encounter, with a fair prospect of success, their entire Navy." In other words, Mallory's initial ironclad strategy was offensive in nature.

The strategy was a failure. Only three of the vessels, the *Arkansas*, *Louisiana*, and *Virginia*, became operational; the other two were destroyed while still under construction. Of the three that were commissioned only the *Arkansas* was used for offensive purposes. During its brief career, it achieved some dramatic success, despite poor design and construction. It was 165 feet in length and carried a battery of ten guns. Its armor was made up of railroad T-rails, and it was powered by inadequate riverboat machinery. The casemate, unlike those found on the other Confederate ironclads, was perpendicular rather than slanted. On July 15, 1862, this awkward-looking warship ran through a large fleet of Union vessels anchored above Vicksburg and successfuliy resisted several planned attempts to destroy it. In August the *Arkansas* was to participate in a combined operation on Baton Rouge, Louisiana, but because of a breakdown in the machinery, the ironclad was blown up by its crew.

Above: To his credit, Secretary of the Navy Gideon Welles, ridiculous wig and all, supported the ironclad idea from the first. Despite his lack of naval experience he saw what many could not, that wooden ships were things of the past. (NA)

Above: The USS Galena *was not a success, its thin iron sheathing proving easily vulnerable to Confederate shore batteries at Drewry's Bluff in May 1862. James Gibson's photo taken in July. (USAMHI)*

Above: But very effective, and very revolutionary, was the design for the USS Monitor. *Much of the vessel was constructed here on Long Island. (U.S. NAVAL HISTORICAL CENTER)*

Above: And here it rests in Gibson's July 9, 1862, photograph, taken on the James River. The turret shows the indentations made by the Virginia*'s solid shot during their epic battle at Hampton Roads. (USAMHI)*

The *Louisiana*'s career was briefer and less successful. As envisioned by its builder, E. C. Murray, the armor-clad was to be 264 feet in length, 64 in beam, with a battery of twenty-two guns and propelled by two paddle wheels and two 4-foot propellers. The most unorthodox feature in his design was twin wheels along the centerline, one abaft the other in a well. The ship was still being fitted out when Admiral Farragut's squadron began its ascent of the Mississippi River. The large Confederate ironclad was towed down the river and moored near Fort Jackson. Here as a floating battery it engaged the Union vessels and was destroyed by its crew when the fort surrendered.

The *Virginia* achieved the most notable success of the initial ironclads. It was converted from the captured and partially destroyed sloop-of-war *Merrimack* at the Gosport Navy Yard in Norfolk. Frequently considered to be the prototype of all the Confederate ironclads, it was in fact an experimental vessel constructed only because the Confederacy needed to get a power-

Above: While monitors would become a mania in the East, on the western waters a different sort of ironclad came about. The first river ironclads were converted snag boats, like the Benton. *With sixteen guns mounted on its deck, it was the most powerful vessel on the Mississippi and flagship of Foote's fleet at Island No. 10 and Davis's fleet in the battle at Memphis. (KA)*

Above: Soon new ships were under construction, however, at places like the Carondelet Marine Railway at Carondelet, Missouri. Here two "city class" ironclads are being built. Their builder, James B. Eads, could construct one in forty-five days, start to finish. (NA, U. S. WAR DEPARTMENT GENERAL STAFF)

Above: Here the finished products rest at anchor at Cairo, Illinois. These "Pook turtles" were the backbone of the Mississippi fleet. At left the USS Baron De Kalb, *in the center the USS* Cincinnati, *and on the right the USS* Mound City. *The* De Kalb *was formerly the USS* St. Louis, *the first of Eads's boats to launch. (NYHS)*

Above: Another converted snag boat became the USS Essex, *an unfortunate vessel that would be much damaged and beset with difficulty throughout the war. A photograph by Dr. J. T. Field taken while the ship lay moored off Memphis in 1864. Mortar boats lie to its left bow. (CIVIL WAR TIMES ILLUSTRATED COLLECTION)*

ful ironclad operational as quickly as possible in that part of the South. The 262-foot vessel had a casemate 170 feet long, inclined on the sides with the ends horizontally rounded. The rounded ends along with the bow and stern of the hull being submerged were unique; no other Confederate ironclad incorporated these features. The armor, rolled at Tredegar Iron Works in Richmond from railroad iron into plates, was 4 inches thick attached in two layers. The ironclad carried a battery of ten guns, four to a side and a pivot rifle at each end. On March 8, 1862, it attacked units of the North Atlantic Blockading Squadron in Hampton Roads and destroyed the frigate Congress and the sloop-of-war Cumberland. The following day it fought the Monitor and for over a month successfully defended the entrance to the James River. Early in May, Norfolk was captured. With no base to return to and a draft too deep to allow it to ascend the James, the ship was destroyed by its crew to prevent its capture.

With the destruction of the *Arkansas*, *Louisiana*, and *Virginia*, the first Confederate ironclad program ended. Mallory's vision of a few powerful armored vessels to sweep Union warships from the seas was a failure. Unlike the Confederates', the Union Navy's initial ironclad program was tentative; professional opinion differed over the type of armored vessel to build. Early in August 1861, Congress appropriated $1,500,000 for the "construction or completion of iron or steelclad steamers or steam batteries," and authorized the creation of a board of naval officers to examine proposals and make recommendations. Then in September the board recommended that contracts be awarded for three vessels; a seagoing broadside type of vessel commissioned *New Ironsides*, a lightly armored wooden vessel, the *Galena*, and a revolving turret vessel, the *Monitor*. While the board of naval officers deliberated, the army had already contracted for seven ironclads for service on the Mississippi River and its tributaries.

These seven ironclads have been called "Pook turtles" after their designer, Samuel M.

Left: Then came the behemoth ironclads, designed by "Dirty Bill" Porter and built by Eads. The USS Lafayette *carried eight heavy guns and a shield of iron laid over rubber, intended to make shot bounce off the casemate. In practice, it did not. (USAMHI)*

Below: Equally formidable in appearance was the USS Choctaw, *it, too, carrying eight heavy cannons. Both ships were ready to ply the rivers by late 1862. (KA)*

Above: William "Dirty Bill" Porter designed the conversion of the Essex and commanded her, while also taking a hand in the fashioning of the ungainly Lafayette *and* Choctaw. *(LC)*

Pook, or the "city class," because they were named after western river ports. They were commissioned the *Cairo, Carondelet, Cincinnati, Louisville, Mound City, Pittsburg,* and *St. Louis* (later *Baron De Kalb*). Pook designed wooden, flat-bottomed light draft and low freeboard center-wheelers measuring 175 feet in length. Each gunboat was to be armed with ten 8-inch shell guns. With slanted casemates covered with 2 1/2-inch armor, they were similar in appearance to Confederate ironclads. These ironclads had defects found on nearly all of the armored vessels of this type built by both sides during the war—they were underpowered, too heavy, and vulnerable to high, arched "plunging fire" directed at their roofs. Nevertheless, they saw more service than any other class of river ironclads, fighting in various engagements from Fort Henry to Vicksburg and beyond. Three of them (*Cairo, Cincinnati,* and the *Baron De Kalb*) would be sunk.

The army was also responsible for the conversion of four large river vessels into ironclads. A snag boat was converted into the casemated ironclad *Benton* while the *Essex*, also casemated, was a rebuilt center-wheel ferryboat. The *Benton* carried sixteen heavy guns while the *Essex* carried six. Two side-wheelers named the *Lafayette* and the *Choctaw* were purchased in St. Louis and converted under the supervision of navy Commander William "Dirty Bill" Porter. Although the *Lafayette* would have a sloping casemate, the *Choctaw* would have a stationary turret with inclined sides and a curved top—"a war dome, like the dome on the Court House in St. Louis"—and be pierced to hold four guns. Just forward and aft of the wheels were two small casemates. On top of the forward casemate, which housed two howitzers to sweep the decks

Above: The USS Ozark *was unusual on the Mississippi. It carried a turret of Ericsson's design forward, and mounted four other cannons on the main deck. (USAMHI)*

Above: A variety of less formidable ironclads and "tinclads" plied the Western rivers, boats like the USS General Grant, *shown here at Kingston, Georgia. (NA)*

Above: David D. Porter had little good to say about any of the Mississippi ironclads. He was a devotee of the conventional Ericsson monitor design. (USAMHI)

Above: And so, obviously, was John Ericsson himself. Arrogant, egotistical, and painfully difficult to work with, he was still a genius of sorts, and the Union turned to him through most of the war for its monitor designs. (NHC)

Above: Admiral Hiram Paulding backed Ericsson's original Monitor *design and worked hard to expedite its building and adoption by the navy. He succeeded. (NYHS)*

if the enemy should board, was located a conical pilothouse, covered with 2 inches of iron. Commander Porter designed the armor himself. The *Choctaw* had two l-inch layers of iron and a l-inch layer of vulcanized India rubber cushions, while the *Lafayette's* sloping casemate was covered with 1-inch iron over 1-inch India rubber. The navy took over the eleven ironclads after they were completed, and they operated as units of the Mississippi Squadron throughout the war.

The navy also contracted for ironclads on the western rivers. Three of them, the *Chillicothe*, *Tuscumbia*, and *Indianola*, were built by Joseph Brown in Cincinnati. Each had a small casemate forward containing two 11-inch rifled guns and a casemate astern between two paddle wheels. All three were regarded as inefficient. The *Chillicothe's* first commanding officer pronounced it a "cumbersome scow," and after the battle of Grand Gulf in April 1863, the *Tuscumbia's* captain referred to his vessel as "a Disgrace."

These river ironclads were all laid down or converted during 1861 and early 1862, months before the engagement between the *Monitor* and the *Virginia*. The *Galena* was also under construction at Mystic, Connecticut, during these months.

The *Galena* was, according to Commodore Joseph Smith, senior officer of the Ironclad Board, "a Lighter boat... intended to have more speed than other ironclads to work in part under canvas." It resembled the wooden steam warships of that day except that the upper part of its sides was rounded inward or "tumbled home" at an angle of about 45 degrees to deflect projectiles. A battery of six guns was mounted on a gun deck protected by armor not quite 4 inches in thickness. It had two l-inch plates of armor on its sides separated by an air space in which there were iron bars. Although it was rigged as a schooner, all the masts, except the fore lower mast kept for a lookout position, were removed. It was built by C. S. Bushnell and Company and commissioned in April 1862. In May, the *Galena* was one of the vessels of the North Atlantic

Blockading Squadron that ascended the James River and engaged the Confederate batteries at Drewry's Bluff. It was badly damaged; its thin armor penetrated thirteen times. Later the armor was removed, and the *Galena* completed the war as a wooden-hulled ship.

The *New Ironsides* was a traditional broadside type warship, but 170 feet of its 230-foot hull were covered with iron armor 4½ inches in thickness. The armor belt covered the sides and deck, generally amidship, with bow and stern unarmored. This citadel protected the main battery of sixteen 11-inch Dahlgren guns. Classified a frigate, this large (more than 4,000 tons displacement) and powerful ironclad was built by Merrick & Sons in Philadelphia. *New Ironsides* spent its entire Civil War career with either the South Atlantic or the North Atlantic blockading squadrons. In April 1863 the armored warship participated in Admiral Samuel F. Du Pont's attack on Confederate positions in Charleston harbor, and in this and subsequent attacks it was hit repeatedly by enemy fire without suffering any damage. In October it was slightly damaged by the Confederate torpedo boat *David*, but after repairs it participated in Admiral David D. Porter's attacks on Fort Fisher. *New Ironsides* was the most powerful ironclad completed by the Union during the war and undoubtedly the most effective in the combined operations along the Southern coastline. It was the only seagoing armored cruiser to be completed during the war. An improved armored cruiser, the *Dunderberg*, was laid down but not completed until after Appomattox. The board of naval officers who had recommended the three original armored vessels wrote that "ocean going [armored] cruisers are for the time being impracticable." This report may have had some effect on Union policy concerning armored vessels, but the major factors were the influence of Assistant Secretary of the Navy Gustavus Fox and the *Monitor's*

Above: Above: Captain Francis H. Gregory, a hero of the era of iron men in wooden ships, superintended the construction of ironclads for Welles. (NYHS)

Above: Chief Engineer Alban Stimers managed most of the construction of the original Monitor, *fought aboard her at Hampton Roads, and later lost his reputation with the unsuccessful Casco class of light-draft monitors. (NHC)*

Below: The first turreted ironclads to follow the Monitor *were those of the* Passaic *class, and they were the workhorse ironclads of the Atlantic coast. Here the launch of the* Camanche *of that class. This launch took place in San Francisco, California, where the vessel was shipped in parts and reconstructed. An 1864 photograph by C. E. Watkins. (CHARLES S. SCHWARTZ)*

Above: Officers working under Gregory, like Chief Engineer James W. King, oversaw individual ironclads to completion. King supervised the Manayunk, Catawba, *and* Tippecanoe. *Later he built the* Ozark, Chickasaw, *and* Winnebago, *out west. (LC)*

Above: The USS Catskill, *photographed in Charleston harbor in 1863, one of the most powerful—and most damaged—Passaics. (USAMHI)*

Above: The anchor well of the Catskill. *Note how the anchor could be raised and lowered from within, without exposing men to fire. (NHC)*

Above: An officer's cabin aboard the Catskill. *A beam of light enters through the skylight scuttle overhead. A watertight bulkhead door is closed behind the desk and above it on the bulkhead is a print of the original* Monitor *at sea. (NHC)*

Above: The Catskill's turret machinery, the enormously heavy turret resting on and being turned by the massive vertical shaft at left. (NHC)

designer, John Ericsson, and the impact of the battle between the *Monitor* and the *Virginia* on Northern public opinion.

As early as December 1861 the Navy Department had requested $12,000,000 to construct twenty additional turreted vessels. As designed, they were to mount a type of turret developed by Captain Cowper Coles of the British Royal Navy. Ericsson, however, persuaded the navy to substitute a turret designed by him for the Coles turret. The *Monitor's* success was primarily responsible for this decision.

The *Monitor* was a unique warship. Designed as a harbor defense vessel, instead of a standard ship hull it had a large armored "raft" 172 feet by 41 feet, 6 inches supported by a lower section of wood 122 feet long and 34 feet wide. The "raft" was designed to increase stability in a seaway and protect the hull from ramming. The vessel's power plant consisted of two boilers and two engines that were of Ericsson's design, as was the revolving turret, which was the armor-clad's most novel feature. The *Monitor* incorporated numerous technical advances for that time including forced ventilation of living spaces, a protected anchor which could be raised and lowered without it or the crew members being exposed to enemy fire, and a protected pilothouse. The turret carried two 11-inch Dahlgren smoothbores. The *Monitor* was completed in early February 1862, and a month later it left under tow to join the North Atlantic Blockading Squadron. Its fortuitous arrival at Hampton Roads in time to challenge the *Virginia* is well known. The *Monitor* won a tactical victory in preventing the destruction of Union vessels in the Roads, and in doing so it produced such an intense enthusiasm in the North that a "monitor fever" swept the Union. From then until the end of the war the Union would concentrate on building monitor-type vessels. It is ironic that the Union Navy which obviously had to assume an offensive strategy in order to win the war, adopted as its principal

Above: The engine room of the Catskill, *showing part of the steam engine that powered not only the screw, but also the turret machinery. (NHC)*

Below: A similar, unpublished view of the engine room of the Camanche *while it was being reassembled in San Francisco. (CHARLES S. SCHWARTZ)*

The USS Nahant *undergoing repairs at Hilton Head, South Carolina, after being heavily damaged in the April 7, 1863, attack on Charleston, carried out largely by* Passaic-*class monitors like the* Nahant. *(USAMHI)*

Left: Rear Admiral Samuel F.I. Du Pont commanded the fleet that attacked Charleston. Seeing the relatively low firepower of the monitors and seeing the heavy damage inflicted on them by Confederate batteries, he formed a poor opinion of monitors as offensive vessels. His entire monitor fleet fired 139 shots in the same time that it received at least 346 hits. (USAMHI)

ironclad a type of vessel that was basically defensive in nature.

On March 21, three weeks after the battle, Ericsson received contracts for six enlarged and improved versions of the *Monitor* while four additional ships of the same class were ordered from other builders. These were the ten *Passaics*—the *Passaic, Montauk, Catskill, Patapsco, Lehigh, Sangamon,* (later renamed *Jason), Camanche, Nahant, Nantucket,* and *Weehawken.* Like the original *Monitor,* each had a single turret, increased thickness of armor, a permanent stack, and a more powerful battery. These vessels as a class were to see more service than any others of the monitor fleet. They were the major ironclad units of both the South Atlantic and North Atlantic blockading squadrons. Monitors of this class participated in the combined operations against Charleston and Savannah, and in the James River.

In 1862 the Navy Department also initiated the construction of double-turreted monitors. The *Onondaga* was built at Continental Iron Works, Greenpoint, New York, under contract with George W. Quintard. Commissioned early in 1864, it was 226 feet long and carried a battery of two 15-inch Dahlgren smoothbores and two 150 pounder Parrott rifles. This vessel spent its entire war career in the James River and was decommissioned after the war. Four additional double turreted monitors were built in navy yards—*Miantonomoh, Monadnock, Agamenticus* (later renamed *Terror),* and *Tonawanda* (later

Left: The next step in improving monitor firepower was two turrets. The Onondaga *was commissioned in March 1864 and proved thoroughly reliable, though it saw very little action. Here it is in the James River, scene of most of its war service. (USAMHI)*

Right: Next came the Miantonomoh *class, ships like the* Tonawanda, *shown here. Only one of them was finished in time to serve in the war, but they were far more seaworthy than their predecessors. (P-M)*

Left: The Miantonomoh *itself actually steamed to Europe, proving the deep-sea capabilities of the monitor type. It appears here at the Washington Navy Yard in 1865. On the left is the USS* Montauk *of the* Passaic *class. In the distance is the light-draft monitor* Chimo *and, just visible behind it, the tall masts of the Confederate ironclad ram* Stonewall. *(NHC)*

Left: Ericsson, meanwhile, turned his mind to much larger seagoing monitors, his Dictator *class. Only two were built, and neither was very successful. Here the* Puritan *peeks out of the shiphouse at the Continental Iron Works at Green Point, New York. (NHC)*

Above: The launch of the USS Dictator, *December 26, 1863, at the Delamater Iron Works. (THE MARINERS MUSEUM, NEWPORT NEWS, VIRGINIA)*

Above: Ready to slide down the ways, the Dictator *looms above the speakers' platform, flag-draped for the dedication ceremonies. (NYHS)*

Above: Stimers's light-draft monitor Casco *on the James River. The* Casco*-type monitors were found to be ill-designed and barely awash, so their turrets were left off and they were turned into torpedo boats instead. (USAMHI)*

Left: The launch of the light-draft USS Modoc, *photographed by the New York artist J. H. Beal in 1864. (NHC)*

Left: James Eads designed powerful light-draft river "monitors" Osage *and* Neosho *to operate in barely four feet of water. Ungainly, they still proved effective against most enemy fire. Here the* Osage, *probably in the Red River in 1864. (LC)*

renamed *Amphitrite).* These vessels were twin-screw, wooden-hulled ironclads over 258 feet in length. Of these four, only the *Monadnock* was completed prior to the end of the war, but it saw no combat. This class, however, was considered the most efficient of the monitor type built during the war and these vessels remained in service for many years afterward.

In September 1862, orders were given to various builders for nine more Ericsson monitors. *Canonicus, Catawba, Oneonta, Mahopac, Manhattan, Tecumseh, Saugus, Manayunk* (later *Ajax),* and *Tippecanoe* (later *Wyandotte)* were similar to the *Passaics*, but with certain significant improvements—a defensive slope around the base of the turret to prevent jamming, a stronger hull, and a heavier battery of 15-inch guns. Five of this class were commissioned in time to see Civil War service, and the *Tecumseh* was sunk during the Battle of Mobile Bay.

The last of the coastal monitors contracted for in 1862 were the two giant single-turret monitors, *Puritan* and Dictator. Displacing more than 3,000 tons each and with large fuel capacities, these vessels were intended as oceangoing vessels. They were built in New York under contract with John Ericsson. Their 312-foot hulls were to be protected by 6-inch side armor. The single turrets would carry two 15-inch Dahlgren smoothbores each. The *Dictator*, after being commissioned in December 1864, joined the North Atlantic Blockading Squadron but saw no action. The *Puritan* was never completed.

The largest single class of monitor-type vessels was the *Casco* class. In the spring of 1863, contracts were signed for the construction of twenty of this type. However, during the war only eight were completed, and they were considered unseaworthy. Five of them were converted to torpedo boats, but none saw action.

Monitors were also constructed for operations on the western rivers. Shortly after the Hampton Roads engagement, James B. Eads received a contract to build three single-turreted monitors of his own design, although the Navy Department insisted that Ericsson's turret be used instead of one designed by Eads. The three river monitors, named *Osage, Neosho,* and *Ozark,* were unlike other monitors in that they were propelled by stern wheels. Unfortunately, the wheels (protected by armored casings) made it impossible for the turrets to turn a full 360 degrees. The *Ozark* was larger and carried additional armament of questionable value—four pivot guns located upon the open deck. They were unusual-looking vessels with virtually nothing showing above the waterline but the turret, the iron-plated house for the stern paddle wheel, and the tall, thin stacks.

Eads received a second contract for monitors. The four vessels built under this contract—*Chickasaw, Kickapoo, Milwaukee,* and *Winnebago* —were double-turreted ironclads, with one turret by Ericsson's design and one by Eads's design. The Eads turret was more sophisticated than Ericsson's. The guns in the turret were mounted on a steam operated elevator which dropped them to a lower deck where they were loaded and then hoisted and run out through ports opened by automatic steam operated shutters. These vessels carried four guns each—two per turret—and were the only monitors ever built with triple screws and rudders. They were principally employed with the West Gulf Blockading Squadron operating in Mobile Bay and its vicinity and were generally considered the most serviceable of the river monitors.

The monitor-type had the great advantage of achieving a maximum of impenetrability through two radical factors—low freeboard and the concentration of guns in the armored turret. The guns could be aimed without moving the ship. In confined and sheltered waters the monitors were excellent defensive ships, but they had serious defects that affected Union naval operations. A majority of them were essentially floating batteries that had to be towed from port to port; even in the rivers they could rarely stem the current. They were unseaworthy and had so little reserve buoyancy that a leak could be fatal. For these reasons they were unsuitable for blockade service, the primary mission of the Union Navy. In anything but a flat calm a monitor's deck was awash. The crew had to remain below with hatches battened down. As Admiral Du Pont wrote: "How can such vesels lay off ports… and protect the wooden vessels."

The western rivers were generally more suitable for the monitor type, but even here there were problems. The gunboats' maneuverability was poor, and they had little protection from plunging shot, a serious defect considering the many miles of bluffs along the waterways.

Even more important was their unsuitability for offensive operations. Loading their guns usually required from six to eight minutes. "This delay," as one authority has written, "violated the cardinal principal of naval gunnery, volume of fire." In the attack by the *New Ironsides, Keokuk,* and seven monitors on Fort Sumter in April 1863, only 139 rounds were fired by the combined batteries of the ironclads' guns. At the same time 76 guns in the Confederate forts rained some 2,206 shots on the Union vessels. As Admiral Du Pont wrote Secretary Welles, "I… remind the Department that ability to endure is not sufficient element where with to gain victories, that endurance must be accompanied with a corresponding power to inflict injury upon the enemy… that the weakness of the monitor class of vessels… is fatal to their attempts against fortifications."

The most unusual turreted vessel commissioned during the Civil War was the converted wooden sloop-of-war *Roanoke.* Like her sister ship, the *Merrimack,* converted by the Confederates into the *Virginia,* she was cut down, and three center-line turrets were installed. With a high freeboard, she was not a monitor-type vessel. Because of instability and a deep draft, she was considered unsuitable for active service and spent the war defending New York harbor from possible attack by Confederate cruisers.

While the Union ironclad building program after 1861 emphasized the monitor type of vessel, the Confederate program on the other hand would change from one which stressed offensive vessels in 1861 to one emphasizing defensive vessels. The apparent unseaworthiness of the *Virginia* and the ironclads built in New Orleans and Memphis, the lack of adequate facilities and qualified technical expertise, the belief that powerful armor-clads could be obtained in Europe, and most important, the growing threat to the Confederacy from invasion and amphibious assault all contributed to this change in poli-

Above: Soon after the Osage *and* Neosho *were begun, Eads started work on another class of light-draft river monitor, the* Winnebagos. *These included turrets designed by Eads, which were far superior to Ericsson's. They did good service on the Mississippi and at Mobile Bay and proved to be the spiritual progenitor of warships for a century to come. Here the USS* Milwaukee, *commissioned at Mound City in August 1864. It struck a "torpedo" on March 28, 1865, and sank. (USAMHI)*

Above: The only three-turreted monitor built during the war, the USS Roanoke. *Originally a steam frigate, sister ship of the* Merrimack, *which the Confederates converted to the CSS* Virginia, *the* Roanoke *also was a conversion. Nearly destroyed by the Confederate ironclad in the battle at Hampton Roads, it was taken to the Brooklyn Navy Yard and the work of making it an ironclad commenced barely two weeks after the battle. The result was not spectacular. The* Roanoke *served two years with the North Atlantic Blockading Squadron, but proved rather ineffective. This previously unpublished photograph shows it at Brooklyn in mid 1865, the old ship-of-the-line USS* Vermont *in the left background . (NHC)*

Above: By the end of the war, sights like these two monitors lying off the Washington Navy Yard were commonplace. The war gave rise to a whole new generation of naval machines in the Union. An unpublished image by Kilburn Brothers of New Hampshire. (USAMHI)

Above: The Confederates looked to a different sort of ironclad, one more compatible with their limited technology and industrial facilities. No photographs of the Virginia *seem to have survived, but all subsequent Confederate ironclads followed the same general pattern originated by John Porter and John Brooke. Here the CSS* Chicora *in Charleston Harbor. On January 31, 1863,* Chicora *and its sister ship* Palmetto State *became the only Confederate ironclads to put to open sea when they steamed out and engaged elements of the blockading fleet successfully, then returned to port. (OLD COURT HOUSE MUSEUM, VICKSBURG)*

Right: Nearly as famous as the Virginia, *the CSS* Albemarle *was equally as unwieldy and slow, yet managed to threaten Albemarle Sound most effectively, sink one enemy warship, and aid materially in the capture of Plymouth, North Carolina. To counter this threat, Lieutenant William B. Cushing attacked it on the night of October 27, 1864, with a torpedo mounted on the end of a spar projecting from a steam launch. The* Albemarle *sank almost immediately and is here shown at the Norfolk Navy Yard in 1865 after being raised by the Federals. (NHC)*

Right: In Georgia's waters, Confederates constructed this casemated ironclad, the CSS Jackson, *only to find themselves so short of iron that it was never completed. The builders destroyed the ship before the Federals could capture it. This image may be by A. J. Riddle, who photographed the Andersonville prison camp in 1864. (TU, LOUISIANA HISTORICAL ASSOCIATION COLLECTION)*

Below: The CSS Atlanta, *now the USS* Atlanta, *patrolling the James. (USAMHI)*

Right: A remarkable unpublished view of the CSS Atlanta, *and perhaps the best illustration extant of the improvised nature of most Confederate ironclads. Taken after the war, this image probably shows the ship laid up at League Island, Pennsylvania, prior to its sale for salvage. It had been converted from the blockade runner* Fingal *in 1862, and the old* Fingal *hull shows clearly below the more streamlined additions that turned it into the* Atlanta. *This deep draft proved its undoing, for in its first engagement it ran aground and surrendered. The Federals later used it to patrol the James River. (THE MARINERS MUSEUM)*

cy. From 1862 until the end of the war, the Confederate naval construction program would concentrate on small, shallow-draft harbor defense armored vessels. Approximately forty of these vessels were laid down, and half of them were completed.

These small defense ironclads were designed by naval constructor John Porter. He developed a standard design which was sent to builders and contractors throughout the Confederacy. The original plan was for a 150-foot flat-bottomed vessel with hull to be partially armored and casemate to be completely covered with iron armor. The iron clad would carry a battery of six guns and be screw propelled. Although this design was utilized by the shipbuilders, it is, nevertheless, almost impossible to generalize about the Confederate armor-clads. There were noticeable differences because of modifications in size, machinery, armor, and battery. In size they ranged from the *Albemarle* and the *Neuse* (139 feet) up to several under construction during the latter months of the war that were over 250 feet in length. The 310-foot *Nashville* was the largest of this class.

The thickness of armor measured from 2 to 8 inches, but all of it was 2-inch laminated iron plate. On several vessels such as the Arkansas and Louisiana railroad iron—T-rails—was substituted because rolled plates were not available. The marine engines and boilers varied from ship to ship. Some of them were manufactured in the South; more of them were salvaged from other vessels. The method of propulsion consisted of either wheel or screw or a combination of both, as in the *Louisiana*, which had two wheels and two screws. A majority of them were screw steamers with either one or two propellers, but several such as the *Nashville* and *Missouri* were paddle-wheelers because of the accessibility of that kind of machinery. The machinery and propulsion units were notoriously inadequate and inefficient.

The Confederacy had more success in arming its ironclads than in providing motive power for them. There was really never a shortage of heavy guns although some of the ships' initial batteries consisted of a variety of guns. Smoothbores were carried at one time or another by nearly all of the armorclads, but in contrast to the Union Navy, which advocated smoothbores during and after the war, the Confederate Navy concentrated on rifled guns. The standard rifled gun used on the Confederate ironclads was the Brooke gun, a cast-iron banded cannon developed by John Brooke, who headed the Confederate Navy's Bureau of Ordnance and Hydrography. The principal types used on the ironclads were 7-inch and 6.4-inch guns. The Confederate Navy also equipped its ironclads in 1863 with spar torpedoes, egg-shaped copper vessels containing from fifty to seventy pounds of powder, fitted to a long pole attached to the bow of the vessel. Although Union naval officers universally referred to the Confederate ironclads as "rams," only a few of them actually had rams built on.

The 150-foot *Richmond*, laid down at the navy yard in Norfolk and completed in Richmond, was the first of Porter's harbor defense vessels completed. Other 150-foot ironclads commenced included the *Chicora*, *Raleigh*, *Palmetto State*, *North Carolina*, *Huntsville*, *Tuscaloosa*, and *Savannah*. Larger vessels included the *Jackson* (renamed *Muscogee), Fredericksburg,* and *Milledgeville* (175 feet); the *Virginia II* and *Charleston* (180 feet); *Missouri* (183 feet); the *Columbia, Texas,* and *Tennessee* (216 feet); and the *Nashville* (310 feet). Porter also designed a smaller vessel of this class to be used in the North Carolina sounds. Only two of these 139-foot ironclads, the *Albemarle* and the *Neuse,* were completed.

Although the casemated ironclad remained the standard "home water" vessel constructed within the Confederacy, two double-ender ironclads with two octagonal casemates were laid down in Richmond and Wilmington. They were similar in appearance to the Union double-turreted monitors, but since the casemates were not moveable turrets, pivot guns were to be utilized. Neither vessel was completed because of the lack of iron armor. No monitor types were constructed in the Confederacy, although one to be built at Columbus, Georgia, was approved. The proposed vessel was apparently never laid down. Secretary of the Navy Mallory preferred the standard casemated ironclad. Less than two months before General Lee surrendered at Appomattox Court House, the secretary was writing, "for river, harbor, and coast defense, the sloping shield and general plan of armored vessels adopted by us... are the best that could be adopted in our situation. In ventilation, light, fighting space, and quarters it is believed that the sloping shield presents greater advantages than the *Monitor* turret."

The ironclads did contribute significantly to the Confederate war effort. They did not break or seriously challenge the Union blockade, but after the spring of 1862, this was not their primary objective. From then until the end of the war their real function was to defend the rivers, inlets, and ports. In this they had some success. Of the five seaports—Savannah, Charleston, Wilmington, Mobile, and Galveston—taken in the last six months of the war, two were taken by land forces from the rear, and two indirectly as a result of pressure from the rear. In all of the cities but one, Galveston, the Confederate Navy had ironclads as part of the harbor defense. Nevertheless, they suffered from serious defects in design and construction. The fundamental problems of weight, speed, seaworthiness, and mechanical inadequacies were never solved.

To a lesser degree the same was true of the Union armored vessels. Yet, they were superior in design and construction—not surprising, considering the available facilities and technological expertise in the North. This was particularly true of the monitors, which would remain the standard armored vessels in the United States Navy until the 1880s.

Like the Confederate ironclads the Union armored vessels played an important role in the Civil War. They were unsuitable for blockade duty, but in the amphibious operations along the coast and in the rivers and confined waters they proved their worth. Truly the Civil War was the ironclad era.

Left: The CSS Tennessee *in Mobile Bay, after its surrender to Farragut. It was commanded in battle by Franklin Buchanan, who commanded the first Confederate ironclad, the* Virginia. *(THE MARINERS MUSEUM)*

Above: The CSS Indianola, *formerly the USS* Indianola. *Captured from the Federals and towed to Vicksburg, the* Indianola *was undergoing refurbishment into a Confederate ironclad when its captors were forced to destroy it before the fall of Vicksburg. (USAMHI)*

Below: A David *class Confederate torpedo boat. These light-draft, semisubmerged "ironclads" were well suited for harbor defense, stealing out in the night to attack blockade ships. They enjoyed little real success, but created considerable consternation among the Federals. (NHC)*

Mr. Cooley of Beaufort and Mr. Moore of Concord

A PORTFOLIO

Two of hundreds of unsung artist, these photographers captured South Carolina long before the Federals

The entrepreneur photographer. (USAMHI)

Two of hundreds of unsung artists, these photographers captured South Carolina long before the Federals

THE WORK of two photographers, Samuel A. Cooley and Henry P. Moore, offers a remarkable view of South Carolina during this period.

Samuel A. Cooley represented that special class of quasi-official photographer, like George Barnard and Alexander Gardner, who sometimes did contract work for the government. Whenever possible, this group made private capital of their army contract work, implying that all of their work bore official sanction. Gardner called himself "Photographer to the Army of the Potomac." Cooley would use two titles—"Photographer Tenth Army Corps" and "U. S. Photographer, Department of the South." Perhaps it helped sales of their commercial views. Certainly Cooley could offer an unusual range of images, for he operated permanent establishments in three South Carolina locations, Folly Island, Hilton Head, and Beaufort, and in Jacksonville, Florida. Houses, hospitals, camps, vessels, forts, landscapes, and everything else came before his lenses, and he sold stereo views of all of them.

By contrast, little is known of Henry P. Moore, of Concord, New Hampshire. He operated at Hilton Head in 1862-63, and probably came chiefly to take marketable views of the 3rd New Hampshire for the folks at home. His remarkable images speak for themselves.

Above: "Cooley's" reads the sign in his Beaufort headquarters, and an unusual "gallery" it is. Clothing, flour, hams, books, butter, stationery, oranges, baskets, watches, and, of course, photographs, all could be bought over Cooley's counter. He stands in the white jacket leaning against his wagon. (USAMHI)

Below: The Fuller House, one of Beaufort's showplaces, and now the headquarters of General Rufus Saxton. A sentry box stands outside the gates to the house. (SOUTH CAROLINA HISTORICAL SOCIETY, CHARLESTON)

Below: Another view of Cooley's Beaufort gallery, with a little less advertising visible. (USAMHI)

Below: Cooley and assistants with his photographic wagon. Cooley himself stands second from the right, his hand resting on one of his cameras. (WRHS)

Right: Cooley's favorite subject, Beaufort, South Carolina, seen from the river. The artist had a wonderful eye for the still-life possibilities of the camera. (USAMHI)

Above: Bay Street in Beaufort, and J. W. Collins & Company's rather unusual clothing store. In addition to coats, vests, pants, and caps, Mr. Collins also sold oats and bran and, as advertised on the sign in his doorway, "cold soda." It certainly seems to attract more customers than the dress shop next door. (WRHS)

Right: A commissary storehouse, shot in October 1864, one of the contract images of government buildings made by Cooley. Right next door stands a fishing tackle and general provisions store. (SOUTH CAROLINA HISTORICAL SOCIETY)

Right: John S. Fyler's store and, next to it, the post office, one example of Cooley's sometimes extraordinary talent for still scenes that have life and seeming movement. (USAMHI)

Above: The Beaufort Hotel and, on its right, the office of the Adams Express Company, one of the early private mail and package carriers in the country. (SOUTH CAROLINA HISTORICAL SOCIETY)

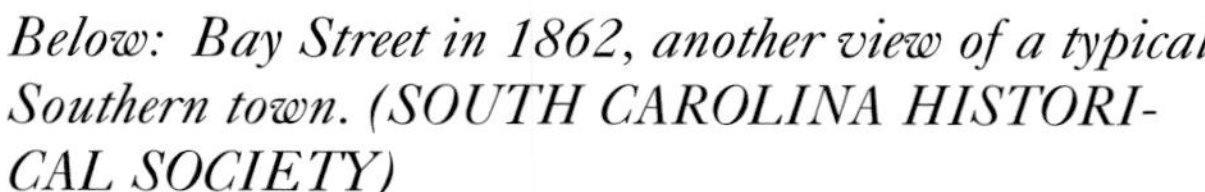

Below: Bay Street in 1862, another view of a typical Southern town. (SOUTH CAROLINA HISTORICAL SOCIETY)

Above: Another Beaufort post office, right next to the Adams Express. Since large sums of money often traveled in the post to and from the soldiers, the ground floor windows are barred with iron mesh to prevent burglary. (USAMHI)

Above: The west side of Bay Street. (USAMHI)

Left: The Beaufort Hotel again and, to its left, the commissary storehouse and fishing tackle shop. The dandies in front of the hotel may be Southern gentlemen who demurred on soldiering, or they may be Yankee traders who followed the army to sell to the soldiers. (USAMHI)

Left: A quiet street scene in Beaufort. (USAMHI)

Above: The one-time home of Dr. John A. Johnson, and now a hospital, with linen and blankets airing on the balcony. (USAMHI)

Left: A house used as a hospital for "contrabands," the slaves who gathered around the Union armies wherever they went, seeking freedom and protection. (SOUTH CAROLINA HISTORICAL SOCIETY)

Below: The Beaufort Arsenal on Craven Street. (SOUTH CAROLINA HISTORICAL SOCIETY)

Left: The United States Marine headquarters on Bay Point, rather a small headquarters, but then it was rather a small Marine Corps. (USAMHI)

Right: A parade, the generals on their white chargers, the men and boys watching from the sideline. Cooley missed no opportunity to shoot a scene with a mass of men. The more subjects in an image, the more who might want to buy a print . . . and perhaps an orange or two from his gallery. (CWTI)

Above: The machine shops at Bay Point and, in the foreground, bits and pieces of the machinery they worked on here, mostly for maintenance on the ships of the South Atlantic Blockading Squadron. (USAMHI)

Above: Hundreds of heavy guns passed through Hilton Head on their way to fight rebellion. They and their accoutrements lie here in some disarray. In the lower left corner, against the sand, can be seen the shadow of Cooley's camera. (USAMHI)

Left: At right the saltwater condenser for purifying water, and in the background several vessels docked awaiting coal. (USAMHI)

Above: The headquarters of Major General David Hunter, now recovered from his Bull Run wound. Cooley did a much more brisk business at Hilton Head than at Beaufort. (USAMHI)

Above: Henry P. Moore, too, went to Hilton Head, where there was more bustle and activity than in sleepy Beaufort. The wharf looked over a bay jammed with warships, transports, tugs, and lighter craft. (USAMHI)

Above: Here immense qualities of supplies for the army besieging Charleston were received. (USAMHI)

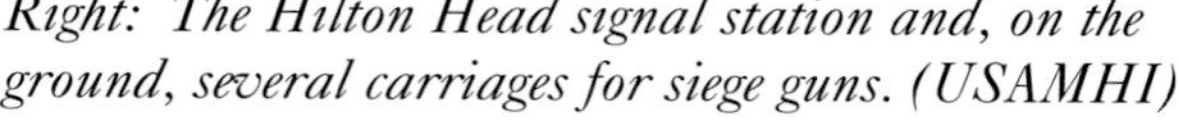

Right: The Hilton Head signal station and, on the ground, several carriages for siege guns. (USAMHI)

Left: Moore took his camera atop the signal station to photograph the hospital in the far distance and an ordnance storeyard in the forground. Cannons and carriages lay awaiting shipment to the front. (USAMHI)

Above: Another, larger, signal station was needed in 1863 on St. Helena Island. The engineers who built it based their tower on four existing trees still growing. (USAMHI)

Above: And on Otter Island they built another, which Moore captures in the act of signaling to a ship out on the horizon. (USAMHI)

Left: But at Hilton Head, Moore's best work was his portraits of the men in their camps, and particularly those of the 3rd New Hampshire. Here Lieutenant Colonel J. H. Jackson stands at left, his son Captain T. M. Jackson second from the right, and his servant Cyrus at his right. (USAMHI)

Left: Signal corpsmen, March 1, 1862.

Right: The 3rd New Hampshire's surgeon, A. A. Moulton, and his somewhat gothic-looking wife. (USAMHI)

Above: Cook's galley of Company H. In the hut in back stand tin plates and cups for the mess. In the center foreground stands the cook, G. N. Wheeler, at his camp stove. The man seated on the small barrel is W. Blake, about to grind coffee beans in the grinder at his feet. In the right background an unknown New Hampshire officer peers from his tent to see what Moore is doing. (USAMHI)

Below: The meal prepared, another cook looks on as the bandsmen of the 3rd New Hampshire dine, their drums and fifes set casually about the area. (USAMHI)

Left: A nonchalant group of the New Hampshire boys pose for the artist, their table reflecting their leisure doings. It lies cluttered with books, a cigar, letters from home, cased ambrotypes of female loved one, dominoes, and an ink bottle from which one man is writing his letter. The man seated on the other side of the table reads a page of crude cartoons from an issue of from an issue of Harper's weekly. *(USAMHI)*

Below: These New Hampshiremen added considerable decoration to their Hilton Head quarters. Seashells, palmettos, cactus, driftwood, all contributed to a scene quite out of the ordinary for Civil War camps. These musicians can enjoy their meal in the most pleasant surroundings. (USAMHI)

Above: The bandmaster's tent with bandmaster G. W. Ingalls at left studying his music while his servant polishes his boots. Sam Brown reads a New Hampshire newspaper at the center of the table, while musician D.A. Brown on the right does the same. Their horns lie on the table. (USAMHI)

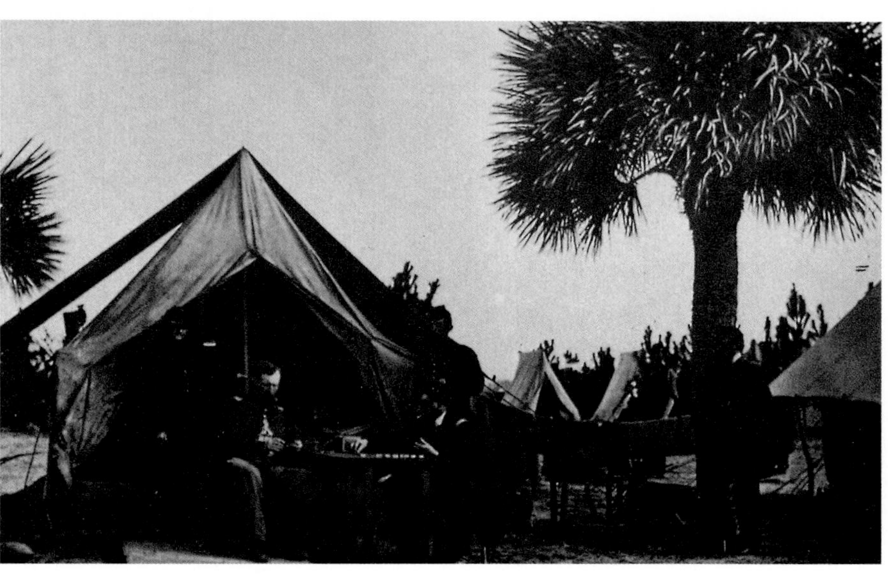

Above: And the officers loved their dominoes. (USAMHI)

Left: The splendid plantation residence of John E. Seabrook on Edisto Island, in 1862. At far left is his library—at right, his wine cellar. Lying like a white carpet on the lawn in front of the house is cotton captured aboard the blockade runner Empire *and spread out to dry in the sun. (USAMHI)*

Left: A closer view of the Seabrook mansion, now headquarters of Colonel E. Q. Fellows and staff. The post adjutant, Martin James, stands under the square marked on the image his office his office by the √, and his sleeping quarters by the #. Made by Moore on April 7, 1862. (KA)

Below: H. P. Moore's images of the Seabrook plantation touched upon art. Here Seabrook's extensive garden as seen from the mansion house. One of Seabrook's slaves, a little boy, stands atop the sundial at right center. Standing with folded arms in the foregrounds in Colonel E. Q. Fellows, commanding the 3rd New Hampshire. It is early spring, April 7, 1862, and already the garden is verdant. Half a continent away, the second day's fighting at Shiloh is raging. (KA)

Above: Seabrook's fishpond, with his house in the distance at left. Bandmaster Ingalls steers the boat. (USAMHI)

Right: More cotton is drying on Seabrook's grounds, being tended by freedmen who were once his slaves. In the distance at center stands the USS Pocahontas. *(USAMHI)*

Left: Seabrook's library. (USAMHI)

Left: Men who died before Moore could catch them in life pose silent and still in death. Almost all are of the 3rd New Hampshire—almost all died of disease. Hilton Head could kill despite its tropical beauty. (USAMHI)

Left: And however easy it might have been to forget the war, they could not, and neither did Moore. Deceptive in its peacefulness, this scene could turn warlike at any time, and the soldiers reading his letter beside the gun carriage in Fort Wells is certainly not far from his weapon. The sights atop the Rodman gun could fill with enemy vessels or blockade runners, and the tranquility of this image could vanish. Moore, for all his commercial instincts, knew as well that he was capturing a special part of the war for posterity. Thanks to him, these scenes will remain captive for all of time. (USAMHI)

The Peninsular Campaign

EMORY M. THOMAS

The first campaign going "on to Richmond," and the emergence of a general called "Granny" Lee

Above: After Johnston and Magruder abandoned Yorktown, the Confederates found Norfolk untenable and evacuated on May 9. Before leaving they did their best to destroy the navy yard. Timothy O'Sullivan's December 1864 photograph shows how thoroughly they did their task. (P-M)

THE ARMY OF THE POTOMAC was awesome. In the spring of 1862 it was the largest, best equipped armed force ever assembled in the Western Hemisphere. From the masses of volunteers who had descended upon Washington, George B. McClellan had fashioned a mammoth war machine—150,000 men, plus the material to support and sustain this host. With such force McClellan confidently intended to deliver the *coup de grace* to the would-be Confederacy.

McClellan had taken command in the aftermath of the Union debacle at Bull Run in July 1861. He began at once to mold his army and endured pleas and pressure to commit to battle prematurely. Termed "Young Napoleon" by the press, McClellan believed he understood the complexity of "modern war." He first had to spar with ranking United States General Winfield Scott until the aged Scott finally retired from the service in November 1861; then McClellan suffered the "help" of his Commander-in-Chief Abraham Lincoln and other martial amateurs in the administration and Congress.

Having built so splendid an army and waited so long to employ it, McClellan could not afford to err; when he marched, he would have to win. As the campaigning season of 1862 loomed imminent, Lincoln felt the need to rebuild his faith in "Young Napoleon." In frustration, the President issued his own General War Order Number One, which prescribed a "general forward movement" to begin on all fronts on February 22. Beyond this action, he and others in Washington could only chafe at McClellan's caution. Lincoln realized his administration had invested too much in McClellan to cut its losses now. Whatever "Young Napoleon" did or did not do would have to be Union strategy and policy.

Beyond the Potomac waited Confederate armies, the chief of which, commanded by Joseph E. Johnston, occupied the ground around Manassas near the battlefield of Bull Run. Johnston, who ironically held much the same low opinion of his President, Jefferson Davis, as McClellan did of Lincoln, had only some 40,000 troops. But he had 10,000 reinforcements nearby, and he had had all fall and winter to improve a position which had proven impenetrable the previous summer.

For the Army of the Potomac to emulate the tactics of First Bull Run and smash headlong into these waiting defenders seemed to McClellan art less and wasteful. Accordingly he determined to strike the Southerners elsewhere. He wanted to transport his army by water to the tiny port town of Urbana on the Rappahannock and interpose the Army of the Potomac between Johnston's Confederates and Richmond. Johnston, however, foiled the Urbana approach by evacuating Manassas and moving to Culpeper Court House where he might counter attacks from the east and north with equal facility. However sound was Johnston's movement, he acted in haste without fully apprising his President of his intentions. And he had had to destroy at Manassas enormous quantities of supplies his government had labored so diligently to collect. Davis, then, had doubts about Johnston nearly equal to Lincoln's about McClellan.

His Urbana landing scrapped, McClellan shifted to a strategic plan which was even more ambitious. He proposed to transport the Army of

Left: Now McClellan could pursue his original intention of campaigning up the Virginia Peninsula toward Richmond. Here he poses for a Brady camera with members of his staff including, standing at right, Van Vliet. (KA)

Right: Lieutenant General Winfield Scott on June 10, 1862, by Charles D. Fredericks. Taken at West Point after his retirement, it shows a man now bitter at his treatment by the younger McClellan. Two weeks from now, however, "Little Mac" will begin to feel his comeuppance on the Peninsula. (USAMHI)

the Potomac by water to Fort Monroe on the tip of the Virginia Peninsula between the York and James rivers. Union troops had maintained possession of the fort throughout the war, and McClellan planned to use this friendly perimeter as a staging area for an assault upon Richmond from the east. The combined army-navy operation and the eastern invasion route may have seemed complicated logistically, but it offered several advantages over a more direct assault. The Peninsular approach would not compel the Federals to cross the many streams and rivers which crossed the direct route to Richmond. The advance would take place on the relatively flat, tidewater coastal plain. The James, York, and Pamunkey rivers would permit the Union Navy to support McClellan's army with both supplies and gunfire during the advance to Richmond. If Johnston or any other commander dared confront the Army of the Potomac on the Peninsula, he would risk the prospect of having a portion of the blue army landed behind him and thus encirclement and destruction. On the other hand, if the Confederates chose to give battle nearer Richmond, McClellan had the siege artillery with which to blast his way into the city and destroy the opposing army at the same time. Withholding McDowell's corps, Lincoln assented to the plan, and McClellan promptly moved his army to the Peninsula and began his month-long siege of Yorktown.

On April 14 in Richmond the Confederate high command met for fourteen hours to plan some response to McClellan's Peninsular approach. Johnston favored a concentration near Richmond because he thought the Federals too strong on the Peninsula. Robert E. Lee, the President's chief military advisor, and Secretary of War George W. Randolph contended that the Southern army would have to confront the threat somewhere and that the Peninsula was as good a place as any. President Davis feared losing his army and capital if the campaign produced siege operations in front of Richmond. Accordingly Davis instructed Johnston to move his entire

Above: One of McClellan's commanders, Brigadier General Edwin V. Sumner, the oldest corps leader of the war. Born in 1797, he was called "bull head" because a musket ball supposedly bounced from his head in Mexico. During the coming campaign, however, he was wounded twice. (USAMHI)

Left: Some of McClellan's generals, on May 14, 1862. Seated from the right they are Brigadier General John Newton, Brigadier General William F. Barry, VI Corps commander Brigadier General William B. Franklin, and Brigadier General Henry W. Slocum. (NLM)

Above: Stewart Van Vliet, McClellan's chief quartermaster in the Peninsular campaign. (KA)

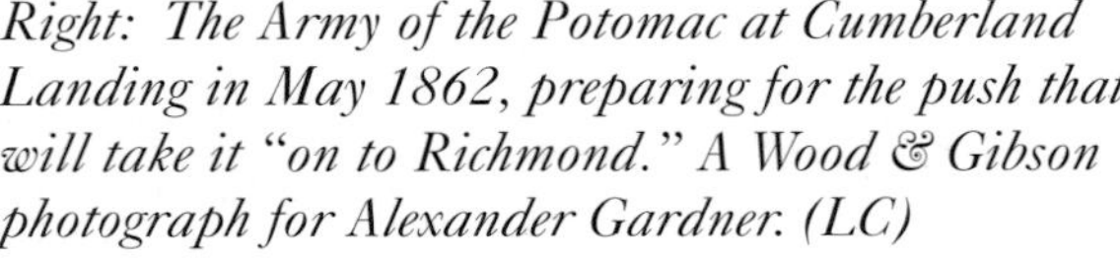

Right: The Army of the Potomac at Cumberland Landing in May 1862, preparing for the push that will take it "on to Richmond." A Wood & Gibson photograph for Alexander Gardner. (LC)

Above: One of Brady's assistants captures a scene at Cumberland Landing. Over 100,000 men await the order to advance against an enemy barely half their numbers. (LC)

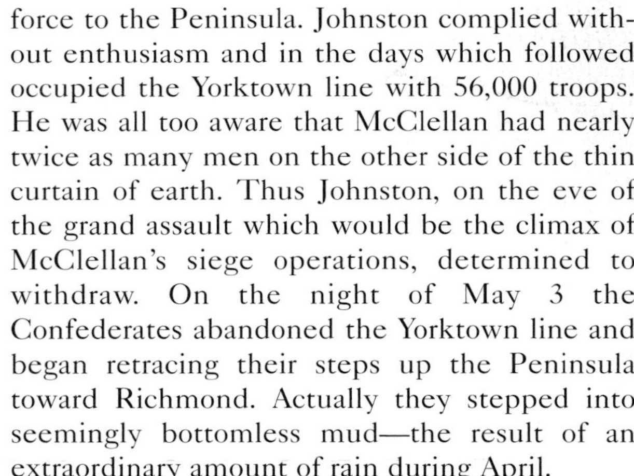

force to the Peninsula. Johnston complied without enthusiasm and in the days which followed occupied the Yorktown line with 56,000 troops. He was all too aware that McClellan had nearly twice as many men on the other side of the thin curtain of earth. Thus Johnston, on the eve of the grand assault which would be the climax of McClellan's siege operations, determined to withdraw. On the night of May 3 the Confederates abandoned the Yorktown line and began retracing their steps up the Peninsula toward Richmond. Actually they stepped into seemingly bottomless mud—the result of an extraordinary amount of rain during April.

As Southern columns clogged the spongy roads westward, McClellan's Federals on May 4 rushed empty earthworks. To Washington McClellan announced a great victory at small cost. Then he set about directing the pursuit of his elusive enemy. Five Union divisions plunged into the Peninsular mud, by now well-churned by the retreating Con federates; four more divisions stood ready to move by water up the York to cut off the Southern withdrawal.

Johnston's rear guard (James Longstreet's division) first felt the pressure of the Federal pursuit near Williamsburg. Just east of the old

Below: A panorama showing the army at camp near Cumberland Landing. (CHS)

Left: Two images by James F. Gibson almost form a panoramic view of troops at Cumberland Landing on the Pamunkey River. The landing appears at right. (left, LC; right, USAMHI)

Above: Another Gibson panorama of the camps on the Pamunkey. (USAMHI)

Below: Probably Gibson's finest panorama. The enormity of an army on campaign is evident and overwhelming. (USAMHI)

Right: In mid-May McClellan moved his base to White House on the Pamunkey, formerly the home of one of Robert E. Lee's sons. James Gibson photographed the house on May 17, 1862. (USAMHI)

Below: And G. W. Houghton, the Brattleboro, Vermont photographer, caught this scene of the camps of the army at White House Landing. (VERMONT HISTORICAL SOCIETY)

Left: Gibson's May 17 image of the destroyed bridge of the Richmond & York River Railroad over the Pamunkey. McClellan's people started the work of repair at once and… (NLM)

Below: … soon it was rebuilt, though the steam engine here is on a barge. Tracks have not yet been laid on the bridge. And within a month, McClellan himself will have to destroy it once again when he retreats. (USAMHI)

colonial capital on May 5 a sharp fight ensued. The Southerners first stopped the Union advance, then counterattacked, and finally withdrew into the darkness. The Battle of Williamsburg was bloody, but inconclusive. Johnston gained the time he needed to make good his escape, but the Confederate counterattack was a costly failure.

McClellan, meanwhile, was trying to hasten Johnston's envelopment by water. William B. Franklin's division made a landing on the Peninsula opposite West Point, but encountered Gustavus W. Smith's Confederates soon after. The wily Johnston anticipated McClellan's move, and the engagement between Smith's and Franklin's troops on May 7 at Barhamsville (Eltham's Landing) convinced McClellan that his trap had failed. Thereafter he contented himself with a methodical pursuit of his quarry up the Peninsula.

The rival commanders each expressed satisfaction at the developments thus far. Johnston was pleased to have made good his escape, and McClellan took pride in his conquest of the Yorktown line and his pursuit of a fleeing foe. Both generals consumed themselves in cautious movement: Johnston to the vicinity of Richmond and McClellan to the vicinity of Johnston.

In the process both ignored their navies and a succession of military "dominoes" involved in the movement up the Peninsula. When Johnston evacuated the Yorktown line, he left the port city of Norfolk exposed and untenable. When Norfolk fell—the Confederates evacuated the city on May 9—the *Virginia* became a ship without a port. When the *Virginia's* crew failed in their attempt to lighten the heavy-draft vessel sufficiently to steam up the James, they had to destroy the ironclad. This in turn opened the James all the way to Richmond to Union gunboats and troop transports.

Curiously, neither field commander appreciated this circumstance. Lee was the first Confederate to react; he hastened the work on gun emplacements, river obstructions, and "torpedoes" at Drewry's Bluff. McClellan was seemingly too preoccupied even to comprehend the city's vulnerability. Indeed, it was President Lincoln himself, while visiting Fort Monroe, who gave the instructions which led to Norfolk's capture. The Federal Navy then pressed the issue, and on May 15 two ironclads, the *Monitor* and *Galena*, led three wooden gun boats up the James toward Richmond. The small fleet encountered little difficulty until it reached Drewry's Bluff, which was only about seven miles from the Confederate capital. There Southern batteries and channel obstructions halted the Union advance. Had McClellan provided the expedition with a supporting army column of any size, the fight at Drewry's Bluff might have turned out quite differently. As it happened though, this repulse ended the Federal threat to Richmond by water.

Indeed water, in the form of rain, seemed to plague instead of assist McClellan's campaign as the Army of the Potomac advanced nearer Richmond. The Federal route lay up the northern half of the Peninsula to take advantage of supply lines from the York and Pamunkey rivers. At Cumberland Landing and White House the navy deposited massive amounts of supplies for transport overland via road and the Richmond &

York River rail line to the troops. Throughout May unseasonal amounts of rain hampered the movements of men and supplies. Yet even though the Army of the Potomac seemed to ooze instead of march, it moved nonetheless ever closer to Richmond.

As he neared the city McClellan recognized the necessity to broaden his front and position his army on the south as well as the north side of the Chickahominy River, which bisects the Peninsula near Richmond. Two Federal corps had crossed the Chickahominy on May 30 when one of the most violent rainstorms in memory descended upon the area. The fresh rain turned the normally sluggish Chickahominy into a torrent which washed away bridges and left Erasmus Keyes's Union corps isolated from the rest of the army. Joe Johnston recognized his opportunity and determined to strike the exposed Federals with four Confederate divisions.

The Confederate attack appeared simple as long as it consisted only of lines drawn on a map. The lines, representing Southern troops moving along roads, converged at the village of Seven Pines, and there Johnston planned to attack a fraction of the blue army with masses of his own men. On the morning of May 31, however, Johnston's plan came unraveled. James Longstreet seemed most at fault; he took the wrong road and in so doing clogged the Confederate advance. As a result the supposedly coordinated attack degenerated into a series of single blows and an aborted Confederate opportunity. In the aftermath of the day's fighting Johnston fell wounded from his horse, leaving the Southerners not only confused, but also leaderless.

On June 1, after an unsuccessful attempt to salvage victory from the Battle of Seven Pines (or Fair Oaks), Robert E. Lee arrived to assume command and lead the march back toward Richmond. To this juncture, Lee had disappointed himself and others in the Southern cause. Possessed of splendid credentials at the outset of the war, he had directed a doomed campaign in the Kanawha Valley of western Virginia, presided over a retreat from the coast in South Carolina and Georgia, and served in the President's shadow as Davis's military advisor. In this last capacity, Lee had ameliorated some what the relations between Davis and Johnston; but of this, no one but Lee was aware. Thus, he took command of Johnston's army in the wake of a bungled battle in the midst of a desperate campaign with little reputation beyond those who knew him. And the first direction he gave to his troops was to dig holes in the ground—to shore up the defensive works in front of Richmond.

Those who crowned Lee with the sobriquet "Granny Lee" or "King of Spades," however, missed his intention. Lee threw up breastworks so that he might defend Richmond with as few troops as possible; with the bulk of his army he determined to attack.

If the new Confederate commander needed time to make Johnston's army his own following the battle, McClellan seemed to be in a cooperative mood. He moved, slowly and cautiously, to consolidate his position before Richmond. Completing his shift of troop units south of the Chickahominy, McClellan stationed four corps (Franklin's, E. V. Sumner's, Samuel P.

Left: George Washington was married in St. Peter's Church near White House. Now it is favored by touring Federals, including white-bearded General Sumner and his staff. (USAMHI)

Left: Another view of St. Peter's, taken by a Brady assistant. (LC)

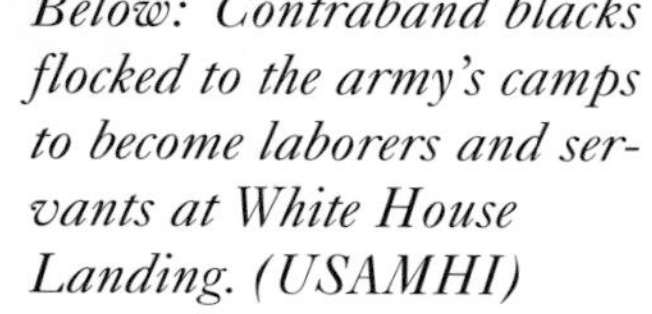

Below: Contraband blacks flocked to the army's camps to become laborers and servants at White House Landing. (USAMHI)

Right: And another sort of man gathered around the army, the romantic secret service men, the operatives and spies whose "intelligence" McClellan believed unquestioningly. The trouble was, their information proved consistently erroneous. Seated in the background, pipe in mouth, is the most unreliable of them all, Allan Pinkerton. Yet McClellan preferred to believe him since his reports of overwhelming enemy numbers confirmed "Little Mac's" own exaggerated fears. (NLM)

Left: On the march again. David Woodbury caught men of the 5th New Hampshire and 64th New York at work on this military bridge over the Chickahominy in the last days of May, as the Federals are on their way to Seven Pines. (USAMHI)

Above: On the battle line at Seven Pines, or Fair Oaks. Gibson's early June photo of Fort Richardson, near the Quarles House. (NLM)

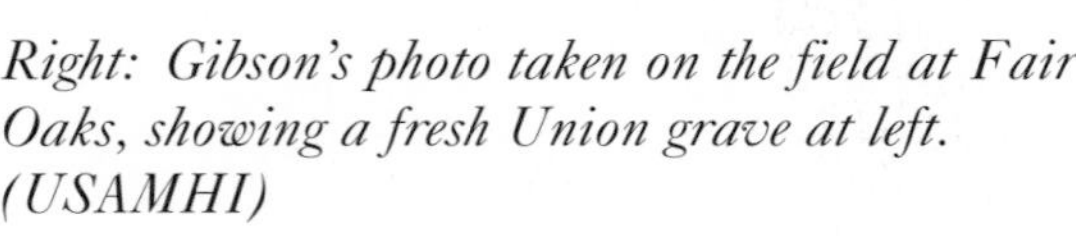

Right: Gibson's photo taken on the field at Fair Oaks, showing a fresh Union grave at left. (USAMHI)

Heintzelman's and Keyes's) directly east of Seven Pines about six miles from its limits and about one mile from the Confederate works. North of the Chickahominy were the 30,000 troops of Fitz John Porter's corps. McClellan was careful for good reason; his intelligence operatives and spies informed him that the Confederate Army numbered 200,000 men. The estimate, largely the product of Allan Pinkerton's civilian agents, was much exaggerated; Lee had perhaps 65,000 to 70,000 troops with which to confront McClellan's 90,000 to 100,000 at this point. Nevertheless McClellan believed the Army of the Potomac was outnumbered, and he renewed his pleas for reinforcements.

While waiting for his government to appreciate his situation and support him as he believed necessary, McClellan brought up his big guns, 101 pieces of siege artillery. These weapons, he believed, would compensate for his numerical inferiority and enable the Federals to blast their way into Richmond. To his wife, McClellan explained that he planned to "make the first battle mainly an artillery combat." The artillery would "push them in upon Richmond and behind their works." Then he would "bring up my heavy guns, shell the city, and carry it by assault."

With uncanny insight into the mind of his foe, Lee wrote to Davis on June 5, "McClellan will make this a battle of posts. He will take position from position, under cover of his heavy guns, and we cannot get at him without storming his works, which... is extremely hazardous." To counter the Union tactics, Lee proposed "to bring McClellan out," to make the Federals fight in the open, away from prepared fortifications and big guns. First he assured himself that his defensive works before Richmond were as strong as he could make them. Then he dispatched almost four brigades to the Shenandoah Valley to provide "Stonewall" Jackson with the strength to conclude his brilliant campaign there. Lee had need of the hard-hitting Valley Army at Richmond. Finally, he sent J.E.B. Stuart and 1,200 cavalry troopers to scout the Federal right flank.

Stuart left Richmond on the morning of June 12 and rode north twenty-two miles before making camp for the night. Next day the column turned east. The Confederates encountered slight resistance as they moved, and Stuart realized that the Union right flank was unsecured. Nevertheless, he pressed on—completely around McClellan's army and back into Richmond from the south on June 15. Stuart's "ride around McClellan" made him a hero and did wonders for Confederate morale; it also seemed to confirm McClellan's fears about Confederate strength. But most importantly the venture provided Lee with valuable information regarding the Federal flank.

During the latter half of June McClellan hesitated. He considered opening an additional supply route from Harrison's Landing on the James to supplement or supplant his bases on the Pamunkey. He contemplated an all-out assault on Richmond. Eventually he decided upon a limited advance to test Confederate defenses east of the city.

Meanwhile Lee was dreaming larger dreams. On June 23 he convened a meeting attended by Longstreet, D. H. Hill, A. P. Hill, and Jackson, and announced his plans. He would station

Above: Battery C of the 1st Pennsylvania Light Artillery, the extreme front line at Fair Oaks. (NLM)

Above: Major General Gustavus W. Smith, center, and his staff. After the wounding of Johnston at Fair Oaks, Smith temporarily commanded the Army of Northern Virginia. (CHS)

Above: Two old frame houses, an orchard, and a well, near Fair Oaks, where over 400 dead Federals were buried after the battle. (NLM)

Left: Union Fort Sumner near Fair Oaks, looking toward the Confederate lines, taken by Gibson a few days after the battle. (USAMHI)

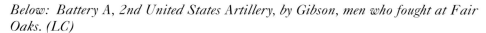

Below: Battery A, 2nd United States Artillery, by Gibson, men who fought at Fair Oaks. (LC)

Above: Another view of the twin frame houses beside the orchard. A central main house was meant to connect the two wings, but it was never built. (USAMHI)

Left: Lowe replenishing the gas in his balloon Intrepid *from the Constitution. Brady's assistant made a series of images of Lowe and his apparatus. (USAMHI)*

Right: While the armies fought at Fair Oaks, Professor T. S. Lowe gained a true bird's-eye view of the fight from his balloon Intrepid. *Here it is being inflated on Gaines's Hill, June 1, 1862. Lowe stands at right with his hand resting against the balloon. (KA)*

Above: "Your message received announcing the success of Balloon and Telegraph combined—the most wonderful feat of the age." So said Thomas T. Eckert of the Union's Military Telegraph. On June 1, 1862, during the Battle of Fair Oaks, a photographer working for Brady captured the scene that made Eckert so ecstatic. Professor Thaddeus Lowe's observation balloon, probably the Intrepid, *is grounded after an ascent. From his observations, telegrapher Parker Spring is sending a dispatch over the portable field key attached to the roll of wire. Lowe may be the man in the white hat seated below him. A third man sits with his back to the camera, sketching the scene on a pad. It was a blending of two new means of rapid communications, a historic moment. "Give my compliments to Prof Lowe and Spring," said Eckert after receiving the first telegram; "if they feel as proud over the enterprise as I do, they have been well repaid and will long be remembered." (KA)*

Right: On his way to the heavens, an officer ascends in Lowe's craft to observe the fighting at Fair Oaks. His climb is controlled by the soldiers anchoring the balloon. (LC)

25,000 men commanded by Magruder and Benjamin Huger in the works to the east of Richmond; these troops would have to fend off the entire Union Army if Lee's plan miscarried. The divisions of Longstreet and the two Hills would mass on the Confederate left and strike the Union right at the village of Mechanicsville. And Jackson's Valley Army by rapid and secret marches would join Lee's force and strike the Federals in the rear of their right flank. If all went well, approximately 66,000 Confederates would assault Porter's 30,000 Federals from the flank and the rear. This would "bring McClellan out" of his works and, perhaps, destroy him. If, on the other hand, McClellan realized in time the weakness of the Confederate force covering Richmond, he was capable of blasting his way into the city. The stakes of Lee's gamble were high—victory or disaster.

Lee's campaign, known as the Seven Days Battles, began on June 25 when McClellan launched his limited attack upon the Confederate lines east of Richmond. Two Federal divisions advanced upon the Southern works, tested their strength, and then threw up field fortifications of their own. McClellan believed what Lee wanted him to believe—that the 25,000 Confederates were 50,000. The same day McClellan also learned that Jackson's army was on the way down from the Valley. Immediately he sent a message to Washington announcing Jackson's presence and emphasizing his peril. "I am in no way responsible..." McClellan insisted, "I have not failed to represent repeatedly the necessity for reinforcements... if the result... is a disaster, the responsibility can not be thrown on my shoulders; it must rest where it belongs." Then having prepared his government for the worst and exonerated himself, McClellan hastened to Porter's headquarters.

On June 26 Lee's three divisions formed for the attack on Mechanicsville. The commands of A. P. Hill, D. H. Hill, and Longstreet formed land waited. Nothing was supposed to occur until Jackson arrived, and Jackson was uncharacteristically late. Finally, at three in the afternoon, A. P. Hill could restrain himself no longer. Acting upon the assumption that Jackson must be nearby and poised for attack, Hill began the battle. The Confederates swept across the Chickahominy and through Mechanicsville. Then they crashed head long into Porter's lines behind Beaver Dam Creek.

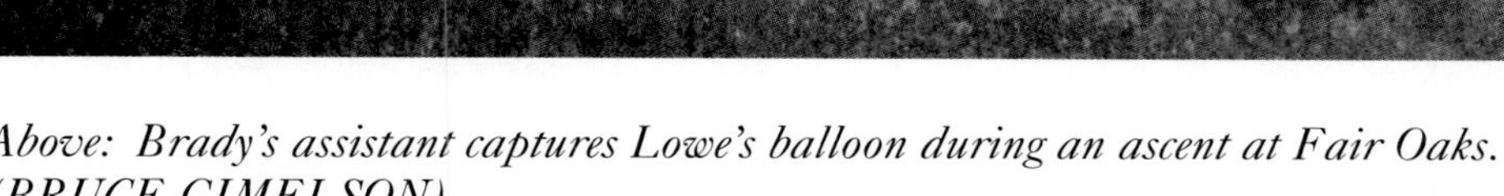

Above: Brady's assistant captures Lowe's balloon during an ascent at Fair Oaks. (BRUCE GIMELSON)

Left: Brigadier General David B. Birney, son of the abolitionist leader James G. Birney, commanded a brigade at Fair Oaks. He was charged with disobeying an order from his superior,... (USAMHI)

Below: ... Samuel P. Heintzelman, during the battle. Birney was acquitted. (CWTI)

Neither frontal assault nor flank attack could dislodge the Federals. The Confederates sustained 1,484 casualties against 361 Union losses and did precisely what Lee had not wanted to do—attacked the Unionists in their prepared works.

Darkness ended the day's fighting in the Battle of Mechanicsville, and still Jackson's troops had not arrived. Actually the Valley Army reached the vicinity at five o'clock in the afternoon; then Jackson, after being unaccountably late, became incredibly cautious. He made camp within the sound of the battle. The most rational explanation of Jackson's behavior focuses upon an irrational response to stress and exhaustion. He had ridden, fought, and marched too long with too little rest. And now a "fog of war" settled over him and clouded his otherwise clear mind. On the morning of June 27, Jackson finally found the battle. But the fact that the first shells fired by the artillery of the Valley Army landed among some of A. P. Hill's troops portended more confusion on Jackson's part. Lee resolved to continue his attack on June 27; he had little choice. During the previous night McClellan had removed Porter's troops to a new position near Gaines's Mill on Boatswain's Swamp. The Southerners attacked in the early afternoon, and again Porter's men withstood the assault. Jackson was supposed to send his troops crashing down upon the Federal flank, but once more he was late. At last, at seven o'clock in the evening, Lee was able to assemble his army for a concerted drive. In the face of this new attack, Porter's troops, who had been repelling piecemeal assaults for five hours, broke. Confederate infantry tore through the center of the Federal lines. In desperation Union General Phillip St. George Cooke, J.E.B. Stuart's father-in-law, ordered his cavalry to charge the oncoming Southerners. The charge only added to the general confusion, however, when it degenerated into a stampede to the rear in the face of Confederate rifle fire. At Gaines's Mill, at a cost of 8,750 Confederate casualties to 6,837 Union losses, Lee won his first clear victory. Yet during the night Porter was able to cross the Chickahominy and unite his battered men with

Left: And General Oliver O. Howard, who fought at Bull Run, commanded a brigade at Fair Oaks. A bullet there cost him his right arm. He still had both arms in this Brady studio portrait. (USAMHI)

Below: Brigadier General Willis A. Gorman, former territorial governor of Minnesota, shown here with his wife, commanded a brigade in Sumner's corps and won acclaim from several superiors. (NA)

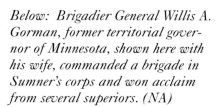

Right: And Brigadier General John J. Abercrombie, born in 1798, was still active enough to lead a brigade at Fair Oaks at the age of sixty-four. Here he was wounded, and he left active service for the duration of the war. (USAMHI)

Above: A house used by the Federals as a hospital after the battle. Image by Gibson in June 1862. (USAMHI)

Below: Another view of the hospital, used by wounded from General Joseph Hooker's division. Even it did not escape the battle, as evidenced in the collapsed chimney and damaged wall. (LC)

Above: The Quarles House near Fair Oaks. Many Federal dead were interred here after the fight. (USAMHI)

Below: Gibson's photo of the house used as a hospital by General Philip Kearny's brigade. The nondescript looking lot of men here may well be walking wounded . (NLM)

the rest of the Army of the Potomac. McClellan's army was much alive and still a potent force.

McClellan himself was unnerved, however. Fearing for his supply lines to the Pamunkey and for the safety of his army, he determined to retreat to the James and open a new base of supply at Harrison's Landing. Some of his subordinates, notably Joseph Hooker and Phil Kearny, perceived that the Confederate forces directly before Richmond were as weak as they actually were. But McClellan rejected their counsel. He gave the order for his retreat and then vented his frustration upon his superiors in Washington. He dispatched a lengthy telegram in which he explained the situation as he understood it. In conclusion he placed the blame for this circumstance where he thought blame belonged. "If I save this army now, I tell you plainly that I owe no thanks to you or to any other persons in Washington. You have done your best to sacrifice this army." Fortunately for McClellan, the telegraph supervisor in Washington did not transmit these two final sentences to the President.

Satisfied that he had absolved himself of the responsibility for his "change of base," on June 28 McClellan set about saving his army. Confederates could see the smoke from burning

Above: For most of the men in McClellan's army, Fair Oaks was their first real fight. One of these was McClellan's chief of cavalry, Brigadier General George Stoneman, shown here in camp after the battle. He and his cavalry took little part, in fact. (USAMHI)

Above: Stoneman, seated at right, and Brigadier General Henry M. Naglee. The dog is nearly as photogenic as the generals. (USAMHI)

supplies and wagons moving to the southeast. Nevertheless Lee had to act on less than confirmed intelligence when he committed his army to an all-out pursuit. Elements of the opposing armies fought on June 28, but the major effort to cut off and destroy the Army of the Potomac began the following day.

On June 29 Magruder was finally to have the chance for offensive, instead of defensive, action. Moving east, near the old battlefield at Fair Oaks, Magruder was in a good position to strike the retreating Federals. Jackson, too, had the opportunity to fall upon the Union rear. As it happened, though, both Confederate generals failed to move fast enough or decisively enough. Jackson never really got his command into action, and Magruder advanced timidly until his troops encountered the Federals near Savage Station. There, late in the day, the Confederates attacked to no significant effect. Understandably Lee was concerned that he would lose the chance to reap the benefits of his hard-won victories thus far. Accordingly on June 30 he again exhorted his subordinates to press the pursuit. He planned to bring the troops of Longstreet, A. P. Hill, Magruder, Huger, and Jackson together for a climactic battle. Once more, however, Magruder and Jackson were slow, and Huger, too, was late. As a result, Hill's and Longstreet's divisions struck the center of the Federal Army in a battle variously named White Oak Swamp, Frayser's Farm, or Glendale. The combat raged in all three of these places, and more, and the Union line held firm amid fierce fighting.

On the morning of July 1 McClellan seemed to have made good his escape. Porter's corps and the huge wagon train of army supplies were safely at Harrison's Landing. The remaining four

Above: On March 18, 1862, with the threat of McClellan coming up the Peninsula, President Jefferson Davis appointed a new Secretary of War, George Wythe Randolph of Virginia. He appears here in an unpublished portrait. One of the few war secretaries to attempt to exercise real control of the War Department, he only lasted in office until November. But he worked well with the man that he and Davis chose to replace the wounded Johnston at the head of the Army of Northern Virginia,... (UNIVERSITY OF VIRGINIA, EDGEHILL RANDOLPH PAPERS)

Above: ... General Robert Edward Lee. Until now, Lee's war service had been less than glorious. Some called him "Granny Lee," and some, like South Carolina Governor Francis Pickens, doubted that his heart was in the cause. The next month on the Peninsula would answer their fears. (SOUTHERN HISTORICAL COLLECTION, THE UNIVERSITY OF NORTH CAROLINA AT CHAPEL HILL)

Above: Ironically, Lee's opposite number in the Confederate Navy on the Peninsula was his own brother Captain Sidney Smith Lee. "There will be no interference with the naval forces under your command by the land forces serving in conjunction with you," the general wrote to the captain, expressing the hope that "the two services will harmonize perfectly." Even among brothers the age-old rivalry between army and navy had to be resisted . (WILLIAM A. ALBAUGH)

Above: One of the cavalrymen with Stuart, the scout who led him on his ride around McClellan, Lieutenant John Singleton Mosby. Previously unknown, he established his reputation in this war. He appears in this unpublished portrait in the uniform of a colonel. (USAMHI)

Above: The pace of the campaign quickened when, on June 12, Lee sent Brigadier General James Ewell Brown "Jeb" Stuart on a four-day reconnaissance around McClellan's army. Lee gained valuable information, but at the price of alerting McClellan that something was in the wind. (VALENTINE MUSEUM, COOK COLLECTION)

Above: Major General Fitz John Porter and his corps were dangerously isolated north of the Chickahominy River, and late in June Lee determined to attack. (USAMHI)

corps of the Army of the Potomac were drawn up on the slopes of Malvern Hill, the last position they would have to occupy before they reached Harrison's Landing and sanctuary. The Federal position seemed impregnable. Still, Lee hoped for total victory, and so he sent Longstreet to investigate "the feasibility of aggressive battle."

Longstreet believed he had discovered locations from which Confederate artillery might catch the Federals in a devastating cross fire. Lee gave the order to mass the guns where Longstreet indicated and instructed the infantry to charge in the wake of the artillery barrage. However, the Southern artillery never got completely into place or action. Hence Confederate infantry remained in place, and it seemed that there would be no battle.

Then in the middle of the afternoon the Federals began to move; they seemed to be with drawing. Lee ordered an immediate attack. Southern troops charged up Malvern Hill to find the Army of the Potomac very much in place. The assault was slaughter. Union artillery raked the advancing ranks, and Federal infantry blazed away at the survivors. Yet the series of charges continued until dark. And in the night 8,000 casualties littered the field, 5,000 Confederate, 3,000 Union.

Lee had seized a last chance to destroy his foe and lost. Perhaps he sensed a moment of truth which might not come again. Regardless of the reason the result was disaster.

Although no one knew it for sure at the time, the Battle of Malvern Hill was the last of the Seven Days Battles and the conclusion of the Peninsular campaign. The Army of the Potomac withdrew to Harrison's Landing to recuperate. The Confederates remained nearby for a time; then Lee left a token force and took the bulk of his army to Richmond. The campaign established Lee as savior of the Confederacy. When he took command, the Army of the Potomac was in the suburbs of Richmond; a month later the same army cowered inert under the protection of naval guns twenty-three miles away. Lee was lavish in his praise of his own army, the Army of Northern Virginia. Later in his official report, however, he admitted, "Under ordinary circumstances the Federal Army should have been destroyed."

Although out-generaled, the Army of the Potomac had fought well. The men who had stood firm against the furious Confederate assaults at Gaines's Mill, Malvern Hill, and elsewhere would be back. But McClellan, the "Young Napoleon" who molded this splendid army, had proven him self unable to command it.

Above: Confederate casualties at Mechanicsville ran high. Colonel Mumford S. Stokes of the 1st North Carolina Infantry took a mortal wound. (WRHS)

Left: A group of staff officers on the eve of the fighting on the Virginia Peninsula. The man lying at right with the dog is a twenty-two year old captain, George Armstrong Custer. He too, like Mosby, made a name for himself in this war. (LC)

Left: Mechanics--ville, Virginia, photographed in April 1865 by Gardner's assistant James Reekie. Here on June 26, 1862, was fought the second of the Seven Days Battles, when Lee attempted to strike Porter's exposed position north of the Chickahominy. (USAMHI)

Left: Reekie's 1865 image of Ellison's Mill on the battlefield at Mechanicsville. The hottest of the fighting raged around and past this little structure as Porter successfully defended himself before withdrawing. (NA)

Above: Colonel Edward L. Thomas of the 35th Georgia took a bad wound at Mechanicsville. He recovered to become a fine brigade commander and, as pictured here, a brigadier general. (VM)

Right: Faced with heavy numbers against him, Porter withdrew across the Chickahominy on bridges like this one on the Mechanicsville road. (LC)

Right: Porter took a new position near Gaines's Mill, and here on June 27, 1862, Lee attacked again. Reekie's photo shows the destroyed mill in April 1865. (USAMHI)

Below: Brigadier General George Morell was instrumental in defending Porter's corps from Lee's attempted encirclement. (USAMHI)

Right: The Gaines House. Less than two months before, Federal generals were posing for Houghton and others on this porch. Now it is Lee's headquarters. (MUSEUM OF THE CONFEDERACY, RICHMOND)

Above: Brigadier General Andrew A. Humphreys served as McClellan's chief topographical engineer. Poor and inadequate maps plagued both sides on the Peninsula, where local traditions twist names and pronunciations. One road pronounced "Darby" was in fact spelled "Enroughty." (USAMHI)

Above: Brigadier General Arnold Elzey—whose real name was Jones—was a hero at Bull Run. At Gaines's Mill he received a terrible wound which left him unfit for field command for most of the rest of the war. (DUKE UNIVERSITY, BRADLEY T. JOHNSON PAPERS)

Above: Colonel James S. Connor, a veteran of Bull Run and the Hampton Legion, took command of the 22nd North Carolina shortly before Gaines's Mill. In this battle a rifle ball broke his leg. (LC)

Above: Major General Ambrose Powell Hill performed the greatest share of the fighting for Lee at Mechanicsville and Gaines's Mill. He became one of Lee's premier commanders. (FRANK DEMENTI)

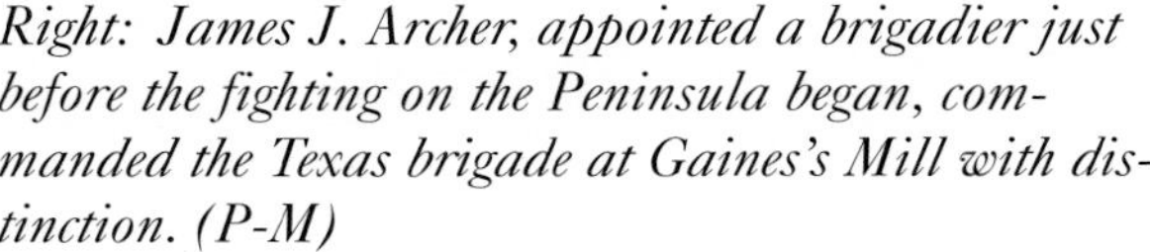

Right: James J. Archer, appointed a brigadier just before the fighting on the Peninsula began, commanded the Texas brigade at Gaines's Mill with distinction. (P-M)

Above: William Dorsey Pender won promotion to brigadier for his service at Fair Oaks, and now led a brigade for A. P. Hill. One of the army's most brilliant young commanders, he died as a result of a wound at Gettysburg a year later. (USAMHI)

Vermont photographer G. W. Houghton found this tent wrecked after a Confederate shell fired during the Gaines's Mill fighting struck it. (VHS)

Left: Part of the cost of Gaines's Mill. Federal soldiers buried hurriedly in shallow graves by their retreating comrades were exposed by later rains. Reekie found them like this in April 1865. (WRHS)

Right: On June 29 the fighting moved to Savage Station on the Richmond & York River Railroad. It is shown here the day before the battle, photographed by James Gibson. (VM)

Above: "Prince John" Magruder had been fighting holding actions south of the Chickahominy while Lee attacked Porter. Now Lee ordered him to attack McClellan's rear. He pushed the Federal advance back to Savage Station. (USAMHI)

Above: In the subsequent fighting, over 1,500 Federals became casualties. Here some wounded from Gaines's Mill and earlier fights await transportation to the rear at Savage Station. (USAMHI)

Left: Vermont soldiers particularly distinguished themselves at Savage Station. Here the Green Mountain Boys of the 6th Vermont's Company I at drill. (LC)

Above: McClellan retreated to White Oak Swamp where the forces joined battle again on June 30. There in furious fighting Brigadier General George G. Meade was wounded twice in almost the same moment. (USAMHI)

Left: Sick and wounded of the 16th New York being tended at Savage Station photographed by Gibson on June 28. (MHS)

Above: John Sedgwick, now a brigadier, was once major of the 1st United States Cavalry, whose colonel was Robert E. Lee. Now he led a division in Sumner's corps, but a bullet at White Oak Swamp put him out of the war for several weeks. (NA)

Above: Major General Erasmus D. Keyes, veteran of Bull Run, commanded McClellan's I V Corps without particular distinction at White Oak Swamp. One of his brigade commanders,... (USAMHI)

Right: ... Colonel Philippe Regis Denis de Keredern de Trobriand, was the son of a French nobleman. He became one of the Union's finest brigadiers. (USAMHI)

Above: Brigadier General James L. Kemper, once speaker of the house in the Virginia capital, now led a brigade in the nightmarish morass of White Oak Swamp. (USAMHI)

Above: George M. Sauerbier's image of the "Westchester Chasseurs," the 17th New York on parade. They are among many regiments mauled in the Seven Days fighting and at White Oak Swamp. (NA, BRADY COLLECTION)

Above: The final battle came at Malvern Hill, where the retreating Federals made their stand. On July 1, 1862, Lee attacked repeatedly and with heavy losses. Regiments like the 4th Georgia, shown here in April 1861, could not move the enemy. (GEORGIA DEPARTMENT OF ARCHIVES AND HISTORY)

Above: Despite heavy support from his artillery, commanded by Brigadier General William N. Pendleton, Lee could not break McClellan's line. Pendleton, an Episcopal clergyman, was often mistaken for Lee. When not fighting, he preached in the camps. This photo was probably taken in 1864 after the death of his son, thus the mourning band on his arm. (TONY MARION)

Below: The 19th Georgia took part in repeated attacks. It was largely a family regiment. Standing at right is Lieutenant Colonel Thomas C. Johnson, and seated at right is Lieutenant William H. Johnson. The sergeant standing at back is R. A. Johnson, and the father of all three is seated second from the left. (EMORY UNIVERSITY, PHOTOGRAPHIC SERVICES, ATLANTA)

Above: A remarkable J. D. Edwards image of Gaston Coppens's Louisiana Zouaves on parade in front of the general staff quarters at the navy yard at Pensacola, April 1861. Here was a real trouble regiment. "They are generally small," said a Richmond newspaper, "but wiry, muscular, active as cats, and brown as a side of sole leather." Mutinous, thieving, they never gave their superiors peace. One day's morning report a year from now would show only one man present for duty, the others being absent without leave or under arrest. But they fought like devils at Malvern Hill. The campaign almost destroyed the unit. (SOUTHERN HISTORICAL COLLECTION, THE UNIVERSITY OF NORTH CAROLINA AT CHAPEL HILL)

Above: What stopped Lee at Malvern Hill was the massed guns of McClellan's artillery chief, Colonel Henry J. Hunt. He gathered a hundred cannons to repel enemy assaults. (P-M)

Above: There were no birds perched on the rammers of the 1st Massachusetts Artillery when it took part in Hunt's massive barrage at Malvern Hill. (USAMHI)

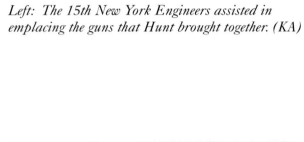

Left: The 15th New York Engineers assisted in emplacing the guns that Hunt brought together. (KA)

Right: Captain August V. Kautz led a company of the 6th United States Cavalry at Malvern Hill, but there was little for the mounted arm to do in this largely infantry campaign. He later became a feared Federal cavalry raider. (AMERICANA IMAGE GALLERY, CUSTODIAN OF THE RINHART COLLECTION)

Above: Lieutenant Colonel Louis Thourot had command of the 55th New York at Malvern Hill when his colonel,... (WRHS)

Above: ... Regis de Trobriand, took over a brigade. He stands at right holding a rammer, while members of the 55th New York look on. (AMERICANA IMAGE GALLERY)

Above: Brigadier General John H. Martindale, seated here in 1864 with his staff, reportedly declared that he would sooner surrender than leave behind his wounded at Malvern Hill. A court of inquiry acquitted him of the charge. (LC)

Above: Defeated in his purpose to take Richmond and unable to withstand Lee's attacks, McClellan finally withdrew to Harrison's Landing on the James River, thus ending the campaign. His troops occupied "Westover," once the plantation estate of William Byrd, a remarkable Virginia gentleman of a century before. For now the war must move elsewhere. (USAMHI)

In Camp with the Commom Soldiers

BELL I. WILEY

The real story of the life of the Civil War Soldier; for every day in battle, fifty in camp

Above: Of all the places remembered in afteryears, it is the camp tent with all its associations that soldiers will most clearly call to mind. Lieutenant J. B. Neill of the 153rd New York sits peacefully in his tent, pictures of his wife on the table with his books, his camp cot in the shadows. Arrayed on the shelf above him are the few simple items that he carries from one field to another in this war. (USAMHI)

WHAT MOST YANKS AND REBS had in mind when they enlisted was to meet their foes in battle, and the sooner the better. Instead they learned after a while that fighting was to occupy only a small part of their army service. The long lulls between battles saw them occupied instead with drills, parades, inspections, and routine activities. However good or bad in the fight they might be, all Yanks and Rebs came to excell in "camp life."

Both in camp and on the march the first concern was food. At the beginning of the war the ration officially prescribed for both sides provided a daily allowance for each soldier of twelve ounces of pork or bacon, or twenty ounces of beef, fresh or salted; twenty-two ounces of soft bread or flour, or sixteen ounces of hard bread, or twenty ounces of corn meal; and to every one hundred rations: fifteen pounds of peas or beans and ten pounds of rice or hominy; ten pounds of green coffee, or eight pounds of roasted coffee, or twenty-four ounces of tea; fifteen pounds of sugar; four quarts of vinegar; three pounds and twelve ounces of salt; four ounces of pepper; thirty pounds of potatoes, when practicable; and one quart of molasses. This allowance exceeded that authorized in any European army. Even so, the Union government increased the allowance in August 1861 and the augmentation remained in effect until June 1864, when it was reduced to that provided at the beginning of the war. Experience had shown that the enlarged issue exceeded the needs of the soldiers and promoted wastefulness.

On the Confederate side authorities ordered a general reduction of the ration in April 1862, and later particular items were curtailed. In the autumn of 1863 Commissary-General Lucius B. Northrop reduced the bacon issue to one third of a pound, and the next year the flour or meal ration was cut to sixteen ounces. More often than not, owing to hoarding, bad management, and the breakdown of transportation facilities in the South, Johnny Rebs got considerably less food than that authorized by Northrop and his associates in Richmond.

In both armies the rations specified in regulations and the fare actually served in camp differed considerably. As a rule, Northerners enjoyed greater abundance and variety of food than did Southerners. Billy Yanks were never reduced to the low level of subsistence experienced by Rebs at Port Hudson and Vicksburg in the summer of 1863, but some of them experienced times of great hunger. Those who marched from Chattanooga to Knoxville and back late in 1863 had to subsist for several days on corn gathered from the places where the horses fed and parched over the coals of their campfires. They experienced similar deprivation in Chattanooga before U. S. Grant and William "Baldy" Smith opened up the "cracker line" in October 1863. A Hoosier soldier wrote from Chattanooga on October 22, 1863, that for the past month he and his comrades had lived on "two meals per day and one cracker for each meal."

Mainstays of rations issued to both Rebs and Yanks were meat, bread (or the flour or meal with which to make it), and coffee. Meat was pork or beef, sometimes fresh from recently slaughtered animals, but more often salt-cured or pickled. Salt pork, widely known as sowbelly or sow bosom by the soldiers, was fried in skillets, boiled in pots, or broiled on the ends of sticks held above hot coals. It was also used as seasoning for vegetables cooked in containers suspended above campfires. Fresh beef was usually boiled. Pickled beef, commonly called "salt horse," was sometimes putrid and so briny as to make it unpalatable. An Ohio soldier wrote from camp in Maryland in 1862 that "we drew meat last night that was so damd full of skippers that it could move alone; some of them is stout enuf to cary a musket." A Mississippi Reb stated that the beef issued to his company was so rotten that "the buzzards would not eat it." An Illinois Yank wrote, "Sometimes we draw sow belly and sometimes old bull. The old bull is very good... but the sow belly, phew!"

The bread most often served to Johnny Rebs was cornbread, though sometimes they drew loaves of flour bread and occasionally they had hardtack. When left to their own resources they often converted the flour into hoecakes or biscuits, which they baked on slanting boards placed near their campfires. Some Rebs preferred to wrap bits of dough around a stick or ramrod and convert them into rolls by rotating them above hot coals. Many Southerners were surfeited on cornbread. A Louisianian wrote near the end of the conflict, "If any person offers me cornbread after this war comes to a close I shall probably tell him to—go to hell."

Yanks rarely ate cornbread. They much preferred flour loaves baked in field ovens or prepared by comrades or black servants who cooked for companies or messes. During seasons of active campaigning and sometimes during periods of inactivity the only bread issued to them was hardtack.

Hardtack were crackers 2 1/2 inches wide, 2 7/8 inches high, and 3/8 inch thick. They weighed about 1 1/2 ounces and were so hard that soldiers referred to them as "teeth dullers," and said they were more suitable for the building of breastworks than for human consumption. They came packed in boxes or barrels stamped "B.C.," probably for Brigade Commissary, but some soldiers insisted that the abbreviation represented the crackers' date of manufacture. Consumers often increased the edibility of hardtack by pulverizing them with rocks or musket butts, or soaking them in water. Hardtack crumbs were sometimes fried in bacon grease or mixed with soup or coffee.

Coffee, boiled in large kettles for quantity distribution or prepared individually in small cans or tin cups which most soldiers slung to their belts while on the march, was one of the most highly cherished items of camp fare. Soldiers of both armies consumed it in vast quantities. When the genuine "Rio" became scarce in the South owing to the blockade, Rebs resorted to "Confederate coffee" brewed from parched particles of corn, sweet potatoes, peanuts, or rye. Lacking sugar, they added molasses for "long sweetening." Some Rebs professed a fondness for their coffee improvisations, but their tributes reflect more of patriotism than actuality.

White "army beans" and brown Boston beans were often issued to Billy Yanks. Southern counter parts were field peas, sometimes of the black-eyed variety but more often the speckled whippoorwills.

Peas and white beans were usually mixed

Above: Where most of Civil War soldiering took place, the camp. Here the winter tents of the 40th Massachusetts Infantry at Miner's Hill, Virginia, in 1863. (USAMHI)

Above: An unpublished photograph showing the camp of the New Orleans Confederate Guards, probably in 1861, a scene that would be unusual for its neatness and well-equipped appearance by 1863. (TU, LOUISIANA HISTORICAL ASSOCIATION COLLECTION)

Below: The 5th Vermont in camp in 1861, a G. W. Houghton photograph. (LC)

Above: Colonel Henry HoDaman of the 230th New York at his camp table, cigar in hand, clay pipe on the table. And... (NA)

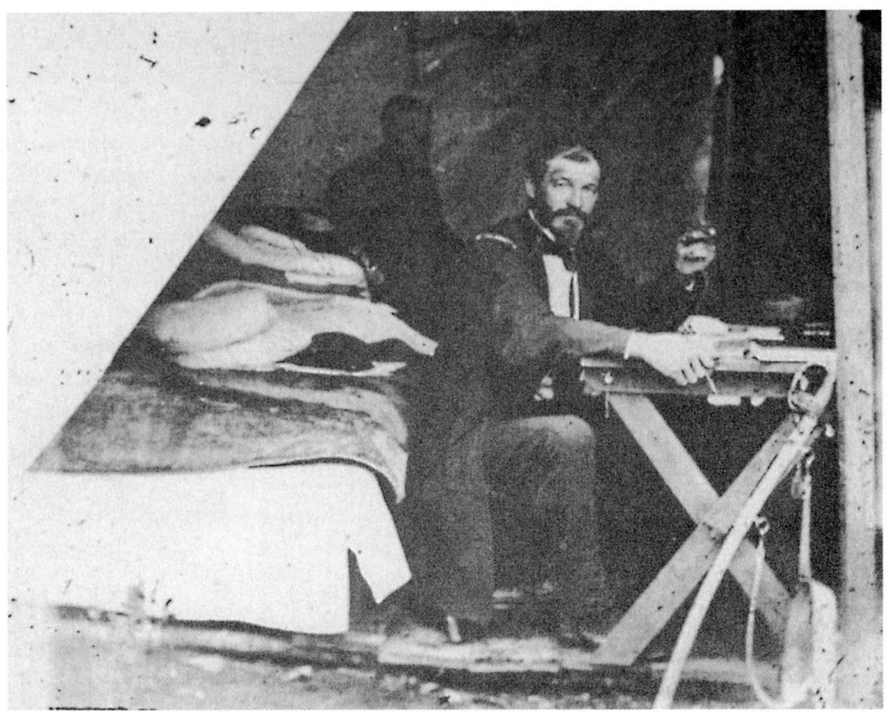

Above: ... his tentmate Major W. M. Gregg at the same table. The occupant of the bed is too tired—or shy—to sit f or the camera. (WRHS)

Above: A typical officer's tent interior. Sabers, binoculars, a home-knitted shawl, a kepi, and a print adorn the canvas wall. On the table, a closed cased ambrotype, comb, candlestick, a few books, scissors, and a small sewing kit (NA)

Above: Some officers enjoyed a bit more space and luxury. The same personal and military items hang on the wall. A plumed hat rests on the bed, and the table is set for a meal. There is almost a look of permanence here. (NA)

with chunks of pork and boiled in iron pots. New Englanders liked to bake their brown beans in submerged pans surrounded by smoldering coals.

Sweet potatoes, Irish potatoes, and dried fruit were consumed in large quantities in both Union and Confederate camps. Potatoes were often baked in their skins and dried fruit was sometimes stewed and used as filler for fried pies.

Soldier life was conducive to the development of hearty appetites. Private Daniel Peck of New York wrote his sister in December 1862, "I am well and tough and as hearty as ever. I can finish twelve tack a day, three quarts of coffee, one half pound pork or beef, some dried apples & beans. But the beans punish me so I don't eat them. The foretaste is better than the after-taste."

Yanks and Rebs supplemented commissary issues with boxes of edibles of all sorts sent to them by solicitous relatives and friends at home. Delays in transit often caused spoilage of perishables, and poor packing or rough handling frequently resulted in breakage. But enough of the foodstuff reached its destination in usable condition to keep recipients asking for more.

Foraging, an army euphemism for stealing, was another frequently used source of enrichment of soldier rations. Yanks, partly because they spent most of their time in "enemy" country, were the greater offenders, but Rebs when subjected to hunger, as they frequently were, foraged freely on fellow Southerners. Pigpens, poultry houses, or chards, watermelon patches, cornfields, vegetable gardens, smokehouses, and turkey roosts were rarely immune to soldier incursions in any locality occupied by either Yanks or Rebs.

Another source of ration supplementation was the sutler who set up shop in army camps. Yanks saw more of sutlers than did Rebs because of the dearth of money among Southerners. Sutlers stocked candy, pies, cakes, pickles, canned oysters, sardines, and other edibles, along with stationery, writing pens, books, beverages, and other articles sought by their clientele. Soldiers usually regarded the sutler's prices as

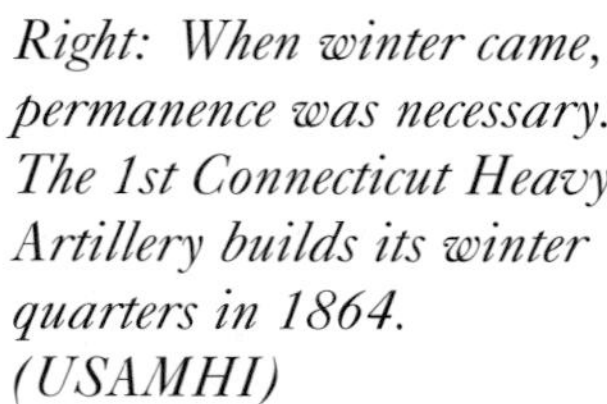

Right: When winter came, permanence was necessary. The 1st Connecticut Heavy Artillery builds its winter quarters in 1864. (USAMHI)

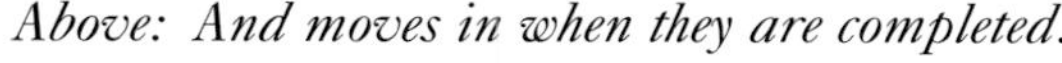

Above: And moves in when they are completed.

Above: Built mostly from scavenged parts and ingenuity, these Confederate huts were good enough that Federals later used them. Manassas, 1862. (WRHS)

exorbitant, and one of their favorite diversions was to raid the merchant's tent and clean out his stock. Civilians too, black and white, residing in areas near army camps often peddled provisions to military personnel. Favorite articles of sale were pies and cakes, which purchasers sometimes referred to as "pizen cakes."

Early in the war soldiers on both sides complained frequently about the quality of their fare. But as the struggle continued and provisions became scarcer, protests centered more on quantity. This was especially true of Confederates. During the Chattanooga campaign a famished Texan of Bragg's army declared that if he ever got home he was going "to take a hundred biscuit and two large hams, call it three days rations, then go down on Goat Island and eat it all at one meal."

The culinary abilities of Yanks and Rebs improved as they adjusted to soldiering and many of them boasted to civilian friends and kin that the food they prepared in camp compared favorably with that served at home. They also bragged about the proficiency acquired in laundering their clothes. On the march they had to wash their garments in streams, lakes, and ponds, as opportunity afforded, and hang them on tree limbs while they lounged naked on the banks waiting for the apparel to dry. But when settled in camp for considerable periods of time, as they usually were in winter, Rebs and Yanks often observed weekly washdays. These resembled the same occasions known at home, except that the washing was done by males with whatever facilities were at hand. Water was usually heated in pots, and clothes were soaped and scrubbed in tubs fashioned from barrels. Sometimes the scrubbing was done on corrugated metal boards, such as those used by the homefolk, but in most instances the dirt was removed by repeated dousing and twisting. Ironing was dispensed with, owing to lack of equipment and the view that wrinkles were an acceptable part of camp life.

Still, practices known at home were considered ideal and in their housing arrangements soldiers were inclined to approximate them to the fullest possible extent. The shelter tents, or pup

Above: Whole cities of log huts dot the Southern landscape every war winter. (USAMHI)

Above: They are Confederate as well as Union. Here Confederate winter quarters of J. E. Johnston's army at Manassas in 1862. (USAMHI)

Left: Union soldiers occupying once-Confederate winter houses at Centreville, Virginia. Winter, rain, and mud erased any care about who built them. "Corduroy" roads and walkways made of logs cross the mud. (LC)

Right: Winter quarters for some were far more luxurious. The 22nd Michigan at Camp Ella in Bishop, Kentucky, had regular barracks to withstand the cold. (GORDON WHITNEY COLLECTION)

Left: Their officers' quarters even boasted a little bit of gingerbread trim. (GORDON WHITNEY COLLECTION)

tents, used during periods of active campaigning were too small to permit much "fixing up." But larger tents, whether the bell-shaped Sibleys, the A tents, or the wall tents, which provided protection from sun and rain during relatively mild seasons when troops were not on the move, gave Rebs and Yanks an opportunity to apply their homemaking instincts. Guns were neatly stacked in the center or near entrances of canvas abodes. Bunks fashioned of boards and filled with leaves, straw, or other soft materials and covered with blankets were placed around the interior to suit the taste and convenience of the occupants. When not used for reclining, bunks served as seats. Additional seating was improvised from kegs, barrels, and cracker boxes. Tables and writing desks were made of boards "liberated" from abandoned buildings or obtained from crates discarded by commissary or quarter master. Canteens, cooking utensils, haversacks, knapsacks and other items of equipment were suspended from tent poles or stacked on the ground. Light came from candles stuck in bayonet sockets.

Homemaking proclivities were indulged to the fullest extent in cold weather when soldiers settled in winter quarters. Winter residences were frequently rectangular cabins made of logs cut from nearby trees, dragged to the building site, notched, and put in place by the soldiers. Slanting roofs were made of boards or split logs covered with pine straw; spaces between the logs were filled with mud. A variation of the log hut was a hybrid structure part wood and part fabric, made by superimposing rectangular tents on log bases. These "winterized" or "stockaded" tents, like the log huts, were usually designed for four men. Sometimes the occupants increased roominess and warmth by excavating interiors to a depth of several feet. In some cases winter dwellings were warmed by stoves, which also were used for cooking, but more commonly heat for comfort and cooking was provided by fireplaces located usually at one end of the room. These were made of small logs chinked with mud and capped by chimneys made of the same materials. Draft was increased by topping chimneys with barrels, but these sometimes caught fire, routing soldiers from their bunks and threatening their abodes with destruction. Some soldiers were content with floors of earth or straw. Others, at considerable labor, covered the soil with split logs or with boards.

The average winter dwelling contained two bunks, one above the other, extending across the side or rear. The occupants made mattresses by filling cloth containers with pine needles, leaves, or straw. Ordinarily they placed knapsacks at the head of the bunks and suspended other equip-

Left: Wherever and whatever their accommodations, however, the soldiers enjoyed winter. There was little or no fighting and, with some protection from the cold, it was a peaceful time. (USAMHI)

Above: These Confederates of the 1st Texas at Camp Quantico, near Dumfries, Virginia, perform their camp chores with a casual air of contentment. They are the "Beauregard Mess," and this winter of 1861-62 they will be warm. (ROBERT MCDONALD)

Above: Some even used civilian skills to build chimneys and fireplaces. They read books and newspapers and letters from home, and they trained mascots like dogs and birds. (LLOYD OSTENDORP COLLECTION)

Left: Music occupied the time of many, as did cards. Here in the quarters of Dr. David McKay of the Army of the James, unusual luxury is evident. Ample space in an old occupied house, a fireplace, instruments galore, all combine to make the "5 Drons" and their "Fun & Fury" quarters more than habitable. (USAMHI)

ment and extra clothing from nails or pegs driven into the walls. Seats, desks, and tables were made of logs, boxes, kegs, and barrels. Almost every company had a few fastidious members who insisted on providing their winter quarters with wallpaper and adding adornments in the form of mantelpieces, pictures, and fancy pieces of furniture.

When family or friends visited camp, as they sometimes did in the winter season, soldiers took great pride in showing off their homemaking prowess. Many described their comforts in letters to the folk at home. A Georgia private wrote his wife from camp near Fredericksburg in early March, 1863, "You would be surprised to know how comfortable a place I have to live in, a white [from snow] hous and a good fire place and a box, chunk, or the ground wich are all used for seats hear. We all take our seats, some reading, som writing, some laughing, some talking, som set up sleeping and some thinking of home.... Finely [finally] Mr. A. begines to tell whare he herd his first bum and how bad it sceard him and Mr. B. not to be out don tells what dangers he has pased through. Mr. C. he tells his tale.... Mr. E.... says that he thinks that he is the man that ought to have the next furlow.... [After a lively argument over who had the best claim to a furlough] H. commenses singing home sweet hom, all the crowd joines in and the hole wood resounds with the music."

In both winter and summer officers generally lived better than their men, and the higher the rank, with some notable exceptions, the greater their comfort. In winter they had more commodious huts, made usually by the soldiers whom they commanded, and when they lived in tents, they normally had relatively spacious wall tents. Sometimes an officer had a dwelling all to himself, save perhaps for a black servant who performed menial duties. His furniture, clothing, and food usually were superior to that of the rank and file. Normally he had no difficulty in obtaining liquor, a commodity often denied to ordinary soldiers. However, most thirsty privates were able to circumvent the prohibitions when they had funds, but the stuff that they obtained on

Left: The average soldier and officer settled for much less, like the quarters of these officers of the 1st Rhode Island Light Artillery, Battery E. But still they have their books, their maps decorating the wall, and a well-stocked table. (USAMHI)

Above and above right: Life in camp was not all relaxation. There were tasks aplenty to keep the men busy and fit. Chopping wood, sweeping, polishing boots, mending socks, and clowning all filled the idle hours. The denizens of "Pine Cottage" did their chores first, then dressed for the camera. (USAMHI)

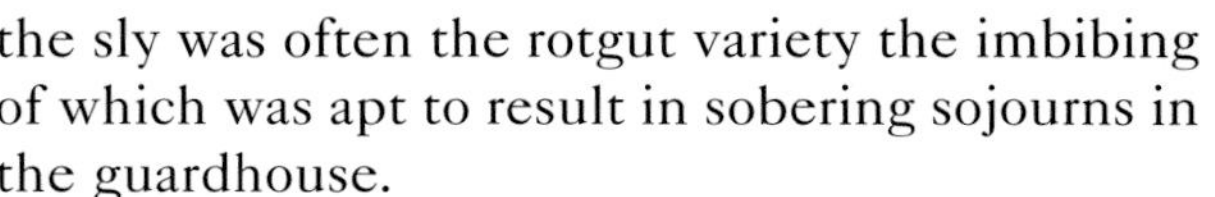

the sly was often the rotgut variety the imbibing of which was apt to result in sobering sojourns in the guardhouse.

Camp life at its best was apt to be monotonous and lonely. Daily drills, Sunday reviews, and periodic parades increased in onerousness with the passing of time. Marches in rain and mud or in heat and dust were irksome and exhausting, and when accompanied by poor rations and polluted water, as they frequently were, they became almost intolerable. Exposure, overexertion, undernourishment, and the ravages of insects and germs produced floods of sickness, and hostile missiles added countless others to the list of the disabled. In the American Civil War the sick and wounded suffered most. Medicines and medical facilities fell far short of needs, especially on the Confederate side.

Both the ailing and the well sought diversion to combat their hardship and boredom. Music was a favorite pastime in both armies. Regimental and brigade bands often gave evening concerts at which they played sentimental, patriotic, and sometimes classical pieces. Occasionally bands would serenade officers, a practice which afforded pleasure to entire camps. General Lee, after listening to an informal band concert in 1864, stated, "I don't believe we can have an army without music." A Rebel private

Right: The "Wigfall Mess" of the 1st Texas Infantry, chop their wood and carry water and wash their dishes. (THE MUSEUM OF THE CONFEDERACY, RICHMOND)

Below: The need for wood was endless. (USAMHI)

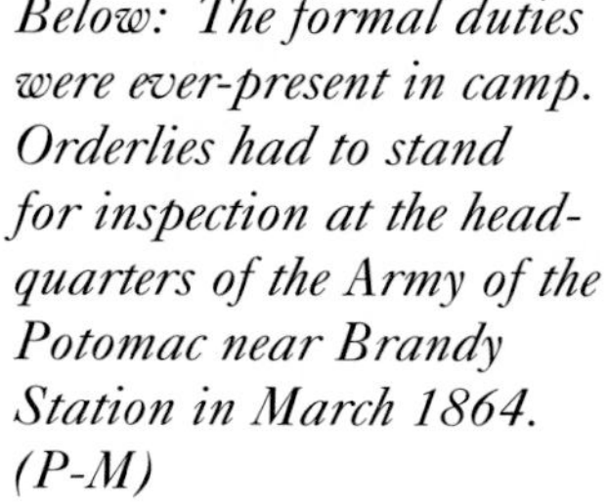

Below: The formal duties were ever-present in camp. Orderlies had to stand for inspection at the headquarters of the Army of the Potomac near Brandy Station in March 1864. (P-M)

Left: James F. Gibson's spring 1862 image of the servants of the Prince de Joinville doing his chores for him. (KA)

Above: Artillerists of the 1st Brigade of Horse Artillery, Brandy Station, in September 1863, studied their maps in off moments. (AMERICANA IMAGE GALLERY)

Above: Signal corpsmen refined their skills, if somewhat lazily. A Brady & Company image from 1864. (CHS)

was prompted to remark at the conclusion of a stirring band concert in a Virginia camp, "I felt at the time that I could whip a whole brigade of the enemy." As a rule Billy Yanks, owing to the relatively greater number of musicians and instruments available in Northern units, enjoyed more and better band music than did Rebs. Some of the best music was provided by the Germans, about 200,000 of whom donned the Union blue.

In both armies the instrumental music heard most frequently was provided by individuals and small groups who brought violins, banjos, guitars, and flutes to camp with them and played informally for the entertainment of themselves and their comrades. A Mississippian wrote to a friend early in the war that he and his associates were experiencing lively times in camp. "Every night," he stated, "fiddlers are plentiful.... I wish you would happen in sometime while Will Mason is playing the violin & see some of his capers."

Many regiments had glee clubs who entertained fellow soldiers with a variety of songs. But, as in the case of instrumental programs, the most frequent, and probably the most appreciated vocal performances, were those given by informal groups brought together by the sheer

Left: And there was always drill. (USAMHI)

Left: And more drill. (MHS)

Left: And still more. The New York Excelsior Brigade. (USAMHI)

Right: George N. Barrlard caught this company drilling amid its own quarters, behind a decidedly decorative fence. (NA)

Above: Fresh bread came from the camp bakery, where the bakers let the dough rise in the sun. (INTERNATIONAL MUSEUM OF PHOTOGRAPHY)

Left: When the drill and the duties were done, however, then came the time for food. Every Civil War soldier was an expert at eating. Here Captain James W. Forsythe—later a brigadier general—sits on the staple of the soldier diet, a box of "Army Bread"—hard tack. (NA)

Left: They baked the loaves twenty at a time. (USAMHI)

Below: And doled the loaves out to each mess's cook or servant, along with the ration of meat and vegetables. The meat was rationed by weight. (USAMHI)

Above: No one was too bothered about sanitation. Keeping the bread in the same tent with the animal hay and letting a dog wander over both seemed not out of order. (USAMHI)

Above: The armies brought their own herds with them, killing and butchering fresh beef daily when possible. These beef quarters have been salted and hung for drying. The salt residue lies on the boards below them. It would help preserve the beef—sometimes. (USAMHI)

Above: Cutting the meat for the stew. Brady & Company published this image in 1861. (T. SCOTT SANDERS COLLECTION)

Above: Doling out commissary stores at Camp Essex, weighing, carving, and—with the red tape so beloved of armies—recording who got how much of what and when. (MHS)

Above: Weighing beef on Morris Island, South Carolina. The more tropical the climate, the more likely the soldier was to receive rancid meat—and eat it. (RONN PALM COLLECTION)

love of music combined with a desire to entertain their comrades. A New York artillery captain wrote to a friend in 1863, "We have pretty lively times in the evenings, the Germans of my company get together and sing very sweetly and I try to join in with them."

Reading was another favorite diversion of Rebs and Yanks. What they enjoyed most was reading the letters of their homefolk. "Mail call" from company headquarters always brought throngs of eager soldiers rushing to claim missives from wives, children, parents, and friends. Arrival of mail was about the only incident that would cause men to interrupt their meals. Those whose names were called proceeded happily to some quiet spot to read and reread the latest word from home; those for whom no letters came slipped away in disappointment and envy to resume the drab routine of camp life. "Boys who will lie on their backs with hardly energy enough to turn over," wrote an Alabamian in 1862, "will jump up and hurry to the captain's tent to get it [mail]." A Texan wrote his wife in 1863, "I feel mightily down when the mail comes in and the other boys get letters and I don't." About the same time another Reb wrote his spouse that he "was almost down in histericks to hear from home." Yanks were less frequently disappointed than Rebs by nonreceipt of mail, because mail service in the North, owing to more and better rail and other communications facilities, was much better than in the South. Sometimes letters from rural areas of the South were not delivered in camp for several months. Slowness of Confederate postal service led correspondents to rely increasingly on personal delivery of letters by friends and relatives. Despite uncertainties and delays a large volume of mail reached its destination in both South and North. Unfortunately for the historian, only a small portion of correspondence received in camp was preserved, owing to the inconvenience of keeping it and fear on the part of recipients that it might fall into the hands of foes and become the subject of derisive comment.

Most soldiers enjoyed answering letters. A

Above: Boiled beef for the soldiers, cooked on the camp stove. (USAMHI)

Above: Not the most nourishing meal, perhaps, but filling. Hardtack and butter on the plate, and bread in hand. Coffee would steam from the cup in good times. (LES JENSEN COLLECTION)

Below: Like soldiers in all armies, Rebs and Yanks complained about their food. But they cooked and ate it nevertheless. (NA)

Right: A few potatoes or other vegetables added variety to the salt pork and boiled beef. Always there was hardtack. A private of the 49th New York. (DALE S. SNAIR COLLECTION, RICHMOND)

Above: Lieutenant Colonel F. M. Bache of the 16th United States Infantry and his mess in January 1864. He sits at left, with other members of the Army of the Potomac headquarters staff at Brandy Station. They dine well, served by a servant with a milk glass pitcher. Alexander Gardner's photograph. (USAMHI)

Right: A noncommissioned officers' mess, Company D, 93rd New York, at Bealton, Virginia, August 1863. They dine with less style than the officers, but they still eat well. (MHS)

Right: And the privates eat as they can, and as much as they can. Bread, hardtack, beef, and coffee are their staples. (COLLECTION OF MICHAEL J. MCAFEE)

likely scene during any respite from camp duties was a Reb or Yank off to himself, with paper resting on stump, box, or knee "dropping a few lines" to the folk at home. Health was a favorite subject of comment and many a soldier complained to the homefolk of recurrent bouts with the "the sh-ts," a malady also known as "the Tennessee quick step." Correspondents almost always requested early responses and stressed a desire for information about the doings of children, the progress of crops, the condition of pets and livestock, and details of life in home and community. In the 165 extant letters that Robert M. Gill wrote to his wife Bettie in Mississippi before he was killed at Jonesboro, Georgia, August 31, 1864, one of his most frequent inquiries was about his little daughter, Callie. "Does she remember me?" he asked in one letter. "You must not whip her," he added, "I have a perfect horror of whipping children." The advice that innumerable Rebs and Yanks sent to their offspring was "mind your mother, say your prayers and don't neglect your books."

Next to letters, newspapers provided the most pleasure for soldier readers. Rebs had considerably less access to journalistic literature than did the men in blue because Southern papers did not approach those of the North in numbers, circulation, or coverage of events. Owing to scarcity of newsprint, deterioration of equipment, and inadequacy of financial resources most Southern newspapers declined in size and quality during the conflict, and some became casualties of war. The Memphis *Appeal*

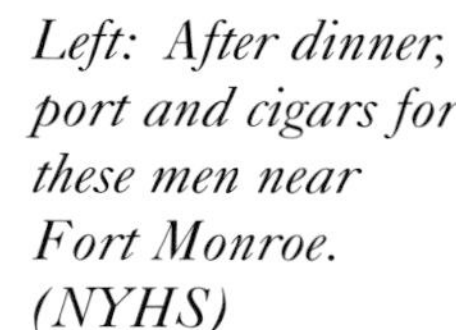

Left: After dinner, port and cigars for these men near Fort Monroe. (NYHS)

Right: And now and then a picnic with sausages and bologna, cider, and sometimes chocolate. (COLLECTION OF MICHAEL J. MCAFEE)

Left: The soldiers supplemented their uninteresting diet with delicacies bought from the sutlers—government-approved vendors—who followed the armies. Here a decidedly seedy-looking lot of them pose amid their wares of liquor and tobacco. (USAMHI)

had to flee invading Federals so often that it came to be known as "the moving Appeal." Both this paper and the Chattanooga *Daily Rebel* devoted considerable attention to military affairs and were eagerly read by soldiers of the Western armies. The same could be said of the Richmond dailies and Rebs serving in the Army of Northern Virginia. These journals were not driven to use wallpaper for newsprint as were the Vicksburg *Citizen* and the Opelousas, Louisiana, *Courier*, but all of them had their troubles. Circulation in Southern camps suffered from various circumstances including scarcity of money among Johnny Rebs and their families. Papers that found their way to news-hungry Confederates were literally worn out as they passed from hand to hand.

The war created a great boom for Northern journalism, and as circulation increased, both at home and in the army, reporters, photographers, and artists frequented camps to gather news and illustrations, and news vendors regularly made the rounds of military units and hospitals hawking the New York *Tribune*, *Herald*, and *Times*, the Boston *Journal*, the Philadelphia *Inquirer*, the Cincinnati *Gazette*, the Chicago *Times*, and other metropolitan dailies. Both Yanks and Rebs gave a high rating to the illustrated weeklies that thrived during the war years, including *Leslie's* and *Harper's* and the Richmond-based *Southern Illustrated News*. County and town newspapers were not often sold in camps but soldiers, and especially Billy Yanks, frequently received issues of local journals sent through the mail by publishers or homefolk.

Sometimes regiments and other units issued their own papers, and in rare instances informal groups wrote out news sheets by hand. Both printed and manuscript newspapers contained military information, poetry, gossip, and jokes. After being read in camp they were usually sent to the folk at home.

Magazines such as the *Atlantic* and *Southern*

Right: They opened their stores wherever the tents and winter huts sprang up. Some, like A. Foulke, followed the same unit throughout the war. Brandy Station, Virginia, February 1863. (USAMHI)

Right: The soldiers bellied up to the "bar" for their whiskey and beer. They bought Bibles and books at the same place. (USAMHI)

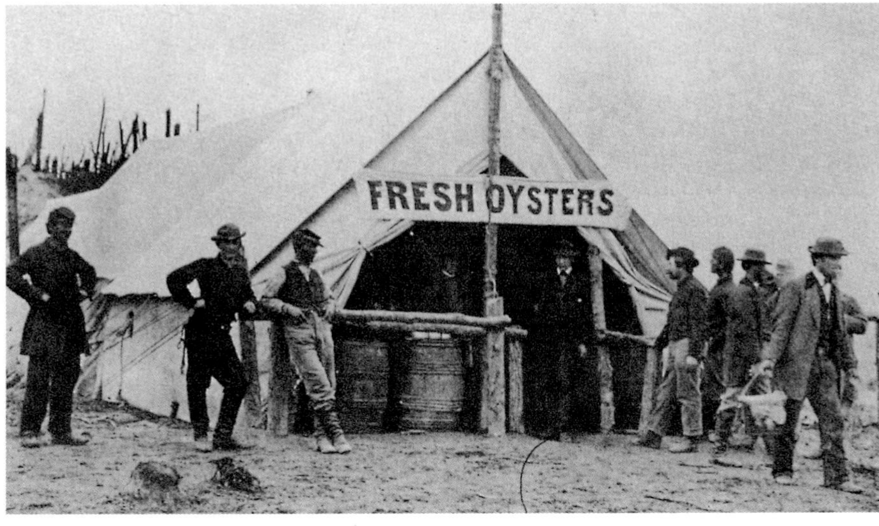

Left: Fresh oysters were a real delicacy, and often not so fresh. Sutlers were frequently charged with selling rancid victuals. (USAMHI)

Above: A "Fruit & Oyster House" in front of Petersburg in 1864. (USAMHI)

Above: Some specialized solely in whiskey and tobacco, where the real money lay. (USAMHI)

Below: Others created virtual shopping centers like this area at Petersburg in early 1865. Sayer's Oyster House sold pipes, cigars, oysters, and soda water. Next door Mr. Shuz sold cakes, and his neighbor sold and repaired boots and shoes. Up on the hill sat an "Eating House," while on the left a clothier sold "Ready Made" army garments. In the center sits the wagon of Bates of New York City, who attached himself strictly to the 7th New York, and behind him stands a wholesale and retail condensed milk "depot." Behind that sits an outhouse. (LC)

Field and *Fireside* had some circulation in camp. Books of fiction, literature, and history never lacked readers in either Northern or Southern camps, but Yanks, owing to better education, more money, and superior distribution facilities had considerably better opportunity to read them than did Rebs. On both sides, but far more often in Northern than in Southern camps, soldiers had access to cheap paperback novels and joke books. Religious organizations flooded camps with tracts, most of them warning readers against the evils of profanity, liquor, and gambling. Among Rebels especially, owing to a dearth of other materials, these tracts always found readers. The most widely read book among both Yanks and Rebs was the Bible.

Religious services provided diversion for many soldiers. Yanks and Rebs often spoke disparagingly of chaplains, and there is considerable evidence to indicate that the better ministers, owing to the poor pay and the great hardships endured by chaplains, preferred service on the home front to that in camp. But "Holy Joes of the Sixties" were often sincere, dedicated individuals whose ministrations were much appreciated by the rank and file. In addition to attending Sabbath services, which usually featured the chaplains' sermons, religiously inclined soldiers often met on their own for prayer meetings led by one of their comrades. In the spring, when the season of active campaigning approached, revivals sometimes swept over the camps, but these occurred more frequently and on larger

Above: Both armies also relied heavily on "foraging," officially sanctioned theft from local farmers who were sometimes—but by no means always—paid in government scrip. G. W. Houghton captured this foraging expedition, decidedly ambitious, leaving to scour the Virginia countryside for edibles. (VHS)

Right: More common was the individual foraging soldier, though there was certainly nothing at all common about this grinning lad, Billy Crump of Company I, 23rd Ohio Infantry. He was orderly to Colonel—later President—Rutherford B. Hayes. In February 1863 he borrowed Hayes's horse and pistol and set off from camp near Gauley Bridge in West Virginia. He traveled twenty miles in two days and came back laden with fifty chickens, two turkeys, one goose, twenty to twenty-five dozen eggs, and between twenty-six and thirty pounds of butter. Here was a good provider. (USAMHI)

scale among Confederates than among Federals. This was due in part to the greater strength among Southerners of evangelistic denominations and to the greater religiousness of their officers, including such high-ranking leaders as Lee, Jackson, and Jeb Stuart. Interestingly, the largest and most fervent revivals experienced by Confederates came after 1862, when owing to the worsening of the military situation and the increasing prospect of exposure to death in combat, Southerners felt a greater need to seek spiritual guidance and comfort.

The religious activity that Yanks and Rebs probably enjoyed most of all was the singing of hymns. Favorites included "Sweet Hour of Prayer," "My Faith Looks Up to Thee," "Rock of Ages," "All Hail the Power of Jesus' Name," "Amazing Grace," "On Jordan's Stormy Banks I Stand," and "There Is a Fountain Filled with Blood." Religious organizations encouraged singing by distributing pocket-size hymn books prepared especially for army use.

When opposing armies were stationed near each other much fraternization occurred. On these occasions Northern newspapers were swapped for those published in the South, and coffee was exchanged for tobacco. Sometimes trade was carried on by means of small boats equipped with sails set in such a manner as to take the vessels across river, lake, or bay separating opposing forces. Throughout fighting areas, Yanks and Rebs swam together, drank together, and even gambled together. Friendly intercourse was sometimes interspersed with communication that was not so cordial. During the siege of Vicksburg, for example, Yanks would call out to Confederates, "Say, Rebs, how do you like your new general?" Southerners would respond, "What do you mean by new general? We've still got old Pemberton." The Federals would retort, "Oh, yes you have, General Starvation." Rebs would come back with the inquiry, "Say, Yanks, have you got yourselves any nigger wives yet? Do you suppose they will improve the Yankee breed any?" The Federal taunt, "Say Reb, haint you got any better clothes than them," once provoked the response, "Who do you think we are, a set of damn fools to put on our good clothes to go out and kill damn dogs in." Then the shooting would resume.

Clowning among themselves, horseplay, teasing, and joking made soldiering more tolerable for many. A person appearing in camp in any unusual garb was almost certain to become the target of much disparagement and ridicule, such as "Come up outer them boots; I know you're in thar; I see your arms sticking out." Or, "Look out, that parrot shell that you're wearing on your head is going to explode." Unpopular officers were sometimes subjected to groans or catcalls as they walked company streets or reclined in their bunks. Some Georgia soldiers once rode their colonel on a rail, letting him dismount only when he promised better behavior.

A Federal officer stationed at Murfreesboro wrote that in March 1863, when General Rosecrans and his staff rode through a camp of Yanks living in pup tents they "were greeted with a tremendous bow-wow. The boys were on their hands and knees, stretching their heads out of the ends of the tents, barking furiously at the passing cavalcade." The general, he added, instead of becoming angry, laughed heartily and

Left: Their hunger satisfied, the soldiers passed their leisure time as best they could. Reading was a favorite in both armies, and literacy was much higher than usually supposed. Those who could not read liked being read to. Gardner caught these news vendors in October 1862. (LC)

Left: In Chattanooga, Tennessee, at the quarters of the 1st Engineers and Mechanics, they read and wrote letters. (MICHIGAN DEPARTMENT OF STATE, STATE ARCHIVES)

Above: A. P. Muben, a somewhat gaily bedecked news vendor, with some of the New York illustrated weeklies so popular with the soldiers. (LC)

Above: In the camp of the 5th Georgia they wrote their letters. (JOE CANOLE, JR.)

Above: The small building in the middle, just left of the tent, is the 13th Massachusetts' library in their camp at Williamsport, Maryland. Few other regiments could boast such an establishment, yet many of the Bay State regiments were almost aggressively literate. (USAMHI)

Above: Field post offices operated with most of the Federal armies, handling a huge volume of soldier mail. Here an unidentified brigadier general hands a letter to the postal clerk. (NA)

Above: In winter quarters such as Brandy Station in February 1864, there were more permanent postal establishments, like this post office with a clerk perched on a mail bag. (USAMHI)

Above: Neither snow nor rain nor gloom of night—not even the enemy—could stay the delivery of the mail to the soldiers. It was one of the single most important factors in preserving morale. Brandy Station in April 1864. (USAMHI)

Below: A group of IX Corps chaplains pose before their "Baltimore Cotton Duck Extra" tent, near Petersburg. (LC)

promised the barkers better living accommodations.

Impromptu diversion was afforded by the appearance of a rabbit in camp or along the route of march. Sometimes the excited animal was pressed so long and so hard by yelling soldiers as to be caught. Then an argument was apt to ensue as to what individual or mess was to have the pleasure of eating the captured hare. Hunting, with or with out guns, and fishing, with hooks or seines, was al ways a welcome diversion, not only for the fun that it provided, but also for the enrichment that it gave to issues of hardtack and sowbelly.

Sports and games flourished during periods of leisure. Football was mentioned occasionally in the letters of both Yanks and Rebs but baseball, of the four-base or two-base "town-ball" variety, was a more popular exercise. The ball was often soft and in one version of the game the mode of putting out the runner was to hit him with the ball. Bats were frequently sticks or boards. Scores sometimes were very high. In a game at Yorktown, Virginia, in 1863, the 9th New York Regiment beat the 51st New York by a score of 58-19.

Holidays such as the Fourth of July and, in Irish regiments, St. Patrick's Day, were celebrat-

Above: Religious revivals frequently swept through the camps even faster than the mail. Devotion, as many soldiers confessed, helped fill idle hours, and sometimes local belles attended as well. Here the 50th New York Engineers built their own church before Petersburg. (P-M)

ed by horse races, boxing, wrestling matches, foot races, leap frog, cricket, broad jumping, and free-for-all scuffles. These festivities were often accompanied by swigging of whiskey or beer on the part of participants and spectators, and at the end of the day guardhouses might overflow with soldiers suffering from black eyes, bruised limbs, and even broken bones.

In winter, when the weather became cold enough to coat lakes and ponds with ice, Yanks found pleasure in skating. Rebs rarely had skates or the skill of using them, but if soles were thick enough they scooted awkwardly over the ice in their shoes. Sleds, often improvised from boards or tubs, carried soldiers down snow-covered hills and merriment was enhanced by occasional spills. Snowball battles were frequent occurrences. Sometimes participants would fight in regiments or brigades, commanded by the same officers who led them in battle. Prisoners were taken and paroled, and the wounded were attended by doctors or nurses. Since contestants occasionally loaded their snow pellets with cores of rock or metal, wounds were sometimes more than superficial. Early in 1863, near Fredericksburg, the 26th New Jersey Regiment and a Vermont unit formed a line of battle and pitched into each other with such fury that "the air was filled with white missles and stentorian cheers went up as one or the other party gained an advantage." After a series of charges and countercharges, each resulting in the taking of prisoners, "victory rested with the Vermonters and the Jersey boys surrendered the field." A Georgia Reb stationed near Fredericksburg wrote his wife in February 1863, "Some times the hole brigade formes and it looks like the sky and the hole elements was made of snow.... General Longstreet and his agitant took regs the other

Left: Mass at Camp Cass for the largely Irish 9th Massachusetts Infantry. Only the officers attend this service. (LC)

Left: At Camp Griffin, Virginia, the 49th Pennsylvania worships as Chaplain Captain William Earnshaw uses stacked drums for an altar. (LLOYD OSTENDORF COLLECTION)

Right: Father Thomas H. Mooney performs Sunday Mass for the 69th New York. Its colonel, Michael Corcoran, stands with folded arms just left of the cleric. Both North and South claimed divine endorsement. (LC)

Below: When chaplains like this one found themselves conducting services in the presence of shot and shell and weapons of destruction, some were inclined to question whether the deity could possibly condone either side. Fort Darling in April 1865, the chaplain's quarters of the 1st Connecticut Heavy Artillery, photographed by J. Reekie. (LC)

Above: With reading and religion exhausted, the soldiers turned to sport. Many opted for something cerebral like chess, but most, like those at the left, preferred cards. (USAMHI)

Right: Gambling filled the long hours of boredom, and not a few pockets as well. Officers of the 82nd Illinois in camp at Atlanta, Georgia, in 1864 gambled with ease and comfort. Outrageous pipes, often handmade, were also the rage in the Western army. (CHS)

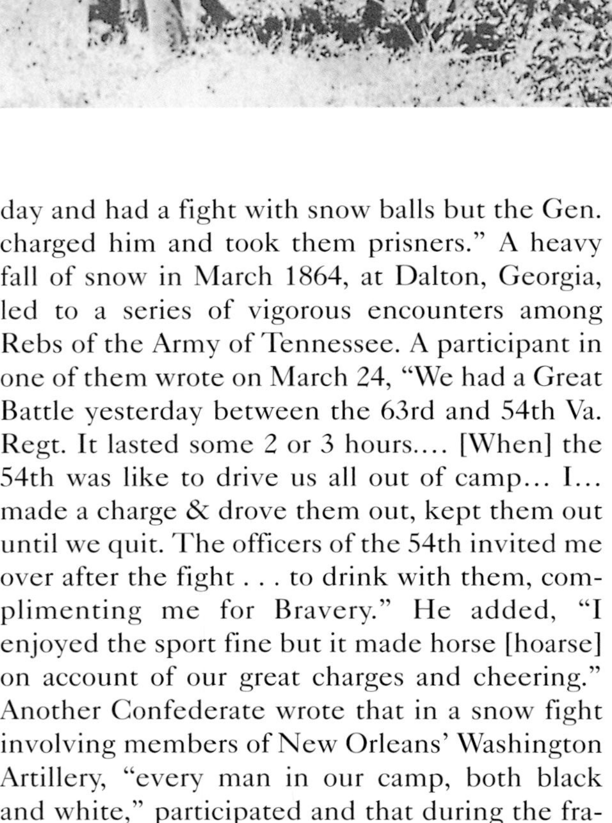

Right: When gambling-failed there was always horseplay, often at the expense of the poor freedman. (LC)

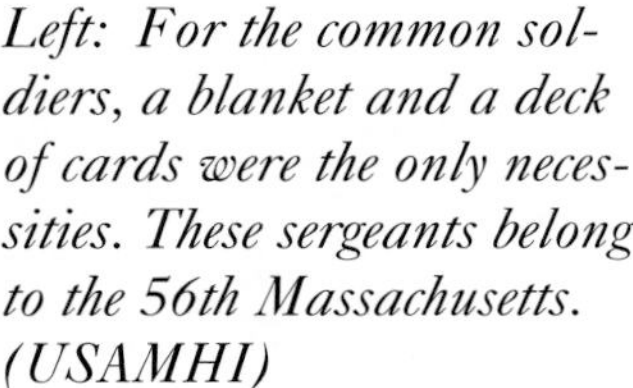

Left: For the common soldiers, a blanket and a deck of cards were the only necessities. These sergeants belong to the 56th Massachusetts. (USAMHI)

Left: A cockfight could also provide entertainment of a gruesome sort, and plenty of money changed hands on a rooster's feet. Even the brass took part. Brigadier General Orlando B. Willcox affects disinterest, looking at a letter, but he cannot help glancing at the start of a fight staged by former slaves George, on the left, and John, and their chickens. Taken at Petersburg in August 1864. (USAMHI)

day and had a fight with snow balls but the Gen. charged him and took them prisners." A heavy fall of snow in March 1864, at Dalton, Georgia, led to a series of vigorous encounters among Rebs of the Army of Tennessee. A participant in one of them wrote on March 24, "We had a Great Battle yesterday between the 63rd and 54th Va. Regt. It lasted some 2 or 3 hours.... [When] the 54th was like to drive us all out of camp... I... made a charge & drove them out, kept them out until we quit. The officers of the 54th invited me over after the fight . . . to drink with them, complimenting me for Bravery." He added, "I enjoyed the sport fine but it made horse [hoarse] on account of our great charges and cheering." Another Confederate wrote that in a snow fight involving members of New Orleans' Washington Artillery, "every man in our camp, both black and white," participated and that during the fracas, "Capt. C. H. Slocomb lost two front teeth, Lieut. Challeron [got a] black eye," and five privates came out with bloody noses. Among the captured property, he added, "is the flag of the Ga. Regiment, 8 or 10 caps and Hats, frying pan and 4 or 5 pones of corn bread."

Less boisterous than snowball fights but equally enjoyable were the sham courts-martial, the minstrels, and the plays staged by Yanks and

Below: Their funning could take a macabre turn at times. Being so close to death, it helped to make fun of it. (T. GORDON, JR.)

Right: A friendly spar for the camera was a favorite picture to send home. Boxing in camp, however, did not enjoy wide popularity. There was too much real fighting to be done. (DON W. MINDEMANN)

Rebs. In the simulated trials, enlisted men derived special pleasure from assigning officer roles to the rank and file and finding them guilty of such offenses as neglect of duty, drunkenness, immorality, and excessive harshness in discipline. Units such as the Richmond Howitzers and Boston's 44th Massachusetts Infantry formed dramatic associations and presented plays in a manner that won hearty applause from both soldiers and civilians. The 44th Massachusetts gave a program consisting of songs by a quartet, musical selections by the band, a scene from The Merchant of Venice, and a concluding drama entitled A Terrible Catastrophe on the North Atlantic R.R.

Minstrels and comedies were the most popular of all the shows presented in camp. The 9th New York Regiment's Zouave Dramatic Club in June 1862 gave a burlesque Combastus De Zouasio, which a soldier observing rated as well-performed. He liked the singing and dancing and the concluding farce Box and Cox. He reported that the theater was crowded with local aristocrats, soldiers, and officers, among them General John P. Hawkins.

Both individuals and units derived much pleasure from pets. George Baxter of the 24th Massachusetts Regiment wrote from camp in Maryland in December 1861, "Last night I was on guard.... Towards morning a little black kitten came purring around my feet, so I picked her up and put her on my shoulder and continued pacing my beat, with a rifle on one shoulder and a cat on the other." In December 1863 a correspondent of the Army of the Cumberland reported, "One of the boys has carried a red squirrel through thick and thin over a thousand miles. 'Bun' eats hard tack like a veteran and has the freedom of the tent. Another soldier has an owl captured in Arkansas & named 'Minerva'. Another has a young Cumberland Mountain bear; but chief among camp pets are dogs, riding on the saddle bow, tucked into a baggage wagon, mounted on a knapsack [or] growling under a gun.... A dog, like a horse, comes to love the rattle and crash of muskets and cannon." Colonel Lucius Fairchild of the 2nd Wisconsin Regiment wrote from near Fredericksburg in July 1862, "We have... a big half bull dog... named McClellan & stolen from a secesh. He attends all drills... is always at dress parade, sometimes marches up & down in front of the regt with the band & always marches to the center with his officers & up to the Col. All this is done with becoming gravity." A Union private wrote his homefolk from Hilton Head, South Carolina, in 1862, "Co. B has got 3 pets in the shape of yong aligators ... captured ... in the swamp.... Our little dog has a big time with them.... Co. A has a yong coon, Co. K has a crow." Soldiers whiled away many hours at cards, checkers, and dominoes, and almost every camp had a few chess enthusiasts. Meetings of Masons and other fraternal groups afforded diversion to a considerable number of men in both armies. Especially gratifying were the visits of wives and children, but these occasions were all too rare. The same was true of furloughs. A poor compensation for the lack of feminine association were the womanless dances at which soldiers and their bogus sweethearts whirled and stomped to fiddled renditions of such pieces as "Arkansas Traveler," "Billy in the Low Grounds," "The Goose Hangs

Above: Shamming for the camera was a favorite, and drinking seemed always the chosen topic, perhaps because it was so important a release for the soldiers. An excellent series ranging from the first toast in "Here is to the gal I love," to "Over the Bay," "Going Home," and finally "Good Night." Taken probably by H. Skinner of Fulton, New York, in 1862. (COLLECTION OF WILLIAM WELLING)

Below: Whenever possible, however, camp life was mostly for relaxation. It was a picture that did not change no matter the year, the place, or the army. J. D. Edwards caught these men of the Perote Guards at Pensacola drinking, reading, drawing, gambling. It was a never-ending scene. (TU)

Left: Edwards found the same scene with the 9th Mississippi in April 1861. (MUSEUM OF THE CONFEDERACY, RICHMOND)

Right: General Robert O. Tyler and his staff presented much the same image two years later in Virginia. Tyler stands second from the right. (USAMHI)

Below: Many fortunate officers North and South were joined in winter quarters by their wives, adding a dimension of domestic tranquility denied to most soldiers. (P-M)

High," "The Blue-Tailed Fly," and "Oh Lord God One Friday." These, like other social activities, sometimes were made more festive by copious draughts of "Oh Be Joyful," "Old Red Eye" and "Rock Me to Sleep Mother."

It is not surprising that many Yanks and Rebs sought relief from boredom in gambling. This was usually done with cards, and the most popular card games were poker, euchre, twenty-one, and faro. Soldiers used dice for craps and chuck-a-luck. They also gambled at keno, a game resembling bingo. Raffling was still another popular form of gambling. Rebel Sam Watkins stated that his comrades in the 1st Tennessee Regiment pitted vermin in trials of speed on tin plates. The owner of the louse that first vacated the plate was adjudged the winner. In one series of contests, one soldier's louse won so consistently as to arouse suspicion. An investigation disclosed that the winning Reb had been secretly heating his plate before each contest, thus giving his louse compelling reason to abandon it.

Gambling peaked in periods following payday. "Yesterday was Sunday," wrote a Mississippian shortly after a visit of the paymaster, "and I sat by the fire and saw the preachers holding forth about thirty steps off, and between them and me were two games of poker.... Chuck-a-luck and faro banks are running night and day with eager crowds standing around with their hands full of money. Open gambling has been prohibited but that amounts to nothing."

Visits to nearby towns and cities provided entertainment for many soldiers. Country lads derived special pleasure from these excursions. Zoos, large shops, tall buildings, and horse-drawn omnibuses were all new and exciting to men accustomed to a way of life devoid of all such attractions. Like soldiers of other conflicts, some of them freed for the first time from home restraints and knowing that the future was uncertain, yielded to the lure of a fling at the fleshpots. They visited grog shops and bawdy houses and in some instances paid a high price for their experimentation. The 10th Alabama Regiment, with a mean strength of 1,063, which went from the rural South in the early summer of 1861 to the environs of Richmond, had in July, according to the surgeon's report, a total of 62 new cases of gonorrhea and 6 of syphilis.

When visits to places beyond camp limits

Below: Wives and daughters quickly became a focal point for attention, many men vicariously paying favor to loved ones at home through women with the armies. (USAMHI)

Below: Many read and wrote letters for illiterate soldiers. Some, like the lady on the porch, even brought their babies. Hers has moved during the exposure, causing the blur with feet in her lap. (USAMHI)

Above: The women's presence helped their men forget for a time that they were at war, especially when they had quarters like these in a casemate at Fort Monroe. (USAMHI)

Left: The younger and prettier maidens became the belles of the armies, the object of every single officer's suit. This young lady attracts a host from an Illinois battery at Chattanooga in 1865. (CHS)

Left: For one of these soldiers of Company G, 95th Illinois Infantry, Camp life was more than exotic. It was a constant tension as he attempted to conceal a perhaps scandalous secret. For the soldier on the right, Private Albert Cashier, is in fact a woman. Born in Ireland, her feminine name was Hodgers, but all her life she was known as Albert J. Cashier. She not only successfully maintained her pose, serving well particularly at Vicksburg, but she eluded detection until 1911 when an automobile caused her hospitalization. It took a twentieth-century machine to expose the life-long sham of a patriotic woman who for so long fooled the men of her own century. (SPENCER H. WATTERSON, PONTIAC, ILLINOIS)

were made without leave, as they frequently were, apprehended offenders were subjected to punishment. Brief absences drew light penalties, prescribed by company or regimental commanders. These included extra stints of guard duty, digging ditches, grubbing stumps, riding the wooden horse—a horizontal pole held aloft by two upright beams—standing in a conspicuous place on barrel, box, or stump, and cleaning company grounds. Unit commanders also punished other minor offenses such as petty theft, straggling on the march, excessive drinking, brawling, and neglect of duty. For these breaches of discipline Rebs and Yanks had to carry weights such as logs, rails, or cannonballs, wear placards specifying the offense, such as "I Stole a Shirt" or "I Am a Thief," promenade the parade ground in a "barrel shirt" with arms extending through holes cut in the sides, or wear a ball and chain, the ball being a cannonball weighing six to thirty-two pounds fastened to the ankle by a chain two to six feet long. One of the most painful penal ties imposed by officers was to hang offenders by their thumbs from boughs or beams, with toes barely touching the ground for periods of time varying with the gravity of the disciplinary breach. This was a common punishment for soldiers who spoke disrespectfully to their superiors. Another loathsome punishment often imposed for "back talk" to officers and for other insubordinate behavior was bucking and gagging. This consisted of seating the offender on the ground, tying a stick in his mouth, fastening his hands together with a rope, slipping them over his knees and inserting a pole between the arms and knees. Sometimes artillery officers strapped a recalcitrant with arms and legs extended in spread-eagle fashion to the extra wheel carried on the rear of a caisson. This punishment was cruel enough when the vehicle was stationary and the soldier's head rested at the top of the wheel; but if the wheel was given a half-turn and the caisson driven over rough ground, the pain was excruciating.

Punishments of the sort mentioned above were sometimes dispensed by regimental or garrison courts-martial instead of by unit commanders. These bodies consisted of three officers, and their jurisdiction was restricted to enlisted men and to noncapital cases. They could not assess fines greater than a month's pay or impose hard labor sentences of more than a month's duration.

Left: The soldiers made their camps as much like vacation spots as they could. The quiet moments were the best, like this one caught by Gardner in 1865. (P-M)

Below: Intimate friendships made in camp lasted for life. Brevet Major General Charles H. T. Collis sits at left with a friend. He won the Medal of Honor for Fredericksburg. (NYHS)

Right: Confederates like these of the 1st Texas at Camp Quantico, Virginia, in the winter of '61 formed especially firm associations, bound tightly together by the shared hardships of the later war years. This recently discovered image is published here for the first time. (ROSENBURG LIBRARY, GALVESTON, TEXAS)

Above left: The fellowship... (TONY MARION)

Above: ... the outrageous sense of fun... (KA)

Left: ... and the smiles of friends made the most memorable of war experiences. Smiling soldiers like Lieutenant John G. Hecksher of the 12th United States Infantry, at left, are rare indeed in Civil War photographs. The men preferred the more somber—nay, glum—aspect of his friend Captain William Sergeant. (P-M)

Below: Camp life was for the generals, too, and they usually enjoyed it even more than their men. Brigadier General George Stoneman sits astride his charger watching men build their winter quarters—or his. (USAMHI)

The most serious offenses, such as murder, rape, arson, desertion, cowardice in battle, striking a superior, and sleeping on sentry post, were tried by general courts-martial, summoned by commanders of separate brigades, divisions, and larger units. They consisted of from five to thirteen officers, and their jurisdiction extended to all types of cases including capital crimes. Army regulations authorized them to issue sentences providing for death, life imprisonment, solitary confinement on bread and water, hard labor, ball and chain, forfeiture of pay and allowances, discharge from the service, reprimand, and, in case of noncommissioned officers, reduction in grade. General courts-martial often specified a combination of legal punishments and sometimes they imposed penalties that violated the spirit if not the letter of the law, such as branding and shaving all or part of the head. The brand, stamped on with indelible ink or burned into the skin of hip, hand, forehead, or cheek, was usually the first letter of the victim's offense, such as "C" for cowardice, "D" for desertion, "T" for theft, and "W" for worthless. The Federals in August 1861 and Confederates in April 1862 enacted legislation prohibiting flogging, but these laws were sometimes ignored.

In both armies deserters, cowards, and other serious offenders who were sentenced to dishonorable discharge sometimes had their scalps shaved, had their buttons or insignia torn off, and were drummed out of camp to the tune of "The Rogue's March"—or in the case of Confederates, to the strains of "Yankee Doodle"—with soldiers fore and aft carrying arms reversed. Some capital offenders were hanged, but most Yanks and Rebs who paid the death penalty were shot by firing squads. Executions, which comrades of the condemned had to witness from a hollow square—a rectangle with one end open—made a tremendous impression. Private Thomas Warrick of Bragg's army wrote to his wife on December 19, 1862, "I saw a site today that made me feel mity bad. I saw a man shot for deserting there was twenty fore Guns shot at him they shot him all to pease... he went home and thay Brote him Back and then he went home again and so they shot him for that. Martha it was one site that I did hate to see But I could not helpe my self I had to do Jest as thay sed for me to doo." A Connecticut soldier reported that two of his comrades fainted while watching thirty executioners fire a fusillade that killed a deserter. Concerning an execution of six other deserters which he was forced to attend the next day, this soldier wrote that he stood within twenty feet of the victim sit ting on the coffin nearest him. "They were all fired at the first time," he stated, "& 2 were killed instantly & 3 were shot the second time & the other one died while they were murdering the other three, for I call it murdering & I was not the olney one." Thomas Clark, a Pennsylvania Yank, registered no disapproval when in February 1864 he wrote his sister of the shooting of two deserters in Florida. "It was a great sight," he stated, "for it came on a Sunday and all of our regiment was out.... They where [were] hauled out in an opin wagon sitting on their coffins with a minister with each one of them and they looked and acted like they where going on an excursion. There was twelve men to shoot each one of them. The men was drawn up in a line nine paces from where the prisoners

Above: Major General John Sedgwick, left, sits with Brigadier General George Washington Getty, seated at right, at their Brandy Station tent. (USAMHI)

Above: Major General Israel B. Richardson and servant pose in the summer shade in1862. (USAMHI)

Left: Brigadier General John A. Rawlins, Grant's chief of staff, was joined at City Point, Virginia, by his family in 1864. (USAMHI)

Left: Brigadier General Marsena R. Patrick lived alone, as befitted Grant's chief policeman, provost-marshal general of the Army of the Potomac. (P-M)

stood by their coffins. Four o'clock came and the order was given to fire and them and day light was no more. There was nine balls went through one of their hearts and eleven passed through the other ones body. They did not live till the doctors came up to see if they were dead." If this report was accurate, the usual custom was not followed by loading only alternate rifles with live ammunition so that members of the firing squad might not know who fired the lethal shots. Clark attributed his indifference to the fact that the victims were recently recruited substitutes for whom "there was no pity."

Higher authorities on both sides showed a reluctance to approve death sentences. Apparently no Civil War soldier was executed for the capital offense of sleeping on sentry. Among Union forces totaling over 2,000,000 men, only 267 were executed and over half of these were deserters. Aggregate figures for Confederates are not available, but it is known that of 245 cases of court-martial convictions for desertion during the last six months of the conflict, mostly in the Army of Northern Virginia, death was prescribed in only 70 instances. President Davis's general amnesty of February 1865 set aside 31 of these sentences.

But death, by whatever means, became commonplace to Yanks and Rebs as the war progressed. Whatever respite they obtained from it came chiefly in the society and distinctly American character of their life in the camps. There the friendships were made, loyalties built, and memories indelibly imprinted on their minds. Here, at the fire, the tent, the mess table, men North and South displayed the true commonality of all Americans in all wars.

Below: Brigadier General Thomas W. Sherman lived in tropical tranquility on Hilton Head, South Carolina, when H. P. Moore took this image on March 8, 1862. (USAMHI)

Left: Brigadier General Edwin V. Sumner was not so old he could not enjoy paying court to a young belle visiting camp. (LC)

Above: And their entertainments were much the same as those of the men they commanded, including even an occasional sleigh ride. Here at Port Hudson, Louisiana, in January 1864, Brigadier General Cyrus Hamlin—son of Vice President Hannibal Hamlin—sits with a companion in the small one-horse sleigh at left. Behind him are the officers of the black regiment he was raising. (USAMHI)

Above: Music proved a pleasant diversion for all. Here a member of the band of the 26th North Carolina Infantry, with his horn. (DALE S. SNAIR COLLECTION, RICHMOND)

Above: Members of the band of the 26th North Carolina, missing only their compatriot of the previous image. Taken at Salem, North Carolina, around 1862. (MORAVIAN MUSIC FOUNDATION, INC.)

Below: This Tennessee fiddler could enliven the coldest winter camp with the "Bonnie Blue Flag" or Dixie. (TENNESSEE STATE MUSEUM)

Left: Now terribly faded, this image of members of the Washington Light Infantry of Charleston once revealed the words "Music Hall" on the tent wall. A bugler stands at left and the soldier seated second from the right cradles a violin in his lap. This March 1861 photograph is ample evidence that music went to the camps with the very first Confederates. (WASHINGTON LIGHT INFANTRY, CHARLESTON, SOUTH CAROLINA)

Above: Special ensembles like this group, with tambourine, banjo, guitar, violin, triangle, and bells, sprang up informally from among the members of several regiments. (T. SCOTT SANDERS COLLECTION)

Above: The bands played for all sorts of occasions, the saddest being funerals and farewells to favorite generals being transferred to other commands. The band at left here serenades Major General Frederick Steele as he leaves Arkansas for another post, probably at the end of the war. Steele is standing second from the left between the columns immediately behind the band. (RONN PALM COLLECTION)

Above: A typical Federal regimental band, this one composed of Pennsylvanians, photographed by S. R. Miller. (RONN PALM COLLECTION)

Above: A concomitant to music was dramatics. This engineer battalion formed its own theatrical club, the "Essayons Dramatic Club," giving performances in a theater of their building at Petersburg in 1864. (USAMHI)

Left: Photographers McPherson & Oliver took this image in Baton Rouge in 1863. It shows an improvised theater which at the moment is advertising a "Benefit to Lieutenant M. W. Morris" and presenting the Lady of Lyons and a Favorite Farce. (ILLINOIS STATE HISTORICAL LIBRARY)

Above: Fraternal orders, chiefly the Masons, came with the army. Here Samuel Cooley photographs an improvised "temple" on Folly Island, South Carolina. (USAMHI)

Above: The men trained pets, like the nationally famous "Old Abe," mascot of a Wisconsin regiment with whom it lived through the war. In battle the eagle would fly from its perch and remain aloft until the fighting subsided . (LC)

Above: Dogs were the favorite. This one is supposed to be saying, "I am the dog that went through the army with the 25th Iowa Infantry. (CHICAGO PUBLIC LIBRARY)

Left: Building and elaborate decoration occupied some, especially the ever-industrious 50th New York Engineers, who made their Petersburg headquarters a virtual arbor. (USAMHI)

Left: And, of course, with idle time on their hands, the men would misbehave. That is where the provost came in. Here the Army of the Potomac's provost marshal's camp at Bealton, Virginia, in August 1863. (P-M)

Left: Wherever the army went in numbers, so the provost went also. Mostly the men drank too much or disobeyed orders. (NA,U.S. WAR DEPARTMENT GENERAL STAFF)

Right: When they did, the provost guard spirited them away to the guardhouse. Here the guard for the Army of the Potomac headquarters at Petersburg in 1865. Behind them is the picketed fence of their stockade. (USAMHI)

Below: Minor offenders were fined pay or made to ride the wooden horse and other such essentially humiliating punishments. (ROBERT L. KOTCHIAN)

Above: The worst cases went before courts-martial like this one meeting at Concord, New Hampshire. (USAMHI)

Left: More serious cases spent time at hard labor in the heavy stockades like this United States Military Prison yard at Chattanooga. (NA,U.S. WAR DEPARTMENT GENERAL STAFF)

Left: ... so was the punishment. Troops stand drawn into a three-sided square to witness a hanging near Petersburg in 1864. The mounds of earth right of the gallows mark the grave of the condemned already dug. (LC)

Right: Another court-martial, at Chattanooga. If the offense was grave enough . . (TERENCE P. OLEARY, GLADWYNE, PENNSYLVANTA)

Left: And like soldiers everywhere, the men of blue and gray loved to celebrate holidays. Here a Christmas feast appears ready for the men who will tightly jam the benches. Turkeys sit on the tables as well as relishes. The hot vegetables will be brought out and served, and every plate has a slab of bread or cake. (NA)

Right: Another wreath-bedecked hall for Christmas. These diners will be a little less crowded. (USAMHI)

Below: Washington's birthday, February 22, was a holiday in both North and South, and here the "New Forage House" ballroom in Beaufort, South Carolina, stands ready for an 1864 observance. (WRHS)

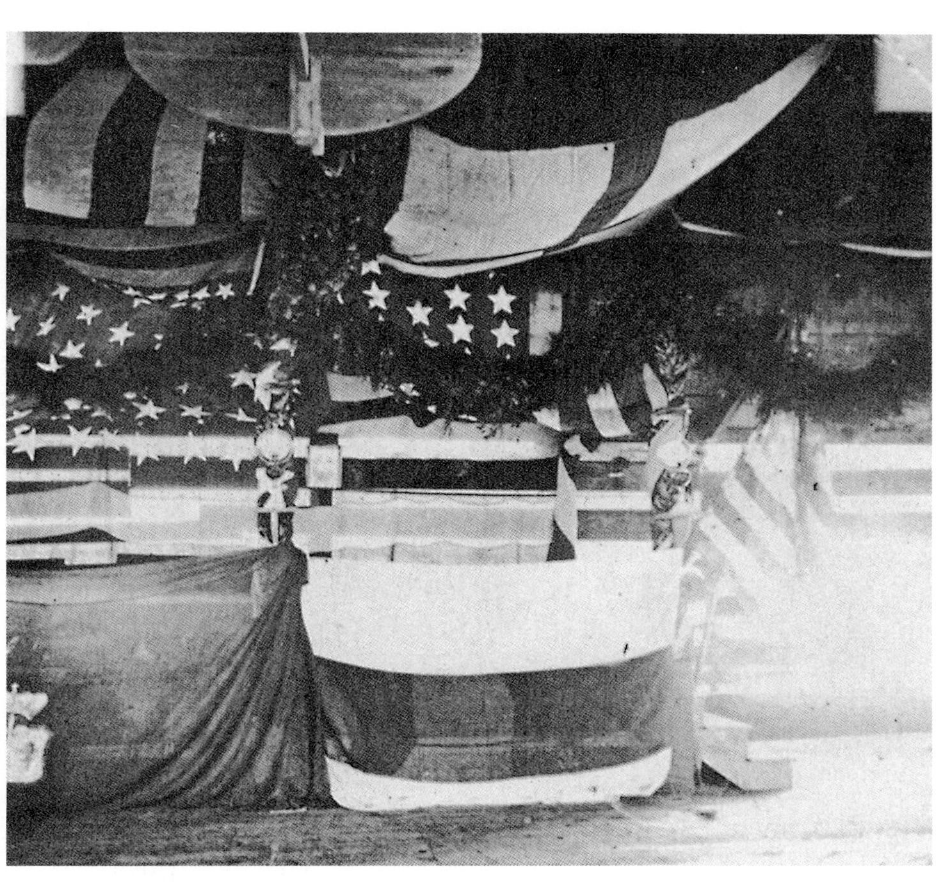

Right: The speakers' stand for the Beaufort celebration, with flags and bunting aplenty. (USAMHI)

Right: The Fourth of July was the greatest of all in the Union armies, and even some Confederates celebrated the day. Here the 50th New York Engineers revel in the day on July 4, 1864. Joining them, and seated at the extreme left, is Charles Francis Adams, Jr., historian, grandson of President John Quincy Adams, and future president of the Union Pacific Railroad. (USAMHI)

The Conquest of the Mississippi

CHARLES L. DUFOUR

The great river spawned great men to contest her waters

Above: The USS Brooklyn, *the first ship to go on blockade off the mouth of the Mississippi. The warship and the river were to see a lot of each other in the years to come. (NA)*

THE USS *Brooklyn* dropped anchor off the mouth of the Mississippi at 2 P.M. on May 26, 1861, and the Union conquest of the great river, so vital to the Confederacy, was underway.

It was the first implementation of General Winfield Scott's "Anaconda Plan," the purpose of which was not only the military envelopment of the Confederacy but its economic strangulation as well. As early as May 3, Scott had discussed his plan with General George B. McClellan, pointing out that a powerful Union movement, by land and by water, down the Mississippi together with an effective blockade of the river's mouth would "envelop the insurgent States, and bring them to terms with less bloodshed than by another plan."

The effectiveness of the Union blockade was almost immediately felt in New Orleans, the Confederacy's greatest city. On May 30, 1861, a ship loaded with Brazilian coffee was captured by the *Brooklyn* and the next day another New Orleans bound vessel carrying foodstuffs was seized. From the moment the blockade was established, not a single ship reached the Confederate city until Farragut's attacking fleet ran past Fort Jackson and Fort St. Philip in April 1862. Although the Union blockading vessels prevented ships from entering the Mississippi, the river's five passes into the Gulf of Mexico offered avenues of escape to blockade runners from New Orleans and several did make it to sea. The most significant escape was that of the Confederate raider *Sumter* commanded by Raphael Semmes, later of *Alabama* fame, which eluded the blockade on June 30 to prey relentlessly on American commerce vessels for more than six months.

The Confederate government was slow to realize the defenselessness of New Orleans and the absolute necessity of making an all-out effort to prepare the city for invasion. Four months after Louisiana seceded from the Union, a general officer had not yet arrived in New Orleans to take command. During that time, the city had been drained of troops; they had been ordered to Pensacola to reinforce Braxton Bragg. On April 10, two days before the guns sounded at Charleston, Governor Thomas O. Moore of Louisiana complained to Confederate authorities, "We are disorganized, and have no general officer to command and direct." Seven weeks went by before seventy-one-year-old General David E. Twiggs, veteran of more than half a century in the United States Army, reached New Orleans to take command.

Although the Common Council of the City of New Orleans praised Twiggs's "integrity, sagacity, and nerve so essential to a commander," it soon became evident that the enfeebled septuagenerian general was not the man to defend the South's greatest city from Federal attack. President Davis had already received complaints of the "infirmities of General Twiggs," when Governor Moore's plea for "an officer... who, with youth, energy and military ability, would infuse some activity in our preparation and some confidence in our people," reached Richmond in September. In closing this appeal to Davis, Moore begged that "this city, the most important to be preserved of any of the Confederacy, and our coast, the most exposed of all the states, be no longer neglected."

President Davis finally conceded that General Twiggs "has proven unequal to his command," but he shifted the blame for Twiggs's appointment to the people of New Orleans: "As in his selection I yielded much to the solicitation of the

Above: Major General Mansfield Lovell would never be fully appreciated in the Confederacy for his talents. Rather, he would be remembered as the man who lost New Orleans. (USAMHI)

Above: David D. Porter did heavy duty on the Mississippi. At the outset of the war, however, he ridiculed the Confederate success at Head of the Passes as a "ridiculous affair." (USAMHI)

Above: Commodore George N. Hollins, who led the successful Confederate attack on the little Union squadron at Head of the Passes. (LSU)

people of New Orleans, I think they should sooner have in formed me of the mistake they had made."

When Major General Mansfield Lovell was assigned to New Orleans, Twiggs got the implied message and prevented an awkward situation by asking, on October 5, to be relieved from duty for reasons of health. Before leaving for New Orleans, Lovell conferred with both President Davis and Secretary of War Judah P. Benjamin and, with almost prophetic insight, declared that the only proper defense of New Orleans would require a unified command. He argued, but in vain, that the employment of naval as well as army forces should be under his direction. Fearing that Lovell had not fully understood the definition of his command responsibilities, Davis hurried off a letter to him stating, "The fleet maintained at the port of New Orleans and its vicinity is not a part of your command." This decision would prove fatal.

Lovell reached New Orleans on October 17 and found, as he reported to Richmond, "great confusion, irresolution, and want of system in every thing administrative." New Orleans was "almost entirely stripped of everything available in the way of ordnance, stores, ammunition, clothing, medicines etc." There existed a frightening shortage of powder, Lovell reported. So he established two powder mills in New Orleans, and moved a third mill from the Mississippi coast to the city.

Before leaving Virginia, Lovell met with his old army friend General P. G. T. Beauregard, a native of New Orleans who, for ten years before the war, had been in charge of the defenses of Louisiana. Beauregard reiterated to Lovell what he had told Louisiana authorities many months earlier, that Forts Jackson and St. Philip, miles downriver from New Orleans, could not prevent steam vessels from passing unless an obstruction in the river held the ships under the cross fire of the forts for half an hour. Such a barricade, talked about in February but not constructed until the

Left: The CSS McRae, *part of Hollins's "fleet." (NHC)*

Left: The USS Richmond *was rammed by Hollins's ironclad* Manassas, *an action that did more damage to the ironclad than to the Federal warship. The* Richmond *served continually on the river in the years to come. (NHC)*

Above: Naval stations at places like Mound City, Illinois, were organized and readied to construct new ships as well as to refit and repair those already in service. (WRHS)

Above: Ironclads were of interest to the Union naval authorities on the Mississippi. Captain John Rodgers was sent by the Navy Department to supervise the construction of the Benton-*class gunboats at Cairo, Illinois. (NA,U.S. WAR DEPARTMENT GENERAL STAFF)*

summer, had been in place about a month when Lovell reached New Orleans. After inspecting this so-called raft, Lovell undertook to strengthen it.

On arrival, Lovell heard much of a recent Confederate naval victory at the Head of the Passes where a bold attack on a Yankee squadron routed it in what David Dixon Porter later described as "the most ridiculous affair that ever took place in the American Navy."

The heroes of this exploit were Commodore George Hollins and the ironclad *Manassas*, popularly known in New Orleans as the "Turtle." The latter, originally the twin-screw tugboat *Enoch Train*, had been purchased by a syndicate of businessmen for conversion into an ironclad to operate as a privateer against the blockaders. The cigar shaped *Manassas*, covered with railroad iron three quarters of an inch thick, mounted one gun, which operated through a trapdoor forward. It had a heavy cast-iron prow, which extended below the waterline so that the vessel could operate as a ram.

Although the project was supposedly a secret one, reports of the "formidable instrument of destruction" the Confederates were building at New Orleans slipped into the Northern press. Fantastic stories, born of imagination and misinformation, told that the *Manassas* was equipped with a powerful auger which could bore holes in a ship below its waterline and that this "hellish engine" had twenty-four hoses with which boiling water could be played upon the crew of an enemy ship. The "Turtle" was, in fact, much more formidable in the Northern press than it proved in the water. Nevertheless, its owners had high hopes that, operating as a privateer, the *Manassas* would reap a rich harvest of prize money by capturing Union block-

Left: Mound City remained in a bustle of activity during most of the war. (LC)

Above: Its shops and ways echoed to the sounds of machinery and workmen. Here, in the foreground, blocks and tackle and lines are visible on the bank where ships were hauled out of the water for hull-scraping and repair. (USAMHI)

Above: Tugboats like the little Daisy *plied the river constantly off Mound City. (NHC)*

ade vessels. But hardly had the *Manassas* been launched and given its trial runs than Commodore Hollins seized it for the Confederacy against the protests of the syndicate.

On the night of October 11–12, 1861, Hollins's little flotilla, consisting of the *Manassas, McRae, Ivy, Calhoun, Tuscarora, Jackson,* and *Pickens*—New Orleanians called it the "mosquito fleet"—attacked a Union squadron of four warships under Captain John Pope at the Head of the Passes, where the various mouths of the Mississippi leave the main stream.

What followed was a comic opera of naval warfare. The *Manassas* rammed the *Richmond,* and the ten-knot impact disabled the Confederate ironclad while causing panic aboard the Union flagship. In the confusion and darkness, three Union ships, *Vincennes, Preble,* and *Waterwitch,* on signals from Captain Pope, slipped their cables and began steaming down Southwest Pass, and the *Richmond* followed. A running fight of no actual consequence ensued, but the aftermath was farcical after the *Vincennes* ran aground on the bar. Commander Robert Handy, believing erroneously that Pope had ordered him to abandon ship, did so after ordering the lighting of a slow fuse to the magazine. Fortunately, a Union quartermaster, after lighting the fuse, cut off the burning end and tossed it into the river, and the *Vincennes* was thus saved. "Pope's Run" as the incident became known, was later characterized by Admiral Alfred T. Mahan as "a move which brought intense mortification to himself [Pope] and in a measure to the service."

Fully believing that he had sunk a Union vessel (he announced it as the *Preble*) in this weird affair at the Head of the Passes, Hollins hurried back to New Orleans with the morale-building news of a great victory. But the expedition had little significance beyond creating popular enthusiasm. Elise Ellis Bragg, writing her husband, General Braxton Bragg, said, "Our 'Turtle,' alias *Manassas* made a grand charge and would have done wonders if it had not been disabled. All these things make a sensation, but I fear they help our cause but little, and a dark and gloomy winter seems closing around us."

When General Lovell arrived, New Orleanians were still talking enthusiastically about the action at the Head of the Passes and also of the two giant ironclads *Mississippi* and *Louisiana,* which were

Above: And frequently an entire fleet of ironclads and "tinclads" appeared at anchor in midstream. The USS St. Louis *rests in the center of the image, while in the distance behind its stern can be seen what is probably the USS* Tyler. *(USAMHI)*

Below: Specialized craft like the hospital boat Nashville *were also needed to serve both the navy and the armed soldiers fighting along the river. (LC)*

Above: Another hospital ship, the R. C. Wood, *on the wharf at Vicksburg in 1863. (OLD COURT HOUSE MUSEUM, VICKSBURG)*

Above: Cairo, Illinois, also hosted an important naval station. Here its wharf boat lies moored on the shore. (USAMHI)

Above: A river fleet at anchor off Cairo in 1865. (AMERICANA IMAGE GALLERY)

Above: At Cairo, soldiers boarded transports like the USS Brown *for the journey to the front at New Orleans or Vicksburg or Port Hudson. (USAMHI)*

Below: And packet boats carrying mail, like the Golden Era, *shared the stream with gunboats like the USS* Tyler *in the crowded waters off Cairo. Shipbuilder James B. Eads first used his skills to convert a steamer into the gunboat* Tyler. *(CHS)*

under construction just above the city, and which were expected to be in operation in January.

Meanwhile, the first Union preparations on the upper Mississippi had been made on August 2, when James B. Eads of St. Louis was authorized to construct seven ironclad gunboats of a new type for use on the western rivers. Three river steamers, the *Tyler, Lexington,* and *Conestoga,* had been con verted into gunboats, and they became the nucleus of the Union naval forces on the Mississippi until Eads's ironclads were completed.

On October 7, the gunboats *Lexington* and *Tyler,* on a reconnaissance from Cairo, steamed toward Lucas Bend, Missouri, to engage Confederate shore batteries at Iron Bluff, not far from Columbus, Kentucky. On October 12, the same date of the ignominious "Pope's Run" from the Head of the Passes, the *St. Louis,* first Federal ironclad, was launched at Carondelet, Missouri.

Initial land operation by Union forces on the Mississippi proved abortive. On November 7,

Brigadier General U. S. Grant descended from Cairo with 3,000 troops on transports supported by two wooden converted gunboats. Landing on the Missouri side, Grant seized the village of Belmont, across the river from Columbus, Kentucky. Grant held Belmont until Confederate reinforcements from Columbus crossed the river, and then he regained his transports and steamed back to Cairo.

Before 1861 ended, the first significant operation concerned with the conquest of the Mississippi occurred when 1,900 Union troops under Brigadier General John W. Phelps landed on Ship Island, in Mississippi Sound, twelve miles off the mainland and sixty miles from the mouth of the Mississippi.

With the coming of the new year, Union efforts on the upper Mississippi were stepped up. On January 14, three Union gunboats descended to the vicinity of Columbus and shelled Confederate encampments along the river. After the fall of Forts Henry and Donelson early in February, 1862, Columbus became the prime Union objective in the West. The Confederate government, recognizing its extreme vulnerability, ordered the evacuation of Columbus on February 20. Withdrawal of troops, guns, and material began at once and by March 2 the evacuation was completed. All but two of Columbus's 140 guns were moved south to Island No. 10 and its adjacent batteries. The next day, as Federal troops occupied Columbus, another force under General John Pope laid siege to New Madrid, Missouri. After a heavy bombardment of their works on March 13, the Confederates slipped out of New Madrid the next day and retreated to Island No. 10, leaving behind a substantial amount of guns and supplies.

Island No. 10, so named because it was the tenth island in the Mississippi south of its confluence with the Ohio, was assumed by the Confederates to be impregnable. Situated in Madrid Bend, between Tennessee and Missouri, Island No. 10 commanded the river in both directions. Earthworks, constructed for two miles along the banks, made Island No. 10 formidable for an attacking fleet, while virtually impassable swamps made a land attack on Island No. 10 unfeasible.

When Pope seized New Madrid, the Confederate naval force—six gunboats under Commodore Hollins—found itself much outgunned and withdrew to Tiptonville, thirty miles below Island No. 10 by river, but less than five miles by land. The stage was now set for a combined army and navy operation against Island No. 10, with Pope attacking by land while Commodore Andrew Foote's flotilla, headed by Eads's formidable ironclad *Benton,* most powerful warship on the Mississippi, engaged the Confederate bastion from the river. While Pope was impatient to begin operations against Island No. 10 as soon as New Madrid fell, it was not until March l4 that Foote's flotilla left Cairo for the fifty-mile run down to Island No. 10. With seven gunboats and ten mortar vessels, and transports carrying troops to occupy Island No. 10 after its capture, Foote dropped anchor two miles from the Union objective on the morning of March 15. The next day, Foote's mortars opened fire on the Confederate works and on

Left: And he did the same with the USS Lexington. *These gunboats were not very effectively armored, but they were a start. (USAMHI)*

Right: Far more effective was the USS St. Louis, *launched at Carondelet, Missouri, the first Federal ironclad. (NA, U. S. WAR DEPARTMENT GENERAL STAFF)*

Below: Active operations on the Mississippi really begin with Brigadier General U. S. Grant, shown here as a major general. His attack on Belmont was staged from Cairo. (LC)

Left: The first real Union success came at Island No. 10, when Brigadier General John Pope cooperated with Foote's flotilla to force the Confederate bastion to surrender. (NA, U. S. SIGNAL CORPS)

Right: In both defense and offense, cannons mounted on rafts and floated into position were used frequently. on the river at places like Island No. 10. (NHC)

Left: Henry Gurney's image of the mightiest ironclad on the river, the USS Benton, *another of Eads's conversions. Foote made it his flagship. This photo was taken at Natchez in 1863 or later. (JOAN AND THOMAS GANDY, NATCHEZ, MISSISSIPPI)*

Right: Commander Henry Walke, a Virginian by birth, ran his Carondelet past No. 10's batteries to assist Pope's land assault. (LC)

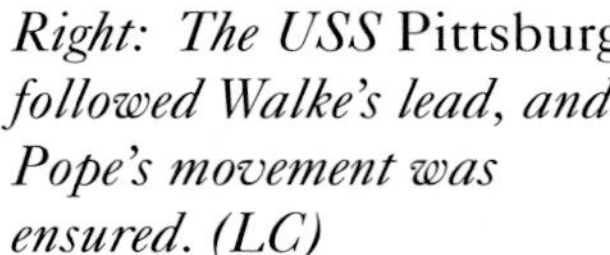

Right: The USS Pittsburg *followed Walke's lead, and Pope's movement was ensured. (LC)*

Right: Captures included the Confederate ship CSS Red Rover, *a barracks ship which the Federals turned into the first hospital ship in the navy. (USAMHI)*

Right: The CSS De Soto *was captured as well, to become the USS* General Lyon. *(NHC)*

March 17 the Benton and Foote's other ironclads went into action, at a range of 2,000 yards.

Meanwhile, Pope had realized he needed transports to get his troops across the Mississippi if the joint operation were to be successful. In an official request, he promised that if Foote were to "... run past the batteries of Island No. 10 with two or three gunboats and reach here, I can cross my whole force and capture every man of the enemy at Island No. 10 and on the mainland." Foote immediately rejected Pope's proposal.

Pope's chief engineer, Colonel Josiah W. Bissell, then proposed that a canal be dug through the overflowed swamps to bypass Island No. 10. Pope approved the project when Bissell assured him that he could open a way for vessels of light draft to cut across the neck of land. He authorized Bissell to employ his entire regiment to open the canal. Working feverishly for nearly three weeks, Bissell cut a twelve-mile-long channel, fifty feet wide.

Before Bissell's canal was ready, Foote had a change of mind when Henry Walke, commander of the *Carondelet*, volunteered to run his ship past Island No. 10's batteries. In a thunderstorm on the night of April 4, the *Carondelet* ran the fiery gauntlet and reached New Madrid at midnight, a few hours after Bissell's engineers had completed the last stretch of the canal. Three nights later, during another storm, the *Pittsburg* ran past Island No. 10's guns and anchored at New Madrid. The same night, four shallow-draft steamers passed through Bissell's canal to provide Pope with the transports he needed to get his troops across the river to assault Island No. 10 from the rear.

Island No. 10 had been subjected to constant fire from Foote's ships, and a bold Union raid on

the *Louisiana* went down to the forts, the *Mississippi*, still far from completed, was launched.

On the night of April 20, Farragut sent Captain Henry Bell with two gunboats to sever the barrier and open a way for the ships to pass through. Bell succeeded in his mission and Farragut, never enthusiastic about the mortar ships' ability to silence the forts, determined to make his run on the night of April 23-24.

Everything was in readiness at the Head of the Passes, but disorganization prevailed among the Confederate defenders. That strange War Department instrument, the River Defense Fleet, refused to take orders from the navy; the navy showed no inclination to cooperate with General Lovell's defense plans; and, to top it, New Orleans was a city verging on panic.

At 2 A.M. on April 24, the *Cayuga* raised its anchors and steamed off into the moonless night, the vanguard of Farragut's attacking fleet. One by one, the warships followed. At 3: 30 A.M., the *Cayuga* passed noiselessly through the breach in the barrier, unchallenged by any Confederate vessel and unthreatened by the fire rafts which were supposed to have been illuminated and sent down the river. Immediately, the guns of Fort Jackson and Fort St. Philip opened up as Farragut's other vessels moved into range, firing their broadsides at the forts. The flashes of their guns and the arching course of mortar shells lit the river in a spectacle of awesome grandeur. Three of Farragut's gunboats failed to make it through the breach in the barrier. The *Kennebec* entangled itself in the raft and the *Winona* suffered the same fate, and both freed themselves with difficulty and drifted out of action. The third, the *Itasca*, was badly crippled by gunfire from Fort Jackson and it retired downriver.

At the first fighting, the Confederate River Defense Fleet hurried off ingloriously, but three Rebel ships fought with valor. Hopelessly outgunned and outnumbered, the *Manassas* ("Turtle"), *McRae*, and *Governor Moore* were in the thick of the melee, each drawing the concentrated fire of several Union ships at various stages of the battle. The forts laid down tremendous barrages, but fourteen of Farragut's ships ran the fiery gauntlet successfully, although his flagship, the *Hartford*, was set ablaze by a fire raft while it was aground off Fort St. Philip. For a while, it was touch and go for the *Hartford*, but discipline and engine power prevailed: The fire was extinguished by the crew and the flagship shivered and shook as it freed itself from the mud and steamed out of range of the forts.

At the peak of the battle, the roaring and flashing of the guns created a spectacular scene. One of General Benjamin Butler's officers wrote, "Combine all that you have heard of thunder, add to it all that you have ever seen of lightning, and you have, perhaps, a conception of the scene." To an officer on the Hartford, "it was like the breaking up of the universe with the moon and all the stars bursting in our midst." Farragut himself described it: "It was as if the artillery of heaven were playing upon the earth."

The *Manassas*, which had rammed the *Brooklyn* and *Mississippi* and fought at close quarter half a dozen other Union ships, was finally disabled and scuttled by its crew. The *McRae*, just as active in the unequal fight, had its tiller ropes shot away and made it with difficulty to the protection of Fort Jackson. The *Governor Moore* engaged the *Varuna* in a running battle, rammed the Union

Right: New Orleans' City Hall. Here Farragut raised the Union flag over the conquered city. (USAMHI)

Left: Looking down the levee from Canal Street. The busy traffic, once interrupted by the war, now flows again. Bales of cotton await shipment. (USAMHI)

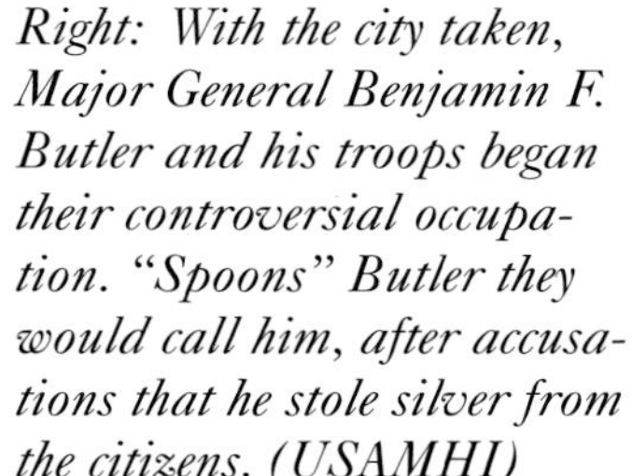

Right: With the city taken, Major General Benjamin F. Butler and his troops began their controversial occupation. "Spoons" Butler they would call him, after accusations that he stole silver from the citizens. (USAMHI)

Below: Before long New Orleans would be designated the headquarters of the new Department of the Gulf. Here officers serving in the department from several services, army, navy, and marines, gather for a group portrait in March 1863. Seated from the left are Lieutenant Edward Terry of the Richmond, Captain James Alden commanding the Richmond, and Brigadier General Godfrey Weitzel. The rest are staff officers. (USAMHI)

Right: Soon after the fall of New Orleans, Farragut's ships took Baton Rouge and, shown here, Natchez. Then it was time to try for Vicksburg. (USAMHI)

Right: Commander S. P. Lee led the small fleet that first tried to force the surrender of Vicksburg, but unsuccessfully. (USAMHI)

Far right: Farragut soon moved north to join Lee, bringing with him the 3,200 men of Brigadier General Thomas Williams, an almost universally disliked commander. The soldiers would attempt nothing, being shattered by disease. Williams retired to Baton Rouge, and there on August 5 he was killed in the Confederate attack. (USAMHI)

Below: On the way to Vicksburg, Farragut learned of the Union fleet victory at Plum Run Bend, a victory won over ineffectual Confederate ships by gunboats like the USS Carondelet. *(USAMHI)*

ship twice and sank it—Farragut's only loss in the passage of the forts. Beverly Kennon, commander of the *Governor Moore,* fired his ship, threw his sword overboard, and surrendered himself as half a dozen Union gunboats descended upon his horribly cut-up craft. The dead on the *Governor Moore* totaled fifty-seven—nine more than the combined dead in Farragut's fleet and in the two forts.

The Louisiana, still anchored above Fort St. Philip, received heavy firing at close range as Farragut's ships passed up the river, but the ironclad was practically undamaged. David Dixon Porter noted in his journal that had Commander Mitch ell, captain of the Louisiana, "possessed the soul of a flea, he could have driven us all out of the river."

The next day, April 25, Farragut pushed up the river to New Orleans. He was amazed at the sight that met his eye: "The levee of New Orleans was one scene of desolation, ships, steamers, cotton, coal, etc., were all in one common blaze," he wrote. "The Mississippi, which was to be the terror of the seas, and no doubt would have been to a great extent... soon came floating by us all in flames, and passed down the river."

Demands that the city surrender met with a scornful refusal by Mayor John Monroe, who pointed out to Farragut that as Lovell had evacuated his militia troops, New Orleans was defense less and "the city is yours by the power of brutal force."

Meanwhile, down at the forts, mutiny broke out on April 27, compelling Duncan to surrender to Porter. During the signing, the *Louisiana* came drifting by ablaze, and moments later it blew up. All Confederate resistance below New Orleans was now ended. When the news reached Farragut he sent a party ashore to haul down the flag of Louisiana from the city hall flagpole and raise the American flag.

On May 1, Major General Benjamin F. Butler landed his occupation troops and New Orleans' days in the Confederacy were over. Mary Baykin Chesnut prophetically recorded the bitter fact in her diary: "New Orleans is gone, and with it the Confederacy! Are we not cut in two? The Mississippi ruins us if it is lost."

After Butler occupied New Orleans, Farragut was faced with a dilemma: What to do in the light of his original orders. These read: "If the Mississippi expedition from Cairo shall not have descended the river, you will take advantage of the panic to push a strong force up the river to take all their defenses in the rear. You will also reduce the fortifications which defend Mobile Bay and turn them over to the army to hold."

Farragut sent Porter and the mortar boats to Mobile Bay and dispatched Commander S. P. Lee with the *Oneida* and several smaller gunboats up the Mississippi, while he remained at New Orleans with the greater part of his fleet. Baton Rouge and Natchez, both undefended, were captured and the American flag was raised above their public buildings. At Vicksburg, however, Lee's demand for surrender was answered defiantly: "Mississippians don't know and refuse to learn how to surrender to an enemy. If... Farragut or... Butler can teach them let them come and try." Lee gave Vicksburg twenty-four hours to remove its women and children to safety, set up a blockade of the city, and awaited orders from Farragut.

When Farragut learned what was happening upriver, he was anxious to push up the Mississippi with his full command. On May 10, one of the few fleet actions of the war had taken place above Fort Pillow at Plum Run Bend when a much-out gunned Confederate flotilla of eight ships—the Confederate River Defense Fleet—with more valor than judgment attacked seven Union ironclads. With four of his ships disabled by the superior fire power of the Yankees' ships, Captain James Montgomery broke off action and retired downstream to Memphis. On May 23, Farragut's fleet, accompanied by 3,200 troops under Brigadier General Thomas Williams, reached Vicksburg. Two days later, Colonel Charles Ellet's nine rams and two floating batteries, completed for the War Department in only forty days, made liaison with the Western Flotilla, now commanded by Captain Charles H. Davis, who had succeeded the ailing Commodore Foote.

Davis's reaction to Ellet's arrival was politely uncooperative. Ellet informed Davis that he was going to operate against Fort Pillow and asked for one gunboat to accompany him. Failing this, he invited Davis to assign some navy observers to the rams for this "daring and patriotic enterprise." Davis's reply reflected the age-old rivalry between military services: "I decline taking any part in the expedition... I would thank you to inform me how far you consider yourself under my authority; and I shall esteem it a favor to receive from you a copy of the orders under which you are acting." Ellet's reply was conciliatory: "No question of authority need be raised." But to Secretary of War Stanton he wrote, "Commodore Davis will not join me... nor contribute a gunboat... nor allow any of his men to volunteer... I shall therefore... go without him."

The fall of Corinth on June 3 made the Confederate evacuation of Fort Pillow inevitable and exposed Memphis to serious threat. At Memphis, the Confederates were building two powerful ironclads, the *Arkansas* and *Tennessee*, and their seizure was a Union objective. Two of Ellet's rams drew sharp fire from the works at Fort Pillow on June 3, but the Confederates had already begun evacuation, and during the night of June 4 it was completed. The only Confederate defense now between the Union vessels and Memphis was a weak Confederate flotilla at that city.

Union gunboats attacked this flotilla on the morning of June 6 in another of the rare fleet actions on the Mississippi. People of Memphis lined the bluffs to watch the battle when Commodore Davis sent five Union ironclads and four rams—a total of sixty-eight guns—against Montgomery's inferior flotilla of eight makeshift vessels mounting only twenty-eight guns. In the unequal struggle, which featured ramming and close-quarter fighting, the Confederates were decimated. Three Rebel ships were destroyed and four were captured, with only the *Van Dorn* escaping. The Union Navy now controlled the entire Mississippi, except at Vicksburg, Mississippi, and at Port Hudson in Louisiana.

The principal concern of the Union fleet on the Mississippi was the uncompleted Confederate ironclad, *Arkansas*, which, when Memphis was under threat, had been sent downriver to safety.

In the late summer of 1861, the Confederate Navy Department authorized the building of four powerful ironclads, easily the most formidable gun boats on the Mississippi. Devastating to the Confederate cause was the policy of "too little and too late" that prevailed with its gunboat building pro-

Right: The USS Louisville, *too, shown here at Memphis, made light work of the enemy River Defense Fleet at Plum Run Bend. It was, in fact, the largest fleet engagement of the war. (NHC)*

Below: Brigadier General John B. Villepigue commanded the defense of Fort Pillow as best he could, until forced to abandon and destroy his fortifications. (P-M)

Above: Then the Union Navy moved against Memphis. The only thing in their way was a little fleet commanded by the flamboyant M. Jeff Thompson who, though never promoted brigadier general, dressed like one anyhow. (DAVID R. O REILLY COLLECTION)

Left: Thompson's flotilla was obliterated, all but one captured or destroyed. The Little Rebel *was one of the captured, and it was later put into Federal service. (TERENCE P. O LEARY, GLADWYNE, PENNSYLVANIA)*

Right: The CSS General Price *had been a cottonclad—bales of cotton stacked on her sides for protection—when she was sunk at Memphis. Raised and remodeled she became the USS* General Price, *commanded by... (USAMHI)*

Below: ... Acting Volunteer Lieutenant J. F. Richardson. (ROBERT G. HARRIS)

Left: Alfred W. Ellet, later a brigadier general, succeeded to command of the ram fleet when his brother Charles died two weeks after the Battle of Memphis. (USAMHI)

Below: One of the ships of Ellet's ram fleet that destroyed Thompson's little flotilla. (NHC)

Below: And now Memphis belonged to the Union again. The city is shown here viewed from the levee. (USAMHI)

jects. The *Louisiana* and the *Mississippi*, as was stated earlier, were to have been completed at New Orleans by the end of January 1862. But neither was finished when Farragut attacked the forts below New Orleans in April, and the *Louisiana* was blown up and the *Mississippi* set afire.

About the time that work was begun on the *Louisiana* and Mississippi in New Orleans, two other formidable ironclads were started in a Memphis shipyard, the *Arkansas* and the *Tennessee.* Patterned on the *Louisiana* and *Mississippi* and perhaps even more formidable, the Memphis ironclads were to be ready by the end of December 1861.

The descent of the Mississippi by the Union fleet found work on both the *Arkansas* and *Tennessee* lagging, and on April 25, the same day Farragut's warships appeared at New Orleans, the *Arkansas* was launched. It was floated 300 miles down the Mississippi to the Yazoo River above Vicksburg and then was towed 200 miles up the Yazoo to Greenwood, where it was expected to be finished shortly. On orders from Richmond, the *Tennessee* was destroyed before launch.

A shortage of workmen, tools, equipment, timber, and other materials needed to complete the *Arkansas* resulted in interminable delays, despite the vigorous efforts of the ship's commander, Lieutenant Isaac Brown, who was charged with the *Arkansas's* completion. Launch day finally came on July 4, but more than six months late, and the *Arkansas* steamed to Yazoo City.

It was Lieutenant Brown's intention to drive his ironclad through the entire combined Union fleet— Farragut had run Vicksburg's fortifications, and had joined Davis above the city—and anchor the *Arkansas* under the protection of the Confederate batteries.

Major General Earl Van Dorn, commanding at Vicksburg, impatiently awaited the *Arkansas*, which he expected to prove a formidable factor in defending the city. It was due on July 14, but it developed that a defective powder magazine admitted steam which dampened the powder. Lieutenant Brown lost a full day drying his powder on canvas spread along the bank. Underway once more, the *Arkansas* ran aground in the darkness.

Instead of reaching the *Mississippi* by daylight, the *Arkansas* was still in the Yazoo when Brown picked up in his glass three Union vessels steaming toward him. They were the ironclads *Carondelet* and *Queen of the West* and the gunboat *Tyler.*

At 6:20 A.M. the *Carondelet* began to fire on the *Arkansas* at less than half a mile away, then turned and headed down the Yazoo, followed by the other two Union vessels. Stern guns opened on the pursuing *Arkansas* as the chase got underway and the Confederate ironclad was badly cut up. Lieutenant Brown was mistakenly believed to have been seriously wounded when struck in the head by a rifle ball. But the *Arkansas's* guns had severely punished the *Carondelet*, shattering its steering equipment and cutting steam-escape, exhaust, and cold-water pipes. The *Carondelet* limped to the bank and did not return the *Arkansas's* broadside and stern guns' fire as the Rebel ironside swept past, still in pursuit of the *Tyler* and the *Queen of the West.* The latter had fled hastily and its commander, James M. Hunter, was later denounced in the *Tyler's* log for his "cowardly and dastardly" behavior. But the *Tyler*, in retreating, kept up its fire as the running fight brought the

Above: *Here the Memphis levee itself, with Federal shipping and barges crowding the shore. (USAMHI)*

Above: *Union Lieutenant John A. Winslow took command of the Memphis naval facilities, turning them to the purposes of Farragut's and Ellet's ships. (USAMHI)*

two vessels into the Mississippi and on toward Vicksburg.

Suddenly, on rounding a bend, the *Arkansas* came upon the combined fleets of Farragut and Davis—thirty-three ironclads, gunboats, rams, river steamers, and mortar boats—and quickly was furiously engaged. Lieutenant Brown reported later, "The shock of missiles striking our sides was literally continuous, and... we were now surrounded without room for anything but pushing ahead... I had the most lively realization of having steamed into a real volcano, the *Arkansas* from its center firing rapidly to every point of the circumference, without the fear of hitting a friend or missing an enemy."

For about two hours, the *Arkansas* fought its way through the Union fleets and at ten minutes before nine o'clock on July 15 it tied up at the Vicksburg wharf, "smokestack... shot to pieces... much cut up... pilot house smashed and some ugly places through our armor," as Lieutenant Brown later reported.

Elation in Vicksburg was unbounded and General Van Dorn, who had watched the fight from the top of the courthouse, said in his report that Brown "immortalized his single vessel, himself, and the heroes under his command by an achievement the most brilliant ever recorded in naval annals."

Below: *The Memphis Navy Yard, where the mighty CSS* Arkansas *was constructed. (USAMHI)*

Below: *Yet much of Memphis sat in ruins, the first Mississippi River city to feel the hand of destruction. (USAMHI)*

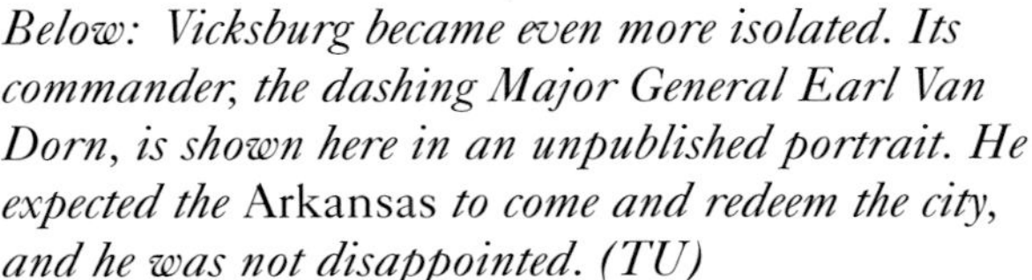

Below: *Vicksburg became even more isolated. Its commander, the dashing Major General Earl Van Dorn, is shown here in an unpublished portrait. He expected the* Arkansas *to come and redeem the city, and he was not disappointed. (TU)*

Right: With Vicksburg secure, Van Dorn sent the Arkansas *downriver to cooperate with Breckinridge in the attack on Baton Rouge, the last real threat to Federal control of the lower Mississippi. Here the waterfront of Baton Rouge, with the state capitol to the right. (LSU)*

Above: Brigadier General Halbert E. Paine commanded in Baton Rouge after Williams's death in battle, but refused to burn the city when ordered to do so by his superior, Butler. (LC)

Above: Colonel Henry W. Allen was prominent in Breckinridge's attack on Baton Rouge until his leg was shattered by a bullet. He was crippled for the rest of his life. (LSU)

Above: "Dirty Bill" Porter took his Essex *after the* Arkansas, *and later claimed credit for destroying the feared Confederate ironclad. (USAMHI)*

Above: To be sure, the Essex *was a formidable ironclad. She appears here off Baton Rouge (which she helped defend) in March 1863. The* Richmond *and* Mississippi *can be seen off her stern. (USAMHI)*

Farragut, not sparing himself in his criticism, wrote Davis, "We were all caught unprepared for him, but we must go down and destroy him.... We must go close to him and smash him in. It will be warm work, but we must do it." That night, Farragut made his run. Mortar fire on Vicksburg opened the action at 6 P.M. and forty five minutes later the fleet was underway. At 8: 20 P.M. it had passed the Vicksburg batteries and anchored below the city. But Farragut had not destroyed the *Arkansas;* in fact, only one of his ships, the *Oneida,* actually saw the Rebel ironclad. How ever, the *Arkansas* did not escape damage, for a shot passed through its armor, penetrated the engine room, and disabled the engine and also caused a severe leak. More casualties were added to the morning's toll of ten killed and fifteen wounded.

All efforts to destroy the *Arkansas* failed during the ensuing days—mortar fire directed at the Rebel craft, a direct assault by the *Essex* and *Queen of the West.* Captain Ledyard Phelps of the *Benton* summed it up in a letter to Andrew Foote: "The whole thing was a fizzle. Every day we heard great things threatened only to realize fizzles." Van Dorn, in a telegram to Jefferson Davis, characterized the attack on the *Arkansas* as a "failure so complete that it was almost ridiculous."

Farragut, chagrined, parted company with the *Arkansas* when he was ordered by the Navy Department to return to New Orleans with his fleet. Departing with Farragut was General Williams's force, which was so riddled with illness that barely a fourth of the 3,000-odd troops was ready for duty. Williams retired to Baton Rouge. With only his gunboats left at Vicksburg, Davis deemed it wise to steam upriver to the mouth of the Yazoo. For more than two months—sixty-seven days—Vicksburg had frustrated the efforts of two powerful Union fleets and more than 3,000 land forces.

The 20,000 to 25,000 shells hurled at the city left Vicksburg undaunted.

Captain Brown took advantage of the respite to visit Granada, Mississippi, where he fell ill. Lieutenant Henry Stevens, left in command of the Arkansas, worked feverishly to repair the engines and to increase the ship's armor. General Van Dorn ordered Stevens to take the *Arkansas* down the river to Baton Rouge to support an attack on that city by Major General John C. Breckinridge.

On August 3 at 2 A.M. the *Arkansas* moved from the wharf and headed for Baton Rouge. Throughout the day, the ironclad's engines functioned efficiently and an eight-knot speed was

Above: A. D. Lytle's 1861 image of Baton Rouge, before the destruction of the war came to visit. (LSU)

Above: Church Street in Baton Rouge, during the Federal occupation. (USAMHI)

Below: Another view of Church Street. These views were made by the Baton Rouge firm of W. D. McPherson and his partner Oliver, whose first name is unknown. (USAMHI)

Above: Breckinridge was initially successful, but later he had to abandon Baton Rouge, which showed the effects of the battle. Most of this damage was done by Federal gunboats, chiefly the Essex, *as they attempted to support Williams's beaten troops. (LSU)*

Above: The Louisiana State House, taken by McPherson & Oliver. (USAMHI)

Above: The Louisiana State Penitentiary, captured by Baton Rouge's other outstanding artist, A. D. Lytle. (USAMHI)

Above: L. I. Prince's image.of the Baton Rouge Arsenal. (ISHL)

Right: Part of the arsenal grounds, by McPherson & Oliver. (USAMHI)

maintained. But shortly before midnight, the starboard engine broke down, and the *Arkansas* tied up while repairs were made throughout the night. At 8 A.M. on August 5, the *Arkansas* was apparently ready to participate in Breckinridge's attack, which was already underway. When the *Arkansas* was within eight miles of Baton Rouge, the engines went dead again. Once more repairs were rushed and once more the engines broke down. By 9:30 A.M. on August 6, the *Arkansas* seemed ready once again. At that time there appeared, steaming toward the *Arkansas*, four Union gunboats, the *Essex*, *Cayuga*, *Katahdin*, and USS *Sumter*. Stevens determined to make a fight of it, but the ironclad's port engine failed as the *Arkansas* headed to engage the enemy. A moment later the starboard engine gave way and the *Arkansas* drifted helplessly toward the advancing Union gunboats.

Both sides opened fire, but ineffectively, and Lieutenant Stevens realized he had no alternative to the destruction of the *Arkansas* to prevent its falling into the hands of the enemy. Ordering the crew ashore and commanding them to take off for the interior, Stevens, with seven officers and petty officers, prepared the *Arkansas* for its end and then abandoned ship, too. For an hour the *Arkansas* floated with the current, its loaded guns firing as the flames reached them, and shortly before noon, it blew up spectacularly.

"It was beautiful," recalled Stevens, "to see her, when abandoned by commander and crew and dedicated to sacrifice, fighting the battle on her own hook."

In a report to the Confederate Congress, Secretary of the Navy Mallory said, "Naval history records few deeds of greater heroism or higher professional ability than this achievement of the *Arkansas*."

With the passing of the *Arkansas*, there passed also the last Confederate offensive challenge on the Mississippi. The Union now controlled the entire river except for the Rebel bastions at Vicksburg and Port Hudson, Louisiana.

Less than a year remained before these last two Confederate strongholds would fall, and the Father of Waters would again go, as Mr. Lincoln expressed it, "unvexed to the sea."

Above: The courthouse as seen by McPherson & Oliver. It was turned into a barracks and later a hospital by the occupying Federals. (USAMHI

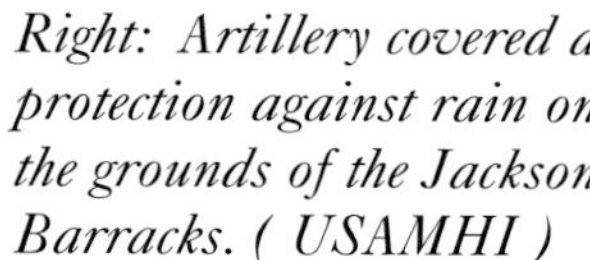

Right: Artillery covered as protection against rain on the grounds of the Jackson Barracks. (USAMHI)

Left: Everywhere in the South, when the Union soldiers came, the slaves flocked to their camps. Here the headquarters of the contraband camps in Baton Rouge. (USAMHI)

Left: General Williams's headquarters before the Battle of Baton Rouge. (USAMHI)

Above: Here Farragut's fleet stands off the city in 1862, on its way north to Vicksburg. The stern of the USS Mississippi *is just visible to the left of the wood pile. The USS* Richmond *is in the center, and the USS* Winona *is to the left of it. (USAMHI)*

Left: The Baton Rouge coaling yard, with the Winona *at right, and the* Richmond *next to it. The other vessels are part of the mortar fleet. (LC)*

Above: Often erroneously identified as the Hartford, *this image shows the USS* Portsmouth *on the right and an unidentified warship astern of it. (LC)*

Above: Two of Porter's mortar schooners lie side by side against the bank at Baton Rouge, while a gunboat, perhaps the Tyler *or* Conestoga, *lies to the left with a damaged stack. (LSU)*

Below: The Hartford *lies off the Main Street levee in this McPherson & Oliver image.*

Above: The Portsmouth *again, with one of the mortar schooners in the distance. (LC)*

Above: A similar view, showing the ruins of a factory at the water's edge. (CWTI)

Above: The same view, perhaps from Lytle's window, shows troops disembarking from the Sallie Johnson *in the spring of 1863. (USAMHI)*

Above: The wharf boat at Baton Rouge, the Natchez, *operated as a warehouse, hotel, and even offered "Fresh Lake Fish" to the soldiers. (USAMHI)*

Above: The Natchez *about to unload supplies from its "warehouse." (USAMHI)*

Above: In March 1863 McPherson & Oliver photographed the Empire Parish *off Baton Rouge. Nathaniel Banks made the steamer his headquarters for a time. (LSU)*

Above: A. D. Lytle's photograph of Federals at leisure on the Mississippi, apparently a celebration. (LSU)

Below: Blacks drafted into service by the Federals worked within sight of the State House. (LSU)

Above: And all around the city the white tents of the soldiers sprouted like mushrooms. (LSU)

Above right: Regiments drilled and reviewed constantly on the old arsenal grounds. (LSU)

Right: And in front of the courthouse. (LSU)

Below: And in front of the Jackson Barracks. (LSU)

Below: One of the final acts of 1862 along the river was the Federal capture of Donaldsonville, Louisiana, in October. Unlike Baton Rouge, Donaldsonville suffered considerably from the fighting. Much of the town lay in ruins. Homes and businesses were burned or battered to pieces. (ISHL)

Below: And in a score of camps on the fringes of the city. Clearly, the Union was here to stay. (LSU)

Left: The Catholic church, damaged. (ISHL)

Left: Everywhere scenes of destruction. (ISHL)

Above: But the flag went up and the rebuilding began. (ISHL)

Below: And by the dawn of 1863, nothing was more commonplace along hundreds of miles of Mississippi banks than the sight of Federal soldiers encamped, as here at Morganza, Louisiana. The Mississippi was truly conquered. Only Port Hudson remained, and Vicksburg. (NHC)

Jackson in the Shenandoah

ROGER G. TANNER

A peculiar professor and a valley whose name meant "Daughter of the Stars"

Above: The men who saved the Valley. Stonewall Jackson and his staff in 1862. The photograph of Jackson was made in Winchester; the composite including all of the portraits is the work of Richmond's distinguished portrait artists Vannerson & Jones. (VM)

IN THE SPRING OF 1862, the Union planned two invasions of Virginia. One is well known: McClellan's seaborne thrust to the Peninsula and Richmond. Less understood is the invasion that was to precede the Peninsula campaign and which was designed to make McClellan's campaign possible. That was the invasion of the Shenandoah Valley.

The Valley lay like a dagger across much of Virginia, running generally north and south between the James and Potomac rivers and bounded by the Blue Ridge and Allegheny mountains. At its northernmost rim, formed by the Potomac, the Valley was actually many miles north of both Washington and Baltimore, so that when Union commanders spread their maps to study the state they were always reminded that the Valley lurked behind them. Confederate forces occupied the northern portion of the Valley, from which they were always in position to thrust across the Potomac. The Baltimore & Ohio Railroad, one of the Union's main east-west highways, was severed by the northern tip of the Valley, as was the Chesapeake & Ohio Canal. The economic impact of the loss of those links was considerable. But worst of all was the fact that Winchester, headquarters of Rebel forces in the Shenandoah, was a scant sixty miles northwest of the Union capital. Geography alone dictated that Confederate forces in the northern Valley must be removed before McClellan launched his Peninsula invasion.

It was initially assumed that ejection of the Rebels posed no significant problem to McClellan's operation. Indeed this was looked upon as an invasion promising major returns for nominal risks. Confederate forces in Winchester were believed to be weak and dispirited after hard campaigning during a savage winter. Federal intelligence reports estimated that Union forces should encounter little difficulty in crossing the Potomac at Harpers Ferry and pushing southward as far as Winchester to destroy Confederate forces there. To ensure success, it was decided that the Federal invasion force would be bolstered by additional thousands of men from McClellan's main army. Once the entire northern Shenandoah had been liberated, garrison forces would be left behind, and the remainder of the invading host would shift east of the Blue Ridge Mountains to take up covering positions around Washington. By protecting Washington these forces would free McClellan to transfer the main Union Army to the doorstep of Richmond.

The two invasions seemed, on paper, to form a sound and perhaps even brilliant plan. And yet, if the invasion of the Valley were disrupted or delayed, the shift of forces eastward would likewise be retarded, which could endanger the Peninsular campaign. Rarely in military history has a major military operation such as the Peninsular campaign depended so substantially for its success upon a seemingly minor and far-removed initial assault.

Rarely, too, has any important military operation been entrusted to one so utterly inexperienced in warfare as Major General Nathaniel P. Banks. Banks was a skilled politician, an ardent abolitionist, and an influential member of the Republican party; during only his second term in the United States Congress he had become Speaker of the House of Representatives. When South Carolina seceded he was retiring from the governor's mansion of Massachusetts; he knew virtually

Above: Major General Nathaniel P. Banks, the perennial loser. Jackson outmaneuvered, out-thought, and outfought him in the Shenandoah, costing Banks 30 percent of his troops in casualties. (LOUIS A. WARREN LINCOLN LIBRARY)

Above: Charlestown, Virginia, in 1862. Here and in the vicinity, the Federals who would face Jackson wintered and readied for the Valley campaign. (USAMHI)

nothing of war, but unemployed governors had a way of finding themselves generals in the Civil War, and Banks was slated to lead the Union's drive into the Shenandoah.

That invasion began in February of 1862, as Banks's forces, totaling almost 40,000 men, spilled across the Potomac River and descended upon Winchester. The Federals advanced deliberately, brushing aside what seemed to be only token opposition. On the afternoon of March 11, 1862, Federal divisions converged upon Winchester from two different directions and found the Rebels drawn up in battle formation. A firefight ensued, and there was prospect of battle in the morning, but dawn found the Rebels gone and Winchester fell without a shot.

Banks trailed the Confederates southward from Winchester but was unable to bring them to a fight. They seemed, to Banks, to be running—just as had been anticipated. Within ten days the Rebels had moved far to the south, and Union forces were regrouping around Winchester. Thousands of Federals were already moving east of the Blue Ridge to take up their assigned positions around Washington. Banks even left the Shenandoah for a rest, a rest which was interrupted when, on the evening of March 23, 1862, the telegraph from the Valley began to crackle.

Opposing Banks in the Shenandoah was the Confederate Valley Army, a force of perhaps 4,500 men rostered into three tiny infantry brigades, six small artillery batteries, and 600 poorly disciplined but splendidly mounted cavalrymen led by Colonel Turner Ashby. The Valley Army was commanded by Major General Thomas J. "Stonewall" Jackson, a West Pointer, retired United States

Above: The headquarters of Brigadier General Alpheus S. Williams, who commanded a brigade under Banks in the Valley campaign, taken at Darnestown, Maryland. (USAMHI)

Above: Camps of men of Banks's command at Darnestown. (KA)

Above: Here in Williamsport, Maryland, the Federals also awaited the order to march south. No one yet knew much about this fellow Jackson. (USAMHI)

Above: The men of the 13th Massachusetts shown here at Williamsport soon had to leave the comfort of their winter quarters. (USAMHI)

Below: The surgeons shown here before their quarters in Williamsport would have plenty of work, thanks to Jackson. (USAMHI)

Above: A brigade headquarters in Banks's command at Martinsburg, Virginia, in March 1862. (USAMHI)

Army Major, and former physics professor at Virginia Military Institute. Jackson was virtually unknown at this point of the war. Except for one brief hour of glory at the First Battle of Bull Run, he had contributed little to the Confederate struggle save a ruthless discipline of his men and a winter campaign in the Alleghenies that had killed or sickened hundreds of them.

But Jackson was full of fight, and that resolve was well adapted to his instructions. His task in the Valley was to keep as many Federal soldiers pinned down there and as far away from McClellan as he could. It was the perfect mission for this fiercely stubborn man. Although outnumbered ten to one he had clung to Winchester even as Banks uncoiled around him; Jackson had even planned an attack on Banks for the night of March 11. He was prevented from striking only when his staff relayed his orders erroneously and moved the army out of position. Jackson retreated, but he left behind his cavalry commander Ashby to cover the rear and to search for openings to attack.

Ashby found an opening as Banks redeployed his forces east of the Blue Ridge to cover Washington in accordance with the overall Union strategy. His mounted scouts detected this eastward shift and relayed word to Jackson. Within hours, Jackson was pushing northward toward Winchester with the bulk of the Valley Army. On March 23, as Banks was reaching Washington for his rest, Jackson was nearing Kernstown, a hamlet three miles south of Winchester. His rapid march had left his troops exhausted and his ranks thinned by straggling; nevertheless, Jackson threw his men into the attack.

What followed was a confused stand-up soldiers' fight called the Battle of Kernstown. The Confederates made good initial headway, then were slowed by unexpected Federal strength. One Confederate wrote his father after the battle, "The crack of rifles and the whistling of balls soon told us what we must expect. Soon volleys of musketry seemed to shake the hills." When one of Jackson's aides reported sighting increasing Federal numbers, the General replied tersely, "Say nothing about it. We are in for it."

Above: Officers of the 2nd Massachusetts in 1861. They and their regiment would feel the full sting of Confederate might in the Shenandoah. (USAMHI)

Left: Colonel John White Geary of the 28th Pennsylvania in an unpublished portrait by McAllister of Philadelphia. Formerly the first mayor of San Francisco and the governor of Kansas Territory, he was, like Banks, a politician turned commander. Unlike Banks, he proved to be a man of genuine military talent. In March 1862 he captured Leesburg before the campaign had fairly begun. (CWTI)

Jackson had blundered into at least 10,000 Federal troops under Brigadier General James Shields. Shields had kept most of his division hidden well enough to fool Ashby's scouts, and then fed them skillfully into the battle. His numbers allowed him to overlap the smaller Southern army on either flank, and by nightfall the Confederates were driven from the field in nearly total rout.

So the Battle of Kernstown ended as a Southern defeat—but a defeat which actually proved some thing of a victory. General Shields was impressed by Jackson's hard fighting; he believed that the Confederates had numbered at least 11,000 men who were the "very flower of the Southern Army."

Shields called for help from Northern forces moving east of the Blue Ridge after the battle; one large division was diverted back to the Valley at once. Shields's reports that the flower of the Southern army had emerged in the northern Shenandoah canceled plans for any further redeployment of Union forces from that area to Washington. Instead, the Union's invasion of the Valley had to begin anew.

Banks returned to the Shenandoah to handle operations there. His army was built up again to 25,000 men and he was directed to drive the Rebels as far south as Staunton. He would be assisted by Federal forces west of the Valley in the Alleghenies. Thus, Kernstown lured the Union to undertake an extended Shenandoah invasion. McClellan henceforth would be operating on one side of Virginia while Banks campaigned on the other; instead of one invasion of Virginia followed by another, the Union was now engaged in a dangerous two-pronged invasion. And every man who was in the Valley would be one man less for McClellan.

Confederate losses at Kernstown totaled almost 25 percent of those engaged; Jackson could not risk battle again for a month. During those weeks, while Federal forces were built up against him, he rebuilt his own battered army. Through March and April he retreated slowly southward up the Valley while he recruited, reorganized, and made his army ready for maneuvers.

Above: Harpers Ferry, Virginia, showing the remnant of the United States Arsenal. Here Banks anchored his army at the outset of the campaign. (USAMHI)

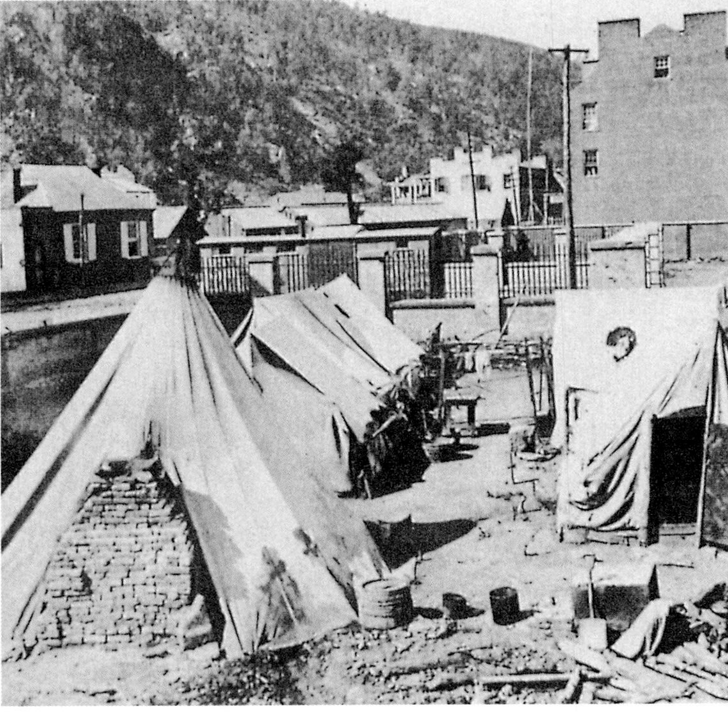

Left: David B. Woodbury's October 1862 image of Federal troops camped on ground which once held the armory buildings. (USAMHI)

Right: The charred remains of a canal boat and steam engine at Harpers Ferry, the scene of repeated destruction in 1862. (USAMHI)

Left: Colonel John Echols was severely wounded leading his 27th Virginia at Kernstown. Three weeks later he was promoted brigadier, and would become—though unsung—one of the finest subordinates in the army. At 6 feet, 4 inches, and weighing 260 pounds, he was a wonderful target. (USAMHI)

Below: Past this sawmill at Kernstown, Jackson advanced against Shields in the Battle of Kernstown, first engagement of the campaign. An 1885 photograph. (USAMHI)

Left: Jackson, with something of an affinity for stone walls, formed his line of battle on the near side of this one at Kernstown. (USAMHI)

In normal usage, because the top of a map represents the northernmost portion of the area depicted, to go *up* is to go *north* and, conversely, to go *down* is to go *south*. The idiom of the Valley is exactly the opposite because its streams drain generally northward and water routes were the principal early means of transportation. To go *down* the Valley is thus to go *northward* and, conversely, to go *up* is to go *southward*. The Shenandoah's northern region is the *lower* Valley, and the southern region is the *upper* Valley.

Before recounting these movements, a glance at the Shenandoah is essential. Up and down the middle of the region runs the great Valley Pike, a macadamized road which was one of the best highways of its time. Other roads in the area tended to be abysmal, so the principal towns clustered along the pike. From Martinsburg and Winchester in the north, the pike passed through Strasburg, New Market, Harrisonburg, and Staunton in the lower—northern—Valley. Staunton, which linked also with the eastern part of the state by the Virginia Central Railroad, served as Jackson's base of supplies. Another salient feature of the Valley is the great Massanutten Mountain. This is actually an interlocking system of ridges which rises precipitously just east of Strasburg and runs up the Valley for fifty miles. For this distance the Shenandoah is actually two valleys, the Luray Valley between the Massanutten and the Blue Ridge, and the Shenandoah proper between the Massanutten and the Alleghenies. There is only one pass through this tangled green wall, a winding and difficult road between New Market, in the Shenandoah, and the village of Luray, in the Luray Valley. From Luray a passable road ran northward to the little town of Front Royal and southward to the village of Port Republic. In the next few weeks Jackson would fight battles at both ends of that road.

While retreating southward after Kernstown, Jackson had not forgotten his primary mission of keeping Federal forces occupied in the Valley. Nevertheless, sheer Union numbers eventually forced Jackson to almost abandon the Shenandoah. By the end of April he had moved into Swift Run Gap, where he completed the reorganization of the Valley Army. He also received a major reinforcement from east of the Blue Ridge. This was the division of Major General Richard S. Ewell, a fine body of some 8,000 well-trained and well equipped infantry. At the end of April Jackson and Ewell were concentrated within supporting range of each other in the vicinity of Swift Run Gap; their combined forces totaled 14,000 men.

The situation confronting Jackson was complex. Staunton, his base of operations, was threatened from two directions. Union Major General John C. Fremont—the "Pathfinder" of America's westward expansion to California—was approaching Staunton from the Alleghenies with an army of 10,000 to 15,000 men. His advance guard, under Brigadier General R. H. Milroy, was pressing forward vigorously against scattered Confederate strength. Banks, with 25,000 men, was located in Harrisonburg and threatened Staunton from the north. In simplest terms, Jackson's dilemma was how to keep Staunton secure and Fremont and

Banks apart but still pinned down in the Valley. The resolution of that dilemma came through a series of dazzling marches and battles rarely equaled in military history.

On April 30, 1862, Jackson slipped out of his camps in Swift Run Gap and headed for Staunton. Ewell's division came across the Blue Ridge and occupied Jackson's camp, attempting thereby to conceal from Banks the start of a Confederate offensive. Winding in and out of the Blue Ridge, Jackson reached Staunton by May 3 with 6,000 men and then plunged westward into the Alleghenies. He soon linked up with the Confederate forces there and drove Fremont's vanguard back. On May 8 Milroy turned to fight near the little mountain town of McDowell. Like Kernstown, the Battle of McDowell was a stand-up soldiers' fight. The mountainous terrain made it impossible to give much direction to the fighting, which broke into small groups of men banging away desperately at each other. Jackson managed to seize the high ground overlooking the Federal camp, and this proved decisive. Though the Rebels suffered heavier casualties than the attacking Federals, they repulsed all attacks, and the next morning found the Union retreat accelerating.

Movement now exploded all around the Valley. Jackson pursued Milroy through the Alleghenies for several days. Banks abandoned Harrisonburg and retreated northward to Strasburg, a signal that the Union again had decided that the Shenandoah invasion was over. Due to Jackson's earlier withdrawal to Swift Run Gap, the Union high command had decided the Shenandoah was secure and Banks could retire to defensive positions along its northern borders and dispatch one division out of the Valley. Unlike the situation in March, however, Banks's redeployment this time was not merely defensive. Instead, Banks was to send Shields's division to Fredericksburg to join forces assembling there which were, in turn, to march south and link up with McClellan outside Richmond. The first step in achieving this redeployment was Banks's withdrawal to Strasburg.

The race began. Jackson hustled his troops back down into the Shenandoah and surged northward after Banks. The movements were rapid; marches of twenty miles a day were typical. The movements were also secret. Jackson had a mania for secrecy and told his subordinates—and his superiors—almost nothing of his location and intentions. His army seemed to simply drop from sight.

That Jackson disappeared during much of the Valley Campaign was true in one literal sense. His movements were such that there is almost no pictorial record of them. Burdened with unwieldy and very heavy equipment, photographers of the day needed a more stationary subject than Jackson's army to bring their talents into play. He simply moved too fast for them to arrive in time to take photographs of his operations. Such pictures as we have are of battlefields and not of the actual battles or marches, with the result that what we know of this campaign comes not from the camera but from the written word.

During May 1862, those words grew increasingly fatigued. "We are very wearied by the march, in fact, virtually worn down. A night's rest appears to do us no good—just as sleepy and languid in the morning as when we sleep in the evening," one Rebel recorded in his diary. Those who had started from Swift Run Gap with Jackson

Left: Captain Pinckney D. Bowles led a company of the 4th Alabama in Jackson's army. Like many junior officers of talent, he gained from the ravages of the bullet, which gave him plenty of opportunity for advancement. He finished the war an unconfirmed brigadier. (USAMHI)

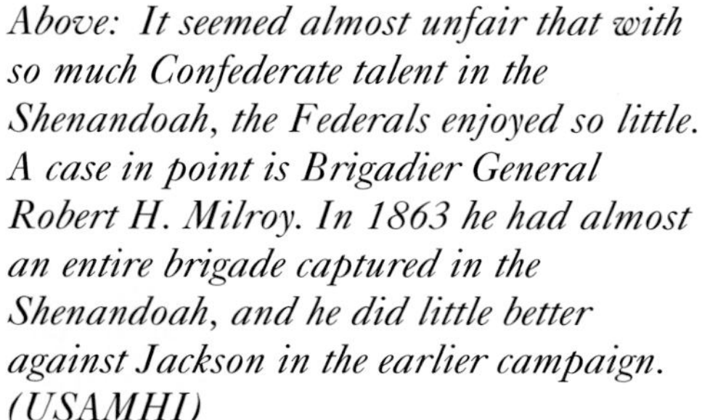

Above: It seemed almost unfair that with so much Confederate talent in the Shenandoah, the Federals enjoyed so little. A case in point is Brigadier General Robert H. Milroy. In 1863 he had almost an entire brigade captured in the Shenandoah, and he did little better against Jackson in the earlier campaign. (USAMHI)

Below: A few days after Jackson's victory at Front Royal, a photographer caught these Confederate prisoners awaiting transport to prison. They keep a respectful distance from their guards and their stacked arms. (LC)

Right: Brigadier General Alpheus S. Williams advanced from brigade to division command at the Battle of Winchester. Few Federals won laurels there. (P-M)

Above: A street in Winchester showing Taylor's Hotel, the building with the columns, where Federal officers made their headquarters in April before the battle. Winchester changed hands in this war fifty-two times. (USAMHI)

Right: Main Street in Winchester, probably taken after the war. Winchester saw more marching armies than any other town in the war. (USAMHI)

Right: Brigadier General William B. Taliaferro, seated left, commanded a brigade for Jackson. He had been in command of the Virginia Militia, as shown here, when it mustered to put down John Brown's attack on Harpers Ferry. (MUSEUM OF THE CONFEDERACY, RICHMOND)

on the last day of April had marched more than 250 miles, most of the way across mountains and over horrible roads. But by force of will and much hard work the Valley Army kept coming. Jackson passed through Massanutten Gap with his forces and those he had collected in the Alleghenies and united around Luray with Ewell's division. He thus assembled all of the Confederates in the Shenandoah, perhaps 17,000 men and 50 cannons. With out a day's rest he turned northward on May 22 and marched to within 10 miles of Front Royal. There would be battle in the morning.

On the morning of May 23, Banks's forces in the Valley were concentrated in two small bodies: 8,000 men at Strasburg, with 1,000 men twelve miles east in Front Royal. Banks's remaining strength was spread along the Manassas Gap Rail road east of the Blue Ridge and beyond supporting distance. Shields's division had completed its shift to Fredericksburg, where it was resting for the march southward to attack Richmond. The Shenandoah had supposedly been secured, a redeployment of forces out of the Valley had been completed, and all available Federal forces were prepared to move on to Richmond. As had happened after Kernstown, however, Union plans were disarranged.

Around midday on the twenty-third, Jackson's 17,000 men engulfed the Union garrison at Front Royal, comprised principally of the 1st Maryland Infantry. As it happened Jackson also had a regiment recruited in Maryland, and he used it as his shock troops. The Marylanders squared off in a brief but fierce skirmish, interrupted by arrival of a freight train that chugged into town between the opposing battle lines. The Rebels swept up the train, the town, and almost one thousand prisoners. Only a few dozen Federals escaped to bring Banks word of the onslaught.

Banks reacted to the situation poorly, first underestimating and then exaggerating Southern strength. His subordinates urged him to evacuate Strasburg at once, but he refused to do so until midmorning of the next day. He then ordered an immediate retreat, with the result that a near frantic collection of wagon trains, cavalry columns, and infantry poured down the pike for Winchester. The column was subjected to repeated Confederate cavalry raids and occasional shellings. Around Middletown the Federal column was severed, and hundreds of Yankees fled to the south and then the west as Rebels fanned out after them.

Banks, meanwhile, reached Winchester by evening with the bulk of his forces. He put them into line of battle on the hills south of Winchester and began to wire Washington frantically for reinforcements. But there was no time for help to arrive.

The Rebels hit again at first light on May 25, and Banks saw his army dissolve. Within two hours his brigades were swept from their positions in total rout. The Federal flight continued throughout the day, carrying them almost to the Potomac that night.

In two days of running battle, Banks had been swept out of the Valley. Three thousand Federals were prisoners. More than nine thousand rifles, warehouses of urgently needed medical stores, herds of cattle, and tons of other stores had been captured from Strasburg to the Potomac. Confederates gloated that the Federal rout was more complete than that at Manassas; total Southern casualties from Front Royal to Winchester were less

Above: Francis T. Nichols led the 8th Louisiana at Winchester, and there took a wound which cost him his left arm. Promoted to brigadier—as shown here—a few months later, he later lost a foot at Chancellorsville. (NYHS)

Above: A ford on the Shenandoah River, crossed and recrossed by Jackson many times in the course of his campaign. (USAMHI)

Left: A postwar view of the Massanutten Mountain, key to Jackson's brilliant success in the Shenandoah. (USAMHI)

than four hundred killed and wounded. One Rebel veteran summarized this highlight of the war long after when he wrote, "We had no general engagement, and our loss was small; it being a kind of one-sided fight all the time. General Jackson 'got the drop' on them in the start, and kept it."

The effect of Jackson's onslaught was immediate. President Lincoln was seriously disturbed by events in the Shenandoah, and he responded with orders to capture or crush the Valley Army. Studying his map of Virginia, Lincoln noted that Jackson had moved dangerously north of both Fremont and the Union forces around Fredericksburg; the Rebels were, in fact, moving into a trap. Even as the Confederates were herding Banks out of the Shenandoah, Lincoln directed Fremont to drive into the Valley from the Alleghenies, while Shields was ordered to retrace the march he had just made and return to the Valley from the east with 20,000 men. Both halves of this pincer were to enter the Valley well south of Jackson so as to cut off his escape.

Lincoln's bold plan, which was, in effect, a third invasion of the Shenandoah, was purchased at the price of assistance to McClellan. With Shields leading 20,000 men back to the Valley, the remaining Union forces at Fredericksburg were too weak to lunge southward, which is just what Jackson desired. Jackson had fulfilled his mission to keep as many Federal troops as possible tied down in and around the Shenandoah. Overall, some 50,000 to 60,000 Federals across northern Virginia were concentrating on the Valley Army instead of Richmond.

Jackson, meanwhile, pushed northward to Harpers Ferry at the end of May and made a vigorous demonstration before a well-entrenched Union garrison hoping to multiply the shock value of his sudden appearance in the lower Valley. But his own situation was now critical. By May 30,

Above: Jackson's brilliant cavalry leader, Brigadier General Turner Ashby, made major contributions to the defense of the Valley. It cost him his life on June 6, 1862, just two weeks after he received his general's stars. The only known photograph of him in uniform is this one, taken in death. (CHS)

Above: Colonel Beverly Robertson succeeded to command of Ashby's cavalry at his death, and three days later he was made a brigadier. (VM)

Right: Brigadier General John P. Hatch commanded Banks's cavalry in the futile attempt to contain Ashby. Shown here in an 1865 portrait made in Charleston, South Carolina, he failed to distinguish himself. (USAMHI)

Far right: The ever-present Brigadier General Louis Blenker had to make a torturous march with his division in March 1862, going from McClellan's army to join the Federals in the Valley. It took six weeks and the War Department forgot to supply him with anything. Cross Keys was his last battle. He fell from his horse during the war, and in October 1863 he died from the effects of the fall. (P-M)

Below: The battlefield at Cross Keys. (USAMHI)

Right: Colonel Wladimir Krzyzanowski, a Pole by birth, led the 58th New York at Cross Keys. "Kriz" rose to brigade command within a year. (P-M)

Jackson learned he was almost surrounded by Federal columns from the west (Fremont), east (Shields), and north (Banks's reorganizing army and the garrison at Harpers Ferry). Jackson's response was calm and to the point: He ordered his men to turn around and march southward very fast. In two days of heroic effort he covered the fifty miles from Harpers Ferry to Strasburg with all his captured stores and prisoners. He collided with Fremont just outside of Strasburg and drove him back into the Alleghenies, clearing the way for the last of his stragglers to slip through the Union ring.

Throughout the first week of June, the Valley Army withdrew from Strasburg under terrific pressure. Fremont trailed the Rebels along the Valley Pike, while Shields pushed his divisions southward into the Luray Valley. Rain poured down in crackling streams. Units lost their wagon trains, officers lost their commands, regiments became intermingled, and confusion reached epidemic proportions. The courageous cavalry leader Turner Ashby was killed protecting the army's rear in a heavy skirmish. The retreat demanded the courage of a battle and was far more costly. The Valley Army had lost four hundred men fighting its way from Front Royal to Winchester; it lost thousands of stragglers and sick on this retreat. One Rebel wrote, "I never saw a Brigade so completely broken down and unfitted for service as our Brigade.... I am satisfied that the Brigade has lost at least 1,000 men broken down, left on the way and captured."

By June 7, Jackson had turned southeastward from Harrisonburg to slip around the Massanutten to the village of Port Republic. There he would stand between Fremont and Shields, and around this village were to occur scenes as thrilling as any of the Valley Campaign.

These events erupted on the morning of June 8, as a surprise Union cavalry raid stormed into Port Republic and almost captured Jackson and most of his staff. Other Union cavalrymen probed to within a few hundred yards of the huge Confederate wagon train. A courageous stand by a dozen sentries stalled the Union raiders just long enough to allow Jackson to move in reinforcements and eject them.

As if in echo, Fremont's guns began to pound Confederate positions west of Port Republic. Jackson feared that he was about to be struck from two sides at once and built up his positions around the village; he left the handling of Fremont to Ewell's division. Ewell did his job well. In what has become known as the Battle of Cross Keys, Ewell sparred with Fremont throughout the day, repulsing every Union attack and driving the Federals back several miles by nightfall. During the day Shields's advanced guards showed themselves briefly to the east of Port Republic but made no advance.

Emboldened by Fremont's weak showing, Jackson planned the most ambitious battle of the campaign for the next morning. He would maneuver all available men across the two small rivers that joined around Port Republic to crush Shields's advance guard east of those streams, then return to rout Fremont. His timetable allowed only four hours to thrash Shields before he would have to rejoin the thin covering force he would leave behind to bluff Fremont. There was equally little time to prepare the attack; Jackson was able to span the river obstacles with only

primitive temporary bridges, and this was to cost more valuable time.

Before dawn on June 9, Jackson's maneuver brigades were on the march, and things promptly began to go wrong. Delays were encountered crossing Jackson's hastily erected bridges, batteries came up without ammunition, and the Confederate at tack began piecemeal about 7:00 A.M. It stalled at once and during the next several hours Jackson was outnumbered and on the defensive. Shields's men, recalling Kernstown, attacked furiously and at one point shattered the main Southern line. The dramatic arrival of Ewell with several fresh regiments reversed the flight, but more anxious minutes passed before Jackson finally assembled an overwhelming numerical superiority and drove Shields's forces back handsomely. Kernstown was revenged by the Battle of Port Republic but Confederate losses were severe, and Jackson abandoned any further hope of attacking Fremont. Instead, he coiled his forces along the slopes of the Blue Ridge out of enemy reach. He need not have worried, for both Fremont and Shields retreated the next day.

The Valley campaign comes to an end with those retreats. Jackson made preparations to join Lee around Richmond as soon as he learned of the enemy withdrawals. As he laid his plans, Jackson found himself something of a hero of the South. Since leaving Swift Run Gap on April 30, he had marched almost four hundred miles. He had inflicted approximately seven thousand casualties on the Union, half of them prisoners, and captured enormous quantities of supplies. His own losses had been less than half of those of the enemy, light losses indeed when compared to the ghastly casualty lists from other encounters of this war. Most important of all, the Valley Army's weeks of marching had been weeks of victory which stalled the Union drive on Richmond. Jackson's successes reinspired a South parched for victory. Robert E. Lee expressed the feelings of the Confederacy when he wrote to Jackson, "Your successes have been the cause of the liveliest joy in this army as well as in the country."

Above left: Colonel Thomas T. Munford led the 2nd Virginia Cavalry under Ashby and at Cross Keys. Like many of these Virginians, Munford found that the dashing Valley service appealed to the romantic in him. (CWTI)

Above: Brigadier General Arnold Elzey distinguished himself and his brigade at Port Republic. His horse was killed under him and he took a painful wound in the head. (VM)

Above: Brigadier General George H. Steuart, called "Maryland Steuart," thanks to his birthplace, led a Virginia brigade and was badly wounded at Cross Keys. At Winchester he had declined to obey an order from Jackson because it did not come through the proper chain of command, and this may have cost the Confederates the chance to entirely destroy the Federals. (SOUTHERN HISTORICAL COLLECTION, THE UNIVERSITY OF NORTH CAROLINA AT CHAPEL HILL)

Below: Port Republic, in a photograph taken fifty years after the battle in which Jackson effectively completed the Valley campaign in victory. (USAMHI)

The Second Bull Run

DAVID LINDSEY

To Manassas once again, another battle, another defeat

Above: Photographer Timothy O'Sullivan's wagon on the road leading into Culpeper. (USAMHI)

AS UNION Major General George B. McClellan's Peninsular campaign sputtered out in the heavy fighting of the Seven Days Battles, the opposing armies drew apart. McClellan backed off his 100,000-man Army of the Potomac to a new base at Harrison's Landing on the James River, where Federal Navy control assured protection, supplies, and future mobility. The newly named commander of the 75,000-man Confederate Army, General Robert E. Lee, had succeeded in beating back the Union drive on Richmond. Both sides now paused, catching their breath, pondering how to proceed next.

From Washington a disappointed President Abraham Lincoln came in person to McClellan's headquarters to assess the situation. When McClellan handed him a lengthy note giving blunt advice on matters of policy, Lincoln kept his own counsel, while mulling over what to do with his balky general and the well-trained, well-equipped army. In a move to pump new blood and spirit into the eastern theater command, Lincoln now brought bewhiskered Major General John Pope from the west to command a newly organized Army of Virginia that combined the forces of Major Generals Nathaniel Banks, John Fremont, and Irvin McDowell. Pope's credits included some earlier victories in the west, strong antislavery views, and an aggressive attitude toward the enemy. He talked too much and had criticized McClellan's "indisposition to active movements." Also from the west came Major General Henry W. Halleck, clean-shaven and bug eyed, whose large forehead inspired his nickname "Old Brains," to be installed as General-in-Chief of all Union armies.

Where McClellan fitted in the new command picture remained undetermined by Washington. Clearly "Little Mac" was extremely popular with his soldiers, one of whom wrote, "the real man of the army is Little Mac. No general could ask for greater love and more unbounded confidence than he receives from his men.... everywhere among his boys, as he calls them,... he is received with enthusiasm." For himself, McClellan says of his plans for midsummer 1862, "I would have crossed to the south bank" of the James River and seized Petersburg from which "I would have operated against Richmond and its communications from the west, having already gained those from the south." Perhaps. McClellan wrote this years later, knowing with hindsight that General U. S. Grant used precisely that approach in 1864-65. At least one of his soldiers thought it possible, agreeing with McClellan that the administration had not given adequate support, noting, "We want 300,000 men raised and sent down here immediately. We've been fooling about this thing long enough.... The army and the people demand such a vigorous prosecution of the war as shall give some hope of ending it."

But the Lincoln Administration decided otherwise by early August. On August 3 Halleck ordered McClellan "to withdraw your army from the Peninsula to Aquia Creek" on the Potomac, some thirty miles south of Washington. McClellan protested, arguing, "Here is the true defense of Washington; it is here on the banks of the James that the fate of the Union should be decided." But Halleck insisted McClellan get moving. But "Little Mac" as always moved with caution, sending first the wounded, followed by the able-bodied troops, on transports down the James, up Chesapeake Bay and the Potomac to Aquia Creek and

Above: Octagon House in Arlington, Virginia, headquarters for Major General Irvin McDowell in the early summer of 1862, when Lincoln held his corps back from McClellan on the Peninsula. (USAMHI)

Above: Culpeper's important railroad depot on the Orange & Alexandria. (USAMHI)

Above: Then once again McDowell marched south into Virginia's heartland, past scenes remembered from his campaign of the year before, scenes like Falls Church. (USAMHI)

Left: Inside Culpeper McDowell's soldiers made themselves comfortable for what they hoped might be a long stay. (USAMHI)

Left: But they would not be there long. In August their wagons loaded to roll toward the enemy. (USAMHI)

Alexandria. All of this took time—too much time as it turned out.

During July Lee watched intently from Richmond seeking to fathom the next Federal move. He learned of Pope's taking command of the new 40,000-man Army of Virginia. If Pope should begin moving south toward Richmond and McClellan should punch again at Richmond from the east, the combined 140,000 Union force would put Lee in deep trouble. To remain inactive was to risk envelopment. Weighing the risks carefully, Lee decided on July 13 to move boldly by sending Major General Thomas J. "Stonewall" Jackson with 12,000 troops sixty miles northwest out of Richmond to Gordonsville. Here where the Virginia Central Railroad crossed the Orange & Alexandria Railroad was the critical point the Confederates had to hold—whether Pope decided to move south or Lee decided to move out from Richmond.

When the Federal command made no immediate response, Lee then sent Major General A. P. Hill's "light division" of 12,000 men forward to join Jackson, saying, "I want Pope to be suppressed." When Jackson probed forward north of

Above: There was a new commander in Virginia, Major General John Pope, a hero from the western campaigns who promised he would lead this army to victory. He led the army first toward Cedar Mountain. Pope here appears as a brigadier. (LC)

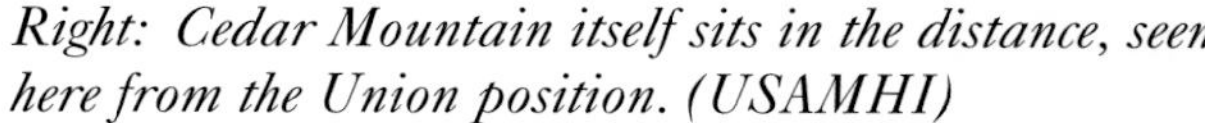

Right: Cedar Mountain itself sits in the distance, seen here from the Union position. (USAMHI)

Above: On August 9, 1862, the armies clashed at Cedar Mountain. That same day O'Sullivan caught this battery fording a tributary of the Rappahannock on its way to the fight. (USAMHI)

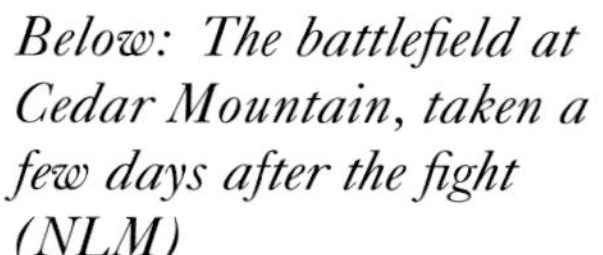

Below: The battlefield at Cedar Mountain, taken a few days after the fight (NLM)

Above: Major General Nathaniel Banks. A failure in the campaign against Jackson in the Shenandoah that spring, he was defeated by Jackson again here at Cedar Mountain. (USAMHI)

Above: The Robinson House near the center of the battlefield at Cedar Mountain. Banks enjoyed some initial success on this line before Jackson smashed him. (USAMHI)

Above: Here the home of the Reverend Mr. Slaughter, an appropriate name for Cedar Mountain. Banks's losses were almost twice those of Jackson. (USAMHI)

Right: Brigadier General John White Geary, hand in blouse, stands with his staff at Harpers Ferry. He fought well for Banks and took two wounds from the field. (LC)

the Rapidan he found a small advance Union force of about 8,000 men under Banks drawn up along a small stream near Cedar Mountain. Characteristically, on August 9 Jackson attacked immediately—probably too soon, since he had only about half his men in position. Banks's troops fought back fiercely, repulsing the first Confederate assaults and pummeling the celebrated Stonewall Brigade (that had won Jackson his nickname at Bull Run a year earlier). But Jackson succeeded in rallying his men, hurried A. P. Hill's division into action, and drove the Federals from the field. After a brief pursuit Jackson withdrew south of the Rapidan.

In itself Cedar Mountain meant little. But over all it meant the military initiative was shifting away from the Federals, who only two months earlier were threatening Richmond. Now Lee, assuming the offensive, would step up pressure on Pope's army. On August 13, learning that McClellan's army was starting to embark from its James River position, he ordered Major General James Longstreet with 25,000 men forward to Gordonsville. Two days later he left some 25,000 soldiers to protect Richmond and he himself moved out to lead the Army of Northern Virginia in person.

General John Pope from his Culpeper headquarters fifteen miles north of the Rapidan River surveyed the military situation. Earlier on arriving from the west, he had issued some bombastic proclamations urging his army to fight tenaciously, not show their backs to the enemy, and not retreat. At mid-August Pope's command of about 55,000 men (including 8,000 of General Ambrose E. Burnside's corps led by Major General Jesse Reno) were encamped north of the Rapidan with the Orange & Alexandria Railroad, their main supply route, running southwest from Alexandria some sixty miles distant. Pope was following Halleck's instructions to remain there until joined by the Army of the Potomac. Some 70,000 to 100,000 of McClellan's troops, withdrawing from the Peninsula via the Potomac and Aquia Creek, were expected shortly to line up alongside Pope's position. At that point, Pope thought, Hal-

Right: Yet Jackson, too, paid a heavy price. Brigadier General Charles S. Winder commanded Jackson's old division in the furious fighting, and in the battle a shell brutally mangled him. He died hours later in this house. (USAMHI)

Left: Officers of the 10th Maine Infantry survey the field of battle some days later. (USAMHI)

Above: The toll in animals, too, proved heavy. O'Sullivan caught this scene a few days after the fight. (USAMHI)

Above: Simple homes became field hospitals, this one for Confederate wounded. (USAMHI)

Right: Men like Brigadier General Samuel W. Crawford—once the surgeon at Fort Sumter—saw their commands almost destroyed. Crawford's brigade suffered 50 percent losses. (NA)

leck would come from Washington and take personal command in the field.

Seeking the weakness in Pope's position north of the Rapidan, with the Rappahannock in his rear, Lee calculated that fast-moving Confederate cavalry could knife swiftly across the Rapidan, drive north, and destroy the rail bridge over the Rappahannock, thus cutting Pope's supply line. But, Lee knew, the strike would have to be lightning fast be cause McClellan's troops would be reaching Pope within about ten days. On August 18 the Confederates tried it, but signals got crossed. Part of the cavalry missed an assignment. A river crossing was left unguarded, and a Federal patrol in a surprise raid south of the river just missed capturing General "Jeb" Stuart but did get his famous plumed hat and silk-lined robe. More important they seized a junior officer carrying Lee's orders. As a result Pope, now aware of Lee's strategy, pulled his troops back to the north bank of the Rappahannock and set strong units at each of the river's fords.

During the intermittent rains of the next few days Lee probed for a crossing of the Rappahannock and pushed farther upstream. Stuart's cavalry crossed after dark on August 22, snaked swiftly through the foothills, and then swinging eastward pounced on Pope's headquarters at Catlett's Station on the Orange & Alexandria Railroad. There Stuart seized a stack of Pope's military papers including an important dispatch book, took personal revenge for the loss of his plumed hat by carrying off Pope's uniform coat, and after trying in vain to fire the rain-soaked rail bridge, withdrew to the Confederate lines.

As the days passed, Lee saw his chance of a quick victory diminishing. From Pope's papers he

Left: The captured were taken back to Culpeper. Here O'Sullivan photographed several Confederates in their rather informal "prison" in Culpeper Court House. (LC)

Below: The Union dead, 314 of them, were buried on the field, in sight of the mountain whose battle killed them. (USAMHI)

Above: Though they lost the battle, the Federals held the field, and here at Cedar Mountain Pope and McDowell made their headquarters. In the background left of the house stands the field wagon for reporters of the New York Herald *who followed the army. (LC)*

Above: On August 18, Pope began to move his army north of the Rappahannock to meet the threat posed by Lee. His engineers had to build several bridges to accomplish the movement. This one crosses the North Fork of the Rappahannock. (USAMHI)

learned that McClellan's V Corps under Major General Fitz John Porter, having landed at Aquia Creek, was marching to join Pope on the upper Rappahannock. Major General Samuel P. Heintzelman's III Corps was scheduled to follow shortly. Lee figured Pope had 70,000 troops within call on August 25 with more on the way. Already outnumbered, Lee would find attack futile if he postponed it even a few days. In fact, it was perhaps already too late for a pitched battle, unless Pope could be maneuvered off balance. Lee was willing to give it a try.

On August 25 Lee sent Jackson with 23,000 "foot cavalry" scurrying out on a long sweep west and north. This division of the army in the immediate presence of the enemy, contrary to all conventional military wisdom, posed a serious military risk. Had Pope pulled all his units together and concentrated on Lee's force remaining south of the Rappahannock, the Rebels might have been badly whipped. But Lee took the gamble, counting on Pope not to move quickly while Jackson circled behind the Bull Run mountains out of sight and around Pope's right flank. If all went well, Jackson would swing in behind and cut Pope's supply and communication lines.

Shedding knapsacks and surplus paraphernalia, Jackson's men sliced swiftly north to Salem Village on the west side of the mountains, then turned east through Thoroughfare Gap in the Bull Run mountains. Having covered a remarkable thirty miles by evening of the first day's march, Jackson proudly watching his columns file forward was heard to murmur, "Who could fail to win battles with such men as these?" The gap, unguarded by Federal troops, was readily negotiated. From its eastern summit the Confederates surveyed the rolling farmland interspersed with woods stretching east ward, with Gainesville lying directly east on the main turnpike that ran northeast to Centreville and southwest to Warrenton. No Federal forces lay in sight on that road. Ten miles beyond lay the Orange & Alexandria rail line, Pope's supply artery and Jackson's target. Pouring out of the mountains, Jackson's troops pushed on swiftly and seized Bristoe Station by dusk on August 26. Capturing most of the astonished garrison, they destroyed the rail bridge over Broad Run, tore up the tracks, cut the telegraph wires, and wrecked two trains. But two trains escaped, one going north to Alexandria, the other south to Warrenton to

Left: The Hazel River, a tributary, afforded a crossing already in place and not destroyed by the Confederates. (USAMHI)

Left: But most bridges had to be built. O'Sullivan took a series of fine images of Franz Sigel's corps crossing this bridge on August 19. (P-M)

Below: Wagons and baggage cross. (LC)

Right: Then horsemen and part of the army's beef herd. (USAMHI)

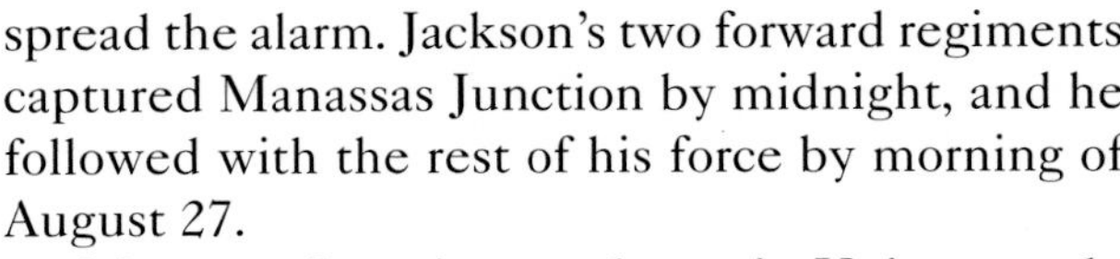

spread the alarm. Jackson's two forward regiments captured Manassas Junction by midnight, and he followed with the rest of his force by morning of August 27.

Manassas Junction, as the main Union supply depot, offered a rich harvest to the tired and hungry Rebels. Here were tons of supplies, hundreds of loaded freight cars, streets of bulging warehouses, fields filled with barrels, boxes, and piles of munitions. After the captured whiskey was carefully destroyed, Jackson's famished men—who had been on short rations for days—tore into the rich stores of food. An enormous picnic resulted as men gorged themselves not only on staples of bread, salt meat, and coffee, but also on canned lobster, oysters, boned turkey, pies, and other delicacies. Shoes, trousers, shirts, toothbrushes, combs, and more were appropriated. The revelry continued all through the day of August 27. Before the bloated army marched that evening, torches were applied to the remaining, unconsumed supplies and munitions, which burned and exploded like fireworks all night.

Meanwhile General Pope with his troops on the north side of the Rappahannock found himself in a position that was both a risk and a challenge—it offered a good opportunity if Pope could seize it, but unless he managed well he would be in increasing danger. Of the three corps comprising his army at the outset, Pope saw McDowell's corps as the only one worth much. Major General Franz Sigel, he thought, was incompetent. Banks's corps, badly mauled at Cedar Mountain, with only 5,000 survivors, was of reduced effectiveness. From McClellan's army, one-armed Major General Phil Kearny brought a reliable division of Heintzelman's corps. Other troops were reported to Pope as at hand or nearby—Heintzelman's other division under Joe Hooker, Reno with most of Burnside's men, and John Reynolds's division from Porter's corps. The rest of Porter's command was reported moving to join Pope. This gave Pope over 70,000 men in the vicinity. If coordinated they could throw overwhelming power against Jackson. At the least they could plug Thoroughfare Gap and thereby prevent Lee and Longstreet's combined force of 30,000 men from using that route to come to Jackson's support. But to do these things, Pope would have to get a good many separate units to do some fast marching under coordinated direction in conditions that would change as the movements of Jackson and Lee changed. Since Pope's wire dispatches to Washington were not reaching Halleck because Jackson had cut the telegraph, Washington had only a faint idea of what was happening in the

Left: Many of the Federals camped at Rappahannock Station, where they skirmished with the enemy on August 23. (LC)

Right: Meanwhile, at Catlett's Station, Lee's cavalry captured Pope's baggage, including vital information on reinforcements coming to him from McClellan. (USAMHI)

Right: The pace of the campaign accelerated quickly. Jackson, occupying Manassas, evacuated just as Pope was set to attack. All he found was ruins, some like these dating to March 1862 and the first Confederate evacuation. George N. Barnard photo. (LC)

Left: All that remained were enemy winter huts and earthworks, and at least one outhouse. (USAMHI)

countryside beyond Manassas Junction. Messages carried by mounted couriers were uncertain. Many slips were possible—Pope could misread enemy movements, his orders to subordinates could be misinterpreted or poorly obeyed, delay and confusion could set in. If any of these things occurred, Lee's gamble would pay off.

From John Buford's effective cavalry Pope learned of Jackson's march west of the mountains—but at first Pope somehow concluded that Jackson was heading for the Shenandoah Valley. Even when he discovered that Jackson's army was coming east through Thoroughfare Gap, Pope seemed unable to deal effectively with the information. Not that Pope was slow or lazy. If nothing else, he was a man of vigor. His response was understandably vigorous. When word reached him of Jackson's sacking of Manassas, Pope pulled his troops back from the Rappahannock to positions running roughly from Gainesville about five miles east of Thoroughfare Gap on the Alexandria-Warrenton turnpike to Warrenton Junction about twenty miles south on the Orange & Alexandria Railroad. This was a well-conceived move.

From Gainesville Pope sent James B. Ricketts's division of McDowell's corps west to cork the bottleneck at Thoroughfare Gap. But from this point forward Pope dispatched curious orders that were often incomprehensible or contradictory or self-canceling. Porter's corps, for example, was marched at top speed for ten miles under a broiling August sun only to be rushed back at the same fervid pace to the point it came from. Heintzelman's III Corps tramped eighteen miles to reach a point only three miles from where it started. Federal troops were being worn down by marching and countermarching on reduced rations, since the Manassas stores had been burned.

Pope pushed other Federal units forward to Manassas Junction to smash Jackson. There they found nothing but smoldering ruins. Leaving after dark the night before, Jackson had sent three columns forward—one across Bull Run and northwest toward Centreville, a second across Bull Run and northwest to Sudley Springs, the third up the west bank of Bull Run. Next day, August 28, he brought all three together near Groveton in a wooded area a short distance west of the Warrenton pike. Puzzled over the invisible Jackson, Pope concluded the enemy was heading north toward the Potomac and ordered troops forward to Centreville to head off such a move. But Jackson wasn't there either. Figuring Jackson was now desperately trying to escape, Pope determined to concentrate his forces on Jackson when he found him.

In making Jackson the sole target of his drive, Pope somehow forgot about Lee and Longstreet. The Federal plug came uncorked from Thoroughfare Gap as Ricketts moved his men back from their forward position there. This was exactly the reverse of what was needed for a Union success. Ricketts should have been strengthened to thwart a juncture between Lee and Longstreet from coming through the pass and joining Jackson. Somehow Pope erroneously developed the notion that McDowell's unit, "ordered to interpose between" Jackson and the enemy's "main body... moving down through Thoroughfare Gap" had "completely accomplished" its mission by driving Longstreet "back to the west side" of the gap. This totally false impression led Pope into mistaken planning for the next day, August 28.

Above: The Barnard & Gibson views taken in March are almost all that survive to give a picture of Manassas. It looked much the same when Pope marched in. (USAMHI)

Left: The fortifications were extensive. (USAMHI)

Left: And so was the clutter and debris. The horse appears to have been hobbled before it was killed, and several pieces of a steer are scattered about it. (USAMHI)

Left: Pope's Federals faced a big task just in cleaning up after the Confederates. (USAMHI)

Right: They occupied the old earthworks. (AMERICANA IMAGE GALLERY)

Right: They restored and refurbished them. (WRHS)

Left: O'Sullivan's July 1862 image shows the eastern range of earthworks at Manassas. (USAMHI)

Below: And this photograph, probably taken by A. J. Russell, reveals Confederate Fort Beauregard. The Federals did not retain the name. (USAMHI)

Arriving at Bristoe by dusk August 27, Pope convinced himself he had Jackson trapped. Out went orders to subordinates to march "at the very earliest blush of dawn" in order to concentrate forces between Gainesville and Manassas and "we shall bag the whole crowd.... Be expeditious, and the day is our own."

In pulling his forces away from Manassas Junction Jackson had ultimately chosen his position well. He brought his various columns together on the western edge of what had been the Bull Run battlefield of a year earlier, under the cover of a wooded area a short distance west of Groveton just off the Warrenton pike. His left was anchored on Bull Run at Sudley Springs, his right on a hill roughly two miles southwest toward Gainesville. His front was protected by a low wooded ridge and a steep embankment of an abandoned railroad line. Here he could rest his men concealed in the shade of the woods, but in a commanding position difficult to assail and with a potential escape route via Aldie Gap in the mountains to his rear. And yet he was close enough for Lee and Longstreet to reach him when they passed through Thoroughfare Gap a dozen miles to the southwest. Here on August 28 Jackson waited in the woods and watched as units of McDowell's corps trudged along the pike to Centreville, past the Stone Bridge to Jack son's left.

Finally as evening approached Jackson determined to make Pope stand and fight rather than let him withdraw to a strong position on the Centreville side of Bull Run. The column of Rufus King's division approached along the pike in the late afternoon heat. "Stonewall" Jackson, after riding out in front of his hidden troops, eyed the Yankees through his glass, then wheeled, galloped back to the ridge, and barked an order. Confederate artillery batteries rolled out and began firing. From the woods Rebel troops charged "with a hoarse roar... like wild beasts at the scent of blood," red battle flags gleaming under the sinking sun. Forming the line of battle they started shooting.

On the Union side Brigadier General John Gibbon's four brigades took the initial shock of the enemy attack. Green, never under fire before, they should have panicked. Instead they wheeled about coolly into their own line of battle and stopped the Rebel attack. Joined by men from Abner Doubleday's brigade, 2,800 Federals faced nearly twice as many Confederates in one of "the hardest close quarter fights of the whole war." The contending battle lines stood face to face "as if they were on parade awaiting inspection, and volleyed away at the murderous range of less than one hundred yards." For two solid hours the deadly firing continued until darkness closed in. By nine o'clock the lines drew apart. On both sides the losses had been staggering. Two of Jackson's generals, William Taliaferro and Richard Ewell, were carried from the field severely wounded. Gibbon's midwestern farm boys, already called the "Black Hat Brigade," won laurels that day and would soon be rightly known as the "Iron Brigade."

By nightfall August 28, Pope, now aware of Jackson's position, decided to destroy Jackson's force the next day. Again orders went to division commanders to move "at the earliest dawn." But as Pope moved his headquarters forward to a hill near the famous Stone House, well-remembered from the first Bull Run battle's intense fighting, he was still fuzzy on several crucial factors. For one, he did not know the current location of McDowell or that Ricketts had moved to Bristoe Station. He still held to his delusion that Lee and Longstreet had been repulsed at Thoroughfare Gap. In addition, his men, after much marching and little eating, were tired and sluggish.

From dawn on August 29 Federal artillery blasted away at Jackson's position in the woods just northwest of the Warrenton pike, while infantry units moved closer. Again, if Pope could get all his forces concentrated, he figured to outweigh Jackson's battered 20,000-man army by three to one. Chance for victory looked bright. Anxious to open the attack, Pope moved hastily while many of his units were still on the road and out of touch.

After the artillery blasts drove in Confederate skirmishers, Sigel's 11,000 men were ordered to attack the center of Jackson's defense line. As a Confederate observer reported, "The Federals sprang forward with a long-drawn 'huzzah' ringing from their 10,000 throats. On they went until half the distance to the [railroad] cut and then the smoke, flash and roar of 4,000 well-aimed guns burst from the Confederate entrenchment, and a wild, reckless and terrifying Southern yell echoed and reechoed through the woodlands." Two more Yankee assaults were made on the center and repulsed.

The attack then shifted to Jackson's left where Pope sent Kearny and Hooker with 12,000 Army of the Potomac veterans aided by Reno's 8,000 seasoned veterans. But organization, timing, and coordination were lacking. Federal units went into action piecemeal, bit by bit, and the full effect of such a massive blow was lost. Besides, the Rebel line here was defended by some of Jackson's best troops under A. P. Hill. The Confederate line bent and at one point snapped temporarily under the impact of six separate attacks, punctuated with vicious hand-to-hand bayonet fighting. Hill's ammunition supply was almost gone and his casualties were enormous, but he managed to hang on as dusk fell.

Meanwhile some 30,000 Union troops nearby had failed to get into action. These men under Porter and McDowell, moving from Manassas toward Gainesville to hit Jackson's right, sighted large clouds of dust ahead. Figuring that Confederate reinforcements were arriving, Porter and McDowell slowed, paused, and shifted course toward Groveton, beyond which fighting raged. Because of their slowness few of McDowell's and none of Porter's troops got into battle before the day's fighting ended. Porter would later be court-martialed and cashiered for holding back here.

Also sitting out the action of August 29 were Longstreet's 30,000 soldiers. They had emerged from Thoroughfare Gap early, marched forward, contacted Jackson's right by noon, and took position just south of the Warrenton pike by 3 P.M., where they blocked Porter's line of advance. Poised to attack the Federal left flank, Longstreet persuaded Lee to wait, arguing that his men needed rest after a long march and that delay might produce new Federal blunders. Toward evening Longstreet sent a reconnaissance unit forward on the pike only to clash with McDowell and to pull back to await the next morning. That night Lee reported to President Davis, "My desire has been to avoid a general engagement, being the weaker force, and by maneuvering to relieve a portion of the country."

Left: Then Pope heard the enemy was at Centreville, and off he went, leaving behind some destruction of his own. Rolling stock of the Orange & Alexandria was burned to the wheels rather than be allowed to fall into Confederate hands. (USAMHI)

Below: Engines were pushed over the railroad embankments. It would take a major effort to right this one. (USAMHI)

Above: And then came another battle at Bull Run. Here Blackburn's Ford is shown on July 4, 1862, a few weeks before the battle. (USAMHI)

Right: Some familiar faces were here again. Major General Richard S. Ewell played a minor role at the first Bull Run. Here at the second he was in the thick of the fighting and lost a leg. (VM)

Below: Brigadier General William B. Taliaferro took a bad wound in the preliminary fighting at Groveton. (USAMHI)

Above: William A. Wallace succeeded to the colonelcy of the 18th South Carolina on the field when its commander was killed. This later image shows him as a brigadier general. (USAMHI)

Above: Major General David R. Jones, called "Neighbor" by friends, was a veteran of the first battle here. During the present campaign he made a major contribution to victory when he took Thoroughfare Gap. (SOUTHERN HISTORICAL COLLECTION, THE UNIVERSITY OF NORTH CAROLINA AT CHAPEL HILL)

That night at his headquarters on a hill close to the Stone House at the junction of the Warrenton pike and the Manassas-Sudley road, the husky Pope with the usual cigar in hand reviewed the day's action with some satisfaction. Jackson, as Pope saw it, was badly bruised, was cornered, and could be captured next day. Annoyed by Porter's failure to advance when ordered, he dismissed as nonsense Porter's claim that Longstreet barred his path with three times his numbers. Reporting optimistically, Pope told Halleck, "We fought a terrific battle... which lasted with continuous fury from daybreak until dark.... The enemy is still in our front, but badly used up.... The news just reaches me that the enemy is retreating toward the mountains."

On August 30 Pope's actions defy comprehension. During the morning he planned cautiously in the belief that Jackson, badly cut up, was pulling out of his position leaving only a rear guard— and of course that Lee and Longstreet were not in the vicinity. But if the Federals' task were simply to mop up the remaining Rebels, why wait until midday to start the process? True, Federal troops were tired after much marching and fighting and they had limited supplies; but the same applied to the enemy. As Pope eyed the situation, the railroad embankment, scene of yesterday's heavy fighting, seemed virtually empty, only a few Rebel sharp shooters replying to the Federal outposts' firing. (Jackson had his men out of sight getting some rest on the wooded hillslope above.) Systematically Pope disposed his units, pulling Porter's corps in on the left to close up with McDowell for a two pronged drive along the pike, sending Heintzelman to drive west from the pike against Jackson and "press him vigorously during the whole day."

As Pope was concentrating his forces, Lee kept Jackson firm on his left and had Longstreet fan his five divisions out on the right to form the lower mandible of a giant jaw. Into this maw Union troops were now marched. About noon Stuart reported to Lee that bluecoats were massing in front of Jackson. Lee forwarded the warning to Jackson, who alerted his men, but kept them concealed in the woods.

At noon without warning Federal troops charged forward in three waves—much heavier than the day before. Rebels rushed to man their line along the railroad bank and fought back doggedly. Determined Yankees slogging forward got within a few yards of the defense position. Confederates, running out of ammunition, began heaving rocks at their attackers. Hill's line wavered, broke, then reformed. Jackson signaled an appeal to Lee for reinforcements.

As Porter's units surged forward on the Union left, Longstreet's men coming out from their forest cover absorbed the first fury of the attack, then began pivoting on a hinge close to Groveton and positioned their artillery for enfilading fire. One observer wrote, "gunners leaped to their pieces..., bowling their shots along the serried rows of Federals who up to now had been unaware of the danger to their flank. The effect was instantaneous. Torn and blasted by this fire, the second and third lines milled aimlessly, bewildered, then retreated... whereupon the first line soldiers [seeing]... their supports in flight, also began to waver and give ground." South of the Warrenton pike two New York volunteer regiments guarded the base of a knoll on which a six-gun Union battery

Above: And, of course, there was meandering Bull Run. Here the ruins of the Stone Bridge, taken by Barnard & Gibson in March 1862. (USAMHI)

Right: Stone Bridge and the heights beyond once again shook with the sound of guns. (USAMHI)

was stationed. As Longstreet swept forward these men caught the brunt of the assault. One regiment was quickly overrun. But the second—Zouaves, nattily dressed with white spats, tasseled fezzes, blue jackets, and fancy scarlet trousers—stood firm while the battery flailed the attackers and then limbered—hitched the guns to their teams—and got away, the New Yorkers then withdrawing. The cost was enormous—of 490 Zouaves, 124 lay dead, 223 wounded when it was over.

By 4 P.M. Porter found his men fighting for their lives on their front and left flank with a prospect of being enveloped by Longstreet. A withdrawal began with Longstreet in hot pursuit. As Porter reeled backwards, Lee ordered his whole army to advance—Jackson's units to drive east and south to block Federal retreat along the Warrenton pike to ward the Stone Bridge. Jackson's revived lines surged forward down the embankment and out onto the plain. Shrieking the Rebel yell, they charged against the backdrop of the setting sun, said a Northern observer, like "demons emerging from the earth."

Federal forces rallied on the high ground of Henry House Hill, where Jackson had won his nickname thirteen months earlier. Sigel's and Reno's troops joined Gibbon's "Black Hat" boys to form a firm shield for the retreating Federal units. Some feared the withdrawal might turn to panic and rout, as it had in July 1861 on this very same ground. Riding up to Gibbon, Phil Kearny, empty sleeve flapping in the breeze, cried, "It's another Bull Run !" When Gibbon said he hoped not, Kearny replied, "Perhaps not. Reno is keeping up the fight.... I am not stampeded; you are not stampeded.... My God, that's about all !" At any rate, battling bluecoats on the hill held the charging Rebels long enough for Pope's army to reach and cross the Stone Bridge over Bull Run. The bridge was then blown up. As darkness and rain came on, these troops, grumbling about their inept leaders, slogged on four muddy miles to camp long after nightfall in positions on the heights of Centreville. These were entrenched fortifications left by Confederates from July 1861. What might have been a disastrous Union rout came off as an orderly withdrawal, quite in contrast to first Bull Run. As Pope saw it in his report

Left: McDowell's engineers had to build bridges to span Bull Run a few days before the battle. (USAMHI)

Left: At the southern end of the field, near Union Mills, the Orange & Alexandria crossed Bull Run. (USAMHI)

Left: But the real fighting took place where it had before, around Henry Hill and along the Warrenton Road. Here a part of the battlefield. (USAMHI)

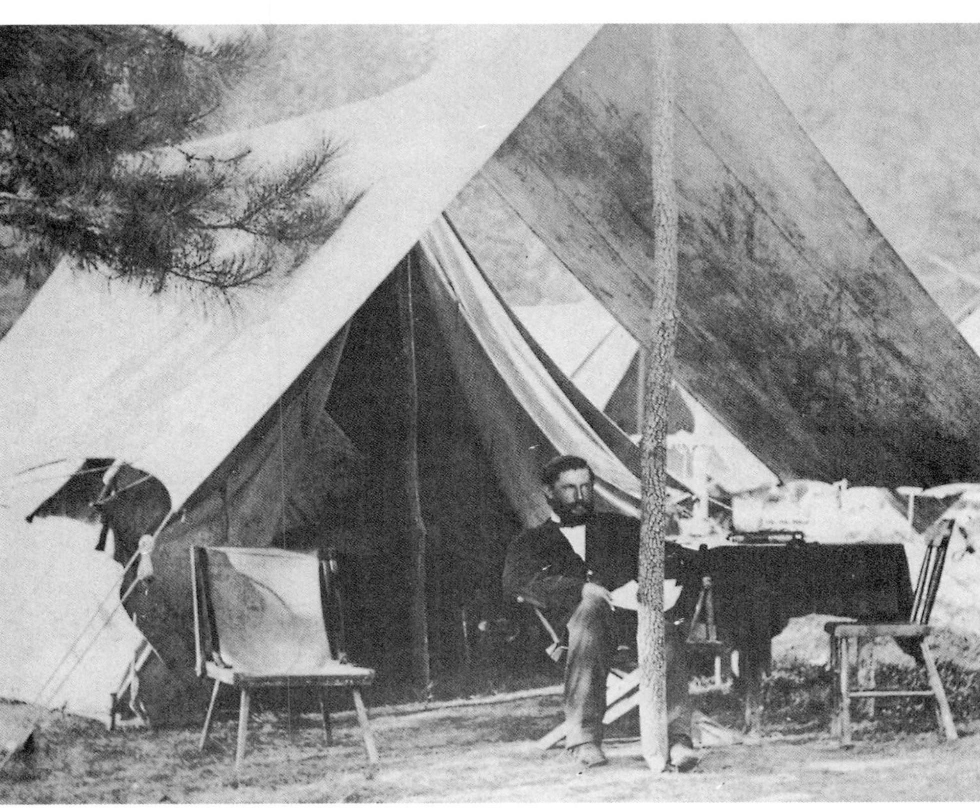

Left: A. J. Myer, the signal officer who could not get his balloon aloft at first Bull Run, operated a more effective signal office for McDowell at the second. Here O'Sullivan's image of Myer in his headquarters in late August. (LC, H. J. MYER COLLECTION)

Right: It must have seemed deja vu *for McDowell. Another Bull Run, another defeat. (USAMHI)*

that night to Halleck, "The battle was most furious for hours without cessation, and the losses on both sides very heavy. The enemy is badly crippled, and we shall do well enough."

But another observer assessed Pope's situation differently, pointing out he had been "kicked, cuffed, hustled about, knocked down, run over and trodden upon.... His communications had been cut; his headquarters pillaged, a corps had marched into his rear...; he had been beaten and foiled in every attempt he had made to 'bag' those defiant intruders; and, in the end, he was glad to find refuge in the intrenchments of Washington."

That night Lee reported proudly if a bit inaccurately to Richmond, "The enemy attacked my left, under Jackson, on Thursday [August 28], and was repulsed. He attacked my right, under Longstreet, on Friday, and was repulsed; and on Saturday I attacked him with my combined armies, and utterly routed" the Federals "on the plains of Manassas."

Casualties on both sides were severe. Lee's losses included 1,481 killed, 7,627 wounded, 89 missing; Pope's, 1,724 killed, 8,372 wounded, 5,958 missing. Some 7,000 Federals appear to have been captured, not counting several thousand wounded left on the field. Over a three-by-five-mile stretch of the Manassas plain, dead and wounded men lay strewn, in some places in heaps. The day after the battle Longstreet's men worked to aid the wounded and bury the dead. Confederate surgeons were so busy with their own as to have no time for Yanks. Shortly Federal ambulances were permitted on the field. Some 3,000 Union wounded were brought to makeshift facilities at Fairfax, where aides, doctors, and nurses were rushed from Washington. Clara Barton, seeking to get medicines and supplies there, estimated that 3,000 wounded men still lay on the straw-strewn ground at Fairfax a week after the battle. "All night," she wrote, "we made compresses and slings, and bound up and wet wounds,

Above: Sending intelligence to the front, though little good it did. (LC, H. J. MYER COLLECTION)

Left: The 2nd United States Sharpshooters, led by officers like Lieutenant B. S. Calef, saw their first real action at Second Manassas. (USAMHI)

Below: Reuben L. Walker fought with distinction at Second Bull Run, working A. P. Hill's artillery. (VM)

Right: A face familiar to the fields along Bull Run, "Shanks" Evans, hero of the first battle. His command, called the "Tramp Brigade," seemed to be everywhere. A year from now his drinking would get him into trouble. (VM)

Above: Brigadier General Abram Duryée, formerly commander of a flamboyant Zouave regiment, took two wounds in the battle while he led a brigade. (USAMHI)

Above: The Stone House on the Warrenton Turnpike would be used as a hospital again, as a year before, when the armies were done fighting around it. (USAMHI)

Above: Few of Pope's high commanders distinguished themselves in the fight. Franz Sigel, commander of a corps, almost never distinguished himself. (USAMHI)

Above: Brigadier General Robert C. Schenck was an exception. He led a brigade in Sigel's corps with distinction until a bullet removed him from further field command . (WRHS)

when we could get water, fed what we could.... Oh, how I needed stores on that field !"

As Pope's wounded were gathered at Fairfax, Union hope, which had been high only a few months before during the drive on Richmond, now lay dashed and broken. All the marching, maneuvering, fighting, dying, sickness, broiling in the Virginia sun had come to nothing by the end of August 1862. Federal troops were back where they had started—resentful, bitter, feeling betrayed and misled by military incompetents. Among Pope's soldiers, noted an officer, "Everyone had an unwashed, sleepy, downcast aspect... as if he would like to hide his head... from all the world." One newsman caught the mood: "We have been whipped by an inferior force of inferior men, better handled than ours."

From the Confederate viewpoint Lee had achieved a miracle—drawing a larger army than his own away from Richmond, running circles around the enemy and then administering a smarting defeat even in the face of superior Union numbers. Southern military fortunes were now at their highest as Lee plunged across the Potomac in early September to invade Union territory. Prospects for European aid to the Confederacy seemed brighter than before, even a possible European intervention that might assure Confederate independence.

In the North a crisis was at hand. Endless lists of wounded and dead filled newspaper pages. Morale sagged. Military leaders and Lincoln's administration were denounced by the surging political opposition. Prospects grew that Republicans would lose control of Congress in the upcoming midterm election, as voters tired of the war. Perhaps some kind of armistice leading to a negotiated peace, some thought, was preferable to continued slaughter and suffering. Obviously Lincoln's plans for wartime emancipation of the slaves—formulated in July—would have to be postponed. Gloom settled over a grim North as the people faced an uncertain future.

And the Widow Henry's house was no more. The war is simply too much for it. (NA, U. S. SIGNAL CORPS)

Right: Samuel P. Heintzelman ended his active field service with an unsuccessful attack on Jackson at Groveton in the opening of the battle. He was photographed here with his staff just a few weeks before the battle. (WRHS)

Above: "Portici," the house that had been headquarters for Johnston in July 1861, saw the armies in its fields once again. (MANASSAS NATIONAL BATTLEFIELD PARK)

Above: A new name attracting much attention was Joseph Hooker, called "Fighting Joe" by the Northern press after his performance on the Peninsula. He led a division for Heintzelman, and would shortly replace Sigel at the head of the I Corps. (USAMHI)

Right: Another Manassas house, again the scene of encamped armies, this time Federals. (USAMHI)

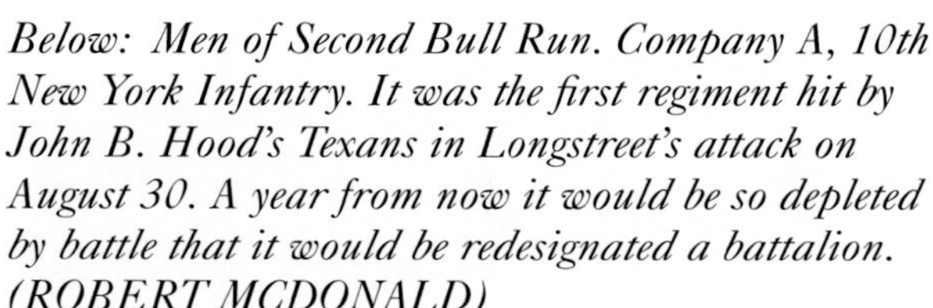

Below: Men of Second Bull Run. Company A, 10th New York Infantry. It was the first regiment hit by John B. Hood's Texans in Longstreet's attack on August 30. A year from now it would be so depleted by battle that it would be redesignated a battalion. (ROBERT MCDONALD)

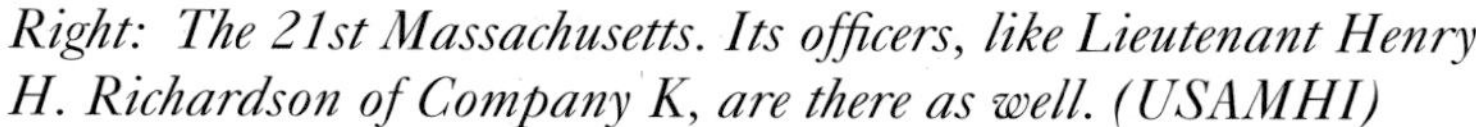

Right: The 21st Massachusetts. Its officers, like Lieutenant Henry H. Richardson of Company K, are there as well. (USAMHI)

Left: The 73rd Ohio Infantry, shown here leaving Chillicothe in 1862, saw its first battle at Second Manassas. They would go on to march through Georgia with Sherman two years later. Photograph by J. A. Simmonds. (WRHS)

Left: This battle was the undoing of Major General Fitz John Porter. Devoted to "Little Mac," he was used in Pope's vendetta against McClellan and charged with disobedience of orders and disloyalty. In January 1863 he was dismissed from the army. Exoneration did not come until 1886. He appears seated here on August 1, 1862, at Harrison's Landing, less than a month before the battle. (USAMHI)

Left: Micah Jenkins had moved up since leading his 5th South Carolina at First Manassas. He is shown here as a colonel, but a severe wound at this second battle interrupted his career for several months. (LC)

Right: Another promising younger officer, William Mahone, called "Scrappy Billy." Shriveled, dyspeptic, weighing less than one hundred pounds, and furiously combative, he was one of Lee's most active brigadiers. (USAMHI)

Below: Colonel Jerome Robertson took a wound while leading his 5th Texas Infantry in its attack on the 10th New York. He became a brigadier a few months later. His son Felix also became a brigadier. A war criminal, accused of the murder of Negro soldiers at Saltville, Virginia, in 1864, Felix was to be the last surviving Confederate general, living until 1928. (P-M)

Above: David A. Weisiger was officer of the day in Taliaferro's Virginia Militia at the hanging of John Brown. At Bull Run he led a regiment in Mahone's brigade. He was seriously wounded but recovered to become a brigadier as shown here. The Confederacy had no distinction of insignia among the various grades of general—brigadier, major, lieutenant, and full general. All wore three stars in a wreath. (USAMHI)

Above: An unusual bearded portrait of Brigadier General Henry Slocum, promoted to major general just before the battle. He materially aided in covering Pope's retreat after the defeat. (NA)

Left: There was a small engagement at Chantilly, the final echo of the Second Manassas battle, and there one of the Union's most promising officers, Brigadier General Philip Kearny, rode accidentally into enemy soldiers. While attempting to escape he was shot and killed instantly. Winfield Scott called him "the bravest man I ever knew." He lost his arm in the war with Mexico. (USAMHI)

Right: Brigadier General Isaac J. Stevens, once governor of Washington Territory, head of the Breckinridge campaign in 1860, died after the Battle of Second Manassas was virtually done, at Chantilly, on September 1. The Union lost great potential in his death and Kearny's. It recognized the loss in the unusual act of promoting Stevens to major general posthumously. (USAMHI)

Left: And so, defeated, Pope retreated to Centreville, and here he stood briefly. There was no rout this time. A Barnard photo from March 1862. (NLM)

Left: Six months before, jubilant Union soldiers had posed gaily here in the old Confederate earthworks. (USAMHI)

Left: The "Quaker guns" once used by the Rebels to fool the Federals were now a taunt. With the bitter memory of two defeats at Bull Run, Union soldiers were not saddened to continue their retreat to Washington. (USAMHI)

Above: Now these fortifications, designed to protect from an attack from the north, were of little use to them against an enemy that might pursue from the south. (USAMHI)

The War on Rails

ROBERT C. BLACK, III

Spiderlike the rails spread over the land, carrying the war everywhere, and feeding its voracious appetites

Above: The railroad, like the camera, came of age just as the nation went to war. Even as the armies were ready to march, so were the routes and rolling stock ready to carry them. Here a locomotive of the Raleigh & Gaston Railroad in North Carolina, around 1850. The South lay far behind the North in its rail system. (NORTH CAROLINA MUSEUM OF HISTORY)

THE IRON HORSE was not bred, on this continent, for war.

Indeed, American railroads have seldom been planned for military purposes. For over a century and a half they typically have been built to serve the economic convenience, either of the public, or of those interests which found it useful to associate their private aspirations with the public good. No railroad was ever designed to create a Southern Confederacy—or to save the Union. The original lines were established for local reasons; subsequent projects remained oblivious to the possibility of war. That such enterprises should have found themselves engulfed in the first significant railroad conflict in all history was as fortuitous as it was unexpected, and it was inevitable that the railroad facilities of 1861 should in few respects perfectly fulfill the wartime needs of either the United or the Confederate States.

At the dawn of the nineteenth century, Americans still thought of transportation in terms of waterways; even when facing inland, they sought out naturally navigable streams and lakes. Canals and steamboats, which came two decades later, were little more than elaborations upon the water concept. Highways were significant chiefly as land bridges, transcending inconvenient terrain between places of navigation. Railroads, when they appeared, were regarded as a special variety of high way, and they assumed for some time a kind of bridge role—Mohawk & Hudson; Baltimore & Ohio; Richmond, Fredericksburg & Potomac; Western & Atlantic—the western waters were meant. That railroads possessed the capacity to supersede waterways was understood at first by almost no one, and even at the outbreak of the Civil War the idea still lacked universal acceptance. As a result, American railroad enterprise was subject for a long time to local influences, frequently petty in nature, that did much to inhibit the growth of anything like a national system; indeed, neither of the famous sections, Northern or Southern, could boast of anything like a unified network.

There did exist, albeit in embryo form, a number of trans-Appalachian railroad routes that straggled across the map between the east coast and the Mississippi River. Three were unquestionably Northern: the New York Central (Albany to Buffalo) and its connections; the Erie (Piermont, New York, to Dunkirk, New York) and its connections; and the Pennsylvania (Philadelphia to Pittsburgh) and its connections. Another was of uncertain status—the Baltimore & Ohio (Baltimore to Wheeling, Virginia) with connections west, which ran so close beneath Mason's and Dixon's line that it found itself, during much of the Civil War, in a kind of no-man's-land; as a carrier it would serve the Union sometimes, the Confederacy never. Authentically Southern trackage, east to west, coalesced at Chattanooga into the single line of a single company, the Memphis & Charleston, a road destined to early fragmentation. Though Northern superiority in terms of number of "routes" was clear, none of the routes could as yet be classified as trunk lines. The tradition of localism continued to be evident in even so fundamental a matter as the distance between the rails of a track. It is true that many Northern companies had adopted the classic British gauge of 4 feet, 8½ inches; moreover, there was an equally strong tendency in the South to use a gauge of 5 feet. But Northern practice could vary; the Erie was committed to an expansive 6 feet. The South contained considerable mileage of the British sort and in other places fancied an unconventional width of 5 feet, 6 inches. Connecting lines, even of an identical gauge, did not always represent unobstructed arteries. In many instances (but particularly in the South) there existed no physical contact between the roads that served a single city or town. Gaps of this sort were naturally cherished by hackmen and drayers, who saw to it that municipal ordinances discouraged their elimination.

The carriers themselves nursed restrictive notions. Many of them—and once more this was most conspicuous in the South—shrank from releasing their rolling stock to the lines of a "foreign" company. Even in the North, railroad executives were happier when such interchanges involved the property of a third company—the germ of the car-line idea. North or South, the advantages of the through trains were as yet only dimly perceived.

Speaking very generally, it may be said that the railroad equipment of the Civil War period, both Union and Confederate, reflected a kind of American standard; that is, nearly all locomotives were of the 4-4-0 classification—two sets of four wheels front and center, and none under the cab—and burned wood; most rails were of wrought iron and weighed no more than 40 pounds to the yard; while the load limit of the average boxcar was established at about 16,000 pounds. This was only natural; most—though not all—of the engines and cars were manufactured in the North, while most—though not all—of the rails were rolled either in the North or in England. But if the Confederacy entered the Civil War with roughly similar patterns of railroad material, it typically possessed less of everything. The South counted 9,000 line miles of track; the North had 21,000. The Pennsylvania Railroad—in 1861 it ran from Philadelphia to Pittsburgh only!—owned more locomotives—220—than did all the lines of secessionist Virginia. The South Carolina Railroad possessed the greatest number of cars of any Confederate property—849. The leading company in the North was the Delaware, Lackawanna & Western with more than 4,000 cars.

Furthermore, if the Southern railroad plant was deficient at the outset, its capacity to grow, or even to maintain itself, was minimal. Confederate inferiority in the metallurgical arts and the steadily more constrictive effects of the Federal blockage are abundantly documented. But it must also be observed that these factors were rendered much worse by an unimaginative public policy, which prevented the most effective use of what the Confederacy did have.

One must, of course, be fair. At the outset, the United States authorities were as naive with respect to the administration of railroads as were the Confederate. Both opponents had sprung from a common military background, and they now faced each other with a common baggage of notions. Prior to 1861, the steam locomotive had played a scant role in American military activity; army transport had depended upon animal-drawn wagons, moving under the orders of commanders in the field and administered by a quartermaster organization whose traditions were as rigid as they were ancient. Enter the iron horse, offering greatly superior speed and almost unimaginable capacity. That the new beast would be useful was obvious, yet the wagon continued to afford an ad-

Above: Secretary of War Edwin M. Stanton, learning from the bitter lesson of the First Battle of Bull Run, which was lost when the enemy used railroads to combine troops against McDowell, knew the vital role to be played by the railroads. As a result, soon after taking his portfolio, he brought to Washington… (USAMHI)

Above: … Herman Haupt, a near-genius who graduated from West Point at age eighteen and thereafter dazzled the railroad industry with his achievements. Stanton made him chief of construction of the United States Military Railroads with the rank of brigadier general. He worked wonders. (NA, U. S. SIGNAL CORPS, BRADY COLLECTION)

Above: Tenuous lifelines, like this viaduct on the Baltimore & Ohio at Relay House, Maryland… (MHS)

vantage that the boxcar could not match: it was not confined to a track and therefore, like its motorized descendant, provided a greater flexibility of movement. This flexibility had conditioned, over the centuries, the very mores of military transport. But now, whenever a field commander applied the traditional procedures to a railroad, the anticipated flood of supplies and reinforcements abruptly ceased. Official wrath would thereupon descend upon the railroaders concerned; "wretched" was an early and probably laundered epithet applied by General Joseph E. Johnston to the Confederate management of the Orange & Alexandria, and it is likely that other comments never saw official print.

The causes of such difficulties quickly became obvious to intelligent railroad men. One was understandable: military authorities were prone to dealing with train crews as if they were teamsters enlisted under the Articles of War, ordering them about without thought of the consequences. Another was inevitable: the temptation to regard railroad cars as convenient storehouses, and the disinclination of field units to unload and release them became notorious. Still another was the absence of any well-understood official relationship between the carriers and the military. None of these problems was ever to be perfectly resolved, but experience brought considerable improvement, especially on the Union side.

Of these principal difficulties, the absence of a formal railroad-army relationship was paramount. Until this was assured, there could be no dealing with the storehouses or the *ad hoc* train orders.

During the first year of the war, both administrations, Federal and Confederate, simply muddled through, relying largely upon quartermaster departments of the conventional kind. True, each side commissioned and inserted into the traditional structure certain knowledgeable railroad of-

Above: ... and the Orange & Alexandria here at Union Mills on Bull Run, were vital to supply and transportation for the armies. A March 1863 image by A. J. Russell . (USAMHI)

Right: Sometimes they could be protected by a detachment of soldiers, as here near Union Mills in a G. W. Houghton photograph. (VHS)

Below left: But not always. Here, Barnard & Gibson's March 1862 picture of a ruined rail crossing near Blackburn's Ford on Bull Run. (USAMHI)

Below: Posing behind the embankment and pretending to defend the bridge after the fact was of little use. Other means, preventive means, had to be found. (AMERICANA IMAGE GALLERY)

ficials; the Pennsylvania's Thomas Scott and William S. Ashe of the Wilmington & Weldon are primary examples. But in neither organization were these men given appropriate authority: in the administrative bureaus their advice was overlooked; in the field it was flouted.

The Federal authorities finally moved, early in 1862, to attack the railroad problem in a serious way. First came a cleansing at the top: Edwin M. Stanton was appointed Secretary of War in place of the dubious Simon Cameron. Mr. Stanton has not enjoyed a universally favorable press; he could be an unpleasant colleague, and his political honesty remains cloudy to this day. But he was both intelligent and efficient, and he was devoted to the proposition that the Confederacy should be subjected to utter defeat. Shortly after Stanton's arrival, an administration railroad bill was pushed through Congress and received President Lincoln's signature on January 31, 1862. Its text was brief: it granted to the President of the United States the authority to assume, whenever the military situation warranted, full control over any railroad in the country. In the face of such a statute, the subordinate status of the railroad industry was clear.

To enact a law is one thing; to carry it out with imagination and dispatch is another. Even under Stanton an effective implementation required a lengthy period of trial and error. The substance of the act was published as a general order of the Adjutant General's office as early as February 4, and on the eleventh the widely respected general superintendent of the Erie, Daniel C. McCallum, was appointed military director and superintendent of railroads in the United States with very broad powers, based upon the statute and its derivative order. But the troubles persisted; they had penetrated so deep that their elimination would require not only an enlightened supervision but also Herculean labors in the field.

The labors were performed by Herman Haupt, a civil engineer of impeccable reputation, who was charged late in April with the restoration of reliable railroad service in the northern Virginia theater. Haupt was a humorless man, born to controversy. Although a graduate of West Point, he utterly lacked a sense of subordination, and his confrontations with certain braided martinets were memorable. He was, in fact, precisely the kind of man the situation demanded. His professional abilities were vast; they embraced every aspect of rail road construction, maintenance, and operation. He furthermore could usually depend upon the support of both McCallum and Stanton. Amid the Virginia disasters of 1862, he pounded out the fundamentals of an organization, the United States Military Railroads, divided specifically into construction and operating corps, and managed upon carefully stated principles perfected by himself. In the course of his service Haupt underwent repeated fits of the sulks, and after the Gettysburg campaign he stamped home to Massachusetts for good. But his military railroad ideas would be enormously and, for the Federals, happily expanded. They would be much recorded by Yankee photographers.

Though the wartime railroad law conveyed sweeping powers to the Lincoln government, this did not mean that every carrier in the United States was subjected to seizure and operation by the Union Army. So Draconian a process was wisely reserved for emergencies—Gettysburg is

Above: Haupt built blockhouses, frontier-style forts to protect bridges in Virginia and Tennessee. Here one overlooks the Orange & Alexandria crossing of Bull Run. (USAMHI)

Left: Even this was not foolproof, as the same blockhouse, now burned, demonstrates. (USAMHI)

Below: But usually they were effective. Here a more elaborate blockhouse built on the East Tennessee & Georgia line to guard the Hiawassee bridge, largely from raiders like Nathan B. Forrest. (USAMHI)

Right: And here Barnard's 1864 image of a fortified bridge on the Louisville & Nashville crossing of the Cumberland River. Giant fortress doors could close each end of the bridge, turning it into a stronghold. (LC)

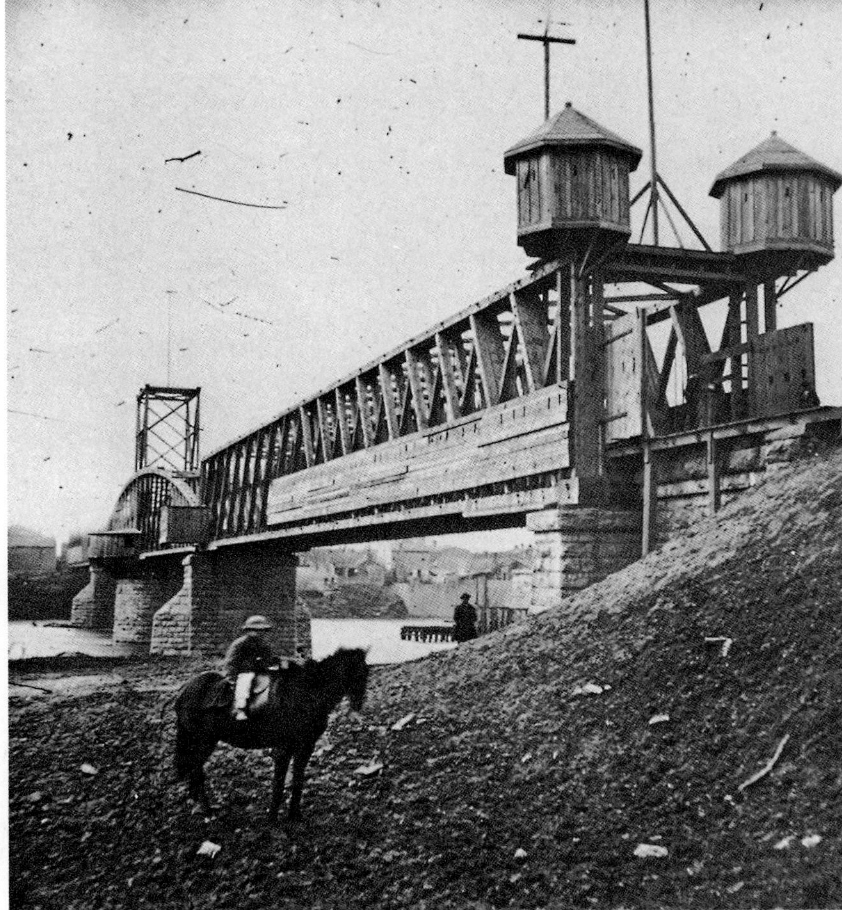

Below: It was men like Brigadier General John D. Imboden that Haupt sought to defeat. Though they were usually troublesome to their superiors, on independent command they were skilled at destroying railroad equipment and installations. Imboden wreaked terrible damage on the Baltimore & Ohio in 1863 and 1864. (USAMHI)

Above right: So did Major Harry Gilmor and his 2nd Maryland Cavalry. On an 1864 raid on the B & O he not only stopped a train, but also robbed the passengers, a feat which got him suspended from command. This portrait was made in Columbia, South Carolina, by W. Weain. (USAMHI)

Left: The Baltimore & Ohio shops at Martinsburg, Virginia, a favorite target of Confederate raiders. Probably an image from the 1850s. Shown are camelback locomotives and several iron pot coal cars. (BALTIMORE & OHIO RAILROAD)

an example—and was routinely applied only to occupied Confederate properties. The statute did, how ever, inspire a healthy cooperation by Northern companies.

Behind the Confederate lines, the railroad situation continued to be in woeful contrast to the improvements on the Union side. Underequipped for the burdens of wartime traffic, hard pressed even to sustain themselves, the Southern carriers were subjected, until nearly the end, to an official policy that can only be pronounced irresponsible. Nothing that was faintly similar to the establishment of McCallum and Haupt was ever achieved. Local, even private, rights were deemed sacrosanct; facts were brushed aside. The South possessed a wealth of natural waterways, especially in the West, but these tended, like the Mississippi, to run in directions favorable to the enemy. The South also enjoyed the means to develop a respectable system of wagon transport, but this was quite inadequate to the supply, over great distances, of the large defensive armies that had become necessary in the face of even larger enemy forces. These, in their turn, had been made possible by both the waterways and the new railroads! Nevertheless, Confederate rails did provide an imperfect skeleton of interior lines, and this just possibly might have been used to so prolong Confederate resistance that the Northern will to fight—always the supreme factor in this war —might have crumbled.

But the Southern leadership failed to make sophisticated use of what was available. It was not until December 1862 that the Richmond government went so far as to bring into its military structure a railroad man of a stature equivalent to that of McCallum and Haupt. This was William M. Wadley, who currently was associated with a half finished enterprise in Louisiana, but who could look back upon a large and fruitful experience with a number of other companies in Georgia and Mississippi. He was, in a professional sense, probably the ablest railroad man in the Southern Confederacy. Wadley was noted for the brevity of his speech and, though not so brusque as Herman Haupt, was deficient in certain military niceties. His Southern loyalties were intense, but he had been born and raised in New England, a circumstance that aroused embarrassing suspicions. But his most serious difficulties were derived from the fact that he had been given rank—a full colonelcy —but no power over either the carriers or over any segment of the military. He tried earnestly to improve matters, but he quickly found himself enmeshed in the thankless role of "ombudsman" between the railroads and the government, neither of which proposed to yield an inch to the other. He did contrive to organize, without clear authority, a quasi-independent Railroad Bureau, with informal lines of communication to a variety of Confederate points. He resigned his commission seven months later, when the Confederate Senate refused, for reasons unspecified, to confirm his appointment.

The activities, such as they were, of the Railroad Bureau were inherited by Wadley's principal assistant, Captain—later Lieutenant Colonel—Frederick W. Sims. Sims enjoyed neither the background nor the reputation of his predecessor, but he was by no means incompetent, and he was endowed with a happy ability to endure frustration. Like Wadley, he carried responsibility without authority, yet he served to the very end as the Confederacy's principal rail transportation officer, devising ineffective "miracles" and accomplishing nothing of lasting consequence. He was invested at last with the kind of power that he and Wadley should have received at the beginning, but the requisite legislation was approved, with open reluctance, by President Jefferson Davis only on March 9, 1865, precisely a month before Appomattox.

Yet the Confederates could sometimes demonstrate a certain brilliance in their use of railroads. On at least three occasions they managed to improvise a steam-powered mass transit system in order to accomplish a particular strategic purpose.

The first took place in the late spring of 1862, when the divisions of W. H. C. Whiting and Jackson were shunted in bewildering sequence between Richmond and the Valley of the Shenandoah and finally were concentrated upon Lee's left wing in the Peninsula. The episode involved at least 20,000 troops, and though they at times exceeded the capabilities of the Virginia Central Railroad, their commanders did achieve a commendable harmony with its operating personnel. The results, from the Confederate viewpoint, were satisfying.

The second occasion came a few weeks later. It witnessed the removal of the greater part of Braxton Bragg's army from Tupelo, in the northeastern part of Mississippi, and its reconcentration at Chattanooga, Tennessee. Like the Virginia episode it was locally conceived and executed—and was carried out with a minimum of fuss. It was a major undertaking; involved was the movement of more than 20,000 men over the tracks of five railroads by a circuitous route through Mobile, Montgomery, and Atlanta. Yet it was completed in little more than two weeks. The consequences were considerable: the disruption over many months of the entire Federal offensive west of the Appalachians.

The third entailed the famous transfer, in September 1863, of Longstreet's corps from Lee's army in Virginia to Bragg's command in northern Georgia. It was a complex affair, organized under difficult circumstances and carried out under the general supervision of Sims's railroad bureau. Federal activities in eastern Tennessee denied to the Confederates the logical routing via Knoxville, and they were obliged to resort to a series of awkward passages through the Carolinas and Atlanta; the situation was further confused by certain unrelated movements in the direction of Charleston. Nevertheless, the thing was brought off successfully. The weather was pleasant, most schedules were kept, and perhaps half the troops arrived in time to participate in the Battle of Chickamauga. The statistics of the operation remain uncertain; the best estimates suggest that the total number completing the journey cannot have much exceeded 12,000. But their presence undoubtedly contributed to the Confederate victory and to a subsequent glimmer of Confederate hope.

The most significant result of Chickamauga, however, was the Union response to it. Hardly had

Left: A somewhat retouched photo showing the junction of the Baltimore & Ohio and Cumberland & Pennsylvania Railroads with the Chesapeake & Ohio Canal at Cumberland, Maryland. The mules are moving the coal cars into position to dump their contents into the canal barges. Another place exceedingly vulnerable to Confederate raiders. (B & O RAILROAD MUSEUM)

Above: Here the Chattanooga depot at Nashville, Tennessee, shows the effects of a Rebel raid . (HERB PECK, JR.)

Left: And Manassas Junction, Virginia, is repeatedly disrupted by the passing of the armies. (USAMHI)

Left: Keeping the U. S. Military Railroads running would be a massive task for the innovative Haupt. He proved equal to it. Here he paddles a small pontoon boat of his own design, used for inspecting bridge foundations. (USAMHI)

Right: Carrying out Haupt's instructions were engineers like these of the Construction Corps, photographed with their tools in Chattanooga in 1864. (LC)

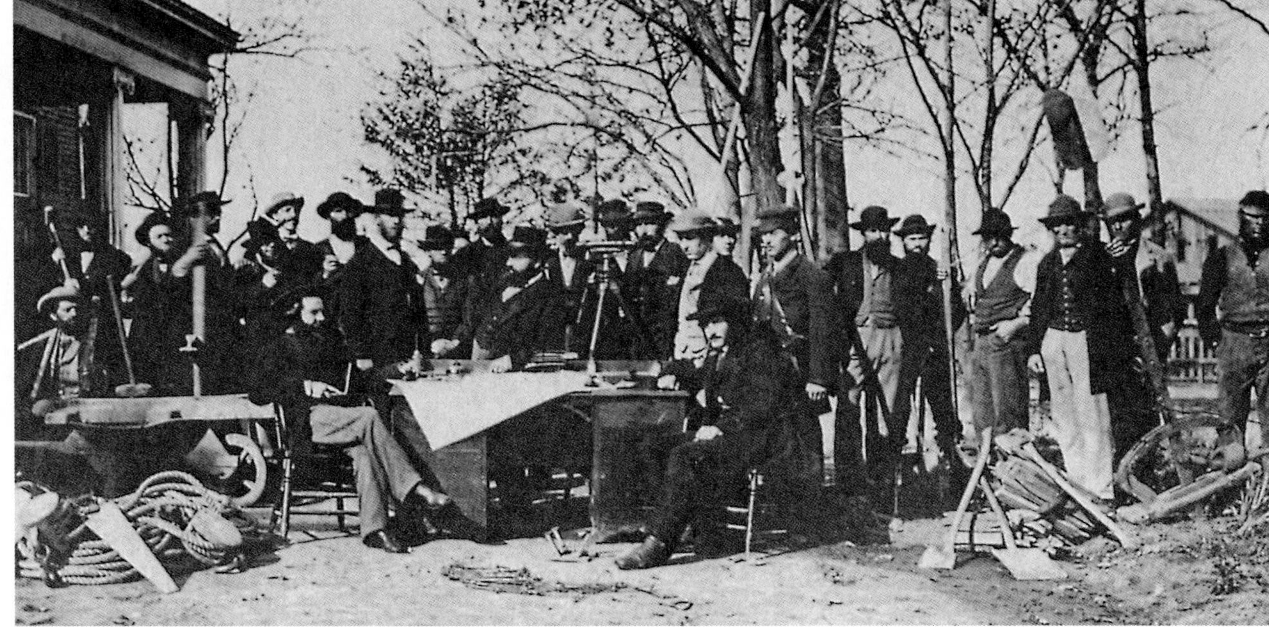

Below: And commissioned to follow the railroads was one of the few officially commissioned military photographers—perhaps the only one—Major A. J. Russell. Here the headquarters of his operations at Petersburg, near City Point, in the summer of 1864. (ROY MEREDITH)

Below: Haupt moved mountains of material over long distances to maintain old lines and build new ones as needed. Here Russell's image of tons of iron rails at Alexandria, ready to go where needed. (USAMHI)

the plight of the defeated General Rosecrans, now trapped in Chattanooga, become clear when plans were being drafted to rectify the situation with massive reinforcements. The most suitable available units were all in northern Virginia; they must proceed by rail, beginning at once and upon an emergency basis, to the vicinity of Chattanooga. The substantive preparations were completed in a single day: General McCallum, President John Garrett of the Baltimore & Ohio, and Thomas Scott assumed the responsibility for specific segments of the route, which was necessarily long and roundabout. It passed through Washington, Benwood—on the Ohio River in West Virginia—then to Indianapolis, south to Louisville and Nashville, and then to Bridgeport, Alabama, on the Tennessee River. Needed cooperation was ensured by reminding participants of the railroad law of 1862, and behind the law stood a no-nonsense administration and a steadily growing U.S. railroad capability.

The first train puffed away from the Virginia encampments on September 25; the last crept down the winding grade into the Tennessee Valley on the evening of October 6. In eleven and one half days, 25,000 infantry, 10 batteries of artillery, and 100 carloads of miscellaneous equipment had been carried 1,200 miles over the lines of a half dozen railroads without a single serious delay or notable interference by the enemy.

Although the reinforcing of Rosecrans at Chattanooga was the most spectacular incident of its kind over the whole course of the Civil War, it was not, in a technical sense, the most impressive. The United States Military Railroads organization was not to be presented with its supreme challenge until the following spring, when it was charged with the supply, over hundreds of miles of single track, of General William T. Sherman's Atlanta campaign. This represented more than a rigorous exercise in logistics; thanks to the renewed activity of enemy guerrillas, very extensive portions of the route required constant rebuilding. The effort—physical and administrative—was staggering, but Sherman and his 100,000 men never lacked for rations or ammunition. Superintending the miracle were three officers of the Military Railroads—W. W. Wright, Adna Anderson, and E. C. Smeed. The Confederates were simply bewildered, and as they were thrust relentlessly back upon Atlanta they wondered aloud whether the

Yankees were not carrying their bridges and tunnels with them in their knapsacks.

During all this, the officers of the United States Military Railroads were always pleased to have their accomplishments recorded photographically. This pleasant liaison between photographer and military railroader in the Civil War was a natural development; railroad gear "held still" frequently enough to serve as a subject for the slow and inconvenient emulsions of the day; moreover, railroad matters enjoyed, in the 1860s, a distinctive appeal to the picture-buying public.

The photographs that follow remind us of something more than the discussions in the text. They are nearly all Northern images and depict Northern activity. To suggest that there nowhere exists a photograph of an authentic Confederate railroad train would be taking a risk, but such a photo has yet to surface.

The South lacked boiler tubes for its locomotives. It also lacked developer and fixer. Consequently Confederate photographers could not undertake to record everything, and likenesses of loved ones must have always been more sought after than prints of the trains that carried them off to battle. Furthermore, the final catastrophe brought grievous disruption to Southern records in all categories. It was therefore inevitable that surviving views of Confederate railroads should be the work of Northerners and that they should portray scenes of occupation and ruin.

It is a fascinating coincidence that the American Civil War should have been the first conflict to encompass, in an extensive way, the techniques of both photography and railroading. And if railroads contributed to the victory of the Union, contemporary railroad photographs dramatically suggest the reasons.

Left: At Burnside's Wharf on Aquia Creek, the Construction Corps joined the rails with the waters to transport supplies. (NA)

Left: The lines of tracks seem endless. Haupt brought his rails to the very water's edge on the James, below Richmond, in 1865. Photograph by Russell. (USAMHI)

Below: Here, opposite Richmond, even locomotives were brought from ship to roadbed at the war's end. (USAMHI)

Below: In the summer of 1864 Russell captured this scene of the camp of the workers of the Construction Corps at City Point, Virginia, their tents bordering the very ties of their tracks. (USAMHI)

Below right: All along the vital arteries of supply Haupt's men could be found. One, at least, proved indifferent to the camera and, turning his back to it, had a mate shine his shoes. (ROY MEREDITH)

Left: A Russell image of a Construction Corps camp on the outskirts of Richmond after the surrender. The Virginia state capitol appears on the skyline at left. (LC)

Below: A Russell view of rolling stock and camps in Virginia. (NA)

Above: Haupt's innovative mind produced many oddities, including the "shad belly" bridge, easily transportable, and speedily assembled. (ROY MEREDITH)

Right: His "beanpole" bridges made him famous, attracting the admiration of President Lincoln. This bridge over Potomac Creek was built in forty hours, utilizing two old piers from its destroyed predecessor. An A. J. Russell image from May 1864. (USAMHI)

Right: Two days before, this creek was an impassable barrier for trains. Now a train can cross in safety. (LC)

Above: Here in 1863 one such bridge is tested. (ROY MEREDITH)

Above: The Bull Run bridge-a-building. (LC)

Below: And completed. The first train crosses. Russell took this scene in the spring of 1863. (KA)

Above: Russell's 1863 print of Bull Run and a bridge under construction in the distance. (KA)

Right: Later there would be time to elaborate and refine the bridge, once it was passing traffic again. The makeshift undergirding of the previous photo is replaced by a sturdy "shad belly" superstructure, complete with ornamental eagle above the entrance. (SOUTHERN RAILWAY SYSTEM)

Left: A similar "beanpole" bridge near Chattanooga. (MHS)

Above: The Howe Turn bridge over the Tennessee at Bridgeport, Alabama, a marvel of Construction Corps engineering. Here, in October 1863, it was just being rebuilt. (MHS)

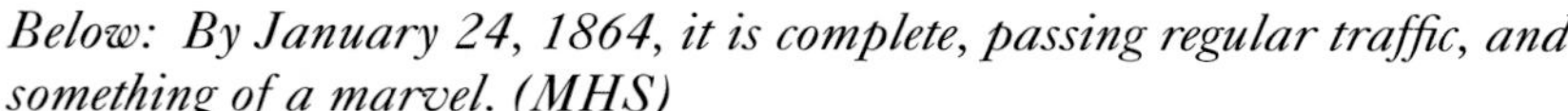

Below: By January 24, 1864, it is complete, passing regular traffic, and something of a marvel. (MHS)

Top and above: And here it is almost finished, with still some temporary shoring at the old piles. (USAMHI)

Left: The same wonders were worked out West. The 1st Michigan Engineers, with Construction Corps help, built the Elk River bridge near Pulaski, Tennessee. It was 700 feet long and 58 feet high. (CHICAGO PUBLIC LIBRARY)

Above: And at every major river and creek between Tennessee and Virginia, similar unheralded feats occurred regularly as Haupt kept the railroads running. (LC)

Above: And a magnificent bridge built over the Tennessee at Chattanooga in 1864, mighty Lookout Mountain brooding in the distance. (MHS)

Left: Conductors and engineers like these actually ran the trains. An A. J. Russell image. (USAMHI)

Right: Their engines were frequently the best that the factories of the North could produce, splendid machines like the Gen. Haupt built by William Mason of Taunton, Massachusetts. (USAMHI)

Left: Their engineers sometimes decorated their locomotives. (USAMHI)

Right: And sometimes the Confederates did the decoration for them. In this Russell photo the men point to enemy shell damage in the stack and tender of the Fred Leach . (USAMHI)

Above: Most major cities soon got—if they did not have them already—major rail yards. Alexandria, at the terminus of the Orange & Alexandria, became the most important in the east by virtue of the O & A's necessary part in supplying armies in Virginia. (USAMHI)

Above: The roundhouse at Alexandria, shown in this Russell image, spun scores of locomotives in the constant traffic moving south. (USAMHI)

Below: The offices of the Orange & Alexandria, photographed by Russell from the top of the roundhouse. (NEIKRUG PHOTOGRAPHICA, LTD.)

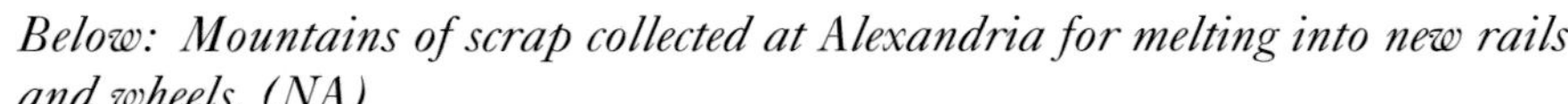

Below: Mountains of scrap collected at Alexandria for melting into new rails and wheels. (NA)

Left: Nashville's Chattanooga depot acted as a principal link in the rail system supplying the Federals in the West. (KA)

Above: Lesser depots like this one at Culpeper, Virgirlia, also played their part. (KA)

Above: And always there was the constant motion of engines and ears. Here a puff of smoke and a blur give testimony to one of hundreds of iron horses at its task. (KA)

Left: A variety of special pieces of equipment came out of the needs of war. Here a private car sits on a siding at City Point in 1864. (ROY MEREDITH)

Left: And here a more elaborate Presidential car, caught by Russell in the Orange Alexandria yard in 1865. It will take Lincoln home to Illinois, in his coffin. (NA)

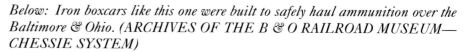

Below: Iron boxcars like this one were built to safely haul ammunition over the Baltimore & Ohio. (ARCHIVES OF THE B & O RAILROAD MUSEUM—CHESSIE SYSTEM)

Left: Car barges like these operated on the Potomac River, shifting trains where bridges could not cross. (NA)

Above: Haupt was not the only innovator, either. The Confederates, with far more limited means, are believed to have created this railroad battery near Petersburg. Such quickly mobile armored artillery could be very useful, if only the rails went to the right places. (USAMHI)

Left: Improvised rail splices like this made quick repairs to old or sabotaged track. (NA)

Left: The Union, too, put guns on rails, and none greater than the mighty 13-inch mortar "Dictator." It weighed 17,000 pounds and performed well at Petersburg. Only rails could move the behemoth gun. (SOUTHERN RAILWAY SYSTEM)

Right: It is unfortunate that so little survives to illustrate the role of Confederate railroads in the war. What does remain is from the cameras of Union photographers, like this tranquil image of an engine of the Atlantic & North Carolina line. Behind it is a "conductor's car." (USAMHI)

Right: And here at Port Hudson, Louisiana, McPherson & Oliver caught two dilapidated pieces of equipment of the Clinton & Port Hudson Railroad. As in so many other areas, the South simply could not compete with the North's industry in railroading, and as shown, was hard pressed to maintain what it already had. (ISHL)

THE EMBATTLED CONFEDERACY

The Onondaga, *a workhorse twin-turreted monitor on the James River. Only two double-turreted monitors saw service during the war, and when Admiral David D. Porter stripped the James fleet for the attack on Fort Fisher in North Carolina in 1864, the* Onondaga *was left to defend the river almost alone.*

The Bloodiest Day: Antietam

JAMES I. ROBERTSON, JR.

Lee the gambler and McClellan the slow do terrible battle in Maryland

The ruins of the Potomac River bridge at Berlin, Maryland. Here and elsewhere in the vicinity Lee began crossing into the North on September 4, 1862. Here the crossing appears a month later, with a Federal pontoon bridge in place. (U. S. ARMY MILITARY HISTORY INSTITUTE, CARLISLE BARRACKS, PA.)

SEPTEMBER 2, 1862, found Virginia virtually free of Federal armies for the first time since the Civil War began. Major General George B. McClellan's huge Army of the Potomac had abandoned the Peninsula east of Richmond following Robert E. Lee's counterattacks in the Seven Days Campaign. A second Federal Army under Major General John Pope had just been all but routed at Second Manassas by the combined forces of Lee and "Stonewall" Jackson. The North's principal assault forces, now sullen and disillusioned, were filing into the fortifications around Washington. The war had returned to where it had begun sixteen months earlier.

Lee then decided on one of his most audacious moves. He would launch an invasion of the North. Based on historical hindsight, this decision appears questionable. Yet less desirable alternatives at the time seemed to justify Lee advancing into enemy territory with a numerically inferior army.

Washington, the North's king in the great chess game of war, was too powerfully defended to be attacked. On the other hand, Lee could not keep his destitute army at Manassas for any length of time. The northern counties of Virginia had been ravaged by war and could not sustain the Confederates. Lee's third choice was to retire to a more defensible site in the Shenandoah Valley or south of the Rappahannock River; but to do so would surrender everything that had been gained at Second Manassas. That left invasion as the most workable alternative, with a number of factors seemingly pointing to success.

The Federal armies were disorganized at the moment and posed no immediate threat. Maryland was a sister state of the South; and if the Army of Northern Virginia could "liberate" the state from Federal occupation troops, Maryland might then cast her lot with the Confederacy—which would have the spontaneous effect of leaving the Northern capital surrounded by seceded territory. An invasion by Lee would also draw the Federals' attention away from Virginia and enable the Old Dominion's farmers to gather the fall crops unmolested. A blow inside the North might trigger widespread demands on Washington for peace. Lastly, such a successful excursion could draw England or France into the Civil War on the side of the South; and foreign recognition seemed the one thing that could most assure victory for the Confederacy.

Therefore, in the pre-dawn darkness on September 4 Lee's columns began wading across the Potomac at the shoals near Leesburg. The Army of Northern Virginia was weaker than it would be at any time during the war, save at Appomattox. Thousands were absent because of wounds, sickness, and exhaustion. Untold others had balked at invasion on the grounds that they had enlisted only to defend their beloved South, and they had simply walked away from the army. The 40,000 ragged Confederates who advanced into Maryland represented barely two thirds of Lee's force. Most of them were barefoot. (Of 300 men in a South Carolina regiment, fewer than 100 were wearing anything akin to shoes.) Yet they were the strongest, the hard core of the Confederacy's main army, and they appeared to one writer as "the scarecrow multitude of lean, vociferous, hairy men who reminded even noncombatants of wolves."

Lee's plan was to strike northward for Harrisburg, Pennsylvania. Capturing that point would break the dual arteries of the Pennsylvania Rail-

Above: The gambler. General Robert Edward Lee took an enormous chance by deciding to invade the North. It was characteristic of the man and of his army. An image from 1862, the year of Antietam. (CIVIL WAR TIMES ILLUSTRATED COLLECTION)

Left: An early postwar view of Frederick, Maryland. On September 6 "Stonewall" Jackson's troops occupied this much-troubled city. It changed hands several times during the war. (USAMHI)

Left: As Lee marched north, another gambler sat in the Executive Mansion in Washington pondering what seemed to be an unending succession of threats and reverses. Lincoln had little time to enjoy the grassy lawns being manicured here in a Brady & Company image from 1862. He had to stop Lee, and the only man who might do it was a high risk... (LIBRARY OF CONGRESS)

road and the Susquehanna River, thereby isolating the Federals' eastern and western theaters of operations from one another. At the same time, the invasion had to be benevolent in tone. The necessity of winning converts in Maryland was such that Lee repeatedly urged his men to show exemplary behavior. That they did so, in the face of raggedness and hunger, is one of the remarkable incidents of the war.

On the morning of September 7 the Confederates paused at Frederick, Maryland. The army was subsisting—as it would throughout the first three weeks of September—on green corn, apples, and an occasional ration of potatoes. Lee himself was in pain. A couple of days earlier he had slipped while mounting his horse. The fall to the ground had broken one hand and badly sprained the other. Yet no time existed for personal discomfort or rest. The army had to move. Maryland had not responded with support for the Confederates. Straggling was on the increase as hard roads tortured already raw feet. Even worse, Lee had received reports that a Federal army was now in pursuit. Indeed, McClellan had been given a second chance. In the latter stages of the Second Manassas Campaign he had found himself at Alexandria, Virginia, a general without an army. Yet Lincoln could not shelve McClellan, whether the President wished it or not. The salvation of the Union at the moment was the Army of the Potomac, and the only general who could make that army respond with any degree of effectiveness was McClellan. So, early in September the dapper little commander once again mounted his black charger, Daniel Webster, and rode to the head of his troops.

The 90,000 men that he greeted at Rockville, Maryland, were not all members of the old Army of the Potomac. Some units had been transferred from Pope's defeated Army of Virginia, while other regiments were entering the field for the first time. Federal soldiers cheered the return of "Little Mac" and morale in the ranks climbed

Above: Major General George B. McClellan. He failed Lincoln badly on the Virginia Peninsula earlier that year and passively contributed to the defeat at Second Manassas. Yet Lincoln offered and "Little Mac" accepted. (USAMHI)

Above: But before he could get to Lee, McClellan had first to pass this stubborn, combative, highly opinionated Confederate, Major General Daniel H. Hill, shown here as a brigadier. At the South Mountain passes this brother-in-law of Jackson's held up the Federal advance for precious hours. (LC)

Right: Colonel Rush Hawkins, organizer and commander of the 9th New YorkóHawkins's Zouavesówas more fortunate than Reno. He lived through South Mountain to fight at Antietam. His first love, though, was old and rare books. (NATIONAL ARCHIVES)

Right: An early postwar view of the Wise House on South Mountain, near Fox's Gap. Out in that field Major General Jesse Reno, commanding the Federal IX Corps, took his mortal wound in the fierce fighting of September 14. (USAMHI)

Above: Alexander Gardner's October 1862 image shows some of the chief culprits in McClellan's consistent failures. These are men of the secret service corps at McClellan's headquarters. Standing, in a checked shirt, just left of the tent pole is Allan Pinkerton. A Scot with a considerable reputation as a detective before the war, he was an utter failure at gathering and evaluating military intelligence. He consistently exaggerated the enemy's numbers, making a cautious McClellan even more timid. (COURTESY OF THE CHICAGO HISTORICAL SOCIETY)

Above: Alexander Gardner's view of Main Street in Sharpsburg, Maryland, taken September 21 or 22. Here Lee came to a halt, his northern invasion stopped. Forced to the defensive, he now had to fight for his army's very life. (LC)

overnight. However, the march north and west in search of Lee was characteristic of McClellan: excruciatingly slow and methodical. In this instance McClellan was not entirely to blame. Scores of false reports relative to Lee's whereabouts poured into his headquarters. Worse, General-in-Chief Henry Halleck provided no stability. One day he would warn McClellan that if the Federal Army moved too far northward, Lee could veer around its right flank and threaten Washington. That same day, or the next, Halleck would warn McClellan that if the Federals advanced too far westward, Lee could lunge unmolested into Pennsylvania.

The self-doubts always lurking in McClellan now festered. He wasted days in reorganizing his army, shifting generals here and there, insuring that supply trains, ammunition wagons, and the like were precisely where they were supposed to be. As a result—and during six critical days when the Army of the Potomac should have been in rapid, concentrated pursuit—it advanced a grand total of thirty miles.

In contrast, it took Lee a day at Frederick to analyze his problems and formulate his strategy. He had expected a Federal garrison at Harpers Ferry to abandon that post when the Confederates swept into Maryland. The garrison was still there. It had to be captured, for its 11,000 Federals lay across Lee's line of communications back to Richmond, and they could be an impediment to a Southern withdrawal into the Shenandoah Valley. The possibility also loomed large that units from

Above: Hall Street in Sharpsburg. At the moment that Gardner made his image, St. Paul's Lutheran Church, in the center background, was filled with wounded from the bloodiest day of the war. Gardner's photographic wagon is in the foreground . (LC)

Above: The Federals had been here before. In August 1862, in more placid days along the Antietam, Colonel W. W. Averell of the 3rd Pennsylvania Cavalry sat with fellow officers for the camera. (USAMHI)

Pennsylvania's huge contingent of militia might move into the valley west of the first range of mountains and present a second front to the depleted Confederate Army.

What Lee decided to do became one of the most daring pieces of strategy in the Civil War. Jackson's fourteen brigades, in three different columns, would march southwestward to Harpers Ferry and overwhelm its defenders. Lee, with nine brigades, would move due west across South Mountain and concentrate at Hagerstown to counter a potential threat from Pennsylvania militia. Daniel Harvey Hill's five brigades would advance only to Boonsborough so as to block both a Federal retreat from Harpers Ferry and a Federal advance toward the South Mountain passes.

These dispositions were spelled out precisely in Special Orders No. 191, which was issued to each of Lee's division commanders, and at dawn on September 10 the Confederates filed out of Frederick. Lee was taking a tremendous gamble: dividing his small army into five parts, with a river separating three of the parts from the other two. Secrecy was imperative for the success of the campaign. However, for the first time in the war, fortune was about to betray Lee.

On September 12, two days after Lee abandoned Frederick, McClellan's army fanned out in the fields surrounding the town. The 27th Indiana was relaxing in a campground formerly occupied by the Confederates when Corporal Barton W. Mitchell spied three cigars wrapped in a piece of paper on the ground. Tobacco was one of the most coveted commodities in the Union armies. Hence, it was a few minutes before Mitchell paid any attention to the wrapping. It was a copy of Special Orders No. 191, and within an hour it was at McClellan's headquarters. The Federal general was a beneficiary of the greatest security leak in American military history.

McClellan now knew precisely where Lee's army was, what Lee was doing, and what he was likely to do. The massive Federal Army at that moment was nearer each of the Confederate wings (Lee and Jackson) than they were to each

Left: But now the whole Federal Army was here, McClellan making his headquarters in the Pry house. Alexander Gardner made this image within a day of the battle. (LC)

Below: The 93rd New York served at Antietam as the headquarters guard for the Army of the Potomac. It kept them from facing the terror of battle with the rest of the army, but they were happy to face Gardner's camera early in October. (USAMHI)

Right: From this site on Elk Mountain McClellan's signalmen watched Lee's movements in his lines along the Antietam. This signal tower was built after the battle. (USAMHI)

Above: The Potomac crossing at Harpers Ferry. Lee wanted the Federal garrison there eliminated to protect his rear. (USAMHI)

Above: One of those sent with Jackson to take Harpers Ferry was Brigadier General Ambrose R. Wright, a Georgian who would be seriously wounded at Antietam following the capture of Harpers Ferry. (VALENTINE MUSEUM)

Left: Colonel Dixon A. Miles of the 2nd United States Infantry commanded the Federals at Harpers Ferry. Accused of drunkenness during the First Manassas fighting, Miles was relegated to a post of lesser importance—lesser, that is, until Lee invaded the North. He stayed longer than he should have and finally surrendered to Jackson. One of the very last shots fired killed him. (USAMHI)

other. McClellan would have to move promptly, for the orders were already four days old; and Lee was not one to waste time or to fall behind schedule. If McClellan took advantage of good roads, balmy weather, and advanced rapidly enough, he could annihilate the fractured Army of Northern Virginia. Yet the Federal commander again fell victim to gnawing uncertainty and self-doubt. Were Lee's "orders" purposefully left to be found? Was Lee where he said he would be? Was it all a trap?

Despite the fact that he outnumbered Lee by more than two to one, McClellan was not willing to take risks. With Jackson at Harpers Ferry, Lee at Hagerstown, and only Harvey Hill's division in his front, McClellan nevertheless began a slow movement westward. Throughout Saturday, September 13, the Federals crawled forward. Hill abandoned Boonsborough and began erecting hasty defenses at the passes atop South Mountain. This eminence, the key to the entire Confederate Army, was a long, irregular range of hills that began at the Potomac and continued some thirty five miles northeastward. The two main passes—Crampton's and Turner's gaps—were about five hundred feet above the valley floor.

Hill had no time to reflect that this was his first independent command involving large numbers of troops. He was a dyspeptic, blunt, and caustic general; but as he looked down from the mountain at endless Federal brigades moving toward him, he confessed that he never felt so lonely in all his life. All of the world's soldiers seemed to be coming toward him. However, McClellan's continuing reliance on Allan Pinkerton's unreliable estimates of Confederate strength caused McClellan to conclude that Hill had five times more than the 6,000 Southerners digging in on the mountaintop.

McClellan therefore made careful, cautious plans that consumed a full day. Not until 9 A.M.

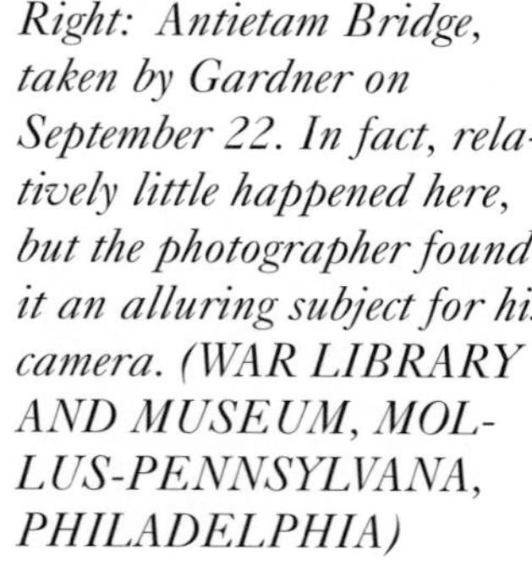

Right: Antietam Bridge, taken by Gardner on September 22. In fact, relatively little happened here, but the photographer found it an alluring subject for his camera. (WAR LIBRARY AND MUSEUM, MOLLUS-PENNSYLVANA, PHILADELPHIA)

Above: The Dunker Church on the Antietam battlefield, taken after the battle damage had been repaired. For the thousands of men who contested the ground around it, this simple structure came to symbolize the bloody horror of Antietam. (USAMHI)

Below: Antietam Bridge again, this time looking northeast. McClellan's headquarters in the Pry house was not far distant, and he used this crossing frequently in sending troops into the battle line. (USAMHI)

on September 14 did the Federal columns start up the slopes. Union troops performed gallantly in scaling the mountainside in the face of sheets of musketry, but the Confederates were just as heroic in holding their position against tremendous odds. It was Thermopylae all over again. It was also the kind of battle that Harvey Hill fought best: hard, close-in combat, with firepower and determination rather than finesse and strategy being the major ingredients. On a more personal note, Hill had no way of knowing that day that one of the Federal brigade commanders assaulting his position was Brigadier General John Gibbon, who had been best man at Hill's wedding a few years earlier.

Intense conflict raged throughout the day as the bulk of two Federal corps swept repeatedly up the mountain, only to be driven back by concentrated fire from thin lines of Southerners massed above. Powder flashes blazed through the battle smoke; hand-to-hand fighting occurred in crevices and along ledges; bodies caromed down the mountain side. One observer likened the Army of the Potomac that day to "a monstrous, crawling, blue black snake, miles long, quilled with the silver slant of muskets at a 'shoulder,' its sluggish tail writhing slowly up over the distant eastern ridge,

Above: The Boonsborough Pike crossed the Antietam at the bridge as it ran from Elk Mountain to Sharpsburg. Behind Newcomer's barn, on the left, Lee laid his first line of defense on the ridge on September 15, awaiting McClellan. (USAMHI)

Above: Newcomer's Mill on Antietam Creek, by Gardner. (USAMHI)

Left: The ruins of the Samuel Mumma house three days after the battle. Here the real fighting in the Battle of Antietam began as the Union I Corps swept against Ewell's and D. H. Hill's Confederates positioned here and nearby. (LC)

Right: Brigadier General George L. Hartsuff led a brigade in Hooker's I Corps in the first attacks against the Confederates, falling with a wound that put him out of action for months. (USAMHI)

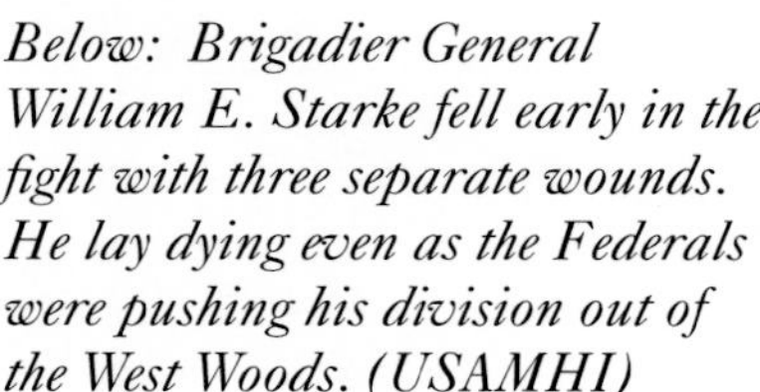

Below: Brigadier General William E. Starke fell early in the fight with three separate wounds. He lay dying even as the Federals were pushing his division out of the West Woods. (USAMHI)

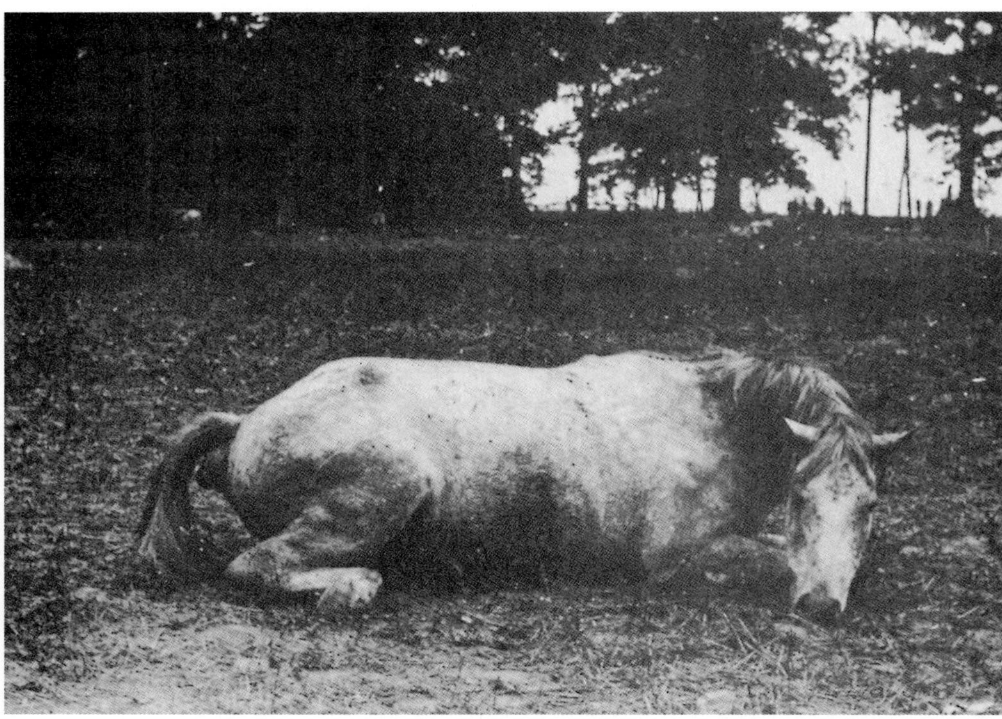

Above: Appearing almost asleep, this dead horse, probably belonging to Colonel Henry Strong of the 6th Louisiana, himself killed in the battle, lies peacefully near the East Woods where Hooker launched his attack. (LC)

Above: Truman Seymour, a brigadier general, led a brigade in Hooker's corps that distinguished itself and him, at Turner's Gap; it continued to perform well at Antietam. Among his regiments was... (USAMHI)

Above: Colonel Hugh W. McNeill's 13th Pennsylvania Reserves, the "Bucktails." McNeill's own bucktail shows in his kepi. He was killed the day before the battle. (USAMHI)

Below: Many fell. Many died. In the fierce fighting along the Hagerstown Pike beside the West Woods and just north of the Dunker Church, hundreds of Confederates of Starke's command sought shelter behind this rail fence. It did them little good. Two days later Gardner found them lying singly... (USAMHI)

its bruised head weltering in the roar and smoke upon the crest above..."

Around 5 P.M. the Federals gained a momentary toehold at Crampton's Gap before Confederate reinforcements sent them scurrying down the ridge. The battle of South Mountain ended at sundown. Hill had suffered 40 percent casualties in a vicious fight that tactically was a draw. Yet the stand at South Mountain had given Lee a full day to react to McClellan's advance; and, as events were to prove, time was a critical factor.

On the Sunday that Hill made his reputation at South Mountain, "Stonewall" Jackson closed in on the Federals defending Harpers Ferry. Jackson was still sore due to a fall from his horse a week earlier, but his concentration, as usual, was totally on the military situation at hand. Six divisions—the largest force Jackson had ever led—methodically took their positions on the mountains overlooking the Ferry. The tiny Federal garrison was caught in a trap. Late in the afternoon of the fourteenth Jackson's batteries began an uncontested bombardment. At dawn the following day Confederate smoothbores and rifled guns opened a concentrated barrage from three different directions. The cannonade lasted barely an hour before aged and ailing Colonel Dixon S. Miles realized the hopelessness of his situation and ordered his command to strike its colors. Miles was subsequently killed in the final shelling from Jackson's guns.

The Confederates bagged 11,500 prisoners, 73 cannon, 13,000 small arms, 200 wagons, and tons of equipment needed by a Southern army that was as destitute as it looked. A Union correspondent at Harpers Ferry noted that Jackson's appearance "was in no respect to be distinguished from the mongrel, bare-footed crew who follow his fortunes." That same reporter then added grudgingly: "I had heard much of the decayed appearance of the rebel soldiers, and yet they glory in their shame."

Jackson, now alerted by Lee to the necessity of rapid concentration, left Ambrose Powell Hill's division to secure Harpers Ferry while he headed northward to rejoin the other units of Lee's army. Meanwhile, Lee had weighed his options. During the fourteenth, with Jackson not in control of Harpers Ferry and Harvey Hill waging a no-win contest at South Mountain, Lee had contemplated withdrawal to Virginia. Then came news early on the fifteenth of Jackson's capture of the Ferry. Lee quickly decided to bring the fragments of his army together on the high ground at Sharpsburg, a village midway between Hagerstown and Harpers Ferry. Throughout that day, therefore, Southern brigades converged on Sharpsburg from the north, east, and south. McClellan could have assailed Lee's columns at any time with 60,000 men—which was far more than Lee could have mustered—but he vacillated too long before moving cautiously down the west face of South Mountain.

Lee's decision to stand and fight at Sharpsburg was, with the exception of Gettysburg, the most controversial decision he made during the war. It was bold, since he was weaker in terms of numbers, with the Potomac to his back and only one major avenue of escape. Yet boldness was characteristic of Lee, and boldness was also the only chance for success that the Confederacy possessed.

So the units of the Confederate Army hastily made for Sharpsburg. Major General James Long street opposed the site as a battleground; Jackson just as sternly endorsed it. Sharpsburg was a village three miles from the winding Potomac River. Only a ford at Shepherdstown offered escape. What attracted Lee to the site was a formidable defense line: a low, crescent-shaped ridge that extended from northwest to southeast of the town. The Confederate left would rest on the Potomac itself; the right would anchor on Antietam Creek, a sluggish north-south stream too deep for the passage of artillery. Hence, the few bridges over it would be of great strategic importance.

Lack of time and tools prevented the Confederates from preparing elaborate entrenchments at Sharpsburg. Brigades arriving on September 15 and 16 simply threw up what defenses they could. It became a truly remarkable battlefield; the three mile Confederate line was so compact that from a number of vantage points its entire length was visible.

September 16 was the day that McClellan lost

Above: ... in groups... (LC)

Below: ... and heaped in piles, their Louisiana blood soaking the soil of Maryland. (LC)

Left: After Hooker's initial attack calmed, Major General John Sedgwick led his division of the fresh II Corps against the Hagerstown Pike and the Confederates in the West Woods. (NA)

Above: Captain Joseph Knap's Battery E, Pennsylvania Light Artillery, joined Sedgwick in his attack, taking a position near the Dunker Church. Gardner photographed them two days later, with the open ground between the East, West, and North Woods beyond. (LC)

Above: Men and colors of the 34th New York, Sedgwick's division. Antietam put more than one tear in their tattered banners. (COURTESY OF MICHAEL J. MCAFEE)

Above: The fighting raged for hours, the casualties falling in rows. Near the Dunker Church, with the West Woods behind it, these Confederate artillerymen died defending their battery, probably Captain W. W. Parker's battery of Virginia Light Artillery. (USAMHI)

Above: Brigadier General Roswell Ripley led a Confederate brigade posted behind the Mumma house. He ordered it burned to prevent its affording shelter to attackers, then later fell wounded himself in the fighting in front of the West Woods. (LC)

Above: Brigadier General Samuel Garland also led a brigade that tried to resist Sedgwick's advance. He could not. He was not with them, having been killed in the fight for Fox's Gap three days before. (MUSEUM OF THE CONFEDERACY)

his opportunity. Lee was at most disorganized and at the very least off balance. Fully half his forces were still not on the field. Absenteeism and straggling had put the whole army in the weakest condition it had ever been in. Lee had barely 40,000 men to contest more than twice that number. Never was the opportunity for Federal victory greater. If McClellan had hurled the mighty Army of the Potomac against the improvised and undermanned Confederate line on the sixteenth, it undoubtedly would have snapped, with perhaps fatal consequences. Yet McClellan spent the day perfecting his own lines, getting cannon into proper position, reconsidering moves, and weighing risks. Thus, while skirmishers bickered and artillerists tested their aim, Jackson's men made a hard march and in the late afternoon were reunited with Lee's army at Sharpsburg.

Through a night of drizzling rain the two armies sat and waited nervously for the battle that would come with the dawn. Jackson's brigades formed Lee's left, Harvey Hill held the center, and Longstreet commanded the right. Movements late on the sixteenth gave ample indication that the battle would begin in Jackson's front, a mile north of Sharpsburg. There, on the west side of the Hagerstown Turnpike, stood a patch of trees known as the West Woods. The area was two hundred to three hundred yards wide and surrounded, on three sides, the white, boxlike Dunker Church standing on a slight knoll. Immediately across the turnpike from the West Woods was another clump of trees. Known as the East Woods and similarly about two hundred yards in width, it extended a quarter of a mile eastward. Between the two woods, adjacent to the east side of the road, was a forty acre cornfield with green stalks head-high at that time of the season.

McClellan's battle plan seemed logical enough, given the preponderance of troops at his disposal. The I and XII Federal Corps would spearhead an assault on Lee's left flank. Two additional corps would act in support. This heavy attack would cause the Confederate left to collapse onto the center and block any further Southern advances toward Hagerstown. Simultaneously, the IX Corps on the Federal left would assail Lee's right flank and turn Lee from his escape route. Then, while the two-pronged attack acted as a vise against Lee's army, McClellan would advance with his remaining divisions and crush the Confederate center.

It was an excellent plan, multifaceted but simple. It depended only on superior numbers and coordination—and McClellan failed on both accounts. Wednesday, September 17, 1862, became the bloodiest single day of the Civil War, in large part be cause the Federals attacked piecemeal, thus allowing a critically outmanned Lee to utilize his inner lines of defense to maximum advantage. Antietam Creek (or Sharpsburg, as the battle is also called) consisted of three heavy engagements piled one atop the other. It was a headlong, day-long explosion of combat, void of memorable tactics—concentrated violence in which thousands of soldiers blazed away in fiery collisions stretching across woods, fields, hillsides, and bottomland. American soldiers never fought harder. Death became commonplace as acts of heroism on one side matched gallantry on the other.

The rain stopped shortly before dawn that morning, and a wet mist quickly gave way to clear skies and the promise of a hot day. In command of the first attack (as well as the Federal I Corps) was handsome and ambitious Major General Joseph Hooker, a hard-fighting, hard-living officer. Thirty-five Federal cannon raked the Confederate positions as an overture. Then, at 6 A.M., ten brigades from the I Corps charged down the Hagerstown Turnpike. Opposing this assault by 12,000 Federals were less than 7,000 Confederates under Jackson. Billy Yanks fought their way through the woods and the cornfield. Confederate musketry took a heavy toll; men fell to the ground with each passing second. Yet Hooker's troops almost reached the Dunker Church and the valuable high ground that was the key to Lee's left flank. A Confederate staff officer wrote of the action: "Such a storm of balls I never conceived it possible for men to live through. Shot and shell shrieking and crashing, canister and bullets whistling and hissing most fiend-like through the air until you could almost see them." As Jackson called for reinforcements, the cornfield became a vast slaughter pen. It was a ghastly sight, bloodied now from the carnage. Never in the history of the Army of Northern Virginia were so many high-ranking officers knocked out of action so quickly. At one point a Confederate colonel was in command of a division because all of his superiors were either dead or wounded. Just as Jackson's line seemed on the verge of snapping, fresh troops under Generals Harvey Hill and John B. Hood rushed on the scene. This new Southern attack a Union officer likened to "a scythe running through our line." Around 7: 30 A.M. the battered I Corps slowly withdrew from the field. A fourth of its number, including Hooker, were casualties; and the remainder were mentally up to nothing more that day.

McClellan then turned to Nathaniel Banks's veterans from the 1862 Valley Campaign. Reorganized as the XII Corps, these soldiers were under the command of Major General Joseph K. F. Mansfield. He was a red-faced, white-haired old regular who had graduated from West Point in 1822—before most of his men were even born. Mansfield rushed his brigades forward into action and was among the first to suffer a mortal wound when a bullet tore through his stomach. His men continued their assault and managed to regain part

Above: Brigadier General John B. Hood was in the fighting early, his brigade suffering terrible losses. The 1st Texas under his command lost 82.3 percent of its men as casualties, the greatest loss in any unit in either army during the war. (VM)

Above: The division of Lafayette McLaws was rushed toward the West Woods as Sedgwick attacked. One of McLaws's brigade commanders was a man who, two years before, sat in President Buchanan's cabinet. Howell Cobb of Georgia, once Secretary of the Treasury and a prominent candidate for Confederate President, was now a brigadier general. (UNIVERSITY

Above: Brigadier General John G. Walker's division came to the West Woods, too. He served in the United States Army during the Mexican War, and appears here as a lieutenant in a photo from the 1850s. (TULANE UNIVERSITY)

Right: The converging Confederates caught Sedgwick and shattered his command, forcing him back to the support of the rest of the II Corps, led by Major General Edwin V. Sumner, the oldest corps commander in the Union Army. (CWTI)

Above: Here the Confederates counterattack, driving Sedgwick and Sumner back. (NATIONAL LIBRARY OF MEDICINE)

Right: Brigadier General Winfield Scott Hancock was a brigade commander in the II Corps. After Sedgwick's repulse, he and others were ordered forward to take possession of ground east of the West Woods. The Confederates met them at a sunken road later to be called Bloody Lane. (P-M)

Right: Colonel Turner G. Morehead led his 106th Pennsylvania in Oliver O. Howard's brigade of Sedgwick's division. In the rout of Sedgwick, Morehead's horse was shot from under him. Retreating on foot, he ran back into the face of the advancing enemy to recover his sword. "I am not going to let them damned rebels get it," he exclaimed . (LC)

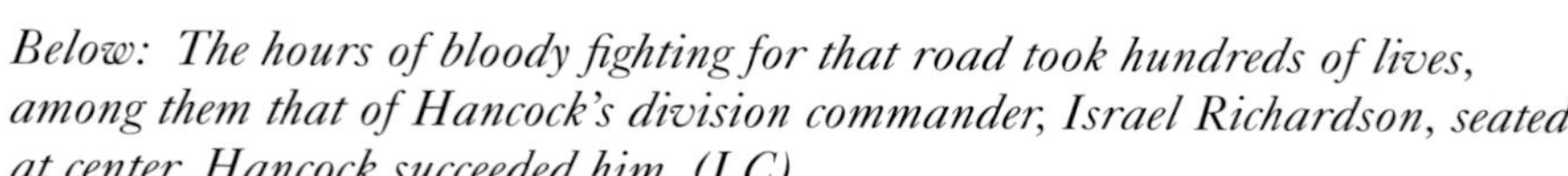

Below: The hours of bloody fighting for that road took hundreds of lives, among them that of Hancock's division commander, Israel Richardson, seated at center. Hancock succeeded him. (LC)

Above: William Harrow, as colonel of the 14th Indiana, fought his regiment for four hours against Bloody Lane, losing half of his numbers. (P-M)

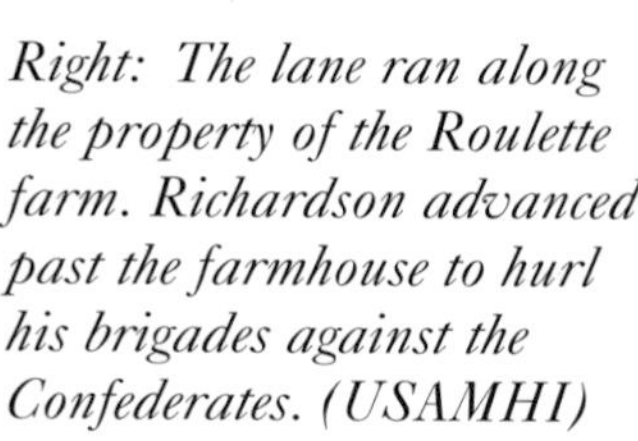

Right: The lane ran along the property of the Roulette farm. Richardson advanced past the farmhouse to hurl his brigades against the Confederates. (USAMHI)

Left: Regular artillerymen from Fitz John Porter's otherwise unengaged corps aided in the attack on Bloody Lane. Captain James M. Robertson led two batteries of the 2nd United States Artillery in the assaults. He stands at right of center. He will become a general after the war. (P-M)

Right: Among the Confederate defenders of the lane, Colonel John B. Gordon of the 6th Alabama took a wound in the head and was only saved from drowning in his own blood by the bullet hole in his hat. (TU)

of the East Woods and the cornfield. Fighting was vicious every foot of the way. Hooker later observed that "every stalk of corn in the northern and greater part of the field was cut as closely as could have been done with a knife, and the slain lay in rows precisely as they had stood in their ranks a few moments before. It was never my fortune to witness a more bloody, dismal battlefield."

This second wave of assaults by Mansfield's corps came in from the northeast, lasted ninety minutes, and also proved fruitless. Confederates firing as rapidly as they could load their guns forced the Federals to relinquish the ground. Had the corps of Hooker and Mansfield attacked in concert and in a concentrated fashion, the outcome would probably have been different. Yet concerted effort and concentration on the part of the Federal Army was lacking throughout the battle.

At 9 A.M., after three hours of killing, McClellan resumed the offensive with a third major attack over the same ground. He ordered the 18,000 troops in the II Corps to assail Jackson from the east-northeast. In command of this corps was Major General Edwin V. "Bull" Sumner, an old Indian fighter with a booming voice and an obsession with rigid discipline. Jackson, meanwhile, had readjusted his lines so that they formed a rough northward-facing arc with the outer points firmly planted.

Sumner's three divisions dashed forward and promptly fell out of alignment, with the result that the sharp point of the attack was blunted before it could pierce the Confedrate lines. Major General John Sedgwick's lead division of 5,000 men lumbered into the battle web that Jackson had spun. Half of those Federals were casualties in less than twenty minutes. Sedgwick himself received three wounds that put this superior combat officer out of action for five months.

A lull in the fighting then gave Jackson a chance to launch an attack of his own, with the three fourths of Lee's army now under his command. Shouting Confederates rushed for the cornfield and were almost at the north end when they came under a withering cross fire from fifty cannon concealed several hundred yards away. The Southern ranks were shredded instantly. Jackson called off the assault; this order brought an end to the four hour fight on the left. Three

Left: Confederate dead in the Bloody Lane, taken by Gardner two days after the battle. (LC)

Left: Dead North Carolinians awaiting burial in Bloody Lane. (USAMHI)

Above: After the fighting on the right and center of McClellan's line, he finally sent Major General Ambrose Burnside forward to attack Lee's right flank. Burnside appears here as a brigadier. (KEAN ARCHIVES)

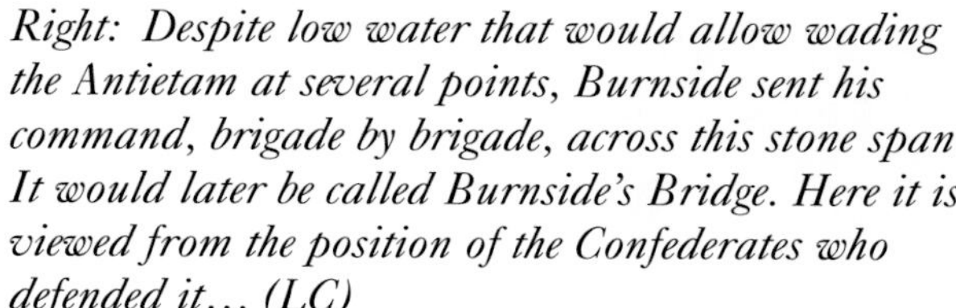

Right: Despite low water that would allow wading the Antietam at several points, Burnside sent his command, brigade by brigade, across this stone span. It would later be called Burnside's Bridge. Here it is viewed from the position of the Confederates who defended it... (LC)

Below: ... and here is how it looked to the attackers who tried to cross it in the face of a wall of fire from Confederates on the ridge beyond. (LC)

Federal corps had gone into action one after another. Two were shattered and the third was broken. Federal losses included over 5,000 men. The extent of Southern casualties can be gauged from the fact that after the battle New England soldiers scouting near the Dunker Church chanced upon 146 Confederate bodies lying in a neat, soldierly line. The celebrated Stonewall Brigade, reduced to 250 men by the Second Manassas Campaign, had 88 new holes in its ranks.

Around 10 A.M. the battle shifted southward to what was the Confederate center. This second stage of Antietam Creek would likewise last four hours. Like the rest of McClellan's strategy, this second stage lacked the coordination necessary for total success. The middle of Lee's line at that moment consisted of little more than two brigades (those of Robert Rodes and G. B. Anderson) in Harvey Hill's division. They were posted in a sunken road that ran eastward along a ravine for a thousand yards, then jackknifed southward for the same distance. The Confederates were frantically placing fence rails along the road as defenses when Federals appeared in force on the hilltop above them.

These columns were part of two divisions from Sumner's II Corps (the third division in that corps had literally been wrecked at the Dunker Church). Confederates massed in the road watched in awe as line after line of Federals advanced in paradelike fashion down the hill toward them. "Their gleaming bayonets flashed like burnished silver in the sunlight," a Southern officer noted, and they marched "with the precision of step and perfect alignment of a holiday parade." However, the two Federal divisions actually attacked in what that day was typical disjointed fashion.

Right: The Sherrick farm buildings just west of Burnside's Bridge. Confederates swarmed all around the farm, and when Joseph Sherrick left to escape the battle, he hid $3,000 in gold in his stone wall. He got it back after the battle. (LC)

The lead division was under Major General William H. French, a hot-tempered, hard-drinking commander whose habit of shutting his eyes tightly when talking caused the men to nickname him "Old Blinkey." French's first wave of troops simply melted away as a result of a heavy volley of musketry from the road. A second wave met the same fate as Federals struggled with the additional obstacle of getting over and around bodies sprawled across the hillside. A third attack produced more casualties for French's battered ranks. Billy Yanks seized whatever protection they could find along the hill; both sides rushed in reinforcements; and a Union officer reported that for three hours "the battle raged incessantly, without either party giving way."

Major General Israel B. Richardson's division then entered the contest in support of French's men. Richardson was a tough veteran of frontier fighting, an unpretentious man who had no use for such military frills as a uniform. He personally led his brigades into action, and he used his sword both to wave his lines forward and to drive skulkers from cover as his profane voice thundered above the action. At one point Richardson shouted: "Where's General _______?"

From the ranks came the reply: "Behind the haystack ! "

"God damn the field officers!" Richardson bellowed as he raced downhill into the battle smoke.

Around 1 P.M. some of Richardson's men succeeded in capturing the high ground near the road's sharp bend. Federals poured an enfilading fire into the 300-odd Confederates still fighting defiantly. The Southerners could not withstand this new fire. Weary, battle-blackened men fell back to a new position. The sunken road was thereafter known as Bloody Lane—and for good reason. A Federal officer who viewed the bodies strewn in the lane commented that a man could walk as far down that road as one could see without stepping on the ground. On the other hand, gaining that road had involved a staggering cost to the Federals. The divisions of French and Richardson suffered combined losses of 509 killed, 2,254 wounded, and 152 missing. Among the slain was Richardson, who died of infection resulting from a bullet wound.

With Lee's center all but broken, the situation was critical. Colonel E. Porter Alexander, a Confederate artillery commander, observed: "Lee's army was ruined, and the end of the Confederacy was in sight." How desperate things were for the Army of Northern Virginia is apparent from two personal incidents. Harvey Hill rounded up 200 stragglers, grabbed a musket, and led a pitiful counterattack that withered in the face of concentrated firepower from the Union lines. Major General James Longstreet, heavyset and somber, was hobbling that day in a carpet slipper because of an infected blister on his foot; nevertheless he helped exhausted gunners man an artillery piece. Yet these acts of devotion did not stop the Federal breakthrough from being complete. Astoundingly, McClellan did that. "It would not be prudent" to deliver another assault, he told Major General William B. Franklin, whose fresh VI Corps—along with Fitz John Porter's entire V Corps—stood poised for the final blow. After the four bloodiest hours to which that day would be witness, McClellan again changed directions and ordered attacks from a different sector. The conflict now moved to its third and final stage.

Left: Once Burnside finally crossed, his men steadily drove back the Confederate defenders. They left their dead, like these on the Sherrick farm, behind them. (LC)

Below: With the threat of dismissal from the army hanging over him as a result of charges about his conduct at Second Manassas, Fitz John Porter sat out the battle on the Antietam, his V Corps being held in reserve. (USAMHI)

Above: Finally forced to leave the field to the enemy, Lee retired from Sharpsburg on September 19. Brigadier General James H. Lane commanded the rear guard as the Confederates withdrew. (VM)

Below: The 139th Pennsylvania arrived on the field on the evening of September 17, too late for the battle. With more Federal reinforcements coming up, Lee would have been foolish to remain. (WESTERN RESERVE HISTORICAL SOCIETY)

Right: The day after the fight. Alexander Gardner began the work of photographing the field. One of his first views was taken from near McClellan's headquarters, showing reserve artillery east of the Antietam. Long thought to be an actual "battle" image showing fighting taking place on the right, the picture actually shows only soldiers lounging in the lowland on the right, while artillery stands idle at left. (LC)

Below: Part of Porter's corps, however, did pursue Lee after the Confederates began their withdrawal. The 2nd Maine, shown here in camp at Hall's Hill, Virginia, crossed the Potomac and skirmished with the enemy on September 20. (WRHS)

Right: And cavalry units, which sat out most of the main battle along the Antietam, managed to snipe at Lee's heels as the Confederates crossed at Shepherdstown. Here, standing in the center, is Colonel David M. Gregg and his officers of the 8th Pennsylvania Cavalry. (LC)

Left: Shepherdstown on the Potomac, where McClellan's feeble attempt to pursue Lee made its only real challenge. (LC)

To the south of the battlefield was a stone bridge that spanned Antietam Creek. The road approaching it from the east ran parallel to the stream, then turned abruptly at the bridge and plunged into a funnel-like valley before crossing the bridge. Immediately at the western end of the structure the road veered sharply to the north because of a ridge several hundred feet high that came to within a short distance of the creek's bank. Atop that hill some small Georgia regiments were entrenched under blustery Brigadier General Robert Toombs.

Commanding the Federal left was Major General Ambrose E. Burnside. A heavily bewhiskered Rhode Islander, he was well liked by all, especially the men in his IX Corps. His four divisions should have acted as a huge sledgehammer against Lee's right. However, instead of employing them en masse against the weak Confederate defenses, Burnside sent them piecemeal into battle that morning. He insisted that the regiments go one at a time across the stone bridge; and as they did, concentrated musketry and canister from the hilltop raked the lines and easily forced each column back from the arched span. Around 1 P.M., as the fight at Bloody Lane came to an end, Federal batteries opened a heavy bombardment at the bridge. The 51st New York and 51st Pennsylvania dashed across the span and established a bridgehead on the west bank of the Antietam. The Georgians, having waged a Thermopylae-like struggle throughout the morning, grudgingly retired from the crest of the hill.

For the Union Army the opportunity again existed for a decisive and fatal thrust into Lee's lines. Yet McClellan was tardy in ordering a concerted attack, Burnside was clumsy in executing it, and coordination was once more lacking. Burnside consumed two hours in reorganizing his numerically superior forces, and it was midafternoon be fore thousands of Federals began moving across the rolling country toward the vulnerable Confederate flank. Long lines of Billy Yanks brushed aside what remained of Toombs's Georgians, then slammed into D. R. Jones's four brigades—which was all that was left of Lee's army south of Sharpsburg.

Lee quickly shifted artillery pieces and fragments of units southward to meet this powerful assault. Longstreet wrote of that moment: "We were already badly whipped and were holding our ground by sheer force of desperation." Indeed they were. By 4 P.M. Sharpsburg was in flames; wounded and demoralized Confederates filled the streets and added a mood of near panic to the frenzy of battle roaring across the countryside; Federal flags were waving in triumph as Burnside's men advanced to within half a mile of Lee's sole escape route. Less than nine hundred yards separated the Union from complete victory against Lee.

Then occurred one of those rare, dramatic moments that history never forgets. The Federal brigades were so intent in pushing northwestward against Lee's flank that apparently no one saw a column of dust rising in the air to the south. Beneath that dust was the Confederate "Light Division" of Major General A. Powell Hill, a hard driving Virginian who sometimes wore red shirts in battle as if to underscore his disdain for danger. After Jackson had captured Harpers Ferry, he had left A. P. Hill's division behind to secure the post. The sound of battle early on September 17 told

Hill that he was badly needed elsewhere; so late that morning he got his troops on the road and started northward. Hill pushed the men hard. Johnny Rebs too exhausted to maintain the pace collapsed along the roadside in droves. Yet Hill urged the men forward, sometimes with the point of his sword. No more than 3,000 of his 5,000 troops reached Sharpsburg; but they marched seventeen miles in seven hours and turned the tide of battle.

Confederates gasping for breath ploughed into Burnside's exposed left flank. Hill himself led the attack, obviously enjoying every second of the in tense fighting (though he was the meekest of men away from battle). Many of his Confederates were wearing blue uniforms captured at Harpers Ferry. This added to the confusion in the unexpected onslaught; shrill screams of the "rebel yell" brought a frightening dimension to weary Federals trying to cope with Hill's attack. It was no use. The conflict in Burnside's sector turned around in a matter of minutes. Federal columns ground to a halt, recoiled, then fell back to the cover of artillery along Antietam Creek. This withdrawal marked the last major action of the day. Night came at last; and when it was impossible to fight any longer, the opposing lines drew apart by mutual consent. In the ensuing darkness there slowly arose a new, more chilling sound: thousands of screams and moans from soldiers too maimed by war to do anything else.

Vicious combat had raged for fourteen hours. Over 100,000 men and 500 artillery pieces had fought a fierce struggle along a 3-mile front. After the long holocaust, Lee's left had been forced back a mile, while his right had retreated half a mile. Those were the day's gains; they paled to in significance when compared to the losses. The Army of the Potomac suffered 12,410 casualties, including 3,000 dead. Lee's losses amounted to 10,700 men. That figure is smaller, to be sure, but it constituted fully a fourth of the Confederate Army. The extent of damage that the Army of Northern Virginia had suffered became obvious that night when Lee held a council of war. All of his lieutenants voiced discouragement. General Hood stated that he simply had no more men left.

"Great God !" Lee exclaimed. "Where is that splendid division you had this morning?"

Above: While part of the army pursued, much of it bled. Back on the Antietam the Federal surgeons set up their makeshift hospitals. Many sprouted in barns like Dr. Otho Smith's place near Keedysville, taken here by Gardner on September 20. (USAMHI)

Left: Huts were built of straw to provide temporary shelter from the sun. (USAMHI)

Left: Dr. Anson Hurd of the 14th Indiana cared for the wounded from Confederate commands in a hasty field hospital. (USAMHI)

Below: Then there were the dead to bury, the men who really purchased this field of blood. They lay everywhere. (USAMHI)

Left: On September 19 Gardner captured burial details working with Federal dead near the North Woods. (USAMHI)

Above: And here is the lonely grave of John Marshall of Company L, 28th Pennsylvania, near the West Woods. (USAMHI)

Left: And the land itself had to recover. St. Paul's suffered heavy damage from artillery fire on both sides. (LC)

Above: And the Federals had time to rest after their greatest test yet in the war. Army blacksmiths had to tend to shodding new stock to replace the hundreds of horses killed. (COURTESY OF THE OAKLAND MUSEUM)

"They are lying on the field where you sent them," the dejected Hood replied. "My division has been almost wiped out."

Displaying stubborn determination, however, on September 18 Lee waited for McClellan to renew the assaults. Lee had only 30,000 ill-equipped men at hand, while McClellan could boast of more than three times that number. On the field were two Federal corps that had seen no action in the slaughter of the previous day. Yet the hills and dales around Sharpsburg remained deathly still for hour after hour that Thursday. The stench of death fouled the air for miles as the two armies eyed each other warily. Meanwhile McClellan weighed his risks, gathered reports, conferred with his generals, awaited reinforcements, and made vague plans for an attack the next day, or the next, or the next. Across the way Lee's position became more untenable as the day passed, particularly with Federal reinforcements fast approaching. Shortly after sundown bone-tired Confederates slipped away from their lines

Below: Soldiers like these relaxed in the calm of the waters beside Antietam Bridge, forgetting the pain of just a few days before. (LC)

Below: The home of Stephen Grove became headquarters for Fitz John Porter. An officer of his staff could leisurely pose for Gardiner in front of the house and headquarters tents. (USAMHI)

Right: And dignitaries could visit to compliment the army and futiley urge McClellan to further action. On October 3 President Abraham Lincoln came to the army. McClellan stands facing him to the left. Just to the right of Lincoln, his hand on his sword, is Porter. To the far right, almost as if not a part of the group, is an aide on McClellan's staff, Captain George Armstrong Custer. (MINNESOTA HISTORICAL SOCIETY

and painfully started southward toward Virginia. An abandoned battlefield greeted McClellan the following morning.

Permitting the Army of Northern Virginia to escape was the worst of McClellan's many failures at Antietam Creek. On the other hand, he must be given some credit in this campaign. He assumed command of demoralized forces early in September; and in the short space of three weeks he had restored morale, reorganized an army, strengthened Washington's defenses, fought two major engagements, forced Lee's retreat to Virginia, and swept Maryland clean of Confederate troops. McClellan felt quite justified in boasting, after Antietam Creek: "I feel that I have done all that can be asked in twice saving the country." Therein lies the tragedy of this general. He never talked of defeating the Confederacy; his only concern was in protecting the Union.

A disappointed Lee found pride in his men as compensation for defeat. "This great battle," he stated, "was fought by less than 40,000 men on our side, all of whom had undergone the greatest labors and hardships in the field and on the march. Nothing could surpass the determined valor with which they met the larger army of the enemy, fully supplied and equipped, and the result reflects the highest credit on the officers and men engaged."

Antietam Creek was not the decisive Union victory that Lincoln had hoped to see, but driving Lee from the North was success enough to prompt Lincoln into an action he had long been considering. On the Monday following the battle, September 22, the President summoned his Cabinet together and announced his intentions of issuing a preliminary emancipation proclamation. The base of the war would thereafter be broadened and its ends appreciably heightened.

Other than Lincoln, few persons at that time sensed that the war's high-water mark may have been reached. Another individual who possibly, and ironically, arrived at the same conclusion was Jefferson Davis. To his Secretary of War shortly after the battle, the Confederate President observed: "Our maximum strength has been mobilized, while the enemy is just beginning to put forth his might."

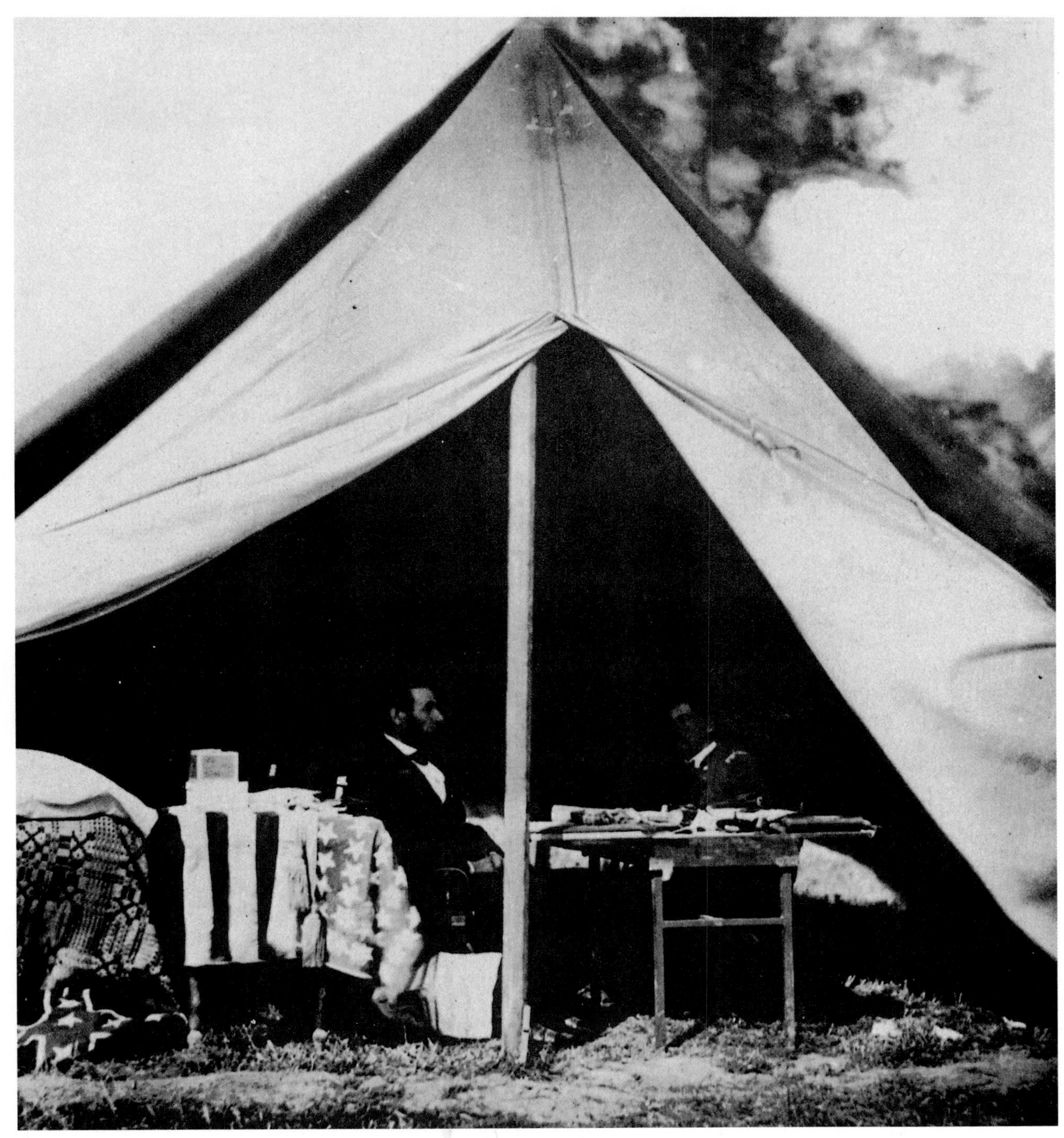

Right: Talking to a general who would not listen. Gardner's October 4 image captured a historic scene as the President patiently tried to persuade "Little Mac" to go after Lee. McClellan was content with his battle trophies, like the Confederate battle flag lying on the ground at left. A month later the President would relieve McClellan of his command and continue his search for a general to bring him victory. (LC)

The Fury of Fredricksburg

PETER J. PARRISH

In a war of mistakes, this battle is the most senseless; even the victor regrets it

In the wake of Antietam, on October 4, 1862, Lincoln posed with Allan Pinkerton and Major General John McClernand at McClellanís headquarters. The President's patience with "Little Mac" was wearing thin. There was pressure for a new commander. (KA)

THE SMALL VIRGINIA TOWN of Fredericksburg lay in the midst of the fiercely contested hundred miles of territory between the Union and Confederate capitals, almost exactly a halfway house between Washington and Richmond. A quiet town dating from the seventeenth century, with a population of some three or four thousand, it had watched the contending armies swirl around it for more than eighteen months, but the full horror of war had hitherto stopped short of its red brick houses and cobbled streets. However, on November 21, 1862, a Union officer brought to the mayor and Common Council of Fredericksburg a letter from Major General Edwin V. Sumner, commanding the Right Grand Division of the Army of the Potomac. He demanded the surrender of the town; if his request was refused, sixteen hours would be allowed for the evacuation of the civilian population before a bombardment began. The arrival of Confederate troops on the high ground behind the town soon altered the situation, but Fredericksburg now found itself in the no man's-land between two armies readying them selves for battle.

The arrival of the war at Fredericksburg's doorstep followed directly from the first major decision taken by the new commander of the Army of the Potomac, Ambrose E. Burnside. When Lincoln had relieved George B. McClellan of the command of that army early in November 1862, he had surprised many observers by the choice of Burnside as his successor. Sensing his own inadequacy, Burnside accepted the appointment only with the greatest reluctance. But the President's range of choice was extremely limited. If the field of candidates was to be confined to corps commanders in the Army of the Potomac, Lincoln did not want to choose a confirmed disciple of McClellan's, such as William B. Franklin, nor an outspoken critic, such as Joseph Hooker. Despite his poor showing at Antietam, Burnside seemed to have much to commend him. He had shown promise in an independent command in North Carolina and courage and loyalty in the Army of the Potomac. He was in many ways an attractive figure, tall and striking in appearance, honest and straightforward in manner. However, his own self-doubt was amply justified; behind the imposing facade lived a man of limited capacity and limited horizons, as the next few weeks were to show. Like many other officers on both sides, Burnside could perform courageously and creditably up to a certain point, but he was quite incapable of effective command of an army incomparably larger than anything for which West Point training or wartime experience had prepared him. Furthermore, whatever he did, he had little hope of satisfying both the defenders of the deposed McClellan and those who assumed that McClellan's removal would be followed by instant success.

When Burnside took command, the bulk of his army was in the area of Warrenton, just east of the Bull Run Mountains. He organized his huge force of over 120,000 men into three Grand Divisions (each comprising two corps), commanded by Sumner, Franklin, and Hooker. His redoubtable opponent, Robert E. Lee, had also reorganized his much smaller army, now numbering some 80,000 men, into two corps of four divisions each, commanded by James Longstreet and "Stonewall" Jackson. With characteristic audacity Lee had separated the two corps of his much smaller army by